MW00331510

Empathy

Social Neuroscience Series

Series Editors John T. Cacioppo and Gary G. Berntson

Series Editorial Board Ralph Adolphs, C. Sue Carter, Richard J. Davidson, Martha K. McClintock, Bruce S. McEwen, Michael J. Meaney, Daniel L. Schacter, Esther M. Sternberg, Steve S. Suomi, and Shelley E. Taylor

Foundations in Social Neuroscience, edited by John T. Cacioppo, Gary G. Berntson, Ralph Adolphs, C. Sue Carter, Richard J. Davidson, Martha K. McClintock, Bruce S. McEwen, Michael J. Meaney, Daniel L. Schacter, Esther M. Sternberg, Steve S. Suomi, and Shelley E. Taylor

Essays in Social Neuroscience, edited by John T. Cacioppo and Gary G. Berntson

Social Neuroscience: People Thinking about People, edited by John T. Cacioppo, Penny S. Visser, and Cynthia L. Pickett

The Social Neuroscience of Empathy, edited by Jean Decety and William Ickes

Empathy: From Bench to Bedside, edited by Jean Decety

Empathy

From Bench to Bedside

edited by Jean Decety

The MIT Press
Cambridge, Massachusetts
London, England

First MIT Press paperback edition, 2014

© 2012 Massachusetts Institute of Technology

All rights reserved. No part of this book may be reproduced in any form by any electronic or mechanical means (including photocopying, recording, or information storage and retrieval) without permission in writing from the publisher.

For information about special quantity discounts, please email special_sales@mitpress.mit.edu

This book was set in Stone Sans and Stone Serif by Toppan Best-set Premedia Limited. Printed and bound in the United States of America.

Library of Congress Cataloging-in-Publication Data

Empathy : from bench to bedside / edited by Jean Decety.
  p. cm. — (Social neuroscience)
Includes bibliographical references and index.
ISBN 978-0-262-01661-2 (hardcover : alk. paper) — 978-0-262-52595-4 (pb.)
1. Empathy. 2. Neurosciences. 3. Social psychology. I. Decety, Jean.
BF575.E55E463 2012
152.4'1—dc22

2011014049

10 9 8 7 6 5 4 3 2

Contents

Introduction: Why Is Empathy so Important?

Jean Decety

Empathy, the natural capacity to share, understand, and respond with care to the affective states of others, plays a crucial role in much of human social interaction from birth to the end of life. Empathy is thought to have a key role in motivating prosocial behavior, inhibiting aggression, and providing the affective and motivational bases for moral development. Empathy is an essential ingredient in psychotherapy and a necessary component of patient-physician interactions. These are some good reasons to be interested in empathy.

This book covers, and helps to integrate, a wide range of topics in empathy theory, research and application including these: How has empathy evolved within the mammalian brain? How does it develop in young infants and children? What are the relationships among empathy, prosocial behavior, compassion, and altruism? How do group processes impact the experience of empathy? What are the neural circuits underpinning empathy? Is a purely cognitive empathy preferable to emotional empathy for clinical practice? What are the costs of empathy?

The first two chapters open the volume with perspectives from philosophy and anthropology. Drawing on phenomenology, Dan Zahavi and and Søren Overgaard outline some of the distinctive features of what the notion of empathy encompasses and then critically compare their view with recent philosophical accounts of empathy. Anthropologist Allan Young explores the place of empathy in the evolutionary history of human nature.

The next part of the volume offers three contributions from social psychology starting with the well-known empathy-altruism hypothesis put forward by C. Daniel Batson. In this chapter Batson suggests a strategy to test the validity of this hypothesis, reviews the empirical evidence that has accumulated during the past three decades, and discusses some important practical societal implications of the empathy-altruism theory. Stephanie Echols and Joshua Correll build on the distinction between the understanding of others' emotions and being concerned by their well-being to demonstrate how group membership can influence the empathic experience as it unfolds, from perceiving an individual in need, to understanding the individual's unique experience, to caring and engaging in helping behavior. In the last chapter of that section Karyn Lewis and Sara Hodges explore the processes involved in achieving empathic accuracy and argue that they are not always as personal as people think.

Empathy is not unique to humans, as many of the mechanisms underlying its functioning are shared with other social animals. Frans de Waal reviews various aspects of empathy such as emotion contagion, concern, and perspective-taking across species, and he makes it clear that even the most advanced forms of human empathy are never fully independent from these simpler processes since we have learned over our lifetimes to internalize what happens to others and how to react.

Section IV of the volume is concerned with the development of empathy in infants and children. First, Sharee Light and Carolyn Zahn-Waxler examine the processes at play in the first year of life that likely serve as building blocks for different aspects of empathy, and they describe ways to assess neural underpinnings of early empathy. Empathic responding is a complex and multifaceted process as argued by Amrisha Vaish and Felix Warneken, who explore some fascinating new work on early relationships between empathy and prosocial behavior in infants and young children. Nancy Eisenberg, Snjezana Huerta, and Alison Edwards argue that empathy-related reactions provide information that fosters socially competent behavior such as friendship, social status, and peer popularity. Children who are high in empathy, sympathy, or both tend to be socially appropriate and well liked by peers; moreover, they tend to have high-quality friendships and to defend peers from bullies.

Section V shows how some remarkable progress in the area of affective and cognitive neuroscience has enabled neuroscientists to study the neurobiological circuits implicated in emotion perception, understanding, as well as empathic concern in both children and adult participants. In the first chapter of that section Jean Decety and Kalina Michalska provide a comprehensive analysis of the neurological mechanisms underlying empathy and concern for others and demonstrate how developmental research and neuroscience can mutually benefit from one another. Next, Abigail Marsh discusses the neural and psychological forces associated with empathy and the drive to help others in distress. In particular she focuses on recent cognitive neuroscience research that highlights the relationship between empathy and the ability to detect and respond to distress in others. In the last chapter of that section Jamil Zaki and Kevin Ochsner review recent cognitive affective neuroscience work on empathy and propose an integrative approach to examining the neural bases of sharing and understanding emotions.

The final section of the book brings together five important contributions on the role of empathy in clinical practice. Whereas everybody will agree that empathy is a necessary component of all patient-physician interactions, and this not only in the case of psychological and psychiatric disorders, medical practitioners have always struggled to achieve an appropriate balance between empathy and clinical distance.

Jodi Halpern starts by asking a difficult question: What kind of empathy, if any at all, should we expect doctors to provide for their patients? She then proposes a coherent model for clinical empathy in terms of a limited number of basic mutually sustaining aims that are important to take into account. In the next chapter Ezequiel Gleichgerrcht and Jean Decety explore the ways in which excessive levels of empathic arousal and poor emotion regulation can lead to professional distress and compassion fatigue and present several ways to regulate empathy to avoid such negative and devastating consequences. They conclude by highlighting the importance of balanced levels of empathic responses in health practitioners for successful interactions with patients. The contribution of Charles Figley focuses on the importance of the empathic response for mental health professionals. He then talk about vicarious trauma and compassion fatigue as healer's burdens and discusses empathy and resilience as goals that prepare healers for clinical practice and, in turn, help patients appreciate the importance of sustainable resilience and helping others—other healers and even patients—to develop tools for healer or practitioner resilience. In her chapter, Johanna Shapiro notes that, although there are a plethora of words expended in support of empathy in clinical training and practice, this has not successfully translated into sustainable and effective attitudes and actions. She analyzes this paradox, identifies possible reasons for its existence, and suggests potential pedagogical alternatives. The final chapter of the book attempts to bridge the new work from affective neuroscience and knowledge and use of empathy in psychoanalysis. David Terman thinks it is quite important that both neuroscientists and psychoanalysts learn from each other with mutual respect and integrity.

Overall, this new volume affords us the opportunity to significantly broaden the interdisciplinary scope of interest on empathy from various disciplines. The reader will gain a deeper understanding of current knowledge of the evolutionary, social, developmental, cognitive, and neurobiological aspects of empathy, and of how this capacity influences key aspects of human communication, including clinical practice and medical education. This multidisciplinary perspective on empathy provides a rich and textured picture of the mechanisms, expressions, social function, and cultural significance of empathy.

I Philosophical and Anthropological Perspectives on Empathy

1 Empathy without Isomorphism: A Phenomenological Account

Dan Zahavi and Søren Overgaard

The concept of empathy is notoriously ambiguous. What is meant by "empathy" seems to vary not only across different disciplines but even within an individual discipline. One reason why philosophers and psychologists alike have been interested in the notion of empathy has been its purported relevance for moral theory—the idea being that it is empathy that leads somebody to respond with sensitivity and care to the suffering of others. At the same time, however, recent research on social cognition has repeatedly emphasized that empathy may hold the key to important and foundational issues in interpersonal understanding (Goldman 1995a; Goldie 1999; Decety and Ickes 2009). In the discussion that follows we focus on the latter issue, that is, the relevance of empathy for the discussion of the nature of social cognition.

In recent decades much of that discussion has taken place within the framework of the so-called theory-of-mind debate. On one side we find the *theory-theory of mind* and on the other the *simulation theory of mind*. Theory-theorists typically argue that we attribute mental states to others on the basis of a theory of mind that is either constructed in early infancy and subsequently revised and modified (Gopnik and Wellman 1995) or else is the result of maturation of innate mind-reading modules (Baron-Cohen 1995). Simulation theorists, on the other hand, deny that our understanding of others is primarily theoretical in nature and maintain that we use our own mind as a model when understanding the minds of others. Some claim that the simulation in question involves the exercise of conscious imagination and deliberative inference (Goldman 1995b); some insist that the simulation although explicit is non-inferential in nature (Gordon 1986); and finally there are those who argue that the simulation rather than being explicit and conscious is implicit and subpersonal (Gallese 2003).

It is in particular within the simulationist camp that the notion of empathy has resurfaced as a central category. In the beginning of his recent book *Simulating Minds*, for instance, Goldman writes that he considers mind reading an extended form of *empathy* (Goldman 2006, 4). As for Gallese, he has in various publications described empathy as a form of inner imitation (2003, 519) and has argued that it is what allows us to understand not only the actions but also the displayed emotions and sensations of others (2001, 45). In fact Gallese has even insisted that empathy "is relevant when accounting for all aspects of behavior enabling us to establish a meaningful link between others and ourselves" (2001, 43). It is consequently not too surprising that some argue that simulationists are today's equivalents of empathy theorists (Stueber 2006, ix).

One noteworthy difference between Goldman's and Gallese's respective uses of the notion of empathy is that the latter is far more interested in the historical origins of the notion. Whereas Goldman makes no significant reference to the extensive discussion of empathy and social cognition found in the phenomenological tradition (cf. Goldman 2006, 18), Gallese refers favorably, not only to Lipps's discussion of inner imitation, but also to Stein's account of empathy and to Husserl's and Merleau-Ponty's understanding of intersubjectivity (Gallese 2001). Indeed, Gallese is quite explicit in considering his own notion of embodied simulation that relies on mirror-resonance mechanisms to be akin to and a further development of the phenomenological proposal (2004, 397; cf. Iacoboni 2008).

In a footnote added in a late Polish translation of his 1918 dissertation—which was supervised by Husserl—Roman Ingarden made the following observation:

At the time when this treatise was written, extensive discussions took place regarding the so-called empathy, a notion that had been proposed by the psychologizing German aesthetes like for instance Theodor Lipps. A number of phenomenologists such as M. Geiger, Max Scheler, Edith Stein and later also Husserl participated in this discussion and it became increasingly clear that the classical theory of empathy which considered it a kind of projection of one's own psychical states into foreign bodies had to be replaced by a theory that took empathy to be a special kind of perception of the psychical states as they are manifest in the bodily expression. (Ingarden, 1994, 170–71)

Ingarden's remark not only highlights the need for a distinction between Lipps's definition of empathy in terms of inner imitation, and the subsequent analyses found in phenomenology. It also suggests that the classical phenomenological account might differ rather markedly from recent attempts to explain empathy in terms of mirroring, mimicry, imitation, emotional contagion, imaginative projection, or inferential attribution.

In the first part of this chapter we outline some of the distinctive features of this alternative phenomenological account of empathy. In the second part of the chapter we compare and contrast the phenomenological account with a recent model proposed by de Vignemont and colleagues (de Vignemont and Singer 2006, de Vignemont and Jacob 2010/under review). We argue that the latter model faces a number of problems that do not arise for the former account.

Empathy and Face-to-Face Interaction

We start with a brief glance at Lipps's account of empathy since this was an account from which all the phenomenologists to varying degrees distanced themselves. In his 1907 article "Das Wissen von fremden Ichen," Lipps argues that we have a tendency to reproduce a foreign gesture of expression when we see it and that this tendency also evokes the feeling normally associated with the expression. He talks of this process as being instinctual in character. He speaks of an *instinct of empathy* and argues that it involves two components: a drive directed toward imitation and a drive directed toward expression (Lipps 1907, 713). It is the feeling in myself evoked by the expression that is then attributed to the other through projection. It is projected into or onto the other's perceived gesture, thereby allowing for a form of interpersonal understanding (Lipps 1907, 717–719). Why is projection involved? Because on Lipps's account we only know of anger, joy, and so forth from our own case. The only mental states we have experiential access to are our own.

It is not difficult to spot the similarities between Lipps's account and contemporary proposals. Hatfield and colleagues, for instance, have recently defended the view that the tendency to automatically mimic and synchronize one's facial expressions, vocalizations, postures, and movements with those of another person is basic to human interaction, and is what allows one to feel oneself into the emotional life of the other (Hatfield, Rapson, and Le 2009).

However, one of the persisting phenomenological objections to Lipps's account targets precisely his suggestion that (inner) imitation constitutes the basis of empathy. According to Lipps when I observe somebody who is afraid, in pain, or happy, this somehow requires me to be afraid, in pain, or happy. Indeed, if the imitation is to serve any explanatory purpose, my own felt pain or joy must precede rather than follow my conscious recognition of the fear, pain, or joy in the other. But as Scheler writes, we might understand from the wagging tail of a dog that he is happy to see us, but this does not require us to imitate the expression ourselves (Scheler 1954, 11). Moreover, how plausible is it after all to claim that I have to be scared myself in order to understand that my child is scared or that I need to become furious myself if I am to recognize the fury in the face of my assailant (Husserl 1973, 188)? As Stein points out there is a discrepancy between the phenomenon that Lipps seeks to explain and the phenomenon he actually does explain (Stein 1989, 23). Lipps's theory might explain why a certain experience occurs in me, but it does not offer an explanation of how I come to understand the other. Rather than explaining empathy, that is, empathy understood as an experience of the minded life of others, Lipps's account is better geared to handle something like *motor mimicry* or *emotional contagion*.

A distinctive feature of what is known as *emotional contagion* is that you literally catch the emotion in question (Scheler 1954, 15). It is transferred to you. It becomes your own emotion. Indeed you can be infected by the jolly or angry mood of others without even being aware of them as distinct individuals. But this is precisely what makes emotional contagion different from empathy. In empathy the experience you empathically understand remains that of the other. The focus is on the other, and the distance between self and other is preserved and upheld. Another distinctive feature of emotional contagion is that it primarily concerns the emotional quality rather than the object of the emotion. You can be infected by cheerfulness or hilarity, without knowing what it is about. This is what makes emotional contagion different from what Scheler calls *emotional sharing*. Think of a situation in which a couple is enjoying a movie together. For Scheler such a situation would exemplify the possibility of sharing both the emotion (joy) and the object of the emotion. But emotional sharing must on its part still be distinguished from empathy. Consider the situation where a common friend interacts with the couple. He might perceive their enjoyment without being joyful himself (perhaps because he finds the movie silly or because he is in a bad mood). In this case the friend would be empathically directed at their enjoyment without experiencing the joy as his own. Indeed, their joy and his empathic under-standing are clearly qualitatively different and distinct. Their joy is the intentional object of his empathy (cf. Scheler 1954, 12–13).

What about the relation between *empathy* and *sympathy*? Compare the following group of cases discussed by Scheler. Consider first the situation in which you see the face of a crying child, but rather than seeing it as expressing discomfort or distress, you merely see certain distortions of the facial muscles, that is, you basically do not see it as emotionally expressive. Compare this (pathological) case with the situation in which you see the same face as emotionally expressive but without feeling any compassion, that is, while remaining indifferent. And finally consider the situation in which you also feel compassion or concern for the child. For Scheler the last situation counts as a case of sympathy, which he considers an ethically relevant act. But in order to feel sympathy, in order to feel compassion with, say, somebody's suffering, you first need to understand that the other is indeed suffering (cf. Batson 2009, 10), and such understanding may be provided by empathy.[1] In short, whereas empathy, for Scheler, has to do with a basic understanding of expressive others, sympathy adds care or concern for the other.

Apart from stressing the difference between empathy and sympathy, the point of Scheler's example is also to remind us that it is possible to empathize with somebody without feeling any sympathy (Scheler 1954, 8–9). Just think of the skilled interrogator or the sadist. A high degree of empathic sensitivity might precisely be of use if one wants to inflict especially cruel pain on somebody.

So far, we find the phenomenologists insisting on the differences among emotional contagion, emotional sharing, empathy, and sympathy. Furthermore, they would reject the proposal that imitation, emotional contagion, or mimicry should be the paradigm of empathy. Indeed, they reject the projective theory of empathy, and they also dismiss the attempt to account for the experience of others in terms of some imaginative transformation. On the phenomenological account, empathy is not a distinct and specific emotion (like embarrassment, shame, or pride); rather, it denotes a basic, sui generis, form of intentionality directed at other experiencing subjects as such (Stein 1989, 6). To have empathy with another person is in short to experience the psychological life of that person. But on the phenomenological account that does not entail that the other's experience is literally transmitted to you. In basic empathy the focus is on the other, on his thoughts and feelings, and not on myself, nor on how it would be like for me to be in the shoes of the other (Scheler 1954, xlviii, 39). To experience, say, the emotion of the other differs from the way you would experience the emotion if it were your own. Thus empathy does not entail that we ourselves undergo the emotion we observe in the other. We might, but this is not a requisite. We might encounter a furious neighbor and become furious ourselves, but our empathic understanding of our neighbor's emotion might also elicit the reverse response, namely a feeling of fear. In either case, however, our emotional reaction is exactly that—a reaction. It is a consequence of our understanding of the other's emotion and not a precondition or prerequisite for this understanding. If presented with Goldman's view that a necessary condition for mind reading "is that the state ascribed to the target is ascribed as a result of the attributor's instantiating, undergoing, or experiencing, that very state" (Goldman and Sripada 2005, 208), the phenomenologists would argue that such an account conflates empathy with other kinds of phenomena and moreover fails to capture the fact that we can and do *experience* other minds. It is no coincidence that Scheler repeatedly speaks of the perception of others (*Fremdwahrnehmung*) and even entitles his own theory *a perceptual theory of other minds* (Scheler 1954, 220).

But is it not preposterous to claim that we are able to *experience* other people's mental states? Does this not overlook the fact that we do not have the same kind of access to the minds of others that we have to our own? To phrase it differently, any convincing account of our understanding of others must respect the asymmetry between self-ascription and other-ascription of mental states and must respect that whereas I enjoy a first-person perspective on my own mental life, I do not have first-personal access to the minds of others. This is true, but neither Husserl nor Stein ignores this fact.

Already in the *Logical Investigations* Husserl wrote that common speech credits us with percepts of other people's inner experiences, we *see* their anger or pain, so to speak. As he then went on to say such talk is to some extent correct. When a hearer perceives a speaker give voice to certain inner experiences, he also perceives these experiences themselves, but as Husserl then adds, the hearer does not have an inner but only an outer perception of these experiences (Husserl 2001, 189–90). So on the one hand Husserl argues that my experience of others has a quasiperceptual character in the sense that it grasps the other him- or herself (Husserl 1973, 24). On the other hand Husserl also says that although the body of another person is perceptually given, this is not the case with the other's experiences. They can never be given to me in the same original fashion as my own experiences; they are not accessible to me through inner consciousness. Rather they are appresented through a special form of apperception, or to use a different terminology, they are co-intended and characterized by a certain co-presence (Husserl 1973, 27).

We find a very similar account in Stein. In her view empathy announces in the most direct manner possible the actual presence of the other's experience, although it does not provide us with first-personal access to it. To exemplify, let us consider a situation in which a friend tells me that he has lost his mother, and I become aware of his distress. What kind of awareness is this? I obviously do not see the distress the same way I see the color of his shirt; rather I see the distress "in" his pained countenance (Stein 1989, 6). In this case it makes sense to say that I experience (rather than imagine or infer) his distress, although I certainly do lack a first-person experience of the distress; it is not *my* distress. Like Scheler, Stein consequently stresses the importance of not conflating empathy with emotional sharing (*Mitfühlen*). In the latter case I feel, say, joy, or distress over the same event as my friend. In the former case I am primarily directed at my friend's experience (and only secondarily at the object of his experience).[2] Thus, Stein takes empathy to be a unique kind of experience in that when I empathize with another, the empathized experience is located in the other and not in myself. Empathy entails by necessity a difference between the subject of empathic experience and the subject of the empathized experience. Stein then goes on to argue that empathy is a sui generis modality of experience, but she also says that its content (the empathized experience) is given nonprimordially (Stein 1989, 10–11). In short, empathy is both like and unlike perception. It is like perception in being direct, unmediated, and noninferential (Stein 1989, 24). It is unlike perception in not being able to offer us the fullest presence of the empathized experience—that presence is only available to the subject of the experience.

To put it differently, when arguing that we are able to *experience* others, and as a consequence do not exclusively have to rely on and employ theoretical inferences, internal simulations, or imaginative projections, the phenomenologists are not denying that second- (and third-) person access to psychological states *do* differ from first-person access. But they would argue that it would be a mistake to restrict and equate experiential access with first-person access. It is possible to experience mental states in more than one way. When I experience the facial expressions or meaningful actions of another person, I am *experiencing* aspects of his or her psychological life and not merely imagining them, simulating them, or theorizing about them. I am experiencing the other him- or herself and not merely some theoretical or imagined construct, some simulation, or simulacrum. Moreover, the fact that my experiential access to the minds of other differs from my experiential access to my own mind is not an imperfection or shortcoming. On the contrary, this difference is constitutional. It is precisely because of this difference, precisely because of this asymmetry, that we can claim that the minds we experience are *other* minds (cf. Husserl 1995, 109).

Phenomenologists would typically not dispute that self-experience is a precondition for other-experience. But there is a decisive difference between arguing that the former is a necessary condition (and that there would be no other-experience in its absence) and claiming that self-experience somehow serves as a model for other-experience, as if interpersonal understanding is basically a question of projecting oneself into the other. Consider, by contrast, Goldman's simulation-plus-projection routine. Goldman explicitly talks of the routine as consisting of "the act of assigning a state of one's own to someone else" (Goldman 2006, 40). But this seems de facto to imprison me within my own mind and to prevent me from ever encountering *others*. It is not insignificant that Lipps, after having argued very much like Goldman, reaches the following conclusion: "Psychologically considered, other human beings are duplications of myself" (Lipps 1900, 418).

Phenomenologists would not deny that in some cases we rely on imagination, memory, or theoretical knowledge when we attempt to understand others. We can for instance attempt to identify the goal of their actions and then imagine how we would seek to accomplish it and what experiences we would be living through. Or we might rely on memory and remember what we went through when, in the past, we sought to realize a similar goal (Schutz 1967, 114). Finally, we can also make use of our general knowledge regarding the kind of action in question and then seek to infer its causes and motives (Schutz 1967, 175). In fact, if we really want to understand the full psychological life of others, if we want to understand what others are up to, why they are doing what they are doing and what that means to them, we have to go beyond a narrow focus on face-to-face interaction and embodied engagement. Although it might be permissible to say that certain aspects of the other's consciousness, such as his joy, sorrow, pain, shame, pleading, love, rage, and threats, are given to us directly and noninferentially, it does not follow from this that we also have a direct access to the *why* of such feelings. And in order to uncover these aspects, it is not sufficient simply to observe expressive movements and actions, we also have to rely on interpretation, and we also have to draw on a highly structured context of meaning (Schutz 1967, 23–24). In short, if we wish to reach a deeper level of interpersonal understanding, we have to go beyond what is directly available (Schutz 1967, 168).

However, even if one concedes all of this, it should not lead one to question the importance of the face-to-face encounter. The latter remains basic in the sense that it constitutes the foundation for all other forms of interpersonal understanding (Schutz

1967, 162). Although it is quite true that theoretical knowledge or past experience might facilitate our understanding of what somebody is up to and what he or she is thinking or feeling (which is why an obstetrician or mother might be better able to understand what a woman giving birth is going through than a teenager), this valid (if somewhat trivial) point regarding concrete facets of interpersonal understanding must be distinguished from the erroneous view that our very conviction that we are faced with a minded creature is to the same extent a result of theorizing or simulation.

To summarize, for the phenomenologists empathy provides us with an experiential access to other minds. But to avoid misunderstandings it is first of all important to realize that empathy, rather than being some mysterious form of telepathy, simply amounts to an experience of the embodied mind of the other, that is, simply refers to our ability to access the life of the mind of others in their bodily and behavioral expressions; it is an ability that can improve with familiarity, learning, and salience. Second, although it is important to recognize the importance of empathy, it is also important to recognize its limitations. There is a limit to how far empathy (plus sensitivity to the immediate context) can get us. Our everyday understanding of others draws on other resources as well. If we wish to unearth *why* somebody is feeling the way he does or *why* he is acting the way he does, we might need to consider the larger social, cultural, and historical context, and this understanding cannot be provided by empathy alone (cf. Stueber 2006).

Isomorphism and Interpersonal Similarity

In this section, we take a closer look at a recent model of empathy that on important points seems to converge with the phenomenological account just outlined. Yet, there are also some significant differences, and as we argue, the former faces some difficulties that do not affect the phenomenological account.

In a number of publications Frédérique de Vignemont and various co-authors have advanced the following ideas about empathy and related notions. First, in order to "enable precise claims to be made about the nature of empathy," we should opt for a narrow definition of empathy that allows us to preserve important distinctions between empathy, on the one hand, and phenomena such as sympathy and emotional contagion, on the other hand (de Vignemont and Singer 2006, 435). Second, whereas emotional contagion is "self-centered," empathy is essentially "other-centered" (de Vignemont 2009). Third, we should resist the temptation to account for empathy in terms of motor mimicry or mirror-resonance mechanisms, both of which are better geared to handle something like emotional contagion.

These are all observations with which we agree, and here we see a clear overlap with the phenomenological proposal. However, whereas de Vignemont and colleagues concede that the similarity between a mind reader's psychological state and her target's affective state is not a necessary, nor even an enabling condition, for ascribing an affective state to the target in standard mind reading, they do claim that such an interpersonal similarity constraint holds true in the case of empathy. More specifically they insist that empathy requires isomorphic emotional or sensory states in empathizer and target. In addition they stipulate a number of other conditions that must be met if empathy is to obtain, and as will become clear from what follows, we suggest that given their definition, it is doubtful whether empathy can play any *foundational* role in our understanding of others. To put it differently, whereas we agree on the importance of defining empathy in such a manner that it is distinct from other forms of interpersonal understanding, we still consider empathy a basic form of interpersonal understanding, and on the definition provided by de Vignemont and collaborators it is anything but that.

So how do they define empathy? There are a handful of slightly different definitions in circulation, but let us focus on the one offered by de Vignemont and Singer:

There is empathy if: (i) one is in an affective state; (ii) this state is isomorphic to another person's state; (iii) this state is elicited by the observation or imagination of another person's affective state; (iv) one knows that the other person is the source of one's own affective state. (de Vignemont and Singer 2006, 435)[3]

Loosely put, the main point of the first condition is to set empathy apart from more theoretical, detached or "colder" ways of working out what another person is feeling. The second condition is supposed to distinguish empathy from sympathy, while the function of the fourth condition is to distinguish empathy from emotional contagion (de Vignemont 2009). But, to start with the latter issue, it is not clear whether the definition is really able to hold all cases of contagion apart from cases of empathizing.

Consider the following example discussed by de Vignemont and Jacob. Suppose a screaming infant is injected with a painful vaccine in a hospital ward, and his six-year-old sister, witnessing the event, tenses up and shrinks "as if she were anticipating her own future painful experience caused by the penetration of the needle into her own skin" (de Vignemont and Jacob 2010/under review, 2–3).[4] This response, de Vignemont and Jacob note,[5] is an example of contagion. Now, of course, this sort of contagion is not just something to which young children are prone—adults sometimes react this way as well. The difference is that, whereas a six-year-old may not realize that the other's pain is the source of her own wincing and tensing up, adults may be fully aware that this is exactly what is going on. But, crucially, this hardly makes the case less a case of contagion. On the contrary it obviously remains contagion, for just like the six-year-old, we adults may primarily be concerned with how unpleasant it is for us to have the needle penetrate our own skin. Our knowledge that the other's pain is the source of our wincing does nothing to change the fact that we are "self-centered."

Let us be clear that this episode *involves* empathy, as we understand it. The initial observation of the infant's expressions of pain qualifies as empathizing, as the phenomenologists understand it. However, we believe that the overall state the observer is in by virtue of meeting de Vignemont and Singer's (2006) four conditions does *not* merit the label "empathy." For the wincing reaction, even when it is coupled with the empathic experience that gave rise to it and with the realization that it is a reaction to another's painful experience, is a phenomenon of contagion, not an empathic phenomenon.

A similar problem arises with respect to the distinction between empathy and sympathy. Suppose someone sees that her friend is depressed and feels sad for him. Following de Vignemont and Singer's scheme, this is a case of sympathy, not empathy, and indeed this seems the most natural way to describe it. However, it is questionable whether the reason why it should be classified in this way is that the two people are in different affective states. For what if someone sees that her friend is *sad* and feels sad for him? Now the "isomorphism" condition is met, and it is likely that the other conditions are met as well.[6] So, according to de Vignemont and Singer, this should be a case of empathy, not sympathy. But this, it seems to us, is wrongheaded. For the two examples are identical in all relevant respects: they are both cases of someone feeling sadness and concern directed at another person's plight. And is it really plausible to suggest that, merely because we change the *target subject's* emotion, what would otherwise have been a clear case of sympathetic concern becomes a case of empathizing instead?

Let us note a further troublesome implication of the isomorphism requirement. A quite common phenomenon, we assume, is that one person expresses a certain emotion—say, anger—and another person sees this and reacts with a different type of emotion—say, fear. This sort of case has no straightforward place in de Vignemont and colleagues' classificatory system. In not meeting the isomorphism requirement, it can count neither as a case of empathy nor as a case of emotional contagion. Nor does it count as sympathy—the frightened person will typically not feel concern or sympathy for the person expressing anger. So the only available option is to classify it as a case of "standard mind reading." In other words if I react with fear to someone else's anger, this is simply standard mind reading; but if I react with anger, I am—if the other conditions are met—empathizing.[7] But is that really plausible? Qua events of *mind reading*, the two cases are surely identical: what varies is the mind reader's emotional *reaction* to the emotion she perceives in the other. And it is just not clear why one should accept that isomorphic reactions yield empathy. Indeed, if we accept this, we should have to say of the youth who reacts with violent rage to another person's anger that the former, *in virtue of reacting in precisely this way and no other way*, "empathizes" with the latter.[8]

Perhaps partly in an attempt to address counterexamples like the ones we have canvassed, de Vignemont and Jacob impose a further requirement on empathy, namely what they call the *"Caring condition."* This condition states that an empathizer must "care about" his or her target's affective life (2010/under review, 21). However, the condition is ambiguous: precisely what is involved in "caring about" someone else's affective life? The most natural reading of this would suggest something characteristic of sympathy rather than empathy: to care about someone else's feelings and emotions, surely, is to feel sympathy or concern for him or her. As this would collapse the distinction between empathy and sympathy, however, we doubt that it is the way de Vignemont and Jacob would want the caring condition to be understood. Alternatively, it might be suggested that the caring condition simply makes explicit the "other-centeredness" that the phenomenologists would agree is central to empathy. If so two comments are in order. First, this surely raises the question of whether de Vignemont and Singer's original four-part definition of empathy—which was after all supposed to have secured the other-centeredness—should not be rethought altogether rather than patched up with further conditions that do the work the original definition was unable to do. Second, on this understanding of the caring condition it is, of course, still the case that the angry youth empathizes with his victim: the problem with this case is not that the youth is not other-centered but that it seems strange to label the violent rage he directs at his victim "empathetic."[9]

This discussion highlights what in our view is the main problem with de Vignemont and colleagues' definition. For them empathy is a less direct and more mediated form of interpersonal understanding than the kind provided by standard mind reading (de Vignemont 2010, 292; de Vignemont and Singer 2006, 439). And they specifically target Gallese's claim that empathy provides a "direct experiential understanding" of others (de Vignemont 2010, 284). The explanation repeatedly offered for why empathy is indirect is that it is influenced by contextual factors and can be modulated, for instance, by appraisal processes (de Vignemont and Singer 2006, 437). But is it impossible for something to be both direct and contextual at the same time? For comparison consider the case of vision. Vision usually counts as the paradigm of direct experience. I can theorize about the aurora borealis, I can imagine what it must be like to see the phenomenon, and I can see and experience it in all its splendor, but—and this is an old insight—when we perceive an object, we perceive it in a perceptual field. We are conscious of it in a particular setting, and the way it is given to us is influenced by what is co-given with it. We see no conflict between this insight and the claim that the perceptual object is directly given. Similarly, consider the case of utensils, say, an iPad. For something to be intended as an iPad, for something to appear as an iPad, a whole network of equipmental contexture, to use a Heideggerian phrasing, must be in place. But again, this fact does not make the perception of an iPad indirect and theory laden in the same way as our positing of black holes or subatomic particles. It does not make our access to the iPad nonexperiential; it does not turn the iPad into an inherently unobservable construct. To put it differently, there is no contradiction in defending the direct and contextual character of perception at the same time. This point also applies to interpersonal understanding.

One possible retort to the claim that empathy provides us with a direct experiential understanding of others is that such a claim is nonsensical since it overlooks the fact that we do not have the same kind of access to the minds of others that we have to our own. To phrase it differently, any convincing account of our understanding of others must respect the asymmetry between self-ascription and other-ascription of mental states; it must respect that, whereas I enjoy a first-person perspective on my own mental life, I do not have first-personal access to the minds of others. This is precisely the objection we find in de Vignemont, since she equates Gallese's (2004) notion of direct experiential understanding with that of having an access to other people's states "as if they were one's own" (de Vignemont 2010, 284). The problem, however, is that there is not one golden standard of what directness amounts to. As Bennett and Hacker (2003) recently remarked, we can speak of indirect evidence or of knowing indirectly only where it also makes sense to speak of a more direct evidence, but there is no more direct way of knowing that *another* is in pain than by seeing him writhe in pain. By contrast, noticing a bottle of pain-killers next to his bedside together with an empty glass of water and concluding that he has been in pain is an example of knowing indirectly or by way of inference (Bennett and Hacker 2003, 89, 93). On this understanding of what "direct access" to another's psychological state amounts to, such direct access is not in any sort of tension with the important point that we do not have access to other people's states "as if they were our own."

There is a further problem facing de Vignemont and Singer's (2006) account. We have noted that they (correctly) attribute to empathy an important role in enabling us to understand the feelings and emotions of others. Empathy "enables us to under-stand what they feel," as de Vignemont and Singer (2006, 439) put it. Now, if what this means is that empathy may, for example, enable us to understand the *type* of emotion someone else is having—that she feels angry, sad, happy, or whatever—then again, along with the phenomenologists discussed above, we would agree. But the problem is that empathy as defined by de Vignemont and Singer seems to *presuppose* such understanding and, if so, cannot be what enables it. To see the problem we must remember that, according to de Vignemont and Singer (2006), it must be "the obser-vation or imagination of another person's affective state" that elicits an empathizing person's isomorphic state. I must imagine or observe someone else's anger, say, and this must be what elicits a feeling of anger in me. But then it seems I must already understand that the other is angry before I can myself get angry, and if so the engendering of the isomorphic state in me, and the knowledge of what caused it, cannot be what enable me to understand that the other is angry: these states themselves must be elicited by such an understanding.[10]

Obviously, one consequence of such a view would be that empathy has a more modest role to play in social understanding than many philosophers and psychologists have believed; but in itself that is maybe not a very damaging criticism of the view. Indeed, de Vignemont and colleagues might cheerfully accept this result. After all they themselves stress the marked difference between the complex machinery of empathy, which must meet four requirements,[11] and the simpler and presumably more widespread "standard mind reading," which has to meet only one requirement—that of attributing a mental state to another (de Vignemont and Jacob 2010/under review, 22).

At this point it might be suggested that the claim of de Vignemont and co-authors (2006, 2010/under review) is not that empathy enables us to understand the type of emotion another person is having. Rather, what empathy enables is an understanding of what it is "like" for the other person—what that person is "going through." In other words, empathy improves or "deepens," as it were, the understanding of others' emotions that we get from other sources, and it does so by giving us more of an "inside-view" of a stretch of their affective lives. We suspect something along such lines may indeed be what de Vignemont and co-authors would want to say. Consider what she and Singer say about the conditions under which a person is able to empathize with someone suffering from vertigo: "An empathizer who does not suffer from vertigo can hardly empathize with a target who is frightened by the void below him because he does not have the specific feeling of vertigo in his repertoire" (de Vignemont and Singer 2006, 438). The point here is surely not that you cannot see that the person suffering from vertigo is frightened unless you yourself suffer from vertigo. Rather, the point must be that you cannot really know "what it is *like*" for the other person unless you share his affliction.

We think, however, that it is far from obvious that empathy, as understood by de Vignemont and colleagues (2006, 2010/under review), will consistently facilitate this sort of deepened understanding of what another person is going through. If the two subjects in de Vignemont and Singer's example—and the description certainly does not rule this out—both have a void below them, one might wonder whether a would-be empathizer who *does* suffer from vertigo would be able to empathize with another person in this situation. Surely, it would be natural to think that his own feelings of vertigo would make him anything but "other-centered" in the sense required for empathy. What seems right about de Vignemont and Singer's (2006) observations is that unless you *have* felt similar things in the past and retain some memory of them, you may not be able to understand "from the inside" what a person suffering from vertigo is going though. But, first, it is not clear that only previous experiences of *vertigo* will fit the bill here. Why can I not achieve an equally good grasp of what the sufferer from vertigo is going through on the basis of having had other experiences of intense fear? Second, and more importantly, empathy, on de Vignemont and Singer's (2006) account, requires you to currently feel such feelings. And it seems plausible that in many situations being oneself in the grip of some affective state is disadvantageous, rather than helpful, when it comes to understanding what another person is going through.

If all this is right, it is questionable whether empathy as understood by de Vignemont and colleagues (2006, 2010/under review) really does contribute much of significance to social understanding. Perhaps this is a consequence that they would be willing to accept. But our hunch is that most researchers working on empathy will prefer to search for other options before embracing such a deflationary conclusion.

Conclusion

To summarize our arguments in the previous section, the definition of empathy offered by de Vignemont, Singer and Jacob is inadequate because:

1. It does not distinguish properly between empathy and emotional contagion.
2. It implausibly counts certain cases of responding with anger to other people's displays of anger as cases of empathizing.
3. It does not distinguish properly between empathy and sympathy.
4. It seemingly deprives empathy of any foundational role in interpersonal understanding.

If our arguments are on the right lines, then the obvious thing to do would be to rethink empathy altogether. In particular we should abandon the idea that an empathizer must be in an affective state that is isomorphic to the target's state.[12] The phenomenological account offers one—in our view quite plausible—way of achieving these aims.

Compared with ambitious attempts—along the lines of de Vignemont, Singer and Jacob—to provide necessary and sufficient conditions for empathy, the phenomenological proposal may seem vague and imprecise. According to the phenomenologists empathy is a kind of direct, noninferential, (quasi-)perceptual awareness of other people's emotions, sensations, and other psychological states. I empathize with another, that is, I have an empathic understanding of another when I see her anger as expressed in her face, for example. This makes empathy look like a simple phenomenon, and per se it gives us no inkling of the "mechanisms" involved in empathizing. But if we understand empathy in this way we have no problem seeing how it can be distinguished from emotional contagion or sympathy, and its pivotal role in interpersonal understanding becomes clear. Sometimes I may catch the mood in a bar, say, without empathizing with any particular person in the bar—which gives us contagion (seemingly) without empathy. At other times it may be the empathic perception of another's fear or sadness that leads me to feel afraid or sad myself—in which case contagion would seem to "build on top of" empathy. In neither sort of case can the two phenomena be confused. Similarly, the empathic detection of someone else's emotion, as we have explained in the first section of this chapter, is clearly different from the element of sympathy that may (or may not) accompany it. Finally, although empathy understood in this way has some clear limitations, its central role in social understanding can hardly be disputed.

Notes

1. "Empathy" is usually considered the standard translation of *Einfühlung*, and it so happens that Scheler himself only used the latter term rather sparingly, and when he did use it his attitude was frequently rather dismissive. However, Scheler's reservation was mainly due to his dissatisfaction with Lipps's projective theory of empathy, and for want of a better term we have decided to use "empathy" as the best way of capturing what Scheler was referring to when he spoke of a basic experience of others. It is telling that other contemporary phenomenologists reasoned in a similar way. Both Stein and Husserl also referred to Scheler's theory of empathy (*Einfühlung*) (Stein 1989, 27; Husserl 1999, 147).

2. The same, by the way, goes for sympathy. As Husserl writes, feeling sympathy with someone who has, say, lost his father, involves feeling sorry about the other's loss and sorrow, rather than simply feeling sorry about the death of the father (Husserl 2004, 194).

3. Strangely, this definition only seems to give us collectively *sufficient* conditions for empathy, whereas we would expect a definition to provide *necessary* and sufficient conditions. That the latter is indeed what de Vignemont and Singer (2006) intended to give is, however, at least implicitly confirmed by the fact that in another paper de Vignemont offers essentially the same definition but now implies that it gives *necessary* (but not sufficient) conditions: "Individual X could not empathize with individual Y unless (i) X were in some affective state or other; (ii) X's affective state were isomorphic with Y's affective state (or target state) in some relevant aspects; (iii) X's state were triggered by Y's state; and (iv) X were aware that Y is the source of X's own affective state" (de Vignemont 2009).

4. One slightly odd thing about this description is de Vignemont's and Jacob's (2010/under review) emphasis on the temporal mode of the experience. Why is the child anticipating a *future* pain of her own? What future are we talking about, the near or the far future? Why is she not simply experiencing vicarious pain in the present moment?

5. Actually, some may wish to classify this as a case of "personal distress" (see, e.g., Batson 2009, 7–8). However that may be, de Vignemont and Jacob (2010/under review) are clearly right in thinking of it as a "contagion-like" phenomenon.

6. The first person *sees* that the other person is sad, so condition (iii) is met. She feels sad herself, so (i) is met, and she is of course aware the other's sadness is the source of her own sorrow—hence (iv) is met too.

7. The case can easily be construed in such a way as to meet all de Vignemont and Singer's (2006) requirements. It obviously meets (i) and (ii); if what causes me to explode is the other person's expression of anger, (iii) is met as well. And finally if I am aware that my anger was caused by the other person—which is surely not implausible—(iv) is met.

8. Note that we have no problem accepting that empathy plays a part in the case that we describe. According to the phenomenological account of empathy, the fearful and the hot-tempered person *alike* empathize when they notice the other person's anger. What is implausible is the suggestion, to which de Vignemont and colleagues (2006, 2010/under review) are committed, that only the hot-tempered person empathizes and that he does so precisely by responding with an isomorphic emotion—that is, anger.

9. Perhaps there is a third way of reading the "caring condition" that escapes the dilemma presented? Maybe so, but then the onus is on de Vignemont and Jacob (2010/under review) to explain how the condition must be understood.

10. To this, de Vignemont and colleagues (2006) might object that ascriptions of "observations" are extensional and thus do not imply understanding of what one sees. Just as I can observe the new iPad without having any inkling that that is what I am looking at, so I can observe another's emotional expression without understanding what I am seeing. This takes care of the circularity problem we have just claimed to detect in de Vignemont and colleagues' (2006) account. However, it does so at an implausibly high cost. For if "observing someone else's emotion" implies no understanding of what one observes *as* an emotion, the following (pathological) case would meet the requirements for empathy: A person notices another person's facial expression without realizing which affective state it expresses, indeed without realizing that it expresses *any* affective state. Yet the expression elicits a certain affective state in the observer (say, anger), and the observer is aware that her anger is somehow caused by the other person's facial contortions. Further, suppose that what the other person is expressing is an emotion of anger. Now if observation does not imply understanding, this example meets all the de Vignemont and Singer (2006) conditions for empathizing with another person's anger. Yet in our example the observer is *entirely oblivious* of the other's anger—indeed she is unaware that the target is feeling any particular emotion. And surely it will not do to classify such a case as one of empathizing with another's anger.

11. According to de Vignemont and Jacob (2010/under review), indeed, a subject must meet no less than five conditions to count as empathizing with someone else.

12. But if what is meant is only that an empathizer's own subpersonal emotional centers must be recruited (Goldman and Sripada 2005), then our criticism is compatible with this idea. But empathy is a personal-level concept; empathizing is something persons do or do not. A definition of empathy should therefore be in terms of what people experience and feel. Once such a definition is in place we can proceed to inquire into the underlying neural states and processes.

Whether empathy is in part enabled by neuronal states that "mirror" states in the target is a question on which we intend to remain neutral (cf. Zahavi 2011).

References

Baron-Cohen, S. 1995. *Mind-Blindness: An Essay on Autism and Theory of Mind*. Cambridge, MA: MIT Press.

Batson, C. D. 2009. These things called empathy: Eight related but distinct phenomena. In *The Social Neuroscience of Empathy*, edited by J. Decety and W. Ickes, 3–15. Cambridge, MA: MIT Press.

Bennett, M. R., and P. M. S. Hacker. 2003. *Philosophical Foundations of Neuroscience*. Oxford: Blackwell.

Decety, J., and W. Ickes, eds. 2009. *The Social Neuroscience of Empathy*. Cambridge, MA: MIT Press.

de Vignemont, F. 2009. Affective mirroring: Emotional contagion or empathy? In *Atkinson and Hilgard's Introduction to Psychology*, 15th ed., edited by S. Nolen-Hoeksema, B. Fredrickson, G. R. Loftus, and W. A. Wagenaar, 63. Florence, KY: Cengage Learning.

de Vignemont, F. 2010. Knowing other people's mental states as if they were one's own. In *Handbook of Phenomenology and Cognitive Science*, edited by D. Schmicking and S. Gallagher, 283–99. Dordrecht: Springer.

de Vignemont, F., and P. Jacob. 2010/under review. What is it like to feel another's pain?

de Vignemont, F., and T. Singer. 2006. The empathic brain: How, when and why? *Trends in Cognitive Sciences* 10: 435–441.

Gallese, V. 2001. The "shared manifold" hypothesis: From mirror neurons to empathy. *Journal of Consciousness Studies* 8 (5–7): 33–50.

Gallese, V. 2003. The manifold nature of interpersonal relations: The quest for a common mechanism. *Philosophical Transactions of the Royal Society of London. Series B, Biological Sciences* 358: 517–528.

Gallese, V., Keysers, C., and Rizzolatti, G. 2004. A unifying view of the basis of social cognition. *Trends in Cognitive Sciences* 8/9: 396–403.

Goldie, P. 1999. How we think of others' emotions. *Mind & Language* 14: 394–423.

Goldman, A. I. 1995a. In defense of the simulation theory. In *Folk Psychology: The Theory of Mind Debate*, edited by M. Davies and T. Stone, 191–206. Oxford: Blackwell.

Goldman, A. I. 1995b. Interpretation psychologized. In *Folk Psychology: The Theory of Mind Debate*, edited by M. Davies and T. Stone, 74–99. Oxford: Blackwell.

Goldman, A. I. 2006. *Simulating Minds: The Philosophy, Psychology, and Neuroscience of Mindreading*. New York: Oxford University Press.

Goldman, A. I., and C. S. Sripada. 2005. Simulationist models of face-based emotion recognition. *Cognition* 94: 193–213.

Gopnik, A., and H. M. Wellman. 1995. Why the child's theory of mind really is a theory. In *Folk Psychology: The Theory of Mind Debate*, edited by M. Davies and T. Stone, 232–258. Oxford: Blackwell.

Gordon, R. 1986. Folk psychology as simulation. *Mind & Language* 1: 158–171.

Hatfield, E., R. L. Rapson, and Y.-C. Le. 2009. Emotional contagion and empathy. In *The Social Neuroscience of Empathy*, edited by J. Decety and W. Ickes, 19–30. Cambridge, MA: MIT Press.

Husserl, E. 1973. *Zur Phänomenologie der Intersubjektivität I, Husserliana XIII*. Den Haag: Martinus Nijhoff.

Husserl, E. 1999. *Cartesian Meditations: An Introduction to Phenomenology*. Dordrecht: Springer.

Husserl, E. 2001. *Logical Investigations I*. London: Routledge.

Husserl, E. 2004. *Einleitung in die Ethik, Husserliana XXXVII*. Dordrecht: Kluwer.

Iacoboni, M. 2008. *Mirroring People: The Science of Empathy and How We Connect with Others*. New York: Picador.

Ingarden, R. 1994. *Gesammelte Werke—Band 6: Frühe Schriften zur Erkenntnistheorie*. Tübingen: Max Niemeyer.

Lipps, T. 1900. Ästhetische Einfühlung. *Zeitschrift für Psychologie und Physiologie der Sinnesorgane* 22: 415–50.

Lipps, T. 1907. Das Wissen von fremden Ichen. *Psychologische Untersuchungen* 1: 694–722.

Scheler, M. 1954. *The Nature of Sympathy,* translated by P. Heath. London: Routledge and Kegan Paul.

Schutz, A. 1967. *The Phenomenology of the Social World*. Evanston, IL: Northwestern University Press.

Stein, E. 1989. *On the Problem of Empathy*. Washington, DC: ICS Publishers.

Stueber, K. R. 2006. *Rediscovering Empathy: Agency, Folk Psychology, and the Human Sciences*. Cambridge, MA: MIT Press.

Zahavi, D. 2011. Empathy and mirroring: Husserl and Gallese. In *Life, Subjectivity and Art: Essays in Honor of Rudolf Bernet*, edited by R. Breeur and U. Melle. Dordrecht: Springer, in press.

2 Empathy, Evolution, and Human Nature

Allan Young

This chapter explores the place of empathy in the evolutionary history of human nature. It is written from the perspective of an anthropologist who studies how the sciences of human nature reach their conclusions. The ordinary language term "human nature" refers to a bundle of faculties and tendencies that distinguishes human beings from other animals and normal people from abnormal individuals. I am not interested in weighing the *truth* of these ideas about human nature but, rather, their *genealogy* and *reality*—that is to say, how the experts—scientists, philosophers, clinicians—reached their conclusions and how these conclusions will affect the conduct of life.

Human nature as we know it today originated in the Enlightenment and the emergence of a naturalistic conception of the mind—that is, a thing that is intimately associated with the brain and fundamentally unlike earlier mind-like conceptions associated with the soul (Ryle 1949, 22–23). Although it would be a mistake to talk about a standard version Enlightenment human nature, we can identify the version that provides the foundations for current conceptions of mind, brain, and empathy and the epistemic foundation for many of our core social institutions and sectors of knowledge production, including the social and behavioral sciences, psychiatry, and the law. This vision of human nature is based on three ideas. The mind is the body's command center and theater of self-awareness. The mind's default setting is rational self-interest: it seeks gratification and avoids distress. The human mind is autonomous and insulated, although its actual independence may be a matter of degree. In Gilbert Ryle's opinion the Enlightenment view of the mind (and our conventional knowledge) is unequivocal on this point: there is "no direct causal connection between what happens in one mind and what happens in another. Only through the medium of the public physical world can the mind of one person make a difference to the mind of another. . . . People can see, hear, and jolt one another's bodies, but they are irremediably blind and deaf to the workings of one another's minds and inoperative upon them" (Ryle 1949, 13). Jerrold Seigel has argued for a more nuanced interpretation of the key Enlightenment author, John Locke. "Far from reducing the self to an avatar of independent reason standing apart from the World, Locke threw the whole of selfhood into crisis, because his notion of the mind as *tabula rasa* or blank slate, formed by the shifting conditions of experience, threaten to deprive the self of any stability. Such a self was hardly a candidate for autonomy or self creation. . ." (Seigel 2005, 42; contrast this with Charles Taylor's remarks on Locke's "punctual self" [1989]).

This vision of human nature is, in some respects, puzzling. For how would self-interested humans ever coalesce into stable, self-reproducing societies? And how would the first simple groups evolve into complex social formations? This is called *the puzzle of the one and the many*. Thomas Hobbes's thesis was that our ancestors, guided by *reason* and driven by *fear*, transferred the private control of violent force to a sovereign who would employ this monopoly to secure the collective peace and defense. David Hume and Adam Smith proposed a different solution, and it is the one that now prevails. Self-interest is tempered by a second, weaker disposition, to "sympathy," the capacity to put oneself in the situation of others and feel some concern for their happiness and misery. Nor is there any good reason to assume that self-interest is intrinsically antisocial, since it mobilizes networks of exchange (goods, gifts, and assistance) and consequent bonds of dependence and obligation. Hume and Adam Smith also understood that sympathy—their notion encompasses our idea of "empathy"—is not only a solution but likewise a puzzle. Given that minds are autonomous and insulated from other minds, how is it possible to put oneself into someone else's situation? This is *the puzzle of other minds*. Reason provides part of the solution: Hume wrote about the capacity to understand others by means of analogy and resemblance, but he was unable to identify the source of this capacity except to suggest that it is innate. The final puzzle concerns my intuition that I, like other normal people, have a sentient self, and it has unity of consciousness. Stream of consciousness, sensory experience, memory, desire, volition, and imagination converge in this self in a way that corresponds with my use of first-person predicates in speech and thought. Hume was a conspicuous dissenter: he appreciated the strength and pervasiveness of this intuition, reflected on it, and concluded that it is unjustified. His contemporaries, notably Kant, disagreed on this, but *the puzzle of self-awareness* remains unresolved.

In the nineteenth and twentieth centuries, Enlightenment human nature became the subject of three scientific revolutions: a Darwinian revolution; a Mendelian revolution and subsequent neo-Darwinian synthesis; and a psychological revolution that is defined by the rise of the new sciences of mind—experimental psychology, neuropsychiatry, and psychodynamic psychiatry. The revolutions bring a fourth puzzle that was of less compelling interest during the Enlightenment: *the puzzle of the mind in the brain*. Are mind and brain one thing or two? Today we are witnesses to one more revolution—the rise of neuroscience and technology that brings the mind-brain puzzle into sharp focus. For the first time we can see, through functional neuroimaging, the mind working inside the brain. It is too early to know whether these developments will contribute only incrementally to the continuing historical evolution of Enlightenment human nature, or whether, as is being increasingly suggested, this is the beginning of a radically different way of knowing human nature, as a thing lacking either a mind or consciousness.

Mindless Human Nature

Here opinion is strikingly divided. On the one hand, there are those who join me in recognizing that *if you leave the Subject in your theory, you have not yet begun!* A good theory of consciousness *should* make a conscious mind look like an abandoned factory . . . full of humming machinery and nobody home to supervise it, or enjoy it, or witness it.
—Daniel Dennett (2005, 70)

According to Dennett consciousness is a real phenomenon but equivalent to a pandemonium in the brain created by neuronal traffic. The conventional version, premised on the unity of consciousness, is a successful illusion: it "resembles *stage* magic, a set of phenomena that exploit our gullibility, and even our desire to be fooled . . ." (Dennett 2005, 57). This is the minority opinion. The prevailing opinion is that consciousness requires a conscious subject (a self). An atomistic approach to studying consciousness—"the view that conscious states can be studied one by one or in small groups without reference to the cognitive system that has them"—is insufficient (Brook 2005, 401–7). Nonetheless, this is what research based on functional neuroimaging generally delivers. According to Ralph Adolphs these images have a "phrenological flavor" since cortical areas are pictured in isolation but, in reality, do not operate in isolation. They form parts of complex and largely unexplored connectional networks and brain systems. If we pick a brain system, however defined, and ask what it does, an analogous effect is produced: "a hodge-podge of different processes" (Uttal 2001; Adolphs 2010; 758, 760; Raichle 2010).

This is *not* how researchers and readers generally interpret task-driven brain images however. The phrenological flavor is absent: researchers and readers effortlessly "connect the dots." This disposition is explained in two ways. First, verbal descriptions (text) that accompany the images are generally "continuous with our commonsense understanding of our minds and the minds of other people" (Adolphs 2010, 760). Second, readers bring a "backstory" when they see the images—a neo-Darwinian history of the human brain, the mind, and empathic human nature—that connects the dots. That backstory is my subject.

A Neo-Darwinian Backstory

The term "backstory" describes a technique employed by writers to construct narratives and films. A narrative's backstory is the fictive or notional history that precedes the events described in the narrative. It allows competent readers to interpret otherwise cryptic elements in the text. An effective backstory makes fictional characters "recognizable" and creates expectations in the reader that the author may manipulate as the narrative develops. A prologue is an overt backstory; the "Introduction" section in science publications performs a similar function. But back-stories are also introduced incrementally within the main narrative's text. The invocation can be didactic, as when a fictional character overtly reflects on his past, or subtle, as when back-stories unfold in a series of clues and strings of bibliographic citations. The effectiveness of these clues for creating such a "subtext" depends partly on the reader's background knowledge.

Before proceeding to the backstory, I want to clarify what neo-Darwinian means in this context of the social brain. Beginning in the 1950s John Maynard Smith, an evolutionary biologist, pioneered an empiricist approach to natural selection that combined the methods and perspectives of population genetics, game theory, and cost-benefit analysis. The approach was the basis for a *dialectical* understanding of human biological evolution and, we shall see, a backstory for the neuroscience revolution (Maynard Smith 1979). In an article "Reconciling Marx and Darwin" published shortly before his death in 2004, Maynard Smith recalls Marx's thesis on human consciousness—thoughts, inferences, perceptions, and desires—the view that consciousness is determined by the material conditions of social life. Marx might reasonably claim to be a materialist, Maynard Smith writes, but he was not a *reductionist*, someone interested in investigating the biological evolution of social life and the brain that made human consciousness possible in the first place. Marx's vision of human nature as malleable—a view still shared by many cultural anthropologists—was unscientific and proved to be "tragically flawed" and a "manifest failure" when put into action by communist regimes.

The neo-Darwinian backstory for the social brain begins with the two puzzles. It is propelled forward, from the emergence of the earliest hominids (perhaps five million years ago) to the advent and dispersion of psychologically modern humans, by a dialectical logic. I consider each puzzle in turn. The first puzzle concerns *altruism*. Population geneticists define altruism as behavior that transfers some or all of the altruist's reproductive potential (fitness) to a beneficiary. In the most extreme case an altruist dies so that a beneficiary might live and reproduce. Altruistic behavior is often observed in animal populations, and it is presumed to be genetically determined. It is a puzzle because it gives the nonaltruist recipients (lacking altruism genes) a reproductive advantage. They will eventually outbreed altruists, and altruists and altruism genes will eventually disappear from the population. This does not happen, however, and that is the puzzle. W. D. Hamilton (1964) solved the puzzle in the 1960s with the theory of kin selection (inclusive fitness). The theory says that altruistic behavior, including self-sacrifice, has favorable cost-benefits if the beneficiaries are closely related to the altruists. When this happens altruism preserves a homogeneous gene pool and a continuing supply of altruism genes for future generations.

Hamilton's solution leads to a new puzzle once biologists discover populations in which altruistic behavior is common but in which the altruists and beneficiaries are often unrelated or too distantly related for Hamilton's solution. Robert Trivers, an anthropologist, solved this puzzle in 1971 by demonstrating that the arrangement works (benefits are greater than costs) if altruism is *reciprocal*. The recipient repays the altruist. Reciprocal behavior is common among nonhuman primates but limited to individuals living in close proximity. It is typically restricted to grooming and, less often, to food-sharing, and the interval between gift-giving and repayment is brief, a few seconds in the case of capuchin monkeys and just minutes with chimpanzees. More complex forms of reciprocity would involve dispersed partners and long intervals between gifts and repayment. In time multiple local groups would be connected, and extensive social networks and coalitions would develop. But these developments depend on the ability of the individuals to keep track of their exchanges and the reputations of potential exchange partners. Thus memory-based reciprocity represented a great leap forward but was cognitively demanding, and it presupposed various developments in the nervous system, including the capacity to inhibit the archaic impulse for immediate gratification.

When altruism and reciprocity are limited to a genetically homogeneous population, *cheating* is impossible. Of course there will be nonreciprocators, and their reproductive fitness will benefit from the costs absorbed by the altruists. But the costs and benefits circulate within a closed system. The term "cheater" is reserved for genetically heterogeneous populations, in which costs and benefits can accumulate within different lineages—circumstances that emerge together with memory-based reciprocity. Once again, there is a solution (reciprocity) that creates a problem (cheaters) and a puzzle. Cheaters are inevitable because all organisms are driven to maximize their reproductive interests and the interests of close kin—a neo-Darwinian premise. The cost-benefits of cheating always favor cheaters. All things being equal, cheaters (nonreciprocators) will outbreed the reciprocators; the nascent social networks will collapse; human social evolution will progress no farther (Nowak and Sigmund 2005; Rosas 2008). Of course the collapse has not occurred. This is a puzzle. There is a neo-Darwinian solution, and it leads to a further contradiction. Puzzle ⇒ solution ⇒ contradiction ⇒ puzzle ⇒ and so forth: this is the dialectic that glues the backstory together.

In this case the solution is in two parts. The social fabric is preserved by the evolution of positive sentiments that include friendship, gratitude, and sympathy. Fast forward to the present time: evidence from game-playing experiments, mathematical modeling and simulation, and ethnographies of small-scale, preindustrial communities indicate that positive sentiments are insufficient to prevent the collapse. Something stronger is needed, and the evidence points to a gene-driven impulse to *punish* cheaters. The solution is efficient except in one respect: it cannot pay for itself; the fitness costs of being an enforcer exceed the benefits. Punishment consumes resources (e.g., energy) and can be terminally expensive if cheaters retaliate violently. For this reason the enforcer's behavior is labeled "altruistic punishment." There is a further problem or contradiction, in that punishment creates a new class of cheaters, namely friends and neighbors who are good reciprocators but unwilling to be enforcers. These are "second order cheaters"; they get the cost-free benefits of punishment, and eventually they should outbreed gene-driven enforcers (Boyd et al. 2003).

Human Nature and Empathic Cruelty

Punishment can prevent entropy, but why would a rational individual—someone innately self-interested and able to estimate cost-benefits—become an enforcer? Benefits are often hypothetical (scheduled to arrive in the distant future) and indirect (dissuading *potential* cheaters), and costs are unpredictable (perhaps bringing retaliation by the cheater or his kin). Even when an enforcer gets his fair share, he cannot know whether this would happen without his intervention. Thus material rewards can provide only a weak motive for altruistic punishment.

A solution reported in the recent experiment, "The Neural Basis of Altruistic Punishment," published in *Science*, provides a solution (de Quervain et al. 2004). The experiment is based on the "trust game." Player A transfers a sum to B, expecting B to return a fair share back to him. If A believes that B has violated the fairness norm, he can punish this "defector" (B) in the next round. Player A must pay to enforce the norm; thus the option simulates altruistic punishment. Player A is given one minute to decide; meanwhile his brain is scanned. PET scan images of enforcers' brains show activation of the caudate nucleus of the dorsal striatum associated with dopamine excretion and the brain's "reward center." Activation occurs when enforcers *anticipate* punishing defectors, and the intensity of activation correlates positively with the severity of the imagined punishment. In effect the enforcer's brain is *paying itself back*. Punishment is its own reward.

The Concise Oxford Dictionary defines "cruelty" as "having pleasure in another's suffering." If so the backstory permits the conclusion that cruelty entered human nature along with our felicitous prosocial disposition to altruistic punishment. (This is an ethnographic observation *not a moral judgment*.) The enforcers in the experiment actively imagined the disappointment that will be experienced by the defectors; they vicariously participated in the defectors' state of mind. This is not simple cruelty but, more precisely, *empathic cruelty*.

Research by Takahashi et al. (2009) on *Schadenfreude* is even more explicit. According to Takahashi *Schadenfreude* (pleasurable response to news that a misfortune has befallen a person who is envied or resented) and envy (a painful feeling of inferiority and resentment that results from awareness of someone else's superior quality, achievement, or possessions) are two sides of one coin. Students in the experiment read descriptions of three fictive students—A, B, and C—and were instructed to see B and C from A's perspective. Student A had average abilities, achievements, possessions, social endowments, and prospects. Student B was superior and successful in each respect and also in life domains important to A. Student C was superior and successful but in domains not important to A. Participants silently read additional texts pertaining to A, B, and C while their brains were scanned (by fMRI). In phase 1 the texts described the successes of B and C, and participants reported how envious the descriptions made them feel. In phase 2, texts described misfortunes that spoiled events and prospects for A, B, and C. Participants reported the intensity of their pleasure (*Schadenfreude*) regarding each of the events. Brain images and self-reports were compared. Intense emotions focused on B. Intense envy (phase 1) correlated with activation of the anterior cingulate cortex. Intense *Schadenfreude* (phase 2) correlated with activation of the ventral striatum—"a central node of reward processing" according to Takahashi. The results replicate the outcome (empathic cruelty) reported by de Quervain (see also Lanzetta and Englis 1989; Knoch et al. 2006; Singer et al. 2006; Fehr and Camerer 2007; Fliessbach et al. 2007; and Shamay-Tsoory et al. 2009).

Empathy and Evolution

The neo-Darwinian backstory of the social brain starts with two puzzles: one of these concerns altruism; the second concerns the brain. The size of the human brain is an evolutionary puzzle. Our ancestors split from the great apes six million years ago. During this period the ancestral human brain quadrupled in volume. The metabolic costs of the human brain are enormous: it constitutes 2 percent of total body weight and consumes 15 percent of cardiac output and 20 percent of body oxygen, and these demands are ceaseless and inflexible. We can assume that the bigger brain paid for itself, yielding favorable cost-benefits. However, efforts to model these developments indicate that increasing metabolic costs would eventually exceed benefits. Why did the brain continue to grow (in size and power) when further growth was no longer adaptive? This is the puzzle, and its solution is a story about how brains adapted to other brains.

The process is a *cognitive arms race* (Byrne and Whiten 1988; Barton and Dunbar 1997; Dunbar 2003). It begins with the emergence of a "mind-reading" capacity: the ability to detect the intentions and predict the behavior of other individuals. Mind reading facilitates more complex social relations, but it also facilitates "cheaters," individuals who use mind reading to manipulate and deceive other individuals. All things being equal, cheating is cost-effective: it gives cheaters a reproductive advantage. As cheaters increased as a proportion of a population, social life would grow more unpredictable, thus undermining the stability of social relations. Entropy loomed. This might have been the evolutionary fate of our hominid ancestors, but it was not. Entropy was avoided through a further improvement to the neural hardware: the emergence of a "cheater detector." This could be no more than a temporary solution however. The next generation of opportunists used their improved brains to subvert the function (or adaptation) of the cheater detector. Entropy was avoided by the evolution of an improved version of the cheater detector that would, of course, facilitate the emergence of a cohort of improved cheaters. And so on over millions of years, following the dialectical logic of the neo-Darwinian backstory.

This part of the story begins with mind reading. Opinion in neuroscience is divided on the biological basis of this ability. One view is that mind reading is facilitated by a *human mirror neuron system*. A mirror neuron functions as a sensory neuron (responding to sight, sound, touch, smell) and a motor neuron (preparing the organism to perform the observed behavior). Activation patterns are a source of the "representations" that enable an observer's brain to infer the actor's immediate intentions. The activation also functions as a mechanism that enables spectators to *passively experience* someone else's situation: a situation that is being observed directly or imagined. Human mirror neurons comprise a *system* in that they extend to multiple regions of the brain and facilitate multiple cognitive functions (Fadiga et al. 1996; Gallese and Goldman 1998; Rizzolatti and Arbib 1998; Gallese 2001; Fogassi, Gallese, and Rizzolatti 2002; Kohler et al. 2002; Rizzolatti and Craighero 2004; Fogassi et al. 2005; Iacoboni et al. 2005; Tettamanti et al. 2005).

These claims are contested by critics who cite (1) contradictory empirical evidence against the existence of specialized sensory-motor neurons in humans; (2) the defective epistemology of key concepts, notably neural "representations"; and (3) plausible alternative interpretations for evidence of a human mirror-neuron system (Jacob and Jeannerod 2005; Singer 2006; Brass et al. 2007; Csibra and Gergely 2007; Dinstein 2008; Dinstein et al. 2007, 2008; Jacob 2008; Turella et al. 2009; cf. Mukamel et al. 2010; see Machamer et al. 2000 and Carr et al. 2003 on the epistemology of "mechanisms"). Thus there are rival explanatory accounts of mind reading: a strong version based on mirror neurons and a weak version based on cognitive mechanisms, notably simulation ("strong" and "weak" are markers, not value judgments).

In the strong version, mind reading emerges at an early stage, prior to the hominid split from the ancestral apes. The process continues through four stages and ends around 50,000 years ago, with the emergence of language. Stage 1: The observer's mirror neurons *resonate* with the neurons of the agent performing a goal-directed action or facial emotion. A transient "primary representation" of the neural activation pattern is produced but is sufficient for the observer to infer the actor's intention. Emotional *contagion* is possible at this stage, but emotional *empathy* is not. The nonhuman primates have not evolved beyond this stage. Stage 2: The primary representation can be *uncoupled* from the transient experience and *copied* inside the brain. The observer now projects the representation back onto its source and perceives it as an attribute (state) of the source. This capacity is the basis for "perspective-taking" as well as cognitive and emotional empathy. Copies are archived in the observer's memory and provide a library of action patterns. True imitation is now possible. Stage 3: The representations are conscious and objectified—they can be put into words. The brain's mirror experience is transformed into first-person knowledge—*my* feelings, *my* awareness—and then projected onto the observed individual, to constitute the observer's third-person knowledge.

In both strong and weak versions the evolution of empathy is understood to be a prosocial development: "the 'glue' of the social world, drawing us to help others and stopping us from hurting others" (Lawson, Baron-Cohen, and Wheelwright 2004, 163; see also Williams et al. 2001; Baron-Cohen, Knickmeyer, and Belmonte 2005; Wheelright et al. 2006; Iacoboni and Dapretto 2006). According to Simon Baron-Cohen, an authority on autism, human evolution produced two (polar) kinds of brains: a "female" brain with highly developed empathic capacities and a "male" brain adapted to manipulating objects and creating systems. Empathy originated as a prosocial adaptation allowing females to detect the wants of preverbal children and the moods of the potentially dangerous males with whom they lived (see also Hrdy 2009). Autistic individuals are characteristically poor empathizers, and autism's epidemiology is biased toward males with a 10 to 1 ratio in high-functioning autistic disorder.

In both versions there is the further assumption that empathy is intrinsically a morally positive disposition. According to Baron-Cohen and Wheelwright (2004), we respond to suffering in three ways: the response mirrors the sufferer's distress (we experience it); the response is culturally appropriate (e.g., pity) but does not mirror the suffering; or the observer takes pleasure in the sufferer's condition. They equate empathy with the first two responses and explicitly exclude the third. De Quervain's (2004) research vindicates a further possibility—empathic cruelty—in which the observer's brain mirrors the sufferer's distress and also takes pleasure in the sufferer's condition.

This is an unexpected twist in the evolutionary backstory: evidence of an evolved empathic disposition that is simultaneously prosocial and cruel. Human nature in the age of neuroscience grows morally complex: a theme that recurs in the story of the cognitive arms race, where an uncomplicated kind of cheating, the refusal to reciprocate, evolves, via mind reading, into *deception*, the effort to represent the current situation as something different from the reality. Deception puts great demands on the brain, which is now required to do two things simultaneously. An individual must construct a lie and also withhold (inhibit) the truth. Experimental and clinical evidence suggests that telling the truth is the brain's default response, a legacy of a prosocial evolutionary adaptation. "[R]esponding with a lie demands something 'extra' and . . . will engage executive prefrontal systems [responsible for planning, decision-making, and monitoring] more than does telling the truth" (Spence 2004, 8;

also Spence et al. 2004: 1756–1757). Thus a deceiver is in constant danger of signaling the truth and betraying himself, for instance, by involuntary and detectable hesitation preceding a lie. To succeed, deception requires a capacity for *self-deception*, the ability to conceal one's true intentions and facts from oneself (Trivers 1971). At this point, two unprecedented objects are created—there is the other (created via projection) and the self (refracted in a *doppelganger*, the fraudulent self).

Empathic Time Travel

The evolutionary origins of the self are brought to life in research on "mental time travel" (Suddendorf et al. 2009). Mental time travel is the capacity to project one's self into situations in the past, future, and subjunctive (an alternative scenario to the actual past or present). Travel to the past evolved first and provided a prototype (an episodic memory in which the thinker is spectator or protagonist) for constructing mental representations of possible futures and also alternative presents and pasts. (See Ingvar 1985 for initial appearance of "memory of the future"; see Busby and Suddendorf 2005 and Schacter et al. 2007 on role of the "prospective brain" in facilitating strategic planning and behavioral flexibility in new situations; and see Okuda et al. 2003, Addis et al. 2007, and Szpunar et al. 2007 on shared and nonshared neural substrates of memories of the past and future.) The emergence of language—notably pronouns and verb forms—and empathy were prerequisite for the evolution of mental time travel (Corballis 2009). The idea that we simply "project" ourselves wholesale into the past or future oversimplifies time travel. It is a first-person experience that requires the splitting of the self: one must be both here-and-now and there-and-then at the same time. The bond between the split-selves is empathic, but not necessarily positive. (In this sense, time travel parallels Triver's account of self-deception.)

Neuroscience makes it possible to see time travel: pain provides an efficient modality. Philip Jackson, Jean Decety, and their collaborators conducted fMRI experiments in which they asked participants to imagine themselves and others in painful situations (Jackson et al. 2006). In other words participants traveled to the subjunctive (an alternative present-time). One expects that, in some participants, the targeted situations stimulated spontaneous time travel to other places as well—notably travel to intensely empathic memories involving loved ones in pain. The imagined situations activated—one might say "mirrored"—brain regions reliably associated with experiencing the emotional content of pain in present-time. There was no phenomenological confusion between the mental act and the experience however. Neuroimages in the self versus other scenarios were similar, but, as one might expect, there were discernible differences—which is what one would expect, given that "a minimal distinction between self and other is essential for social interaction in general and for empathy in particular" (Decety and Batson 2009: 123).

In the neo-Darwinian backstory human evolutionary history begins with a great leap forward. Up to this point social exchange is based on altruism and simple kinds of reciprocity between genetically similar individuals. Afterwards, relations take the form of networks of exchange (reciprocity) among individuals genetically unrelated or only distantly related. Many problems were encountered along the dialectical road to modern times. The "future" was one of these problems. Where reciprocity entails long delays between giving and repayment, exchange partners must share some awareness of time as a continuum that connects past-time to future-time and is the sine qua non for "debt." It is assumed that the concept of time would emerge from incessant travels between memories of the past and the future.

The benefits of having or knowing "time" are obvious. Time travel promotes behavioral flexibility in novel situations, and it is the basis for long-term strategic planning targeted to preselected goals. With the emergence of language transient memories of individuals could be transformed into reproducible narratives that could be accumulated and circulated within groups, creating a powerful collective memory. But human nature can be uncooperative since there is a demonstrable tendency for people to treat present-time and future-time unequally when they calculate costs and benefits: they discount future benefits while they inflate costs incurred in the present. Thus self-interest is intrinsically impulsive and opportunistic, going for immediate gain. If unrestrained it limits reciprocity and would have curtailed the dialectical developments described in the backstory. We have already seen this worked in the genesis of punishment in the cost-benefits of being an enforcer and the benefits (rewards) provided by empathic cruelty and time travel to the future. A suitable countermotivation device was needed, and there was one available (see above discussion on the evolutionary origins of empathic cruelty):

> Memory for emotions . . . does not align with our current goals. This is striking in the common phenomenon of rumination, the unwanted but persistent activation of thoughts concerning an unpleasant past situation. . . . Time travel . . . provides emotions that bypass current goals, as well as time discounting and . . . provide[s] us with immediate counter-rewards against opportunistic motivation. (Boyer 2010, 222)

Clinical psychiatry was acquainted with mental time travel *avant la lettre* as early as the 1880s. Today, posttraumatic stress disorder (PTSD) is the most widely known time-travel syndrome (Young 2004). PTSD comprises an etiological event, a distressful and intrusive memory of this event, and a behavioral syndrome that represents an adaptation to the memory. Traumatic memories are a pathological expression of the "phenomenon of rumination" mentioned by Boyer (Berntsen and Hall 2004). In the language of psychiatry, traumatic memories are "reexperiences," and their exemplar is the "flashback." *Schreckneurose* or fright neurosis is especially interesting in this regard. The disorder, the German variation of shellshock during World War I, was characterized by the victim's terrifying dreams of a traumatizing experience. In the view of influential German doctors the syndrome could be caused by reexperiences (memories, nightmares) of the future in combination with the past. The theory is that the soldiers were fixated on visions of their own deaths. The man is overcome by an *empathic tenderness* for himself—the subject in the nightmares and intrusive images. The remembered event is a composite of two events: a real past event and an imagined future event. The past is reenacted in the future but with a significant change. The past event was harmless; the future event is fatal. He experiences two events as a single, etiological event in the past. His abnormality is a weakness of will and an excess of self-empathy. His symptoms, which often include psychogenic paralysis, are an unconscious effort to hide from the future. His true defect is moral, not medical. A real man (a soldier) lives in the present moment. The doctor's job is to terminate the patient's pathogenic time travel with the most effective means, including electrical torture (Young 1995; Lerner 2003; also Young 2002, on "self-traumatized perpetrators," a clinical phenomenon that intersects pathological time travel and empathic cruelty).

Conclusion

Human nature, as portrayed in the backstory, was fully formed during the Upper Paleolithic period. The story tells us that we are innately empathic but that "empathy" may include unexpected and undesirable attitudes: dissimulation, self-deceit, spitefulness, *Schadenfreude*, and cruelty. Western normative institutions—religion, secular ethics, clinical psychology—regard these attitudes as antisocial and self-destructive. The dialectical history in this chapter views these attitudes from a different perspective, as the causes and consequences of human social evolution and self-awareness. Leaving aside the professional cynics, no one is claiming that these attitudes form the core or essence of human nature. Mind reading, perspective-taking, hormonal responsiveness, and mental time travel were likewise responsible for psychological altruism, the propensity to adjust one's desires and intentions to the perceived needs or wishes of others. (In contrast the starting point for the neo-Darwinian backstory is "biological altruism," which is defined by fitness costs and unconcerned with altruists' perceptions and intentions.) Human nature as described in the backstory is morally complex, even contradictory, certainly inclined to "read and share the concern of others" (Hrdy 2009) but likewise prepared for cruel pleasures.

References

Addis, D. R., A. T. Wong, and D. L. Schacter. 2007. Remembering the past and imagining the future: Common and distinct neural substrates during event construction. *Neuropsychologia* 45: 1363–1377.

Adolphs, R. 2010. Conceptual challenges and directions for social neuroscience. *Neuron* 65: 752–767.

Baron-Cohen, S., R. C. Knickmeyer, and M. K. Belmonte. 2005. Sex differences in the brain: implications for explaining autism. *Science* 310: 819–823.

Baron-Cohen, S., and S. Wheelwright. 2004. The empathy quotient: an investigation of adults with Asperger syndrome or high functioning autism, and normal sex differences. *Journal of Autism and Developmental Disorders* 34: 163–175.

Barton, R. A., and R. I. M. Dunbar. 1997. Evolution of the social brain. In *Machiavellian Intelligence II*, edited by A. Whiten and R.W. Byrne, 240–263. Cambridge, UK: Cambridge University Press.

Berntsen, D., and N. M. Hall. 2004. The episodic nature of involuntary autobiographical memories. *Memory & Cognition* 32: 789–803.

Boyd, R., H. Gintis, S. Bowles, and P. J. Richerson. 2003. The evolution of altruistic punishment. *Proceedings of the National Academy of Sciences of the United States of America* 100: 3531–3535.

Boyer, P. 2010. Evolutionary economics of mental time travel? *Trends in Cognitive Sciences* 12: 219–224.

Brass, M., R. M. Schmitt, S. Spengler, and G. Gergely. 2007. Investigating action understanding: Inferential processes versus action simulation. *Current Biology* 17: 2117–2121.

Brook, A. (2005). Making consciousness safe for neuroscience. In *Cognition and the Brain: the Philosophy and Neuroscience Movement*, edited by A. Brook and K. Akins, 397–422. Cambridge: Cambridge University Press.

Busby, J., and T. Suddendorf. 2005. Recalling yesterday and predicting tomorrow. *Cognitive Development* 20: 362–372.

Byrne, R. W., and A. Whiten. 1988. *Machiavellian Intelligence*. Oxford: Oxford University Press.

Carr, L., M. Iacoboni, M.-C. Dubeau, J. C. Mazziotta, and G. L. Lenzi. 2003. Neural mechanisms of empathy in humans: A relay from neural systems for imitation to limbic areas. *Proceedings of the National Academy of Sciences of the United States of America* 100: 5497–5502.

Corballis, M. C. 2004. The origins of modernity: Was autonomous speech the critical factor? *Psychological Review* 111: 543–552.

Corballis, M. C. 2009. Mental time travel and the shaping of language. *Experimental Brain Research* 192: 553–560.

Csibra, G., and G. Gergely. 2007. "Obsessed with goals": Functions and mechanisms of teleological interpretation of actions in humans. *Acta Psychologica* 124: 60–78.

Decety, J., and C. D. Batson. 2009. Empathy and morality: Integrating social and neuroscience approaches. *The Moral Brain: Essays on the Evolutionary and Neuroscientific Aspects of Morality*, edited by J. Verplaetse, J. Braeckman, and J. De Schrijver, 109–127. Dordrecht, Netherlands: Springer.

Dennett, D. 2005. *Sweet Dreams: Philosophical Obstacles to a Science of Consciousness*. Cambridge, MA: MIT Press.

de Quervain, D. J.-F., U. Fischbacher, V. Treyer, M. Schellhammer, U. Schnyder, A. Buck, and E. Fehr. 2004. The neural basis of altruistic punishment. *Science* 305: 1254–1258.

Dinstein, I. 2008. Human cortex: Reflections of mirror neurons. *Current Biology* 18: R956–R959.

Dinstein, I., U. Hasson, N. Rubin, and D. J. Heege. 2007. Brain areas selective for both observed and executed movements. *Journal of Neurophysiology* 98: 1415–1427.

Dinstein, I., C. Thomas, M. Behrmann, and D. J. Heeger. 2008. A mirror up to Nature. *Current Biology* 18: R13–R18.

Dunbar, R. I. M. 2003. The social brain: mind, language, and society in evolutionary perspective. *Annual Review of Anthropology* 32: 163–181.

Fadiga, L., L. G. Pavesi, and G. Rizzolatti. 1996. Motor facilitation during observation: A magnetic simulation study. *Journal of Neurophysiology* 73: 2608–2611.

Fehr, E., and C. F. Camerer. 2007. Social neuroeconomics: The neural circuitry of social preferences. *Trends in Cognitive Science* 11: 419–427.

Fliessbach, K., B. Weber, P. Trautner, T. Dohmen, U. Sunde, C. E. Elger, and A. Falk. 2007. Social comparison affects reward-related brain activity in the human ventral striatum. *Science* 318: 1305–1308.

Fogassi, L., P. F. Ferrari, B. Gesierich, S. Rozzi, F. Chersi, and G. Rizzolatti. 2005. Parietal lobe: from action organization to intention understanding. *Science* 308: 662–667.

Fogassi, L., V. Gallese, and G. Rizzolatti. 2002. Hearing sounds, understanding actions: action representation in mirror neurons. *Science* 297: 846–848.

Gallese, V. 2001. The "shared manifold" hypothesis: from mirror neurons to empathy. *Journal of Consciousness Studies* 8: 33–50.

Gallese, V., and A. Goldman. 1998. Mirror neurons and the simulation theory of mind reading. *Trends in Cognitive Sciences* 2: 493–501.

Hamilton, W. D. 1964. The genetical evolution of social behaviour. I. *Journal of Theoretical Biology* 7: 1–16.

Hrdy, S. B. 2009. *Mothers and Others: the Evolutionary Origins of Mutual Understanding*. Cambridge, MA: Harvard University Press.

Iacoboni, M., and M. Dapretto. 2006. The mirror neuron system and the consequences of its dysfunction. *Nature Reviews Neuroscience* 7: 942–951.

Iacoboni, M., I. Molnar-Szakacs, V. Gallese, G. Buccino, J. C. Mazziotta, and G. Rizzolatti. 2005. Grasping the intentions of others with one's own mirror neuron system. PLoS *Biology* 3: e79.

Ingvar, D. H. 1985. "Memory of the future": An essay on the temporal organization of conscious awareness. *Human Neurobiology* 4: 127–136.

Kohler, E., C. Keysers, M. A. Umlitá, L. Fogassi, V. Gallese, and G. Rizzolatti. 2002. Hearing sounds, understanding actions: Action representation in mirror neurons. *Science* 297: 846–848.

Jackson, P. L., E. Brunet, A. N. Meltzoff, and J. Decety. 2006. Empathy examined through the neural mechanisms involved in imagining how I feel versus how you feel pain. *Neuropsychologia* 44: 752–761.

Jacob, P. 2008. What do mirror neurons contribute to human social cognition? *Mind and Language* 23: 190–223.

Jacob, P., and M. Jeannerod. 2005. The motor theory of social cognition: a critique. *Trends in Cognitive Sciences* 9: 21–25.

Knoch, D., A. Pascual-Leone, K. Meyer, V. Treyer, and E. Fehr. 2006. Diminishing reciprocal fairness by disrupting the right prefrontal cortex. *Science* 314(5800): 829–832.

Lawson, J., S. Baron-Cohen, and S. Wheelwright. 2004. Empathising and systemising in adults with and without Asperger syndrome. *Journal of Autism and Developmental Disorders* 34: 301–310.

Lanzetta, J. T, and B. G. Englis. 1989. Expectations of cooperation and competition and their effects on observers' vicarious emotional responses. *Journal of Personality and Social Psychology* 46: 543–554.

Lerner, P. 2003. *Hysterical Men: War, Psychiatry, and the Politics of Trauma in Germany, 1890–1930.* Ithaca, NY: Cornell University Press.

Machamer, P., L. Darden, and C. F. Craver. 2000. Thinking about mechanisms. *Philosophy of Science* 67: 1–25.

Maynard Smith, J. 1979. Game theory and the evolution of behaviour. *Proceedings of the Royal Society of London. Series B. Biological Sciences* 205: 475–488.

Maynard Smith, J. 2001. Reconciling Marx and Darwin. *Evolution; International Journal of Organic Evolution* 55: 1496–1498.

Mukamel, R., A. D. Eckstrom, A. Kaplan, M. Iacoboni, and I. Fried. 2010. Single-neuron responses in humans during execution and observation of actions. *Current Biology* 20: 750–756.

Nowak, M. A., and K. Sigmund. 2005. Evolution of indirect reciprocity. *Nature Reviews. Neuroscience* 437: 1291–1298.

Okuda, J., T. Fujii, H. Ohtake, T. Tsukiura, K. Tanji, K. Suzuki, R. Kawashima, H. Fukuda, M. Itoh, and A. Yamadori. 2003. Thinking of the future and past: the roles of the frontal pole and the medial temporal lobes. *NeuroImage* 19: 1369–1380.

Raichle, M. E. 2010. Two views of brain function. *Trends in Cognitive Sciences* 14: 180–190.

Rizzolatti, G., and M. A. Arbib. 1998. Language within our grasp. *Trends in Neurosciences* 21: 188–194.

Rizzolatti, G., and L. Craighero. 2004. The mirror-neuron system. *Annual Review of Neuroscience* 27: 169–192.

Rosas, A. 2008. The return of reciprocity: A psychological approach to the evolution of cooperation. *Biology and Philosophy* 23: 555–566.

Ryle, G. 1949. *The Concept of Mind*. London: Hutchinson.

Schacter, D., D. R. Addis, and R. L. Buckner. 2007. Remembering the past to imagine the future: the prospective brain. *Nature Reviews. Neuroscience* 8: 657–661.

Seigel, J. 2005. *The Idea of the Self: Thought and Experience in Western Europe Since the Seventeenth Century*. Cambridge: Cambridge University Press.

Shamay-Tsoory, S.G., M. Fischer, J. Dvash, H. Harari, N. Perach-Bloom, and Y. Levkovitz. 2009. Intranasal administration of oxytocin increases envy and schadenfreude (gloating). *Biological Psychiatry* 66: 864–870.

Singer, T. 2006. The neuronal basis and ontogeny of empathy and mind reading: review of literature and implications for future research. *Neuroscience and Biobehavioral Reviews* 30: 855–863.

Singer, T., B. Seymour, J. P. O'Dougherty, K. E. Stephan, D. J. Dolan, and C. D. Frith. 2006. Empathic neural responses are modulated by the perceived fairness of others. *Nature* 439: 466–469.

Spence, S. A. 2004. The deceptive brain. *Journal of the Royal Society of Medicine* 97: 6–9.

Spence, S. A., M. D. Hunter, T. F. D. Farrow, R. D. Green, D. H. Leung, C. J. Hughes, and V. Ganesan. 2004. A cognitive neurobiological account of deception: Evidence from functional neuroimaging. *Philosophical Transactions of the Royal Society of London B* 359: 1755–1762.

Spence, S. A., M. D. Hunter, and G. Harpin. 2002. Neuroscience and the will. *Current Opinion in Psychiatry* 15: 519–526.

Suddendorf, T., D. R. Addis, and M. C. Corballis. 2009. Mental time travel and the shaping of the human mind. *Philosophical Transactions of the Royal Society B* 364: 1317–1324.

Szpunar, K. K., J. M. Watson, and K. B. McDermott. 2007. Neural substrates of envisioning the future. *Proceedings of the National Academy of Sciences of the United States of America* 104: 642–647.

Takahashi, H., M. Kato, M. Matsuura, D. Mobbs, T. Suhara, and Y. Okubo. 2009. When your gain is my pain and your pain is my gain: Neural correlates of envy and *schadenfreude*. *Science* 323: 937–39. Supporting Online Material at www.sciencemag.org/cgi/content/full/323/5916/937/DC1

Taylor, C. 1989. *Sources of the Self: The Making of Modern Identity*. Cambridge, MA: Harvard University Press.

Tettamanti, M., G. Buccino, M. C. Succaman, V. Gallese, M. Danna, P. Scifo, F. Fazio, G. Rizzolatti, S. E. Cappa, and D. Perani. 2005. Listening to action-related sentences activates fronto-parietal motor circuits. *Journal of Cognitive Neuroscience* 17: 273–281.

Trivers, R. L. 1971. The evolution of reciprocal altruism. *Quarterly Review of Biology* 46: 35–57.

Turella, L., A. C. Pierno, F. Tubaldi, and U. Castiello. 2009. Mirror neurons in humans: Consisting or confounding evidence? *Brain and Language* 108: 10–21.

Uttal, W. R. 2001. *The New Phrenology: On the Localization of Cognitive Processes in the Brain.* Cambridge: MIT Press.

Wheelwright, S., S. Baron-Cohen, N. Goldenfeld, J. Delaney, D. Fine, R. Smith, and A. Wakabayashi. 2006. Predicting autism spectrum quotient (AQ) from the Systemizing Quotient-Revised (SQ-R) and Empathy Quotient (EQ). *Brain Research* 1079: 47–56.

Williams, J. H. G., A. Whitten, T. Suddendorf, and D. I. Perrett. 2001. Imitation, mirror neurons and autism. *Neuroscience and Biobehavioural Review* 25: 287–295.

Young, A. 1995. *The Harmony of Illusions: Inventing Posttraumatic Stress Disorder.* Princeton, NJ: Princeton University Press.

Young, A. 2002. The self-traumatized perpetrator as a "transient mental illness." *L'Évolution Psychiatrique* 67: 26–50.

Young, A. 2004. When traumatic memory was a problem: On the antecedents of PTSD. In *Posttraumatic Stress Disorder: Issues and Controversies*, edited by G. Rosen, 127–46. Chichester, UK: John Wiley.

II The Contribution of Social Psychology

3 The Empathy-Altruism Hypothesis: Issues and Implications

C. Daniel Batson

I came to empathy as a research topic through a back door—and, going through the door I did, some would say I never got to empathy. My interest was in motivation for helping those in need: Is helping ever, in any degree, motivated by concern for the needy, or is our motivation always and exclusively self-interested? That is, are we humans capable of altruism—a motivational state with the ultimate goal of increasing another's welfare—or only egoism—a motivational state with the ultimate goal of increasing our own welfare. ("Ultimate" in these definitions refers to means-end relations not to a metaphysical first or final cause and not to evolutionary function. An *ultimate goal* is an end in itself. In contrast, an *instrumental goal* is a stepping stone to reach an ultimate goal.)

A review of the egoism-altruism debate in Western thought revealed that the most likely source of altruistic motivation was an other-oriented emotional response elicited by and congruent with the perceived welfare of the person in need. Over the centuries this other-oriented emotion has been called by many names—pity, compassion, tenderness, and sympathy. It involves feeling *for* the other, not feeling *as* the other feels. In social psychology in the 1970s, when I got interested in the question of the existence of altruism, this emotion was called *empathy* (Stotland 1969; Hoffman 1975; Krebs 1975), so that is the term I used. But to emphasize my specific interest in emotional response to another's suffering, I also used the term *empathic concern*. I called the claim that empathic concern produces altruistic motivation the *empathy-altruism hypothesis*.

Since the 1970s the term empathy has been used in a variety of other ways. (It was used in other ways before that time as well.) So to try to forestall confusion let me list some of the things that "empathy" in the empathy-altruism hypothesis does *not* mean (for a discussion of each of these, see Batson 2009).

- Knowing another's thoughts and feelings
- Adopting the posture or matching the neural response of another
- Coming to feel as another feels

- Feeling distress at witnessing another's suffering
- Imagining how one would think and feel in another's place
- Imagining how another thinks and feels
- A general disposition (trait) to feel for others

The empathy-altruism hypothesis makes no claim that any of these phenomena, each of which has been called empathy, produces altruistic motivation—except as the phenomenon evokes empathic concern.

The Research Problem

Given the definitions of altruism and egoism above, helping another person—even at great cost to self—may be altruistically motivated, egoistically motivated, or both. To know whether the motivation produced by empathic concern is altruistic, we must determine whether benefit to the other evoked by empathy is (1) an ultimate goal, and any self-benefits that result are unintended consequences (altruism), or (2) an instrumental means to reach the ultimate goal of gaining one or more self-benefits (egoism).

If empathy-induced helping benefits both a person in need and the helper, as it often does, how are we to know which is the ultimate goal? This puzzle has led many scientists to give up on the question of the existence of altruism, concluding that it cannot be addressed empirically—and often adding that motivation does not really matter anyway, only behavior matters (e.g., de Waal 2008). I think their surrender is premature. I think we *can* empirically discern people's ultimate goals; indeed, we do it all the time. We do it when we infer whether a student is really interested or only seeking a better grade (What happens to the student's interest after the grades are turned in?), why a friend chose one job over another, and whether politicians mean what they say or are only after votes. We also do it when someone does us a favor or is kind.

Four principles are important when we are attempting to determine a person's ultimate goal: (1) We cannot trust self-reports. People often do not know—or will not tell—their ultimate goals. (2) We do not observe goals or intentions directly; we infer them from behavior. (3) If we observe a behavior that has two potential ultimate goals, the true ultimate goal cannot be discerned. It is like having one equation with two unknowns. However, (4) if we change the situation so that this behavior is no longer the best route to one of these goals, and we still observe the behavior, then that goal is not ultimate. We can cross it off the list of possible ultimate goals.

These principles suggest a strategy for testing the empathy-altruism hypothesis. First, we need to identify plausible egoistic ultimate goals of the motivation to help evoked by empathy. Second, we need to vary the situation so that either the altruistic goal or one or more of the egoistic goals can be better reached without having to help.

Finally, we need to see whether this variation reduces helping. If it does, this goal may be ultimate. If it does not, we can cross this goal off the list.

Testing the Empathy-Altruism Hypothesis

Over the past thirty-five years this general strategy has been used to test the empathy-altruism hypothesis against its egoistic alternatives. Three general classes of possible self-benefits of empathy-induced helping have been identified, producing three classes of egoistic alternatives: (1) aversive-arousal reduction—reducing the empathic concern caused by witnessing another in need; (2) punishment avoidance—avoiding empathy-specific material, social, and self-punishments; and (3) reward seeking—gaining empathy-specific material, social, and self-rewards. Advocates of the empathy-altruism hypothesis do not deny that relieving an empathy-inducing need is likely to enable the helper to reduce aversive arousal, avoid punishments, and gain rewards. However, they claim that these benefits to self are not the ultimate goal of the motivation to help produced by empathic concern, only unintended consequences. Advocates of the egoistic alternatives disagree. They claim that one or more of these self-benefits is the ultimate goal.

Experimental Designs to Test the Empathy-Altruism Hypothesis against Its Egoistic Alternatives

Pursuing the strategy outlined above other social psychologists and I have conducted a series of experiments to test the empathy-altruism hypothesis against one or more of the three egoistic alternatives. Typically, although not always, we provide research participants with an opportunity to help a person in need. We manipulate not only the level of empathic concern felt for that person but also some cross-cutting variable that changes whether helping is the most effective means (1) to reach the altruistic ultimate goal of removing the other's need or (2) to reach one or more of the possible egoistic ultimate goals. Table 3.1 lists the cross-cutting variables we have used. These variables do not change the goal(s); they change the attractiveness or availability of behavioral routes to the different goal(s). As a result each variable listed in table 3.1 allows us to make competing empirical predictions from the empathy-altruism hypothesis and at least one of the egoistic alternatives.

Let me illustrate with an example. The most popular egoistic alternative to the empathy-altruism hypothesis has long been aversive-arousal reduction. This alternative claims that to feel empathic concern for someone in need is unpleasant, and we help those for whom we feel empathy because doing so eliminates the stimulus causing our concern.

To test this alternative we need to vary the situation so that empathic concern can be eliminated in a less costly way than by helping. One way to do this is by varying

Table 3.1

Variables That Can Differentiate Altruistic and Egoistic Motives for Helping

Variable	Altruistic motive	Egoistic motive		
		Arousal reducing	Punishment avoiding	Reward seeking
1. *Viability of escape*: Can the goal be reached by escape without helping?	Escape not viable	Escape viable (from victim's distress)	Escape viable (from own shame, guilt)	Escape not viable
2. *Necessity of one's help being effective*: Must one's help be effective to reach the goal?	Necessary	Necessary	Not necessary (if ineffectiveness justified)	Not necessary (if ineffectiveness justified)
3. *Acceptability of other helpers*: Whose help can attain the goal?	Oneself; others	Oneself; others	Oneself; others	Only oneself
4. *Need for rewards of helping*: What is the effect of increased need for the rewards of helping?	No effect	No effect	No effect	Increased motivation
5. *Salient cognitions*: What cognitions are salient when deciding whether to help?	Victim's welfare; costs of helping	Unclear	Anticipated punishments; costs of helping	Anticipated rewards; costs of helping

Adapted from Batson (1987).

whether the potential helper can—without helping—easily escape continued exposure to the other's suffering, the stimulus causing empathic concern. If the ultimate goal of empathy-aroused helping is to remove the empathic concern (egoism), then people who can easily escape should help less than those who cannot. If, on the other hand, the ultimate goal is to reduce the other's suffering (altruism), they should not help less. Reducing the empathic concern without helping does nothing to reduce the other's suffering.

Over a half-dozen experiments have been conducted employing this logic. Results consistently reveal that, when empathic concern is low, the rate of helping is high when escape is difficult but low when escape is easy. This is what we would expect if the ultimate goal of the motivation to help among those feeling little empathy is to relieve the distress caused by witnessing the other's suffering. However, when empathic concern is high, the rate of helping is high even when escape is easy. This is what we would expect if the ultimate goal of the motivation produced by empathic concern is to reduce the other's suffering not the empathic concern. These results clearly contradict the aversive-arousal reduction explanation of the motivation to help produced by empathy. They support the empathy-altruism hypothesis instead. Following a similar logic, experiments have tested the other two egoistic accounts proposed to explain empathy-induced helping—avoid social or self-punishments (shame, guilt) and gain social or self-rewards (praise, esteem-enhancement).

Because the three egoistic alternatives involve quite different psychological processes, it is not surprising that none of the proposed cross-cutting variables listed in table 3.1 allows a clear test of the empathy-altruism hypothesis against all three. As a result it is necessary either to conduct an experiment in which several cross-cutting variables are manipulated at once—which seems unwieldy and unwise—or to conduct a series of experiments in which the egoistic alternatives are tested one after another. In following the latter approach, care must be taken when moving from testing one egoistic alternative to testing another. Experimental situations must remain comparable so that cumulative comparisons can be made. The best way to maintain comparability is to use the same need situations, the same techniques for manipulating empathy, and the same dependent measures, changing only the cross-cutting variables. It is also important to test any given alternative in multiple experiments using different need situations, different techniques for inducing empathic concern, and if possible, different cross-cutting variables. Both procedures have been consistently employed in the research testing the empathy-altruism hypothesis.

Current Status of the Empathy-Altruism Hypothesis

Reports have been published of more than thirty experiments in which one of the cross-cutting variables in table 3.1 has been manipulated and empathy for a person in need has been either manipulated, measured, or both (see Batson 1991 for a review of over twenty of these experiments; Batson 2011 provides a complete review). Cumulatively, these experiments have tested all of the competing predictions in table 3.1. To cite but one example of research using each cross-cutting variable, (1) viability of escape was manipulated by Batson, Duncan, Ackerman, Buckley, and Birch (1981); (2) necessity of one's helping being effective was manipulated by Batson and Weeks (1996); (3) acceptability of other helpers was manipulated by Batson, Dyck, Brandt, Batson, Powell, McMaster, and Griffitt (1988, Study 1); (4) need for rewards of helping was manipulated by Batson, Batson, Griffitt, Barrientos, Brandt, Sprengelmeyer, and Bayly (1989); and (5) salient cognitions were measured by Batson et al. (1988, Study 5).

Overall, results of these experiments have consistently patterned as predicted by the empathy-altruism hypothesis; results have failed to support any egoistic alternative. To the best of my knowledge there is at present no plausible egoistic explanation of the cumulative evidence from these experiments. The evidence has led me to conclude—tentatively—that the empathy-altruism hypothesis is true, that empathic concern produces altruistic motivation. Moreover, the evidence suggests that this motivation is surprisingly powerful.

As early as 1990 after reviewing the empathy-altruism research as well as related research in sociology, economics, political science, and biology, Piliavin and Charng reached a similar conclusion:

There appears to be a "paradigm shift" away from the earlier position that behavior that appears to be altruistic must, under closer scrutiny, be revealed as reflecting egoistic motives. Rather, theory and data now being advanced are more compatible with the view that true altruism—acting with the goal of benefiting another—does exist and is a part of human nature. (1990, 27)

In apparent contradiction to this conclusion Maner, Luce, Neuberg, Cialdini, Brown, and Sagarin (2002) claimed to provide evidence that, once the effects of negative affect are removed, there is no longer a positive relation between empathic concern and motivation to help, altruistic or otherwise. But in their measure of negative affect, Maner et al. included only empathic emotions (feeling *sympathetic, compassionate,* and *soft-hearted,* as well as *sad, low-spirited,* and *heavy-hearted*—sadness items that in response to the need situation they used likely tapped other-oriented sadness for the person in need). So, when controlling for negative affect, Maner et al. actually removed the effect of empathic concern. It is not very surprising—but also not very informative—to find that once the effect of empathic concern on helping is removed, there is no longer an effect of empathic concern on helping.

Twenty years after Piliavin and Charng (1990) reached their conclusion, it still seems correct. Indeed, there is considerably more support for it now than then. Pending new evidence or a plausible new egoistic explanation of the existing evidence, the empathy-altruism hypothesis appears true.

How Could Empathy-Induced Altruism Have Evolved?

Support for the empathy-altruism hypothesis raises questions about the evolution of empathic concern. What evolutionary function might this other-oriented emotion serve? Despite their recent popularity, I think the most plausible evolutionary account is not in terms of inclusive fitness (Hamilton 1964), reciprocal altruism (Trivers 1971), sociality (Caporeal, Dawes, Orbell, and van de Kragt 1989), or group selection (Sober and Wilson 1998). The most plausible account is that empathic concern evolved as part of the parental instinct among higher mammals, especially humans (McDougall 1908; Hoffman 1981; Zahn-Waxler and Radke-Yarrow 1990; de Waal 1996; Bell 2001; Batson 2010).

If mammalian parents were not intensely interested in the welfare of their very vulnerable progeny, these species would quickly die out. Humans have doubtless inherited key aspects of their parental instinct from ancestors they share with other mammalian species, but in humans this instinct has become considerably less automatic and more flexible. The human parental instinct goes well beyond nursing, providing other kinds of food, protecting, and keeping the young close—the activities that characterize parental care in most mammalian species. It includes inferences about the desires and feelings of the child ("Is that a hungry cry or a wet cry?" "She won't like the fireworks; they'll be too loud."). It also includes goal-directed motives and appraisal-based emotions (Scherer 1984).

Antonio Damasio (1994, 1999, 2003) has repeatedly pointed out that one of the virtues of relying on goal-directed motives and appraisal-based emotions to guide action—rather than relying on hard-wired, automatic responses to environmental cues (his "regulatory mechanisms")—is that goal-directed motives and their associated emotions can be adaptive under a wide range of environmental conditions, circumstances, and events. Such flexibility seems highly desirable when caring for human offspring, where complex, novel situations abound.

To illustrate the flexibility that appraisal-based emotions introduce with an emotion quite different from empathic concern, consider anger. Aggressive responses occur in many species that likely do not experience anything like the emotion we would call anger. Among humans, however, aggressive responses are stimulated, tempered, and generalized by feelings of anger that are a product of complex cognitive appraisal of the situation, including appraisal of the intentions of others. Similarly, tender, empathic feelings permit more flexible and adaptive parental care, care that is not simply reflexive or reactive to distress cues but is directed toward the goal of enhancing the child's welfare in whatever way is needed in the particular situation. This flexibility includes anticipation and prevention of needs, even evolutionarily quite novel ones, such as the need to avoid sticking a pin in an electrical socket.

Of course, the human capacity for empathic concern extends well beyond our own children. As long as there is no preexisting antipathy, people can feel empathic concern for a wide range of targets, including nonhumans (Shelton and Rogers 1981; Batson 1991; Batson, Lishner, Cook, and Sawyer 2005). From an evolutionary perspective this extension is usually attributed to cognitive generalization whereby one "adopts" the target making it possible to evoke empathic concern and altruistic motivation when the target is in need (Hoffman 1981; Batson 1987).

Such cognitive generalization may be facilitated by two factors: (1) human cognitive capacity, including symbolic thought and analogic reasoning; and (2) lack of evolutionary advantage in early human hunter-gatherer bands for strict limitation of empathic concern and parental nurturance to offspring. In these bands those in need were often one's children or close kin, and survival of one's genes was tightly tied to the welfare even of those who were not close kin (Kelly 1995; Sober and Wilson 1998; Hrdy 2009). To the extent that the human nurturant impulse relies on appraisal-based, other-oriented emotions such as empathic concern, it would be relatively easy to generalize. In contemporary society the prospect of such generalization appears more plausible when one thinks of the emotional sensitivity and tender care typically provided by nannies and workers in day care centers, by adoptive parents, and by pet owners.

Implications of Empathy-Induced Altruism: Some Good News

The empathy-altruism hypothesis has wide-ranging practical implications. Let me mention a few. Empathic concern has been found to direct attention to the long-term welfare of those in need producing more sensitive care (Sibicky, Schroeder, and Dovidio 1995). It has also been found to improve attitudes toward and action on behalf of stigmatized outgroups. Empathy inductions have improved racial attitudes, as well as attitudes toward people with AIDS, the homeless, and even convicted murderers and drug dealers (Batson et al. 1997, 2002; Dovidio, Gaertner, and Johnson 1999; Vescio, Sechrist, and Paolucci 2003).

Empathy-induced altruism has also been found to increase cooperation in competitive situations (e.g., a Prisoner's Dilemma)—even when one knows that the target of empathic concern has acted competitively toward oneself (Batson and Moran 1999; Batson and Ahmad 2001). In schools empathy-based training has been used to increase mutual care among students (e.g., the Roots of Empathy project—Gordon 2007). And, as Stephan and Finlay (1999) pointed out, the induction of empathic concern is often an explicit component of techniques used in conflict-resolution workshops. Participants in these workshops are encouraged to express their feelings, their hopes and fears, and to imagine the thoughts and feelings of those on the other side of the conflict (Kelman 1990). These techniques affect perception of the other as in need and adoption of the other's perspective, two conditions that, in combination, have been used to produce empathic concern. (See Batson and Ahmad 2009, for a review of different programs that use empathy to improve intergroup attitudes and relations.)

Some Bad

Not all the effects of empathy-induced altruism are positive. People may at times wish to suppress or avoid feeling empathic concern. Aware of the extreme effort involved in helping or of the impossibility of helping effectively, caseworkers in the helping professions, nurses caring for terminal patients, and pedestrians confronted by homeless persons may try to avoid empathic concern in order to be spared the resulting altruistic motivation (Stotland et al. 1978; Maslach 1982; Shaw, Batson, and Todd 1994). That is, there may be an egoistic motive to avoid altruistic motivation.

Many people take it for granted that altruism is a moral motive (e.g., Hoffman 2000). The empathy-altruism hypothesis does not. The ultimate goal of altruism is to increase another's welfare. If pursuit of this goal leads one to act in accord with some moral standard or ideal, as it can, the result may be judged moral. But this is not the only possibility. Results of two experiments in which participants were given an opportunity to distribute benefits to others either fairly or unfairly provide evidence that empathy-induced altruism, much like self-interested egoism, can at times lead us to violate our moral standards of fairness (Batson, Klein, et al. 1995). In each experiment participants who were not induced to feel empathic concern for any of several individuals in need tended to act fairly. Participants induced to feel empathy for one of the individuals did not; they were more likely to show partiality toward this individual. It was not that the high-empathy participants abandoned fairness as a moral standard; they agreed with other participants that partiality was less fair and less moral than impartiality. However, they were willing to violate their moral standard to benefit the person for whom they had been led to care.

In related research, colleagues and I (Batson et al. 1999; Batson, Batson, et al. 1995) have found that empathy felt for one person in a social dilemma can lead participants to violate the Utilitarian principle of the Greatest Good for the Greatest Number. Overall, these studies provide considerable evidence that empathy-induced altruism and motivation to act morally are distinct motives that can conflict as well as cooperate.

Empathy-induced altruism can hurt those in need in another way. If, as suggested earlier, altruistic motivation is based on cognitive generalization of human parental nurturance, then it involves seeing the person in need as metaphorically childlike—as vulnerable, dependent, and in need of care. It also implies a status difference, at least in terms of ability to address the need in question. Sometimes, such a difference poses no problem. Most of us happily defer to the expertise of physicians, police, fire fighters, plumbers, and mechanics when we need their help. At other times the consequences can be tragic. Teachers and tutors can, out of genuine concern, fail to enable students to develop the ability and confidence to solve problems themselves, instead fostering dependence, low self-esteem, and a reduced sense of efficacy (Nadler, Fisher, and DePaulo 1983). Physical therapists, physicians, nurses, friends, and family members can do the same for patients with physical or mental disabilities, as can social welfare efforts to care for the poor and disadvantaged (Nadler and Halabi 2006).

Effective parenting requires sensitivity about when to intervene and when to stand back, as well as how—if possible—to structure the child's environment to foster coping, confidence, and independence. Effective empathy-induced altruism requires the same. Loving one's child is not all that is required for sensitive, effective parenting; empathy-induced altruism is not all that is required for sensitive, effective help (Fisher,

Nadler, and DePaulo 1983). Recall the adage about teaching the hungry to fish rather than giving them fish.

Imagining how the other feels about his or her situation—perspective-taking—seems particularly important in making generalized parental nurturance sensitive to what another person really needs. Drawing on her practice as a physician and psychiatrist, Jodi Halpern (2001) reports the case of "Mr. Smith," a successful executive and family patriarch. Mr. Smith had experienced sudden paralysis from the neck down and was now ventilator dependent. Seeing his helpless condition, Halpern felt—and tried to provide comfort by communicating—her deep sympathy and sorrow for him. He reacted with anger and frustration. Only after Halpern made an active effort to imagine "what it would be like to be a powerful older man, suddenly enfeebled, handled by one young doctor after the next" (2001, 87) was she able to appreciate and address his anger and frustration—and to set the stage for working *with* him rather than working *on* him. Halpern (2001) reflects, "My initial sympathy was an unimaginative response to Mr. Smith's obvious vulnerability, which led me to treat him gently. . . . [His case] highlights the practical importance of imagining how a particular upsetting situation feels versus simply recognizing that a patient is upset" (87–88).

Summary and Conclusion

Why do people help others, often at considerable cost to themselves? What does this behavior tell us about the human capacity to care, about the degree of interconnectedness among us, about how social an animal we humans are? These classic philosophical questions have resurfaced in the behavioral and social sciences in the past several decades. Social-psychological research has focused on the empathy-altruism hypothesis, which claims that empathic concern—other-oriented emotion elicited by and congruent with the perceived welfare of another in need—produces altruistic motivation—motivation with the ultimate goal of increasing the other's welfare by removing the need.

Results of the over thirty experiments designed to test this hypothesis against various egoistic alternatives have proved remarkably supportive, leading to the tentative conclusion that empathic concern felt for a person in need does indeed evoke altruistic motivation to have that need removed. But the empathic concern that produces altruistic motivation should not be confused with other psychological phenomena called empathy. Support for the empathy-altruism hypothesis provides no evidence that any of these other phenomena produces altruistic motivation—except as they serve as stepping-stones to empathic concern. The most plausible evolutionary account of the origins of empathy-induced altruism seems to be generalized parental nurturance.

Research reveals that empathy-induced altruism is a powerful motive. Yet it is not always a force for good. On the one hand there is evidence that it can (1) produce more and more sensitive care for those in need, (2) improve attitudes toward and action on behalf of members of stigmatized groups, and (3) increase cooperation in competitive situations, including international and interethnic conflict. On the other hand there is evidence that (1) people can at times be egoistically motivated to avoid experiencing empathic concern and the altruistic motivation it produces, and (2) empathy-induced altruism can lead people to violate their own standards of fairness and justice, showing partiality to those for whom empathy is felt at the expense of the common good. Finally, if, as suggested, empathy-induced altruism is based on cognitive generalization of parental nurturance, (3) it can lead to a paternalistic or maternalistic response to those in need.

The evidence that empathic concern produces altruistic motivation provides us with a powerful additional resource in trying to build a more caring, humane society. But in order to harness this power and use it wisely, it is important to understand the full potential of empathy-induced altruism—both for good and for ill.

References

Batson, C. D. 1987. Prosocial motivation: Is it ever truly altruistic? In *Advances in Experimental Social Psychology*, vol. 20, edited by L. Berkowitz, 65–122. New York: Academic Press.

Batson, C. D. 1991. *The Altruism Question: Toward a Social-Psychological Answer*. Hillsdale, NJ: Lawrence Erlbaum Associates.

Batson, C. D. 2009. These things called empathy: Eight related but distinct phenomena. In *The Social Neuroscience of Empathy*, edited by J. Decety and W. Ickes, 3–15. Cambridge, MA: MIT Press.

Batson, C. D. 2010. The Naked Emperor: Seeking a more plausible genetic basis for psychological altruism. *Economics and Philosophy* 26: 149–164.

Batson, C. D. 2011. *Altruism in Humans*. New York: Oxford University Press.

Batson, C. D., and N. Ahmad. 2001. Empathy-induced altruism in a Prisoner's Dilemma II: What if the target of empathy has defected? *European Journal of Social Psychology* 31: 25–36.

Batson, C. D., and N. Ahmad. 2009. Using empathy to improve intergroup attitudes and relations. *Social Issues and Policy Review* 3: 141–177.

Batson, C. D., N. Ahmad, J. Yin, S. J. Bedell, J. W. Johnson, C. M. Templin, and A. Whiteside. 1999. Two threats to the common good: Self-interested egoism and empathy-induced altruism. *Personality and Social Psychology Bulletin* 25: 3–16.

Batson, C. D., J. G. Batson, C. A. Griffitt, S. Barrientos, J. R. Brandt, P. Sprengelmeyer, and M. J. Bayly. 1989. Negative-state relief and the empathy-altruism hypothesis. *Journal of Personality and Social Psychology* 56: 922–933.

Batson, C. D., J. G. Batson, R. M. Todd, B. H. Brummett, L. L. Shaw, and C. M. R. Aldeguer. 1995. Empathy and the collective good: Caring for one of the others in a social dilemma. *Journal of Personality and Social Psychology* 68: 619–631.

Batson, C. D., J. Chang, R. Orr, and J. Rowland. 2002. Empathy, attitudes, and action: Can feeling for a member of a stigmatized group motivate one to help the group? *Personality and Social Psychology Bulletin* 28: 1656–1666.

Batson, C. D., B. Duncan, P. Ackerman, T. Buckley, and K. Birch. 1981. Is empathic emotion a source of altruistic motivation? *Journal of Personality and Social Psychology* 40: 290–302.

Batson, C. D., J. L. Dyck, J. R. Brandt, J. G. Batson, A. L. Powell, M. R. McMaster, and C. Griffitt. 1988. Five studies testing two new egoistic alternatives to the empathy-altruism hypothesis. *Journal of Personality and Social Psychology* 55: 52–77.

Batson, C. D., T. R. Klein, L. Highberger, and L. L. Shaw. 1995. Immorality from empathy-induced altruism: When compassion and justice conflict. *Journal of Personality and Social Psychology* 68: 1042–1054.

Batson, C. D., D. A. Lishner, J. Cook, and S. Sawyer. 2005. Similarity and nurturance: Two possible sources of empathy for strangers. *Basic and Applied Social Psychology* 27: 15–25.

Batson, C. D., and T. Moran. 1999. Empathy-induced altruism in a Prisoner's Dilemma. *European Journal of Social Psychology* 29: 909–924.

Batson, C. D., M. P. Polycarpou, E. Harmon-Jones, H. J. Imhoff, E. C. Mitchener, L. L. Bednar, T. R. Klein, and L. Highberger. 1997. Empathy and attitudes: Can feeling for a member of a stigmatized group improve feelings toward the group? *Journal of Personality and Social Psychology* 72: 105–118.

Batson, C. D., and J. L. Weeks. 1996. Mood effects of unsuccessful helping: Another test of the empathy-altruism hypothesis. *Personality and Social Psychology Bulletin* 22: 148–157.

Bell, D. C. 2001. Evolution of parental caregiving. *Personality and Social Psychology Review* 5: 216–229.

Caporeal, L. R., R. Dawes, J. M. Orbell, and A. J. C. van de Kragt. 1989. Selfishness examined: Cooperation in the absence of egoistic incentives. *Behavioral and Brain Sciences* 12: 683–739.

Damasio, A. R. 1994. *Descartes' Error: Emotion, Reason, and the Human Brain*. New York: Avon Books.

Damasio, A. R. 1999. *The Feeling of What Happens: Body and Emotion in the Making of Consciousness*. New York: Harcourt Brace & Company.

Damasio, A. R. 2003. *Looking for Spinoza: Joy, Sorrow, and the Feeling Brain*. Orlando, FL: Harcourt.

de Waal, F. B. M. 1996. *Good Natured: The Origins of Right and Wrong in Humans and Other Animals*. Cambridge, MA: Harvard University Press.

de Waal, F. B. M. 2008. Putting the altruism back into altruism: The evolution of empathy. *Annual Review of Psychology* 59: 279–300.

Dovidio, J. F., S. L. Gaertner, and J. D. Johnson. (1999, October). *New Directions in Prejudice and Prejudice Reduction: The Role of Cognitive Representations and Affect.* Paper presented at the annual meeting of the Society of Experimental Social Psychology, St. Louis, MO.

Fisher, J. D., A. Nadler, and B. M. DePaulo, eds. 1983. *Recipient Reactions to Aid.* Vol. 1 of *New Directions in Helping.* New York: Academic Press.

Gordon, M. 2007. *Roots of Empathy: Changing the World Child by Child.* Toronto: Thomas Allen.

Halpern, J. 2001. *From Detached Concern to Empathy: Humanizing Medical Practice.* New York: Oxford University Press.

Hamilton, W. D. 1964. The genetical evolution of social behavior (I, II). *Journal of Theoretical Biology* 7: 1–52.

Hoffman, M. L. 1975. Developmental synthesis of affect and cognition and its implications for altruistic motivation. *Developmental Psychology* 11: 607–622.

Hoffman, M. L. 1981. Is altruism part of human nature? *Journal of Personality and Social Psychology* 40: 121–137.

Hoffman, M. L. 2000. *Empathy and Moral Development: Implications for Caring and Justice.* New York: Cambridge University Press.

Hrdy, S. B. 2009. *Mothers and Others: The Evolutionary Origins of Mutual Understanding.* Cambridge, MA: Harvard University Press.

Kelman, H. C. 1990. Interactive problem-solving: A social psychological approach to conflict resolution. In *Conflict: Readings in Management and Resolution*, edited by J. W. Burton and F. Dukes, 199–215. New York: St. Martin's Press.

Kelly, R. L. 1995. *The Foraging Spectrum: Diversity in Hunter-Gatherer Lifeways.* Washington, DC: Smithsonian Institution Press.

Krebs, D. L. 1975. Empathy and altruism. *Journal of Personality and Social Psychology* 32: 1134–1146.

McDougall, W. 1908. *An Introduction to Social Psychology.* London: Methuen.

Maner, J. K., C. L. Luce, S. L. Neuberg, R. B. Cialdini, S. Brown, and B. J. Sagarin. 2002. The effects of perspective taking on helping: Still no evidence for altruism. *Personality and Social Psychology Bulletin* 28: 1601–1610.

Maslach, C. 1982. *Burnout: The Cost of Caring.* Englewood Cliffs, NJ: Prentice Hall.

Nadler, A., J. D. Fisher, and B. M. DePaulo, eds. 1983. *Applied Perspectives on Help-Seeking and -Receiving,* Vol. 3 of *New Directions in Helping.* New York: Academic Press.

Nadler, A., and S. Halabi. 2006. Intergroup helping as status relations: Effects of status stability, identification, and type of help on receptivity to high-status group's help. *Journal of Personality and Social Psychology* 91: 97–110.

Piliavin, J. A., and H.-W. Charng. 1990. Altruism: A review of recent theory and research. *American Sociological Review* 16: 27–65.

Scherer, K. R. 1984. On the nature and function of emotion: A component process approach. In *Approaches to Emotion*, edited by K. R. Scherer and P. Ekman, 293–317. Hillsdale, NJ: Lawrence Erlbaum Associates.

Shaw, L. L., C. D. Batson, and R. M. Todd. 1994. Empathy avoidance: Forestalling feeling for another in order to escape the motivational consequences. *Journal of Personality and Social Psychology* 67: 879–887.

Shelton, M. L., and R. W. Rogers. 1981. Fear-arousing and empathy-arousing appeals to help: The pathos of persuasion. *Journal of Applied Social Psychology* 11: 366–378.

Sibicky, M. E., D. A. Schroeder, and J. F. Dovidio. 1995. Empathy and helping: Considering the consequences of intervention. *Basic and Applied Social Psychology* 16: 435–453.

Sober, E., and D. S. Wilson. 1998. *Unto Others: The Evolution and Psychology of Unselfish Behavior.* Cambridge, MA: Harvard University Press.

Stephan, W. G., and K. Finlay. 1999. The role of empathy in improving intergroup relations. *Journal of Social Issues* 55: 729–743.

Stotland, E. 1969. Exploratory investigations of empathy. In *Advances in Experimental Social Psychology*, vol. 4, edited by L. Berkowitz, 271–313. New York: Academic Press.

Stotland, E., K. E. Mathews, S. E. Sherman, R. O. Hansson, and B. Z. Richardson. 1978. *Empathy, Fantasy, and Helping*. Beverly Hills, CA: Sage.

Trivers, R. L. 1971. The evolution of reciprocal altruism. *Quarterly Review of Biology* 46: 35–57.

Vescio, T. K., G. B. Sechrist, and M. P. Paolucci. 2003. Perspective taking and prejudice reduction: The mediational role of empathy arousal and situational attributions. *European Journal of Social Psychology* 33: 455–472.

Zahn-Waxler, C., and M. Radke-Yarrow. 1990. The origins of empathic concern. *Motivation and Emotion* 14: 107–130.

4   It's More than Skin Deep: Empathy and Helping Behavior across Social Groups

Stephanie Echols and Joshua Correll

Human beings are a social species. We form social connections, share resources, work together to protect ourselves from threats, experience social pain when separated from the group, and even depend on others to raise viable offspring (Cacioppo et al. 2006). This *obligatory interdependence* arguably evolved because understanding and coordinating with group members was integral for our survival (Brewer 2004). But in order to successfully thrive in social groups, humans developed particular group-focused affective and cognitive characteristics, with specific underlying neural systems (Adolphs 1999). Critical among these characteristics is empathy, the capacity to perceive, anticipate, and respond with care to the unique affective experiences of another individual (Decety and Batson 2007). It stands to reason that identifying and understanding the causes and consequences of conspecifics' internal states played an integral role not only in child rearing but also in communication, recognizing marginalized in-group members, and detecting deceit in other group members.

Empathy for members of one's social group is particularly important because it promotes behaviors that contribute to the fitness of the group as a whole. Compassion may have evolved as a distinct affective state because it afforded unique survival and reproductive advantages to in-group members (i.e., enhanced the chance of survival of offspring, enabled cooperation and reciprocity integral to group living; Goetz, Keltner, and Simon-Thomas 2010). Further, theories such as kin selection and reciprocal altruism point to the long-term advantages of expending energy to help in-group members (Hoffman 1981). Whether the goal is to ensure the fitness of those who share one's genetic material, or to extend help with the expectation that it may be returned sometime in the future, Hoffman and others suggest that helping one's social group may be inherent to human nature.

The purpose of the chapter is to explore how group membership affects our ability to understand and respond with care to the unique internal experiences of others. How do groups influence the empathic process? Can we use capacities that presumably developed within the context of the in-group to understand members of other groups? Or is there impairment in recognizing, understanding, and responding to the experiences of out-group members? If an out-group impairment in empathy exists, where and how does the empathic process break down? We turn to research exploring how group membership, social identity, in- and out-group attitudes and status hierarchies influence empathy and prosocial behavior.

Empathy is a complex construct, and to understand how group membership moderates empathy, we must first define the term. Batson (2009) identified several qualitatively distinct uses of the term "empathy" in psychology research from behavioral mimicry, emotion contagion and neural resonance, to perspective-taking and feeling compassion for others. Batson ultimately argues that research on empathy addresses two separate questions: (1) How does one come to understand another person's unique affective state? This refers to *empathic understanding*. And (2) what guides the development of concern and a motivation to respond with care for another individual's plight? This refers to *empathic concern*. The current chapter makes use of this distinction to frame a discussion about how group membership can influence the empathic experience as it unfolds, from perceiving an individual in need, to understanding the individual's unique experience, to caring and engaging in helping behavior.

Group Membership and Empathic Understanding

Empathic understanding refers to the capacity to share and understand another person's affective or emotional experience (Decety and Jackson 2004). This understanding represents the culmination of a number of subsidiary automatic and controlled processes (Decety 2011a). Low-level processes involved in face perception and emotion recognition are integral to identifying the internal states of others. Observing another individual in distress may also induce affective arousal in the perceiver, shaping the evaluation of the target's experience. In addition, top-down processes involved in emotion and mental state inference allow prior knowledge, experience and the emotional context to influence the perceiver's attributions. These processes are distinct, but they interact with one another throughout the empathic process (Decety 2011a). For example, autonomic arousal may influence attention to emotional cues, and inferences about another person's mental state may constrain the types of emotions a perceiver will recognize. For ease of presentation, we divide our discussion of empathic understanding into three sections, exploring how group-level processes influence (1) emotion recognition, (2) affective arousal, and (3) emotion understanding.

Group Membership and Emotion Recognition

Empathic understanding begins with the perception of emotional signals from another individual. Recent research suggests that not all affective signals are processed equally. Even basic face perception and emotion recognition may be moderated by group membership. One of the most reliable group differences in face perception is the finding that perceivers are faster and more accurate at recognizing members of an in-group as compared to members of out-groups. Called the cross-race or own-race effect, this in-group advantage is typically demonstrated as increased sensitivity in differentiating faces from one's own race as compared to those of a different race (Meissner and Brigham 2001). The advantage may emerge because fundamentally different processes underlie the perception of in- and out-group faces. For example, researchers showed that participants relied on holistic processing when viewing in-group members, but they relied on feature-based processing when viewing out-group members (Michel et al. 2006). Group-level processes thus influence *how* faces are processed, which can have important implications for emotion perception more generally as well as for the attribution of emotion to a specific individual's experience.

How might differences in face processing affect a perceiver's understanding of a target person's experience? A recent meta-analysis showed that, despite generally high accuracy at identifying facial expressions of emotions, perceivers have an advantage when viewing the emotional displays of racial and ethnic in-group members, particularly when the emotion is spontaneously produced (Elfenbein and Ambady 2002). Perceivers were 9.3 percent more accurate at recognizing the expressions of an in-group than an out-group member. The authors suggest that subtle differences in display and decoding rules produce stylistic differences in emotion expression across populations, regions, and cultures, resulting in an in-group advantage in emotion cue processing (Elfenbein and Ambady 2002).

This in-group advantage in emotion recognition was recently replicated in a functional magnetic resonance imaging (fMRI) study of native Japanese and Caucasian-American individuals (Chiao et al. 2008). Participants viewed Japanese and Caucasian faces displaying happy, angry, fearful, and neutral facial expressions. Both Caucasian and Japanese participants were faster and more accurate at recognizing fear in their in-group and demonstrated greater amygdala activation when viewing an in-group member's fear rather than an out-group member's.

It is interesting to note that the cross-race effect and in-group advantage in emotion recognition seem to depend heavily on the motivation to attend to one's own social group. Young and Hugenberg (2010) presented Caucasian participants with Caucasian faces, but, using a minimal group paradigm, the researchers divided these faces into two groups: one set of faces (randomly selected) was presented as an in-group, the other set was presented as an out-group. Because the faces were all members of the racial in-group and because the sets were randomly assigned, there is no reason that preexisting differences in familiarity or encoding rules should improve processing for one set of faces over the other. Nonetheless, the results showed that participants were more accurate at recognizing emotional expressions of ostensible in-group members than out-group members. Moreover, this in-group advantage in emotion recognition occurred as a result of holistic processing of in-group faces. The authors suggest that the in-group advantage can be driven by a motivation to process in-group faces. Although important exceptions may occur when an emotion is associated with a particular out-group (i.e., Ackerman et al. 2006), these results indicate that when perceivers encounter an out-group member, they are generally less motivated to attend to that individual's facial expression.

Group Membership and Affective Arousal

Perceivers may evaluate an emotional stimulus in a relatively fast and effortless manner to determine whether it is appetitive or aversive and whether it should be approached or avoided (Decety 2011a). This evaluation may lead to undifferentiated arousal of the sympathetic nervous system (Cacioppo, Berntson, and Crites 1996), influencing the perceiver's nascent empathic understanding (Piliavin, Piliavin, and Rodin 1975; Batson, Fultz, and Schoenrade 1987).

A number of researchers in the past five years have utilized fMRI to explore how hemodynamic markers of affective arousal might differ depending on the group membership of the target. In particular, investigations have focused on exploring affective arousal in response to in- and out-group members in pain. Pain is a useful way to investigate the role of affective arousal in empathic understanding because perceivers can generally understand the distress and discomfort of another's pain while maintaining a clear distinction that it is the target, not the perceiver, who is experiencing that discomfort. Further, a great deal is known about the physiology of pain including how it is represented in the brain. For example, the first-hand experience of pain and the observation of another individual in pain activate a number of shared regions in the brain including the anterior cingulate cortex, the anterior midcingulate cortex, and anterior insula (see Decety and Jackson 2004, for a review of neurological resonance in pain perception). It is important to note, however, that hemodynamic activity in these areas of the brain is not limited to pain processing but is implicated in processing arousing and negative stimuli more generally. As such, shared activation in these areas between the observer and target may simply reflect general affective arousal associated with classifying a stimulus as appetitive or aversive, and may be a necessary (but not sufficient) component of empathic understanding (Decety 2011b).

When viewing disliked (rather than liked) targets experience pain, perceivers show reduced hemodynamic activation in areas associated with pain processing (Singer et al. 2006). Other work shows similar increases in neurological resonance when viewing loved ones as compared to strangers (Cheng et al. 2010). This suggests that the perceiver's attitude toward the target moderates affective arousal. Translating this principle to the realm of group processes, researchers asked Chinese and Caucasian participants to view pictures of neutral in- and out-group faces being pricked by a needle (pain) or a Q-tip (no pain) during fMRI scanning (Xu et al. 2009). Greater activation was observed in the anterior cingulate cortex, an area associated with the affective dimension of pain, when viewing in-group faces in pain as compared to out-group faces in pain.

But perceivers do not treat all out-group members in the same fashion. Just as the perceiver's evaluation of individual targets moderates his or her affective arousal (e.g., Singer et al. 2006), his or her attitude toward the out-group moderates neurological resonance in response to out-group pain. In one fMRI investigation (Decety, Echols, and Correll 2010), healthy participants viewed in-group members (other healthy people) versus out-group members (people ostensibly diagnosed with AIDS) as they experienced pain. Moreover, participants viewed these out-group targets with the knowledge that they either were or were not "responsible" for their condition (having contracted the disease either due to intravenous drug use or due to a contaminated blood transfusion, respectively). Perceivers showed greater activation in pain-processing areas (i.e., anterior insula and anterior midcingulate cortex) when viewing the pain of AIDS patients who were not responsible for their condition as compared to AIDS patients who were responsible—that is they were more responsive to the pain of the stigmatized-but-blameless out-group. This pattern was mirrored in explicit pain ratings: participants were more sensitive to the pain of not-responsible AIDS targets as compared to healthy controls and less sensitive to the pain of responsible AIDS targets as a function of how much they blamed these targets for their condition. These results suggest that affective arousal is moderated by a priori attitudes toward the target group. If perceivers experience less affective arousal when viewing an out-group member in pain, there may be fewer cues from the observer's body to help interpret the out-group target's emotional state and/or to signal the need to respond with care. This difference might contribute to an impairment in empathic understanding for out-group members.

Group Membership and Emotion Understanding

Emotion perception and arousal may be necessary steps in sharing and appreciating the affective state of others, but they are not sufficient to account for complete emotion understanding. At minimum, emotion understanding requires an acknowledgment of the other individual's internal state, and at maximum, it involves effortful perspective-taking to precisely understand the other's unique experiences as distinct from one's own (Decety 2011a).

Models of mental state inference suggest that the process by which one attributes thoughts, motivations, and emotions to another individual may be influenced by the similarity and likeability of the target, both of which typically covary with group membership. Participants in one study read a vignette of a target who was either similar or dissimilar to themselves based on the participant's self-reported preferences. Participants then rated a number of different targets: the person described in the vignette, themselves, and a group to which the target belonged (e.g., medical students). Participants who read about a target similar to themselves projected their own thoughts onto that target, but those who read about a dissimilar target used group stereotypes to infer the target's mental state (Ames 2004). Perceivers also tend to attribute more complex mental states to targets they like (and less complex states to those they do not like). For example, participants described a target's actions in more complex and abstract terms (i.e., taking goals and contexts into account) for liked targets than disliked targets, and they made fewer complex attributions for a suffering, victimized target than for a neutral target (Kozak, Marsh, and Wegner 2006).

Similar patterns of intergroup biases are observed when attributing emotions to in- and out-group members. Classifying an individual as an out-group member can lead perceivers to deny them certain "human" characteristics (Leyens et al. 2000). Research reveals that participants more readily ascribe secondary, complex emotions such as pride and guilt to their in-group than to an out-group. This pattern of *infrahumanization* was also demonstrated in a study that examined the attribution of emotions experienced by black and white Hurricane Katrina victims. Participants attributed fewer secondary emotions (i.e., grief, sorrow, and guilt) to racial out-group members than racial in-group members (Cuddy, Rock, and Norton 2007). Even more striking, this denial of secondary emotions to out-group members actually predicted decreases in helping behavior for out-group targets. These investigations show that a perceiver's understanding of emotion may be moderated by the group membership of the target.

Group-level processes can impact empathic understanding in multiple ways. Whether it is emotion recognition, arousal, or mental state attribution, the components underlying empathic understanding may depend on the group membership of the target. We now turn to research exploring a different question: How does group membership influence our *empathic concern* and the motivation to respond with care to disadvantaged in- and out-group members?

Group Membership, Empathic Concern, and Helping Behavior

Empathic concern is an other-oriented emotional reaction that can occur when perceiving an individual in distress. It leads the observer to experience a unique profile of emotions, including feelings of sympathy, compassion, warmth, and tenderness for the target (Batson, Fultz, and Schoenrade 1987). It has been proposed that sharing and understanding the affective experiences of another individual (i.e., the processes reviewed above) may evoke this concern. For instance, participants asked to take the perspective of an individual experience significantly more empathic concern for their plight than participants asked to remain objective (Coke, Batson, and McDavis 1978; Batson, Sager, et al. 1997). In general, then, empathic concern often stems from empathic understanding.

Turning to downstream consequences of concern, research suggests that experiencing empathic concern may evoke a prosocial motivation to help the individual (Batson 1998; for a review, see Eisenberg and Miller 1987). For example, people who score high in dispositional empathic concern are more likely to help others in a variety of situations (Davis et al. 1999). Complementary findings are observed when participants are induced to feel empathic concern via a perspective-taking manipulation (Coke, Batson, and McDavis 1978). Thus, whether it is a general disposition or an experimentally induced state of mind, concern can result in an increased tendency to help that individual in need. In this section we examine the influence of group membership both the antecedents and consequences of empathic concern.

Group Membership and the Antecedents of Empathic Concern and Helping

The vast majority of the research reviewed above suggests that, when perceivers consider members of an out-group, empathic *understanding* is compromised. To the extent that empathic understanding promotes empathic concern and helping behavior, we might expect perceivers to experience reduced concern for out-group victims as well. Recent research provides support for this hypothesis (Hein et al. 2010). Soccer fans in one study observed either another fan of their favored team (in-group) or a rival team (out-group) experiencing painful shocks. Participants showed increased empathic understanding for in-group than out-group targets, reporting higher pain ratings and showing greater activation in the anterior insula for in-group targets. Participants also reported feeling more empathic concern for in-group targets, and they were more likely to volunteer to help by sharing the pain of in-group than out-group targets. Moreover, the difference in anterior insula activation when viewing in- vs. out-group members in pain (arguably a marker of empathic understanding) predicted the group difference in helping behavior. This investigation demonstrates that empathic understanding is more likely to lead to empathic concern and helping behavior for in-group members than out-group members.

Attitudes toward a particular out-group may further moderate the relationship between empathic understanding and empathic concern. Participants in one study watched short video clips of African-American and Caucasian men expressing pain, and reported empathic understanding (i.e., how intense was the pain?) and how much they were willing to help (i.e., how much medication would you provide?). Participants also completed several measures of both implicit and explicit racial attitudes. Critically, the relationship between empathic understanding and helping behavior was moderated by implicit racial attitudes: implicitly biased participants showed a stronger relationship between empathic understanding and helping behavior for Caucasian than African-American men, whereas the reverse was true for participants low in implicit bias (Echols, Decety, Correll, unpublished data). This investigation provides early evidence that negative attitudes about out-groups can interfere with the relationship between empathic understanding, and empathic concern and helping behavior.

Group Membership and the Consequences of Empathic Concern

Given the fairly consistent group differences in empathic understanding and empathic concern reviewed above, it seems reasonable to anticipate similar group differences in helping behavior. And, indeed, when it is salient, group membership can significantly impact the probability that one will empathize and respond with care to the suffering of another individual.

Models of empathic concern and prosocial behavior based in the tradition of Social Identity/Self-Categorization theory (i.e., Tajfel and Turner 1979) specify how group membership can impact these processes. According to Social Identity theory, individuals instinctively categorize themselves into salient social groups, and tend to view these groups as positive. Once classified, individuals may view themselves according to this *social identity:* they will define themselves according to group stereotypes, and automatically minimize the differences between in-group members and maximize the differences between in-group and out-group members (Turner and Onorato 1999). Accentuating in-group similarity should make the importance of another in-group member's welfare self-relevant, increase perceived responsibility to help, and increase the costs of not helping (i.e., Levine et al. 2005). These processes may therefore increase both empathic concern and helping behavior for in-group members relative to out-group members.

A number of investigations have provided empirical support for this perspective (i.e., Levine et al. 2005; Stürmer et al. 2006). For example, White participants were significantly less likely to help a Black victim than a White victim when their responsibility to help was ambiguous (Gaertner and Dovidio, 1977). In more recent work, Levine and colleagues demonstrated that soccer fans who had been primed with their favored team identity were significantly more likely to help another fan of their team than a fan of the rival soccer club (Levine et al. 2005; see also Levine et al. 2002).

But these in-group biases in empathic concern and helping behavior do not always emerge. A recent meta-analysis of 48 studies found no evidence of discrimination in helping behavior toward African-Americans (compared to Caucasians) on average (Saucier, Miller, and Doucet 2005). In fact, White participants in one research study were significantly *more* likely to help a Black confederate over a White confederate (Dovidio and Gaertner 1981). To better understand these discrepant findings we will discuss several different theories that explore how group-level processes might impact helping behavior, highlighting how each model sheds light on the conditions in which one will respond with care to another individual's suffering.

Empathy-Altruism Hypothesis

According to the empathy-altruism hypothesis, individuals are *altruistically* motivated to engage in helping behavior when they experience empathic concern to alleviate the distress of the target (Batson 1998). Importantly, Batson argues that this relationship does not depend on similarity (which he operationalizes through the group membership of the target). In an illustrative study, participants were asked to listen to an audiotape of a woman expressing distress and asked either take her perspective or to remain objective (Batson, Sager, et al. 1997). To manipulate similarity (i.e., group membership), this woman was either described as a student from the participant's own university or from a rival university. Results showed that participants' empathic concern predicted their helping behavior, and that the relationship did not depend on the target's group membership. Moreover, path analysis showed that the relationship between empathic concern and helping behavior could not be explained by measures of observer/target similarity. The authors argue that shared group membership does not necessarily predict empathic concern and helping (Batson, Sager, et al. 1997). However, these data also show a trend such that levels of empathic concern were higher for the in-group victim than the out-group victim. Although empathic concern may drive helping behavior in all cases, if perceivers experience greater concern for in-group members and reduced concern for out-group members, group-based differences in helping should emerge.

Different Groups, Different Mechanisms

In contrast to the contention that concern predicts helping regardless of group membership (Batson, Sager, et al. 1997), some research suggests that fundamentally different processes drive helping behavior for the in-group and the out-group. These different systems are the focus of this subsection. Stürmer argues that, while empathic concern drives helping for the in-group, a sense of *similarity* drives helping for the out-group (Stürmer et al. 2006). In one study, participants of German or Muslim background read a message from a German or Muslim individual in distress and reported both their empathic concern and how much time they would volunteer to help. Although no group differences emerged in mean levels of empathic concern or helping behavior, empathic concern emerged as a significant predictor of helping for ethnic in-group members, but not out-group members. Instead, the extent to which participants felt "one" with out-group members predicted helping behavior. These effects were also replicated in a minimal-group paradigm. The authors argue that empathic concern promotes altruism for the in-group, but that for the out-group, feelings of similarity lead to helping.

Pryor and colleagues offer a related, but distinct account. These researchers have proposed a dual-process model of responses to out-group members (Pryor et al. 2010). According to this model, reflexive negative emotional reactions to an out-group member in pain can be overcome by deliberative, top-down processes, transforming avoidance into an appropriate prosocial response. Critically, this latter process is an effortful, controlled process that requires cognitive resources to enact. DeWall et al. (2008) offer some support for this position. In their investigation, participants imagined that either a family member or a stranger had been evicted from their apartment, and indicated the help they were willing to provide. Critically, some participants had previously performed a demanding task that depleted their cognitive resources. Results showed that both depleted and non-depleted participants helped family members equally; however, depleted participants helped a stranger significantly less than non-depleted participants. Based on these data, the authors argue that participants critically rely on cognitive resources when making deliberative helping decisions for out-group members, but not in-group members.

Individuals may also help out-group members for selfish reasons. The Competitive Altruism Hypothesis posits that individuals compete to provide prosocial behavior to others because it enhances status and affords downstream benefits within a group hierarchy (Hardy and Van Vugt 2006). Extending these findings to inter-group processes, out-group helping may provide an individual or group with "positive-distinctiveness," or the feeling that the in-group is unique and superior to other comparison groups (Van Leeuwen and Täuber 2010). In particular, helping can be strategically offered by an individual or a group to signal status or the possession of valued knowledge and skills. For example, threatened groups can offer *defensive help*: help that is offered as a means of restoring the subordinate role of the out-group (Nadler, Harpaz-Gorodeisky, and Ben-David 2009). Participants who were highly identified with their school were given the opportunity to provide help to a student from a neighboring school that either academically out-performed (status threat) or performed equally (no status threat) to the participant's own school. Students offered help on both easy and difficult problems to the student from a threatening out-group, whereas they only provided help on the difficult problems to the student from the non-threatening out-group. The authors interpret these findings as evidence that in-group members provided help to a threatening out-group as a means to restore their own perceptions of superiority, regardless of the group's actual need state.

Arousal

Finally, group membership may influence the physiological arousal of the observer, which can differentially impact the relationship between empathic concern and helping for in- and out-group members. Two opposing theoretical models may shed light on how group membership may impact this relationship. First, Batson and colleagues postulate a curvilinear relationship between similarity of the observer/target experience and the observer's affective response for that target (Batson, Fultz, and Schoenrade 1987). They argue that, the more similar an observer is to a target, the more difficult it is for the observer to regulate his or her emotional reaction to that target's distress. As a consequence, the observer may experience higher levels of personal distress when viewing close others, impairing their ability to feel empathic understanding and concern for the target. Researchers in one study asked participants to either *imagine themselves in place of* a target expressing pain or to *imagine how the target felt*. Perceivers exhibited significantly more activation in pain processing areas (i.e., anterior insula, anterior mid-cingulate cortex) and reported significantly more personal distress when imagining themselves in place of the victim (Lamm, Batson, and Decety 2007). Without a clear distinction between self and other, participants may experience more personal distress in response to the pain of close in-group targets than distinct out-group targets. This increased distress may manifest itself as physiological arousal when viewing in-group members in pain (as compared to out-group members) and lead the perceiver to focus attention and resources on regulating their own arousal rather than on understanding or helping the target. Counterintuitively, distress and egocentric arousal could reduce empathic understanding or concern for in-group targets as compared to out-group targets.

However, the opposite pattern of effects can also be predicted. Interacting with an out-group member may evoke threat and fear in the perceiver. For example, participants interacting with out-group confederates exhibit patterns of physiological arousal associated with threat (i.e., cardiac responses signaling an activation of the sympathetic-adrenal-medullary axis; Blascovich et al. 2001). In the context of this arousal, perceivers may either fail to understand the situation or fail to help when they encounter an out-group member in need of assistance. In an intergroup interaction, empathy may then depend heavily on the perceiver's ability to regulate his or her emotional response. Unfortunately, evidence also suggests that (at least with respect to race), interacting with an out-group member can compromise this regulatory capacity (Richeson and Trawalter 2005). Richeson and colleagues argue that during interracial interactions, individuals attempt to carefully regulate their behavior in an effort to appear non-prejudiced. This self-regulation depletes a limited reserve of cognitive resources (i.e., Muraven and Baumeister 2000), ultimately impairing self-control. If interracial interaction both increases arousal and decreases regulatory capacity, it may impair the perceiver's ability to accurately understand an out-group member's affective experiences, which could lead to reductions in empathic concern and helping behavior.

Reducing Group Differences in Empathy and Helping Behavior

In this chapter we have explored how group-level processes can impact our ability to understand and respond with care to the unique affective experiences of out-group members. We would be remiss if we failed to address strategies that might help mitigate these biases. Interestingly, the tendency to favor the in-group (the very tendency that *creates* in-group biases in the first place) can also help to *reduce* group differences when employed strategically. The Common In-Group Identity Model (Dovidio et al. 2010) predicts that when members of two separate groups recategorize themselves as one superordinate group, attitudes toward former out-group members will become more positive. By including former out-group members in a larger, more inclusive in-group, perceivers may begin to see the health and welfare of these out-group members as more self-relevant. In early work testing this hypothesis, groups of three participants were assigned to a team and given an opportunity to develop a group identity (Dovidio et al. 1997). Two different groups were then brought together. In one condition, the two groups formed a new inclusive six-person group with a new group name, integrated seating assignments, etc. In another condition, the two groups maintained their separate group identities. A member of each group was then given an opportunity to help either an in-group member or an out-group member. Results showed that participants who developed an inclusive group identity were equally likely to help a previous in-group or out-group member, whereas participants who maintained their separate group identity tended to help their in-group more than the out-group (Dovidio et al. 1997). Similarly, Manchester United football (soccer) fans primed with the superordinate category of "football enthusiast" were more likely to help a confederate when that confederate was wearing a Manchester United *or* Liverpool football club jersey than when he was wearing a plain t-shirt (Levine et al. 2005). Although recategorization may not be equally effective for all groups (see Dovidio et al. 2010), it affords a first step in reducing intergroup biases in empathic concern and helping behavior.

We have also discussed strategies for reducing in-group biases that involve effortful perspective-taking to understand the unique affective experiences of out-group members (Pryor et al. 2010). Though they may be mentally taxing, these strategies may have several positive consequences for downstream intergroup relations. For example, taking the perspective of an out-group member leads to a decrease in the use of explicit and implicit stereotypes for that individual, and to more positive evaluations of that group as a whole (Galinski and Moskowitz, 2000). Perspective-taking is a classic method to induce empathic concern for targets (i.e., see Batson, Sager, et al. 1997), and feelings of empathic concern induced by perspective-taking can lead to valuing the welfare of an out-group target. In a series of experiments, Batson asked participants to listen to a short radio broadcast of a stigmatized out-group member and report both their empathy for that individual and their attitudes toward the stigmatized group. Results showed that taking the perspective of the stigmatized target increased empathic concern for the target, which in turn caused more positive evaluations of the out-group in general (Batson, Polycarpou, et al. 1997). Follow-up research showed that empathy for a stigmatized individual promotes helping behavior for the out-group as a whole (Batson et al. 2002). Although boundary conditions exist on the positive effects of perspective-taking in intergroup interactions (i.e., Vorauer and Sasaki 2009), if perceivers have the motivation and cognitive resources to overcome these challenges, emotion understanding may have long-term positive effects on inter-group relations.

When It Comes to Empathy and Helping, Groups Matter

We have reviewed theory and empirical evidence from multiple levels of analysis to demonstrate that group-level process critically moderate the conditions in which empathic understanding and empathic concern are expressed. This is an important research question with a variety of real-world applications. Why was the response to victims of Hurricane Katrina inadequate and delayed? What are effective ways to encourage charitable giving? In today's multicultural world, how do we understand and interact with others who are not like us? Moreover, how and when does this understanding break down and lead to dehumanization and intergroup violence? Understanding how group membership can influence the processes involved in inter-personal understanding and behavior is integral to navigating our complex social world.

References

Ackerman, J. M., J. R. Shapiro, S. L. Neuberg, D. T. Kenrick, D. V. Becker, V. Griskevicius, J. K. Maner, and M. Schaller. 2006. They all look the same to me (unless they're angry): From out-group homogeneity to out-group heterogeneity. *Psychological Science* 17: 836–840.

Adolphs, R. 1999. Social cognition and the human brain. *Trends in Cognitive Sciences* 3: 469–479.

Ames, D. R. 2004. Inside the mind reader's tool kit: Projection and stereotyping in mental state inference. *Journal of Personality and Social Psychology* 87: 340–353.

Batson, C. D. 1998. Altruism and prosocial behavior. In *Handbook of Social Psychology*, 4th ed., vol. 2, edited by D. T. Gilbert, S. T. Fiske, and G. Lindzey, 282–316. New York: McGraw-Hill.

Batson, C. D. 2009. These things called empathy: Eight related but distinct phenomena. In *The Social Neuroscience of Empathy*, edited by J. Decety and W. Ickes, 3–15. Cambridge, MA: MIT Press.

Batson, C. D., J. Chang, R. Orr, and J. Rowland. 2002. Empathy, attitudes and action: Can feeling for a member of a stigmatized group motivate one to help the group? *Personality and Social Psychology Bulletin* 28: 1656–1666.

Batson, D., J. Fultz, and P. A. Schoenrade. 1987. Distress and empathy: Two qualitatively distinct vicarious emotions with different motivational consequences. *Journal of Personality* 55: 19–39.

Batson, C. D., M. P. Polycarpou, E. Harmon-Jones, H. J. Imhoff, E. C. Mitchener, L. L. Bednar, T. R. Klein, and L. Highberger. 1997a. Empathy and attitudes: Can feeling for a member of a stigmatized group improve feelings toward the group? *Journal of Personality and Social Psychology* 72: 105–118.

Batson, C. D., K. Sager, E. Garst, M. Kang, K. Robchinsky, and K. Dawson. 1997b. Is empathy-induced helping due to self-other merging? *Journal of Personality and Social Psychology* 73: 495–509.

Blascovich, J., W. B. Mendes, S. B. Hunter, B. Lickel, and N. Kowai-Bell. 2001. Perceiver threat in social interactions with stigmatized others. *Journal of Personality and Social Psychology* 80: 253–267.

Brewer, M. B. 2004. Taking the social origins of human nature seriously: Toward an more imperialist social psychology. *Personality and Social Psychology Review* 8: 107–113.

Cacioppo, J. T., G. G. Berntson, and S. L. Crites Jr. 1996. Social neuroscience: Principles of psychophysiological arousal and response. In *Social Psychology: Handbook of Basic Principles*, edited by E. T. Higgins and A. W. Kruglanski, 72–101. New York: Guilford Press.

Cacioppo, J. T., L. C. Hawkley, J. M. Ernst, M. Burleson, G. G. Berntson, B. Nouriani, and D. Spiegel. 2006. Loneliness within a nomological net: An evolutionary perspective. *Journal of Research in Personality* 40: 1054–1085.

Cheng, Y., C. Chen, C. Lin, K. Chou, and J. Decety. 2010. Love hurts: An fMRI study. *NeruoImage* 51: 923–929.

Chiao, J. Y., T. Iidaka, H. L. Gordon, J. Nogawa, M. Bar, E. Aminoff, N. Sadato, and N. Ambady. 2008. Cultural specificity in amygdala response to fear faces. *Journal of Cognitive Neuroscience* 20: 2167–2174.

Coke, J. S., C. D. Batson, and K. McDavis. 1978. Empathic mediation of helping: A two-stage model. *Journal of Personality and Social Psychology* 36: 752–766.

Cuddy, A. J. C., M. S. Rock, and M. I. Norton. 2007. Aid in the aftermath of Hurricane Katrina: Inferences of secondary emotions and intergroup helping. *Group Processes & Intergroup Relations* 10: 107–118.

Davis, M. H., K. V. Mitchell, J. A. Hall, J. Lothert, T. Snapp, and M. Meyer. 1999. Empathy, expectations and situational preferences: Personality influences on the decision to participate in volunteer helping behaviors. *Journal of Personality* 67: 469–503.

Decety, J. 2011a. Dissecting the neural mechanisms mediating empathy. *Emotion Review* 3: 92–108.

Decety, J. 2011b. The neuroevolution of empathy. *Annals of the New York Academy of Sciences*. E-pub ahead of print.

Decety, J., and C. D. Batson. 2007. Social neuroscience approaches to interpersonal sensitivity. *Social Neuroscience* 2: 151–1157.

Decety, J., S. Echols, and J. Correll. 2010. The blame game: The effect of responsibility and social stigma on empathy for pain. *Journal of Cognitive Neuroscience* 22: 985–997.

Decety, J., and P. L. Jackson. 2004. The functional architecture of human empathy. *Behavioral and Cognitive Neuroscience Reviews* 3: 71–100.

DeWall, C. N., R. F. Baumeister, M. T. Gailliot, and J. K. Maner. 2008. Depletion makes the heart grow less helpful: Helping as a function of self-regulatory energy and genetic relatedness. *Personality and Social Psychology Bulletin* 34: 1653–1662.

Dovidio, J. F., and S. L. Gaertner. 1981. The effect of race, status, and ability on helping behavior. *Social Psychology Quarterly* 44: 192–203.

Dovidio, J. F., S. L. Gaertner, N. Shnabel, T. Saguy, and J. Johnson. 2010. Recategorization and prosocial behavior: Common identity and a dual identity. In *The Psychology of Prosocial Behavior: Group Processes, Intergroup Relations, and Helping*, edited by S. Stürmer and M. Snyder, 191–207. Malden, MA: Wiley-Blackwell.

Dovidio, J. F., S. L. Gaertner, A. Validzic, K. Matoka, B. Johnson, and S. Frazier. 1997. Extending the benefits of recategorization: Evaluations, self-disclosure, and helping. *Journal of Experimental Social Psychology* 33: 401–420.

Echols, S., J. Correll, and J. Decety. (unpublished data). The effect of racial attitudes on the relationship between empathic understanding and helping behavior.

Eisenberg, N., and P. A. Miller. 1987. The relation of empathy to prosocial and related behaviors. *Psychological Bulletin* 101: 91–119.

Elfenbein, H. A., and N. Ambady. 2002. On the universality and cultural specificity of emotion recognition: A meta-analysis. *Psychological Bulletin* 128: 203–235.

Gaertner, S. L., and J. F. Dovidio. 1977. The subtlety of white racism, arousal, and helping behavior. *Journal of Personality and Social Psychology* 35: 691–707.

Galinski, A. D., and G. B. Moskowitz. 2000. Perspective-taking: Decreasing stereotype expression, stereotype accessibility, and in-group favoritism. *Journal of Personality and Social Psychology* 78: 708–724.

Goetz, J. L., D. Keltner, and E. Simon-Thomas. 2010. Compassion: An evolutionary analysis and empirical review. *Psychological Bulletin* 136: 351–374.

Hardy, C. L., and M. Van Vugt. 2006. Nice guys finish first: The competitive altruism hypothesis. *Personality and Social Psychology Bulletin* 32: 1402–1413.

Hein, G., G. Silani, K. Preuschoff, C. D. Batson, and T. Singer. 2010. Neural responses to ingroup and outgroup members' suffering predict individual differences in costly helping. *Neuron* 68: 149–160.

Hoffman, M. L. 1981. Is altruism part of human nature? *Journal of Personality and Social Psychology* 40: 121–137.

Kozak, M., A. A. Marsh, and D. M. Wegner. 2006. What do I think you're doing? Action identification and mind attribution. *Journal of Personality and Social Psychology* 90: 543–555.

Lamm, C., C. D. Batson, and J. Decety. 2007. The neural substrate of human empathy: Effects of perspective-taking and cognitive appraisal. *Journal of Cognitive Neuroscience* 19: 42–58.

Levine, M., C. Cassidy, G. Brazier, and S. Reicher. 2002. Self-categorization and bystander intervention: Two experimental studies. *Journal of Applied Social Psychology* 7: 1452–1463.

Levine, M., A. Prosser, D. Evans, and S. Reicher. 2005. Identity and emergency intervention: How social group membership and inclusiveness of group boundaries shapes helping behavior. *Personality and Social Psychology Bulletin* 31: 443–453.

Leyens, J. P., M. P. Paladino, R. T. Rodriguez, J. Vaes, S. Demoulin, A. P. Rodriguez, and R. Gaunt. 2000. The emotional side of prejudice: The attribution of Secondary Emotions to ingroups and outgroups. *Personality and Social Psychology Review* 4: 186–197.

Meissner, C. A., and J. C. Brigham. 2001. Thirty years of investigating the own-race bias in memory for faces: A meta-analytic review. *Psychology, Public Policy, and Law* 7: 3–35.

Michel, C., B. Rossion, J. Han, C. Chung, and R. Caldara. 2006. Holistic processing is finely tuned for faces of one's own race. *Psychological Science* 17: 608–615.

Muraven, M., and R. F. Baumeister. 2000. Self-regulation and depletion of limited resources. Does self-control resemble a muscle? *Psychological Bulletin* 126: 247–259.

Nadler, A., G. Harpaz-Gorodeisky, and Y. Ben-David. 2009. Defensive helping: Threat to group identity, ingroup identification, status stability, and common group identity as determinants of intergroup help-giving. *Journal of Personality and Social Psychology* 97: 823–834.

Piliavin, I. M., J. A. Piliavin, and J. Rodin. 1975. Costs, diffusion, and the stigmatized victim. *Journal of Personality and Social Psychology* 32: 429–438.

Pryor, J. B., G. D. Reeder, A. E. Monroe, and A. Patel. 2010. Stigma and pro-social behavior: Are people reluctant to help stigmatized persons? In *The Psychology of Prosocial Behavior: Group Processes, Intergroup Relations, and Helping*, edited by S. Stürmer and M. Snyder, 59–80. Malden, MA: Wiley-Blackwell.

Richeson, J. A., and S. Trawalter. 2005. Why do interracial interactions impair executive function? A resource depletion account. *Journal of Personality and Social Psychology* 88: 934–947.

Saucier, D. A., C. T. Miller, and N. Doucet. 2005. Differences in helping Whites and Blacks: A meta-analysis. *Personality and Social Psychology Review* 9: 2–16.

Singer, T., B. Seymour, J. P. O'Doherty, K. E. Stephan, R. J. Dolan, and C. D. Frith. 2006. Empathic neural responses are modulated by the perceived fairness of others. *Nature* 439: 466–469.

Stürmer, S., and M. Snyder. 2010. *The Psychology of Prosocial Behavior: Group Processes, Intergroup Relations, and Helping*. Malden, MA: Wiley-Blackwell.

Stürmer, S., M. Snyder, A. Kropp, and B. Siem. 2006. Empathy-motivated helping: The moderating role of group membership. *Personality and Social Psychology Bulletin* 32: 943–956.

Tajfel, H., and J. Turner. 1979. An integrative theory of intergroup conflict. In *The Social Psychology of Intergroup Relations*, edited by W. G. Austin and S. Worchel, 94–109. Monterey, CA: Brooks-Cole.

Turner, J., and R. S. Onorato. 1999. Social identity, personality, and the self-concept: A self-categorization perspective. In *The Psychology of the Social Self*, edited by T. R. Tyler, R. M. Kramer, and O. P. John, 11–46. Mahwah, NJ: Lawrence Erlbaum Associates.

Van Leeuwen, E., and S. Täuber. 2010. The strategic side of out-group helping. In *The Psychology of Prosocial Behavior: Group Processes, Intergroup Relations, and Helping*, edited by S. Stürmer and M. Snyder, 81–99. Malden, MA: Wiley-Blackwell.

Vorauer, J. D., and S. J. Sasaki. 2009. Helpful only in the abstract? Ironic Effects of empathy in intergroup interaction. *Psychological Science* 20: 191–197.

Xu, X., X. Zuo, X. Wang, and S. Han. 2009. Do you feel my pain? Racial group membership modulates empathic neural responses. *Journal of Neuroscience* 29: 8525–8529.

Young, S. G., and K. Hugenberg. 2010. Mere social categorization modulates identification of facial expressions of emotion. *Journal of Personality and Social Psychology* 99: 964–977.

5 Empathy Is Not Always as Personal as You May Think: The Use of Stereotypes in Empathic Accuracy

Karyn L. Lewis and Sara D. Hodges

You never really understand a person until you consider things from his point of view . . . until you climb into his skin and walk around in it.

—Atticus Finch, *To Kill a Mockingbird*

Empathy is one of those ordinary everyday miracles. Although it is impossible to "climb into someone else's skin and walk around in it" as Atticus Finch suggests is necessary to understand another person, we still frequently feel as though we *do* come to understand others' experiences. What makes this possible? How do we mentally walk a mile in another person's shoes? As the opening quote suggests, the idealized view of empathy seems to involve an "empathizer" paying careful, close attention to the specific words and cues of the individual who is the empathizer's target. However, we propose that a substantial part of understanding others comes from within the empathizer's own head, including falling back on very impersonal information such as stereotypes associated with the target person's roles or group memberships. In this chapter we focus on one specific component of empathy, empathic accuracy—that is, people's everyday attempts to accurately understand the specific thoughts and feelings going on in the heads of others. We explore the processes involved in achieving empathic accuracy, and we argue that understanding others is not always as personal as people think.

Top-Down Empathy

Several scholars contrast between two forms of empathy (e.g., Hodges and Wegner 1997; Stueber 2006): a basic form where perceivers (perhaps automatically) detect and decode cues such as facial expressions to understand another's emotions and a more advanced form that requires complex cognitive abilities to understand another's behavior, thought processes, or intentions. Recent research from our lab suggests that these basic and advanced empathic abilities may be separate abilities, orthogonal to one another. Across two studies (Lewis 2008; Locher 2009) participants were given a simple nonverbal decoding task (the DANVA; Nowicki and Duke 2001) that required them to observe and label facial expressions as happy, sad, angry, or fearful. Participants also completed a more complex empathy task in which they inferred the thoughts and feelings of a target person discussing a personal experience (the standard-stimulus empathic accuracy task; Ickes 1993). For this second task, coders then rated the accuracy of these inferences by comparing them to the thoughts and feelings the target actually reported experiencing. Unexpectedly, the correlation between accuracy for decoding facial expression and accuracy for inferring thoughts and feelings was very low and nonsignificant in both studies.

One explanation for the surprising lack of correlation between these two types of empathy may be that they draw on different skill sets. Whereas basic empathy is a "bottom-up" strategy that requires a perceiver to detect and decode cues that are directly available in an interpersonal situation, advanced empathy may instead rely less on decoding cues in the immediate interaction and more on "top-down" strategies that require the use of mental representations that exist in the perceiver's own mind. In line with such an explanation, of the many strategies people use to solve the "other minds problem" (that is, knowing what is going on in other people's heads), social cognition researchers have identified several that rely on information and ideas that are extraneous to the actual behavior displayed by the target of empathy (for a thorough discussion see Malle and Hodges 2005). For instance, perceivers may project their own mental states onto a target or mentally simulate how a target may think, feel, and behave in a certain situation. What these strategies have in common is that they draw on experiences, knowledge, and stored constructs within the mind of the empathic perceiver. What is more, these strategies include a role for imagination and synthesis rather than relying solely on simple perception.

Myers and Hodges (2009) have gone so far as to suggest that empathic accuracy may actually be more a product of good imagination rather than acute perceiving. They propose that good mind readers construct a mental representation, or schema, of another person and then use this schema to model how that person may think or feel at a specific moment. These schemas are helpful when inferring a person's mental contents because they provide a wider base to draw on than the target's outward behaviors alone. Consistent with the hypothesis that people construct and rely on schemas when empathizing, Stinson and Ickes (1992) found friends were more accurate at inferring one another's thoughts than were strangers. This difference was explained by strangers' relative *in*accuracy for inferring thoughts regarding events unrelated to the immediate context of the experiment. Friends had more experience with one another across time and other situations and were accordingly better able to imagine how their partner would think or feel in different types of contexts.

Likewise, Thomas and Fletcher (2003) found accuracy at inferring a target's thoughts was a stair-step function of intimacy between the target and the perceiver—on average a target's dating partner was more accurate than a friend, who was in turn more accurate than a stranger. The authors suggested that, due to rich histories and experiences with one another, dating partners had constructed extensive schemas of the target person that informed their inferences. Friends, and especially strangers, had less varied and deep experiences with the target; thus, their schemas of the target person were comparatively impoverished, and they instead had to rely more heavily on behavioral "data" to inform their inferences. Because a person's words and behaviors alone do not provide a direct portal to his or her private thoughts and feelings, accuracy suffered when perceivers had less extensive schemas to use when imagining what the target was thinking.

These two studies provide observational evidence that empathic accuracy increases with intimacy and acquaintanceship, presumably because a perceiver's target-schema becomes more extensive. These types of schemas can be built with knowledge of past interactions and experiences with a person, and they help us to flesh out the contents of a close other's mind. However, what remains unclear is what perceivers do in the absence of this type of personal information gained from acquaintanceship and experience. We must frequently interact with people with whom we are not intimately acquainted and who are not quick to share personal information. How do we attempt to understand their thoughts and feelings? In the absence of the schemas that come along with acquaintanceship and access to personal information, it seems unlikely that we would revert to relying solely on perceptions of a person's immediate behaviors to make judgments about what they are thinking about.

As one answer to this question, Gesn and Ickes (1999) provided experimental evidence that schemas based on something other than extensive experience with another person aid in achieving empathic accuracy—and they further showed that perceivers begin to build these schemas very quickly. In their study, perceivers watched a videotape of a target (who was a stranger to the research participants) discussing a personal problem and saw the tape either in its naturally occurring order or in a mixed-up sequence. The authors posited that participants who saw the target videotape in its original order would be able to build a schema of that target based on what the target shared about his or her experience; however, the ability to construct such a schema would be compromised for perceivers who saw the target videotape in a random order. Their results showed that perceivers in the natural-order condition showed more accuracy than those in the random-order condition but *only* when the target's thoughts to be inferred were consistent with the ongoing dialogue of the interview. In other words, people who viewed the target's interview in the original order were able to construct a schema of that person to draw on when making inferences about the target's thoughts. When those thoughts were schema consistent, accuracy was high; when the thoughts were schema inconsistent, accuracy was low. This pattern was not observed for participants in the random-order condition. Because those participants saw the target's interview in randomly presented scenes, their ability to collect information and construct a schema of the target was impaired, and they were thus more likely to use behavioral cues over schemas to infer the target's thoughts. Consequently, accuracy for perceivers in the random-order condition did not suffer when the thoughts to be inferred were schema inconsistent.

Thus, the work of Stinson and Ickes (1992) and Thomas and Fletcher (2003) suggests that we naturally accumulate information about the people we have relationships with, and the results from the Gesn and Ickes (1999) study suggest that even when we do not know other people well, we still form expectations about what they are likely to be thinking or feeling. We can expect then, that as time goes by and we gather more and more information about a person, the mental schemas we construct will become richer, providing a basis for more accurately inferring detailed thoughts that would be difficult, if not impossible, to read by simply observing the person's behavior in the immediate situation.

When Stereotypes Help

What other information might perceivers who lack extensive individuated schemas of their targets use to make inferences about that person's thoughts and feelings? We believe that stereotypes serve as an important source of information that perceivers use in such cases. Stereotypes associated with membership in social categories have been suggested as an additional source of information that perceivers use to form broad impressions about others (Brewer 1988; Fiske and Neuberg 1990). Stereotypes get a bad rap as the basis of negative bias in person perception (e.g., Devine 1989), and to the extent that stereotypes lead to prejudice, this reputation is deserved. Furthermore, being on the receiving end of a stereotype can be depersonalizing, even when the stereotype is neutral or positive—and can be devastating when the stereotype is a negative one.

Thus, it may be surprising to suggest that stereotypes play a role in facilitating something associated as much with understanding and caring as empathy. However, stereotypes, like other category generalizations (Macrae, Milne, and Bodenhausen 1994; Fiske and Taylor 2008), come to exist in part because they allow us to make judgments efficiently, which makes them particularly useful when engaging in complex and cognitively demanding tasks such as trying to guess what another person is thinking. Moreover, research suggests that stereotypes can increase the accuracy of social perceptions (for a review see Jussim et al. 2005), particularly when individuating information is unavailable (Kunda and Thagard 1996). Thus, basing mental state inferences on stereotypes (although an imperfect strategy to be sure) may actually buy a perceiver some accuracy in guessing a target's thoughts that would otherwise be hard to come by.

We are unfamiliar with any research specifically examining whether perceivers use stereotypes when inferring a target's ongoing thoughts and feelings over the course of an interaction. However, other social cognition research is suggestive. Ames (2004a, 2004b) has shown that perceivers use stereotypes to infer the intentions and general mental states of an imagined other. Furthermore, Ames found that perceivers used stereotypes more when the target seemed dissimilar to themselves, suggesting that stereotypes were strategically applied to infer mental states when alternate strategies (e.g., projecting one's own mental states onto the target) made less sense.

Similarly, research from the related realm of personality judgments also suggests that stereotypes may play a role in understanding others. Kenny's (2004) theoretical model of interpersonal perception suggests that stereotypes play a role in forming impressions of another person's personality, particularly when acquaintance with that person is low so there is very little other information to go on. Consistent with this model, Biesanz, West, and Millevoi (2007) found that as people became more acquainted with a target, their judgments of that target's personality were less a reflection of stereotype accuracy (e.g., accuracy at judging the average person) and more a reflection of differential accuracy (e.g., accuracy at judging that person specifically). Stated differently, perceivers who were less acquainted with a target and had less individuating information about a target made judgments based more on knowledge about what the average, or stereotypical, person was like. As with Ames's work, the results of Biesanz et al.'s (2007) study suggest that reliance on stereotypes to make personality judgments increased when other strategies were not available.

Other research suggests that increased knowledge about or exposure to a particular stereotype may aid in forming more accurate perceptions of the stereotyped group's attitudes. In a study by Hodges et al. (2010) female perceivers were asked to watch videotapes of new mother targets and guess the targets' general attitudes toward motherhood. Perceivers for whom new motherhood was salient (either because they themselves were also new mothers, or because they were pregnant and about to become new mothers) were more accurate in guessing the targets' attitudes than women who had never been pregnant or raised a child. Specifically, the women for whom new motherhood was salient were more accurate because they were better at stereotype accuracy—guessing the part of a target's attitudes that was generally shared by all new mothers. When it came to differential accuracy—that is, guessing how a specific target's attitudes differed from the prototypical mother, new mothers and pregnant women were no better than never-pregnant nonmothers.

Taken together, we can surmise that when people have individuating information about another person available to them, it allows them to construct and then draw on a personalized schema of the person when inferring that person's thoughts. However, in the absence of this type of personal information gained from acquaintanceship and experience, people may also use stereotypes to inform thought inferences. Specifically, we hypothesize that when inferring the thoughts of someone with whom a perceiver is not intimately acquainted, perceivers draw on group or role-based stereotypes associated with a target person's social categories, and they are particularly likely to do this when individuating information is unavailable. As evidence of this process, we expect that perceivers would be more accurate at inferring thoughts that were stereotypical of a target's social role, especially when that target did not share much personal information.

In order to empirically investigate the hypothesis that perceivers use stereotypes when inferring the contents of a target's mind, we focused our investigation at the level of each distinct thought instead of considering the specific target person as the lowest unit of analysis. In the past, empathic-accuracy researchers have typically aggregated accuracy across thought inferences within a target to circumvent violations of the assumption of independence required by traditional single-level modeling techniques. However, one downside to collapsing accuracy in this way is that it ignores potentially meaningful variation between the different thoughts that a target individual reports. It seems probable that the thoughts experienced by a target vary across a number of characteristics that may also be related to empathic accuracy, and examination of thought-level variables has gone largely uninvestigated up to this point.

One possible reason that previous researchers have chosen to use the target—not individual thoughts—as the lowest unit of analysis may be the difficulty of modeling nested data structures (in this case, individual thoughts nested within targets) using traditional single-level linear modeling strategies. However, the use of hierarchical linear modeling (HLM) is becoming increasingly more common as an approach for disentangling multilevel effects. Because HLM allows us to simultaneously study thought-level variables, target-level variables, and perceiver-level variables, it is possible to test cross-level interactions (e.g., whether differences in the relationship between lower-level variables and outcomes could be explained by higher-level variables). Specifically, by using HLM we are able to test the hypothesis that the effect of stereotypicality (assessed at the individual thought level) on empathic accuracy depends on how much personal information about the target is available (assessed at the target level).

To test whether perceivers use stereotypes to infer the thoughts of a target particularly when little individuating information is available, we asked a sample of college students ($N = 81$) to watch videos of targets who all belonged to the same social category. Specifically, the targets were all women who had recently given birth to their first child and were videotaped while discussing their experiences of becoming a new mother (see Hodges et al. 2010 for a complete description of the collection of the target videos). Following the Ickes (1993) empathic accuracy paradigm, immediately after the original videos were made each target watched the video of her interview and was asked to report any time she remembered having had a specific thought or feeling. The target's description of the actual content of that thought was recorded as well as the time on the video counter that corresponded to the point in the video at which the target remembered having the thought.

The college student participants served as perceivers and were shown the target videos, which were stopped at the same points corresponding to the times in the video when the target reported experiencing a thought or feeling. The perceivers were asked to infer what the target was thinking at that moment. Independent coders then rated the accuracy of the perceivers' inferences by comparing them to the actual thoughts earlier reported by the targets (steps also consistent with Ickes' paradigm). An average accuracy score was computed for each thought inference for each perceiver, and this score was scaled from 0 to 100 (higher numbers reflected higher ratings of accuracy by the coders).

For our measure of thought stereotypicality, another set of coders were shown the actual thoughts reported by the targets and rated how characteristic they were of what the average new mother would report about her experience. In order to measure the availability of individuating information about a particular target, we showed another set of coders the target videos, and after watching the video in its entirety, they rated overall how personal the information shared by the target was. Thus, stereotypicality was assessed for each reported *thought*, whereas the extent that the target shared personal information in general was assessed one level up, for each *target*.

Using HLM, we modeled accuracy for a specific thought as a product of how stereotypical that thought was and how personal the information shared by the target was. Recall that we predicted that perceivers would rely on new mother stereotypes to infer a target's thoughts, and thus we expected higher accuracy for thoughts with content that was consistent with new mother stereotypes and poorer accuracy for more idiosyncratic thoughts whose contents were inconsistent or irrelevant to the stereotype. In addition we expected that participants would be most likely to rely on stereotypes in the absence of person-specific information. Thus, we predicted that the accuracy boost for stereotypical thoughts would depend on how much personally individuating information the target revealed. Consistent with past empathic accuracy researchers (e.g., Gesn and Ickes, 1999), we also included a rating provided earlier by our coders of how difficult each thought was to infer as a covariate in all our analyses. This was done to ensure that any effect of stereotypicality was not confounded with ease of inference.

Overall, the results confirmed our hypotheses. In support of the idea that stereotypes can contribute to people's accuracy in understanding others' thoughts, perceivers showed greater accuracy for stereotypical thoughts and worse accuracy for less stereotypical thoughts. What is more, the boost in accuracy for stereotypical thoughts was present even when controlling for how difficult a thought was to infer. In other words, perceivers were more accurate at inferring stereotypical thoughts, and this could not be explained by these thoughts simply being easier to infer.

The stereotype-based accuracy boost was present for men and for women. Interestingly, however, we did find a sex difference in the extent to which the stereotypicality effect interacted with the availability of personal information about the target. The three-way interaction is broken down in Figure 5.1. As this graph shows, women were more accurate at judging stereotypical thoughts, but more so when the target revealed

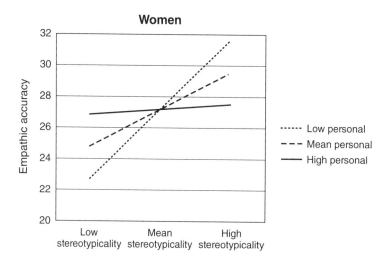

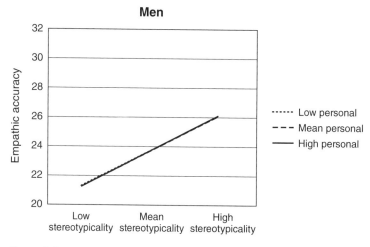

Figure 5.1

Empathic accuracy as a function of thought/feeling stereotypicality and how personal the information revealed by the target was. Low denotes 1 SD below the mean, and high denotes 1 SD above the mean.

little personal information; when a target revealed highly personal information, women's accuracy was similar across all levels of stereotypicality. However, a different pattern was found for men. Across the board men showed higher accuracy for more stereotypical thoughts, regardless of whether or not the target revealed personal information (indeed, the lines for the men's data in figure 5.1 are virtually entirely overlapping!).

In other words, men appear to consistently rely on stereotypes to guess the targets' thoughts, as evidenced by the fact that they had greater accuracy when stereotypes were actually relevant to guessing the target's thoughts. In contrast, women seemed to moderate their use of stereotypes as a strategy for guessing targets' thoughts. Women also relied on stereotypes—but only when a target revealed little personal, individuated information. In this way women's data looked like the extreme version of men's data: much greater accuracy for thoughts that contained more stereotypic content. However, for targets that did share personal, individuated information, women's accuracy depended much less on how stereotypic a specific thought was. It was as if women knew when to pay attention to individuating cues in order to guess a target's thought and when inferring a "one size fits all" thought was their best option. This flexibility in strategies appeared to help women, as women's accuracy was higher than men's overall.

It is interesting to speculate as to why the women were able to switch strategies better than men (as evidenced by the three-way interaction). Notably, we found no two-way interaction of sex and stereotypicality, so being dealt stereotypic thoughts to guess did not generally advantage women over men. Had such a pattern been present in our data, it could possibly be explained by increased familiarity with new-mother stereotypes on the part of women. However, instead, the special sensitivity that women seemed to possess was an awareness that when targets were sharing highly individuated information, it was better to use that information rather than stereotypes to infer what the target was thinking at a particular time.

Biesanz and Human (2010) found that perceivers without an explicit accuracy motivation goal judged others' personality more stereotypically, whereas perceivers with an explicit motivation goal judged others' personality more distinctively, individuating more among targets. Thus, one plausible explanation for our three-way interaction is that, compared to men, women were more motivated to accurately infer thoughts, and this resulted in greater reliance on individuating information when it was available. This interpretation is in line with several past studies finding evidence of subtle motivators that affect women's accuracy more than men's (for a review see Hodges, Laurent, and Lewis 2011).

All told, our results suggest that there may be sex differences in which strategy is employed when guessing another person's thoughts, but overall there was strong support for the idea that all perceivers—men and women—were able to use stereotypes to achieve greater accuracy, as evidenced by the fact that the more stereotypic a target's thought was, the more accurately a perceiver guessed it. When presented with what has historically been seen as the nearly impossible "other minds" problem of reading another person's thoughts, it seems people make good use of shared content in the form of stereotypes.

Stereotypes are learned, but their content does not always reflect having personally experienced any covariation between category membership and characteristics associated with the stereotype (Hamilton and Gifford 1976). For example, many Americans who have experienced minimal or no interactions with certain ethnic or religious groups can nonetheless rattle off the stereotype for these groups, which are often negative and furthermore, frequently inaccurate. However, in a more positive light, our ability to learn stereotypes without having to observe firsthand instances of covariation creates a vast potential for empathic understanding. We learn from after-school TV specials that children of divorced parents often feel their parents' split is somehow their fault. We learn from magazine articles that victims of crimes, especially personal assaults, are victimized twice—once by the actual crime and again by the fear and distrust that lingers. We know from interacting with neighbors and co-workers that chemotherapy patients miss their hair and widows and widowers miss their spouses. We can know all these things without directly experiencing them ourselves (see Hodges 2005; Hodges et al. 2010), and we can effectively call on this knowledge— maybe even without consciously bidding it—in our social interactions, creating a depth of understanding well beyond that which could occur simply by trying to read facial expressions of emotion or via sympathetic resonance between motor cortices.

Conclusions

In conclusion, including generalized knowledge such as stereotypes in the big tent that encompasses empathy overall—and among the tools for achieving empathic accuracy more specifically—certainly runs counter to many intuitions about empathy. One of the defining features of a folk concept of empathy may be the near-magical quality of feeling as if we are directly perceiving what is inside another person's head— with no apparent mechanism bridging our two minds. Indeed, even more formal definitions of empathy may relegate understanding based on stereotypic knowledge to be something other than empathy. However, rather than damaging its mystique, we think uncovering the secrets that lead to empathic understanding simply makes it all the more amazing.

Acknowledgments

The authors thank Brian Clark, Scott John, Nicole Lawson, and Michael W. Myers for their helpful comments on earlier drafts of this chapter, and Alan Phillips for his provocative perspective on folk theories of empathy.

References

Ames, D. R. 2004a. Inside the mind reader's tool kit: Projection and stereotyping in mental state inference. *Journal of Personality and Social Psychology* 87: 340–353.

Ames, D. R. 2004b. Strategies for social inference: A Similarity Contingency Model of projection and stereotyping in attribute prevalence estimates. *Journal of Personality and Social Psychology* 87: 573–585.

Biesanz, J. C., and L. J. Human. 2010. The cost of forming more accurate impressions: Accuracy-motivated perceivers see the personality of others more distinctively but less normatively than perceivers without an explicit goal. *Psychological Science* 21: 589–594.

Biesanz, J. C., S. G. West, and A. Millevoi. 2007. What do you learn about someone over time?: The relationship between length of acquaintance and consensus and Self-Other agreement in judgments of personality. *Journal of Personality and Social Psychology* 92: 119–135.

Brewer, M. B. 1988. A dual process model of impression formation. In *Advances in Social Cognition*, edited by T. K. Srull and R. S. Wyer, 1–36. New York: Academic Press.

Devine, P. G. 1989. Stereotypes and prejudice: Their automatic and controlled components. *Journal of Personality and Social Psychology* 21: 281–295.

Fiske, S. T., and S. L. Neuberg. 1990. A continuum of impression formation, from category-based to individuating processes: Influences of information and motivation on attention and interpretation. In *Advances in Experimental Social Psychology*, edited by M. Zanna, 1–74. San Diego, CA: Academic Press.

Fiske, S. T., and S. E. Taylor. 2008. *Social Cognition: From Brains to Culture*. Boston: McGraw-Hill.

Gesn, P. R., and W. Ickes. 1999. The development of meaning contexts for empathic accuracy: Channel and sequence effects. *Journal of Personality and Social Psychology* 77: 746–761.

Hamilton, D. L., and R. K. Gifford. 1976. Illusory correlation in interpersonal perception: A cognitive basis of stereotypic judgments. *Journal of Experimental Social Psychology* 12: 392–407.

Hodges, S. D. 2005. Is how much you understand me in your head or mine? In *Other Minds: How Humans Bridge the Divide between Self and Others*, edited by B. F. Malle and S. D. Hodges, 298–309. New York: Guilford Press.

Hodges, S. D., K. J. Kiel, A. D. I. K. Kramer, D. Veach, and R. Villanueva. 2010. Giving birth to empathy: The effects of similar experience on empathic accuracy, empathic concern, and perceived empathy. *Personality and Social Psychology Bulletin* 36: 398–409.

Hodges, S. D., S. M. Laurent, and K. L. Lewis. 2011. Specially motivated, feminine, or just female: Do women have an empathic accuracy advantage? In *Managing Interpersonal Sensitivity: Knowing When and When Not to Understand Others*, edited by J. L. Smith, W. Ickes, J. A. Hall, and S. D. Hodges, 59-73. Hauppauge, NY: Nova Science Publishers.

Hodges, S. D., and D. M. Wegner. 1997. Automatic and controlled empathy. In *Empathic Accuracy*, edited by W. Ickes, 311–339. New York: Guilford Press.

Ickes, W. 1993. Empathic accuracy. *Journal of Personality* 61: 587–610.

Jussim, L., K. D. Harber, J. T. Crawford, T. R. Cain, and F. Cohen. 2005. Social reality makes the social mind: Self-fulfilling prophecy, stereotypes, bias, and accuracy. *Interaction Studies: Social Behaviour and Communication in Biological and Artificial Systems* 6: 85–102.

Kenny, D. A. 2004. PERSON: A general model of interpersonal perception. *Personality and Social Psychology Review* 8: 265–280.

Kunda, Z., and P. Thagard. 1996. Forming impressions from stereotypes, traits, and behaviors: A parallel-constraint-satisfaction theory. *Psychological Review* 103: 284–308.

Lewis, K. L. (2008). *Empathic Accuracy and Nonverbal Decoding: Related or Distinct Constructs?* Unpublished master's thesis, University of Oregon.

Locher, B. (2009). *Empathic Accuracy and the Use of Stereotypes in Inferring the Thoughts and Feelings of Others*. Unpublished Honors College thesis, University of Oregon.

Macrae, C. N., A. B. Milne, and G. V. Bodenhausen. 1994. Stereotypes as energy-saving devices: A peek inside the cognitive toolbox. *Journal of Personality and Social Psychology* 66: 37–47.

Malle, B. F., and S. D. Hodges, eds. 2005. *Other Minds: How Humans Bridge the Divide between Self and Others*. New York: Guilford Press.

Myers, M. W., and S. D. Hodges. 2009. Making it up and making do: Simulation, imagination and empathic accuracy. In *The Handbook of Imagination and Mental Simulation*, edited by K. Markman, W. Klein, and J. Suhr, 281–94. New York: Psychology Press.

Nowicki, S., and M. P. Duke. 2001. Nonverbal receptivity: The diagnostic analysis of nonverbal accuracy (DANVA). In *Interpersonal Sensitivity: Theory and Measurement*, edited by J. A. Hall and F. J. Bernieri, 183–98. Mahwah, NJ: Lawrence Erlbaum Associates.

Stinson, L., and W. Ickes. 1992. Empathy accuracy in the interactions of male friends versus male strangers. *Journal of Personality and Social Psychology* 62: 787–797.

Stueber, K. 2006. *Rediscovering Empathy: Agency, Folk, Psychology, and the Human Sciences*. Cambridge, MA: MIT Press.

Thomas, G., and G. J. O. Fletcher. 2003. Mind-reading accuracy in intimate relationships: Assessing the roles of the relationship, the target, and the judge. *Journal of Personality and Social Psychology* 85: 1079–1094.

III Evolutionary Roots of Empathy

6 Empathy in Primates and Other Mammals

Frans B. M. de Waal

Definitions of empathy commonly emphasize two aspects, which are the sharing of emotions and the adoption of another's viewpoint. Empathy allows the organism to quickly relate to the states of others, which is essential for the regulation of social interactions, coordinated activity, and cooperation toward shared goals. Even though the cognitive capacity of perspective-taking assists in this, it is secondary. This is even true for our own species, as Hoffman (1981, 79) noted: "Humans must be equipped biologically to function effectively in many social situations without undue reliance on cognitive processes."

In the scientific literature, however, a mentalistic definition, closer to theory-of-mind, has become popular. Accordingly, empathy is a way of gaining access to another's mind by pretending to imagine yourself in their situation. For example Goldman (2006) sees empathy as a combination of simulation and projection: inside its own head, the subject simulates how it would feel being in the other's situation and proceeds to assign mental states of its own to the other. Similarly, Baron-Cohen (2005, 170) describes empathy as involving "a leap of imagination into someone else's headspace." Most of these definitions sound so cognitively demanding that it is hardly surprising that until recently animal empathy was rarely considered.

But what if the beginnings of empathy are simpler? What if it does not require the subject to sort through information gained from the other as well as digging inside itself to arrive at an evaluation of what might be going on with the other? What if subjects share in the other's state of mind via bodily communication? The immediacy of the empathic response hints at this possibility. If we see a child fall and scrape its knee, we flinch, and exclaim "ouch!" as if what happened to the child happened at the same instant to ourselves. This was already known to Theodor Lipps (1903), who developed the concept of empathy and aptly called it *Einfühlung* (German for "feeling into"). We are in suspense watching a high-wire artist, Lipps wrote, because we vicariously enter his body and thus share his experience. It is as if we are on the rope with him. We obviously cannot feel anything that happens outside of ourselves, but by unconsciously merging self and other, the other's experiences echo within us as if they are our own. Such identification, argued Lipps, cannot be reduced to other capacities, such as learning, association, or reasoning. Empathy offers access to "the foreign self."

Empathy as feeling one with another's state, rather than some sort of cognitive deduction, was already a major point of discussion in early twentieth-century philosophy, from Wittgenstein to Max Scheler (Zahavi 2008). This bottom-up view has the advantage of explaining the unconscious reactions demonstrated by Dimberg et al. (2000) that are unexplained by the more cognitive view. With small electrodes registering facial muscle movements, investigators presented human subjects with pictures of angry and happy faces on a computer screen. Even if the pictures flashed too briefly for conscious perception, subjects still mimicked the faces and experienced corresponding emotions. Subjects exposed to happy faces reported feeling better than those exposed to angry ones, even though neither group was aware of what its members had seen. Clearly, empathy with the perceived emotions was brought about unconsciously without cognitive simulations or projections. Interpersonal emotional connections seem to run as much via bodies as minds (Niedenthal 2007).

If this is true for humans, it is probably even more true for other animals. We should not forget that mirror neurons, which some believe to facilitate these reactions (Gallese 2005), were first discovered not in humans but in monkeys (di Pellegrino et al. 1992), in which we must assume they serve a similar function. Bodily synchronization is as adaptive for prey as it is for cooperative predators. Social animals need to coordinate movements, collectively respond to danger, communicate about food and water, and assist others in need. Responsiveness to the behavioral states of conspecifics ranges from a flock of birds taking off all at once because one among them is startled by a predator to a mother ape returning to a whimpering youngster to help it from one tree to the next by draping her body as a bridge between the two. The first is a reflex-like transmission of fear that may not involve any understanding of what triggered the initial reaction, but one that is undoubtedly adaptive. The mother-ape example is more discriminating, involving anxiety at hearing one's offspring whimper, assessment of the reason for its distress, and an attempt to ameliorate the situation.

These synchronization responses are measurable in primates, for example, by demonstrating that they prefer experimenters who mimic their body movements over experimenters who do not (Paukner et al. 2009). It is also known that chimpanzees, like humans, yawn when they see another individual yawn (Anderson, Myowa-Yamakoshi, and Matsuzawa 2004), or even when they see an animated apelike drawing yawn (Campbell et al. 2009; figure 6.1). This kind of research is still in the beginning stages, but the reactions are strong and predictable and very much in line with what we know about the human tendency for mimicry.

Figure 6.1
Because yawning is an involuntary reflex, yawn contagion is close to empathy. Chimpanzees are so sensitive to the yawns of others that even a three-dimensional animation of a yawning head, of which this drawing shows eight stages, induces yawns in chimpanzees watching it on a computer screen. (Animations by Devyn Carter, from Campbell et al. 2009)

Rodent Empathy

Emotional connectedness in humans is so common, starts so early in life (e.g., Hoffman 1975; Zahn-Waxler and Radke-Yarrow 1990), shows neural and physiological correlates (e.g., Adolphs et al. 1994; Decety and Chaminade 2003) as well as a genetic substrate (Plomin et al. 1993), that it would be strange indeed if no continuity with other species existed. Emotional responses to displays of emotion in others are in fact so commonplace in animals (Plutchik 1987; de Waal 1996) that Darwin (1982 [1871], 77) already noted that "many animals certainly sympathize with each other's distress or danger."

The selection pressure to evolve rapid emotional connectedness likely started in the context of parental care. Signaling their state through smiling and crying, human infants urge their caregiver to come into action, and equivalent mechanisms operate in other animals in which reproduction relies on feeding, cleaning, and warming of the young. Offspring signals are not just responded to but induce an agitated state, suggestive of parental distress at the perception of offspring distress (MacLean 1985). Avian and mammalian parents alert to and affected by their offspring's emotions must have outreproduced those who remained indifferent.

Once empathic capacities existed they could be applied outside the rearing context and play a role in the wider fabric of social relationships. The fact that mammals retain distress vocalizations into adulthood hints at the continued survival value of care-inducing signals. For example primates often lick and clean the wounds of conspecifics, which is so critical for healing that injured migrating adult male macaques have been observed to temporarily return to their native group, where they are more likely to receive this service (Dittus and Ratnayeke 1989).

One of the first experimental studies on animal empathy was Church's (1959) entitled "Emotional Reactions of Rats to the Pain of Others." Having trained rats to obtain food by pressing a lever, Church found that if a rat pressing the lever perceived another rat in a neighboring cage receive a shock from an electrified cage floor, the first rat would interrupt its activity. Why should this rat not continue to acquire food? The larger issue is whether rats that stopped pressing the lever were concerned about their companions or just fearful that something aversive might also happen to themselves.

Church's work inspired a brief flurry of research during the 1960s that investigated concepts such as "empathy," "sympathy," and "altruism" in animals. This included studies on monkeys, which showed a much more dramatic empathy response than rats. Monkeys will for many days refuse to pull a chain that delivers food to themselves if doing so delivers an electric shock to a companion (Masserman, Wechkin, and Terris 1964). In order to avoid accusations of anthropomorphism, however, authors often placed the topic of their research in quotation marks, and their studies went largely ignored in ensuing years.

Half a century after Church's study, however, there is a revival of interest in animal empathy, and a basic mechanism common to humans and other animals has been proposed. Accordingly, seeing another in a given situation or displaying certain emotions reactivates neural representations of when the subject was itself in similar situations or had experienced similar emotions, which in turn generates a bodily state resembling that of the object of attention. Thus, seeing another individual's pain may lead the observer to share the bodily and neural experience. The perception-action mechanism (PAM) seems to operate in both humans and other mammals (Preston and de Waal 2002).

Langford et al. (2006) put pairs of mice through a "writhing test." In each trial two mice were placed in two transparent Plexiglas tubes such that they could see one another. Either one or both mice were injected with diluted acetic acid, known to cause a mild stomach-ache. Mice respond to this treatment with characteristic writhing movements. The researchers found that an injected mouse would show more writhing if its partner was writhing, too, than it would if its partner had not been injected. Significantly, this applied only to mouse pairs who were cage mates.

Male (but not female) mice showed an interesting additional phenomenon while witnessing another male in pain: its own pain sensitivity actually dropped. This counter-empathic reaction occurred only in male pairs that did not know each other, which are probably also the pairs with the greatest degree of rivalry. Was that rivalry suppressing their reaction, or did they actually feel less empathy for a strange rival?

Finally, Langford et al. (2006) exposed pairs of mice to different sources of pain— the acetic acid as before and a radiant heat source. Mice observing a cage mate writhing due to the acid injection withdrew more quickly from the heat source. In other words

their reactions could not be attributed to mere motor imitation but involved emotional contagion because seeing a companion react to pain caused sensitization to
pain in general.

Preconcern

Once an organism is sensitive to another's pain or distress, the next step is to approach
and provide comfort. This goes beyond "personal distress" (i.e., self-focused distress
in response to another's distress) in that it is other-oriented, even though the motivation behind it may still be to comfort oneself. Seeing someone else cry, we get upset,
so that by contacting the other we also reassure ourselves. I am quite familiar with
such behavior in young rhesus monkeys. Once, when an infant had been bitten
because it had accidentally landed on a dominant female, it screamed so incessantly
that it was soon surrounded by other infants. I counted eight of them climbing on
top of the poor victim, pushing, pulling, and shoving each other as well as the first
infant. That obviously did little to alleviate its fright. The infant monkeys' response
seemed automatic, as if they were as distraught as the victim and sought to comfort
themselves as much as the other (de Waal 1989).

This cannot be the whole story, though. If these monkeys were just trying to calm
themselves, why did they approach the victim? Why did they not run to their
mothers? Why seek out the actual source of distress and not a guaranteed source of
comfort? Surely, this is more than emotional contagion. The latter can explain a need
for comfort—but not the magnetic pull toward a crying peer.

In fact both animals and young children often seek out distressed parties without
any indication that they know what is going on. They seem blindly attracted, like a
moth to a flame. We like to read concern about the other into their behavior, but the
required understanding may not be there. I will call this blind attraction *preconcern*.
It is as if nature has endowed the organism with a simple behavioral rule: "If you feel
another's pain, get over there and make contact."

One might counter that such a rule would prompt individuals to waste energy on
all sorts of distraught parties, many of which they would far better stay away from.
Approaching others in a predicament may not be the smartest thing to do. But I do
not think we need to worry about this given the evidence that emotions are picked
up more readily between parties with close ties than between strangers. This was the
case in the above-mentioned mouse study (Langford et al. 2006) and is well known
of many species, including humans (reviewed in Preston and de Waal 2002). A simple
approach rule would automatically propel individuals toward those distressed parties
that matter most to them, such as offspring and familiar companions.

If true, the sort of behavior that we associate with sympathy arose in fact before
sympathy itself. If this seems like putting the cart before the horse, it is really not as

strange as it sounds. There are other examples of behavior preceding understanding. Language development, for example, does not start with children naming things or expressing thoughts. It starts with *babbling:* babies crawl around uttering nonsensical strings of "ba-ba-ba-ba-ba," advancing to "do-ko-yay-day-bu." When our species claims to be the only talking primate, babbling is obviously not what we have in mind, but this is no reason to belittle it. The fact that everyone's linguistic career starts with this baby *lingua franca* illustrates how deeply ingrained language is. It develops out of a primitive urge without any of the refinements of the final product, exactly what I am proposing for the impulse to attend to someone else's distress.

Preconcern goes beyond personal distress, but not by far, since it does not require imagining yourself in the other's situation, and indeed the capacity to do so may be wholly absent, such as when a one-year-old child is already drawn toward upset family members (Zahn-Waxler and Radke-Yarrow 1990). Children of this age are not yet capable of grasping someone else's situation. Preconcern may also explain why certain animals, such as household pets, contact others in pain (Zahn-Waxler, Hollenbeck, and Radke-Yarrow 1984), or why infant monkeys pile on top of a hapless vocalizing peer.

Perspective-Taking

With preconcern in place learning and intelligence can begin to add layers of complexity, making the response ever more discerning until full-blown sympathy emerges. Since this is the level of sympathy that we, human adults, are familiar with, we think of it as a single process, as something you either have or lack, but in fact it consists of many layers added by evolution over millions of years. Most mammals show some of these—only a handful show all of them.

Some large-brained animals may share the human capacity to put themselves into someone else's shoes. Whether they do or do not has been debated ever since an American primatologist, Emil Menzel (1974), conducted his pioneering studies. Do chimps have any inkling of what others feel, want, need, or know? Menzel's work is rarely mentioned anymore, but he was the very first to see the importance of this issue.

Working outdoors with nine juvenile chimpanzees, Menzel would take one of them out into a large, grassy enclosure to reveal hidden food or a scary object, such as a (toy) snake. After this he would bring this individual back to the waiting group and release all the chimps together. Would the others appreciate that one among them knew something of importance, and if so, how would they react? Could they tell the difference between the other having seen food or a snake?

They most certainly could. They eagerly followed a chimpanzee who knew a food location, but they were hesitant to stay close to one who had seen a hidden snake

Figure 6.2
The very first theory-of-mind research was conducted by Emil Menzel (1974) with a focus on emotional body language to see what apes know about what others know. One juvenile chimpanzee, poking with a stick at a snake in the grass, is the only one who knows what is there. Before having seen the danger themselves, the onlooking apes know to be cautious from this individual's body language. (Drawing by Frans de Waal)

(figure 6.2). This was emotional contagion in action: they copied the other's enthusiasm or alarm. Menzel's guesser versus knower test has inspired a huge following as reflected in numerous studies on children, apes, birds, dogs, and so on. Unfortunately, the topic was soon redefined with a more abstract focus, such as knowing what others know (Premack and Woodruff 1978). The precise mechanism of such "theory of mind" (ToM) remained unaddressed, however, and to this date it is questionable if the process is as bodiless and theoretical as implied by the chosen terminology (de Gelder 1987; Hobson 1991).

The acquisition of ToM probably starts with emotional connections. Children pass traditional ToM tasks around the age of four, but they appreciate the feelings, needs, and desires of others already at the age of two or three (Wellman, Phillips, and Rodriguez 2000). They often rely on emotional communication to deduce what kind of situation the other faces, showing reactions similar to Menzel's (1974) apes, who recognized if one among them had spotted hidden food or danger. It should not surprise, therefore, that after many studies in which apes were challenged to guess what human experimenters knew or did not know, the greatest research progress arrived when scientists adopted a more emotionally relevant approach by testing how one ape perceives the knowledge of another in a dominance-subordination context (Hare, Call, and Tomasello 2001). For further experimental evidence for ape ToM see Shillito et al. (2005) and Hirata (2006).

An important spontaneous manifestation of empathic perspective-taking is "targeted helping," which is help fine-tuned to another's specific situation (de Waal 1996). For an individual to move beyond being sensitive to others toward an explicit other-orientation requires a shift in perspective. The emotional state induced in oneself by the other now needs to be attributed to the other instead of the self. A heightened self-identity allows a subject to relate to the object's emotional state without losing sight of the actual source of this state (Hoffman 1982; Lewis 2002). The required self-representation is hard to establish independently, but one common avenue is to gauge reactions to a mirror. The *co-emergence hypothesis* (de Waal 2008) predicts that mirror self-recognition (MSR) and advanced expressions of empathy appear together in both ontogeny and phylogeny.

Ontogenetically, there is compelling support for the co-emergence hypothesis in human children (Bischof-Köhler 1988, 1991; Zahn-Waxler et al. 1992; Johnson 1992). Gallup (1983) was the first to propose phylogenetic co-emergence, a prediction empirically supported by the contrast between monkeys and apes, with compelling evidence for both MSR, consolation, and targeted helping only in the apes (see below). Apart from the great apes, the animals for which we have the most striking accounts of consolation and targeted helping are dolphins and elephants (reviewed in de Waal 2009), which are also the only mammals other than the apes to pass the mark test in which an individual needs to locate a mark on itself that it cannot see without a mirror (Reiss and Marino 2001; Plotnik, de Waal, and Reiss 2006; figure 6.3).

Sympathetic Concern

Yerkes (1925) reported how a young bonobo showed intense concern for his sickly chimpanzee companion, and Ladygina-Kohts (2001 [1935], 121) noticed similar tendencies in her home-reared chimpanzee toward herself:

If I pretend to be crying, close my eyes and weep, Yoni immediately stops his play or any other activities, quickly runs over to me, all excited and shagged, from the most remote places in the house, such as the roof or the ceiling of his cage, from where I could not drive him down despite my persistent calls and entreaties. He hastily runs around me, as if looking for the offender; looking at my face, he tenderly takes my chin in his palm, lightly touches my face with his finger, as though trying to understand what is happening, and turns around, clenching his toes into firm fists.

What better evidence for the power of simian sympathy than the fact that an ape who would refuse to descend from the roof of the house for food that is waved at him would do so instantly on seeing his mistress in distress? Ladygina-Kohts also described

Figure 6.3
An Asian elephant with a visible X-shaped mark on the right side of her head and an invisible sham mark on the left side, touches the visible mark with the tip of her trunk thus indicating self-recognition, which is thought to correlate with perspective-taking. This still image was collected by a lipstick video camera embedded in the mirror. (Video still from Plotnik et al. 2006)

how Yoni would look into her eyes when she pretended to cry: "the more sorrowful and disconsolate my crying, the warmer his sympathy" (2001 [1935]). If she would slap her hands over her eyes, he tried to pull them away, extending his lips toward her face, looking attentively, slightly groaning and whimpering. She described similar reactions for her son, Roody, adding that he went further than the ape in that he would actually cry along with her. Roody cried even when he would notice a bandage over the eye of his favorite uncle or when he would see the maid grimace while swallowing bitter medicine.

A monkey or rat reacting to another's pain by stopping the behavior that caused it may simply be "turning off" unpleasant signals. But such self-protective altruism cannot explain Yoni's reaction to his surrogate mother. First, because he had not caused her distress himself and second, because he could easily have moved away when he saw her crying from the roof of the house. If self-protection were his goal, he also should have left her hands where they were when she cried behind them. Clearly, Yoni was not just focusing on his own situation: he felt an urge to understand what was the matter with Kohts.

Yoni's reaction is typical of apes. The *consolation* he showed is the best documented nonhuman-primate example of what in humans is known as *sympathetic concern.*

Figure 6.4
Consolation is common in humans and apes but largely absent in monkeys. A juvenile chimpanzee puts an arm around a screaming adult male, who has been defeated in a fight. The latest analyses suggest that this behavior expresses sympathetic concern. (Photograph by Frans de Waal)

Consolation is usually defined as reassurance provided by an uninvolved bystander to one of the combatants in a previous aggressive incident. For example, a third party goes over to the loser of a fight and gently puts an arm around his or her shoulders (see figure 6.4). After the first few studies of chimpanzee consolation (de Waal and van Roosmalen 1979; de Waal and Aureli 1996), other studies have confirmed this behavior in different ape species (Palagi, Paoli, and Borgognini 2004; Cordoni, Palagi, and Borgognini 2004; Mallavarapu et al. 2006). But when de Waal and Aureli (1996) set out to apply the same observation protocol to detect consolation in monkeys, they failed to find any, as did others (Watts, Colmenares, and Arnold 2000). The consolation gap between monkeys and the hominids (i.e., humans and apes) extends even to the one situation where one would most expect consolation to occur: macaque mothers fail to comfort their own offspring after a fight (Schino et al. 2004).

Spontaneous consolation is so common in apes that scientists have collected data on literally thousand of cases. Studies confirm that this behavior reduces the

recipient's arousal, is biased toward socially close individuals, and shows a sex difference, with females showing more of it than males (Fraser, Stahl, and Aureli 2008;
Romero, Castellanos, and de Waal 2010) consistent with sex differences in human
empathy (Zahn-Waxler et al. 1992; Han, Fan, and Mao 2008). Given the morphological
similarity between ape consolation behavior and expressions of sympathetic concern
in young children, which also touch and embrace distressed individuals, we follow
the Darwinian principle of parsimony that if two related species show similar behavior
under similar circumstances the psychology behind their behavior is likely similar, too
(de Waal 1999).

Altruistic Behavior

An old female named Peony spends her days with other chimpanzees in a large
outdoor enclosure near Atlanta, Georgia. On bad days when her arthritis is acting up
she has great trouble walking and climbing. But other females help her out. For
example, Peony is huffing and puffing to get up into the climbing frame in which
several chimpanzees have gathered for a grooming session. An unrelated younger
female moves behind her, places both hands on her ample behind and pushes her up
with quite a bit of effort until Peony joins the rest.

Even though there are abundant examples of spontaneous helping among primates,
the modern literature still depicts humans as the only truly altruistic species, since all
that animals care about are return benefits (e.g., Dawkins 1976; Kagan 2000; Fehr and
Fischbacher 2003). The problem with this view is that the evolutionary reasons for
altruistic behavior are not necessarily the animals' reasons. Do animals really help
each other in the knowledge that this will ultimately benefit themselves? To assume
so is cognitively demanding in the extreme, requiring animals to anticipate the future
behavior of others and to keep track of what they did for others versus what others
did for them. Thus far there is little or no evidence for such expectations. Helpful acts
for immediate self-gain are indeed common, but it seems safe to assume that future
return benefits remain largely beyond the animal's cognitive horizon.

Once evolved, behavior often operates with *motivational autonomy*, that is, its motivation is relatively independent of evolutionary goals (de Waal 2008). A good example
is sexual behavior, which arose to serve reproduction. Since animals are, so far as we
know, unaware of the link between sex and reproduction, they must be engaging in
sex (as do humans much of the time) without progeny in mind. Just as sex cannot be
motivated by unforeseen consequences, altruistic behavior cannot be motivated by
unforeseen payoffs such as inclusive fitness or return benefits in the distant future.

The helping impulse must therefore stem from immediate factors, such as sensitivity to the emotions and/or needs of others. Such sensitivity would by no means contradict self-serving reasons for the evolution of behavior so long as it steers altruistic

behavior into the direction predicted by theories of kin selection and reciprocal altruism. Apart from assisting an aging female in her climbing efforts, chimpanzees occasionally perform extremely costly helping actions. For example, when a female reacts to the screams of her closest associate by defending her against a dominant male, she takes enormous risks on behalf of the other. Note the following description of two long-time chimpanzee friends in a zoo colony: "Not only do they often act together against attackers, they also seek comfort and reassurance from each other. When one of them has been involved in a painful conflict, she goes to the other to be embraced. They then literally scream in each other's arms" (de Waal 1982, 67). Or take high-risk helping such as when Washoe, the world's first language-trained chimp, heard another female scream and hit the water. Fouts and Mills (1997, 180) describe how Washoe raced across two electric wires, which normally contained the apes, to reach the victim and waded into the slippery mud to reach the wildly trashing female and grab one of her flailing arms to pull her to safety. This was a courageous act given that chimpanzees do not swim and are extremely hydrophobic. Washoe barely knew this female, having met her only a few hours before.

For both practical and ethical reasons, however, there is a scarcity of experiments on emotionally charged situations that could trigger costly altruism. This is not only true for animal altruism but equally so for human altruism. Instead, experiments usually concern low-cost altruism, sometimes called "other-regarding preferences." A typical paradigm is to offer one member of a pair the option to either secure food for itself by manipulating part A of an apparatus or to secure food for both itself and the other by manipulating part B of the same apparatus. In the first such experiment Colman, Liebold, and Boren (1969) found one of four tested macaques to be consistently other-regarding. When replications failed to find the same tendency in chimpanzees, however, this led to the suggestion that other-regarding preferences may be uniquely human (Silk et al. 2005). It is impossible to prove the null hypothesis, however, and recent studies with different methodologies have yielded results more in line with what we know about naturalistic primate behavior.

In one chimpanzee study investigators tried to rule out reciprocity by having the apes interact with humans they barely knew, and on whom they did not depend for food or other favors, and found significant expressions of altruism (Warneken et al. 2007). Spontaneous helping has also been experimentally demonstrated in both capuchin monkeys (de Waal, Leimgruber, and Greenberg 2008; Lakshminarayanan and Santos 2008) and marmosets (Burkart et al. 2007). In our study two capuchin monkeys were placed side by side separated by mesh. One of them needed to barter with us with small plastic tokens, which we would first give to a monkey, after which we would hold out an open hand to let them return the token for a tidbit (figure 6.5). The critical test came when we offered a choice between two differently colored tokens with different meaning: one token was "selfish," the other "prosocial." If the bartering

Figure 6.5
One capuchin monkey reaches through an armhole to choose between differently marked pieces of pipe while her partner looks on. The pipe pieces can be exchanged for food. One token feeds both monkeys; the other feeds only the chooser. Capuchins typically prefer the "prosocial" token (de Waal et al. 2008). (Drawing from video by Frans de Waal)

monkey picked the selfish token, it received a small piece of apple for returning it, but its partner remained unrewarded. The prosocial token, on the other hand, rewarded both monkeys with apple at the same time. Since the monkey who did the bartering was rewarded either way, the only difference was in what the partner received.

Monkeys preferentially bartered with the prosocial token. This preference could not be explained by fear of future punishment, because dominant partners (which have least to fear) proved to be more prosocial than subordinate ones. Familiarity biased the choices in the predicted direction: the stronger the social tie between two monkeys, as measured by how much time they associated in the group, the more they favored the prosocial token (de Waal et al. 2008).

In short there is mounting evidence from both naturalistic observations and experiments that primates care about each other's welfare, and they follow altruistic impulses that are probably based on empathy, which in both humans and other animals increases with familiarity. The empathy mechanism automatically produces a stake in the other's welfare, that is, the behavior comes with an intrinsic reward, known in the human literature as the *warm-glow* effect. Actions that improve another's condition come with pleasant feelings (Andreoni 1989), so that humans report feeling good when they do good and show activation of reward-related brain areas (Harbaugh, Mayr, and Burghart 2007). It will be important to determine if the same self-reward system extends to other primates.

Empathy as Umbrella Term

At the core of the empathic capacity lies a mechanism that provides the subject with access to the subjective state of another through the subject's own neural representations. When the subject attends to the other's state, the subject's neural representations of similar states are automatically activated. This lets the subject get "under the skin" of the other, bodily sharing its emotions and needs. This neural activation, which Preston and de Waal (2002) dubbed the perception-action mechanism of empathy, fits with Damasio's (1994) somatic marker hypothesis of emotions, Prinz's (1997) common coding theory of perception and action, as well as evidence for a link at the cellular level between seeing and doing, such as the mirror neurons first discovered in macaques.

This view of empathy is a layered one. Instead of driving wedges between, let us say, emotional contagion and empathy, compassion and sympathy, or automatic and deliberate empathy, all of these capacities are connected, I believe. None of them could probably exist without the others. For example, what would empathy be without emotional engagement? Psychopaths may be capable of perspective-taking that superficially looks like empathy, but given their lack of emotional investment they cannot truly be called empathetic (Mullins-Nelson, Salekin, and Leistico 2006). Instead of viewing emotional contagion, personal distress, and other emotional reactions as distinct from empathy, I see them as being at the heart of it.

In the Russian Doll model visualized in figure 6.6, empathy is the *umbrella term* that encompasses all levels. Adult humans show all of them, but many animals show only a few layers as do human infants. I see perspective-taking as another level of empathy, not as separate. In normal development (and also in evolution) perspective-taking is *added* to the emotional processes. The child begins to wonder what causes emotions in others, rather than just being affected by them, and so begins to focus on the situation of the other. The same applies to some large-brained animals. They add perspective-taking to the emotional process, without replacing it. Since it is integrated with the emotional core, I speak of empathetic perspective-taking.

This reflects a typically biological way of thinking, stressing the unity behind a phenomenon and the realization that evolution rarely throws out anything. It rarely replaces one trait with another. Traits are transformed, modified, co-opted for other functions, or "tweaked" in another direction in what Darwin called "descent with modification." Thus, the frontal fins of fish became the front limbs of land animals,

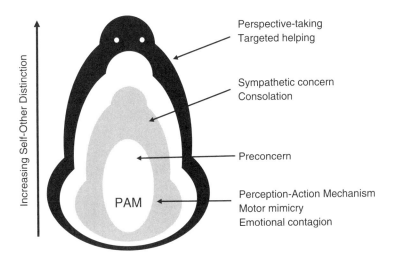

Figure 6.6

The Russian doll model of empathy and imitation. Empathy induces a similar emotional state in the subject as the object. At the core of emotional contagion is the perception-action mechanism (PAM). The doll's outer layers, starting with preconcern and followed by sympathetic concern and targeted helping, build on this hard-wired socio-affective basis. The complexity of empathy grows with increased self-other distinction and perspective-taking abilities. Even though the doll's outer layers depend on learning and prefrontal functioning, they remain fundamentally linked to its inner core.

which over time turned into hoofs, paws, wings, hands, and flippers. In the case of empathy this means that the simple forms remain present in the advanced ones.

Even the most advanced forms of human empathy, which do not require physical closeness and body language, are never fully independent from these simpler processes since we have learned over our lifetime to internalize what happens to others and how to react. Even if we just read about another's situation in a novel, our reaction still draws on well-established neural representations of similar situations that we have encountered, allowing us to have empathy for a fictional character based on our imagination. Human empathy is truly remarkable, but as argued here, it is hardly unprecedented in the animal kingdom.

References

Adolphs, R., D. Tranel, H. Damasio, and A. R. Damasio. 1994. Impaired recognition of emotion in facial expressions following bilateral damage to the human amygdala. *Nature* 372: 669–672.

Anderson, J. R., M. Myowa-Yamakoshi, and T. Matsuzawa. 2004. Contagious yawning in chimpanzees. *Proceedings. Biological Sciences* 271: S468–S470.

Andreoni, J. 1989. Giving with impure altruism: Applications to charity and Ricardian equivalence. *Journal of Political Economy* 97: 1447–1458.

Baron-Cohen, S. 2005. Autism—"Autos": Literally, a total focus on the self? In *The Lost Self: Pathologies of the Brain and Identity*, edited by T. E. Feinberg and J. P. Keenan, 166–80. Oxford: Oxford University Press.

Bischof-Köhler, D. 1988. Über den Zusammenhang von Empathie und der Fähigkeit sich im Spiegel zu erkennen. *Schweizerische Zeitschrift für Psychologie* 47: 147–59.

Bischof-Köhler, D. 1991. The development of empathy in infants. In *Infant Development: Perspectives from German-Speaking Countries,* edited by M. Lamb and M. Keller, 245–273. Hillsdale, NJ: Erlbaum.

Burkart, J. M., E. Fehr, C.Efferson, and C. P. van Schaik. 2007. Other-regarding preferences in a non-human primate: Common marmosets provision food altruistically. *Proceedings of the National Academy of Sciences of the United States of America* 104: 19762–19766.

Campbell, M. W., J. D. Carter, D. Proctor, M. L. Eisenberg, and F. B. M. de Waal. 2009. Computer animations stimulate contagious yawning in chimpanzees."*Proceedings. Biological Sciences* 276: 4255–4259.

Church, R. M. 1959. Emotional reactions of rats to the pain of others. *Journal of Comparative and Physiological Psychology* 52: 132–134.

Colman, A. D., K. E. Liebold, and J. J. Boren. 1969. A method for studying altruism in monkeys. *Psychological Record* 19: 401–405.

Cordoni, G., E. Palagi, and T. S. Borgognini. 2004. Reconciliation and consolation in captive Western gorillas. *International Journal of Primatology* 27: 1365–1382.

Damasio, A. R. 1994. *Descartes' Error: Emotion, Reason, and the Human Brain.* New York: Putnam.

Darwin, C. 1871/1982. *The Descent of Man, and Selection in Relation to Sex.* Princeton, NJ: Princeton University Press.

Dawkins, R. 1976. *The Selfish Gene.* Oxford: Oxford University Press.

Decety, J., and T. Chaminade. 2003. When the self represents the other: A New Cognitive Neuroscience View on Psychological Identification. *Consciousness and Cognition* 12: 577–596.

de Gelder, B. 1987. On having a theory of mind. *Cognition* 27: 285–290.

de Waal, F. B. M. 1989. *Peacemaking among Primates.* Cambridge, MA: Harvard University Press.

de Waal, F. B. M. 1996. *Good Natured: The Origins of Right and Wrong in Humans and Other Animals.* Cambridge, MA: Harvard University Press.

de Waal, F. B. M. 1999. Anthropomorphism and Anthropodenial: Consistency in Our Thinking about humans and other animals. *Philosophical Topics* 27: 255–280.

de Waal, F. B. M. 1982/2007. *Chimpanzee Politics: Power and Sex among Apes*. Baltimore, MD: Johns Hopkins University Press.

de Waal, F. B. M. 2008. Putting the altruism back into altruism: The evolution of empathy. *Annual Review of Psychology* 59: 279–300.

de Waal, F. B. M. 2009. *The Age of Empathy*. New York: Harmony.

de Waal, F. B. M., and F. Aureli. 1996. Consolation, reconciliation, and a possible cognitive difference between macaque and chimpanzee. In *Reaching into Thought: The Minds of the Great Apes*, edited by A. E. Russon, K. A. Bard, and S. T. Parker, 80–110. Cambridge: Cambridge University Press.

de Waal, F. B. M., K. Leimgruber, and A. R. Greenberg. 2008. Giving is self-rewarding for monkeys. *Proceedings of the National Academy of Sciences, USA* 105: 13685–13689.

de Waal, F. B. M., and A. van Roosmalen. 1979. Reconciliation and consolation among chimpanzees. *Behavioral Ecology and Sociobiology* 5: 55–66.

Dimberg, U., M. Thunberg, and K. Elmehed. 2000. Unconscious facial reactions to emotional facial expressions. *Psychological Science* 11: 86–89.

di Pellegrino, G., L. Fadiga, L. Fogassi, V. Gallese, and G. Rizzolatti. 1992. Understanding motor events: A neurophysiological study. *Experimental Brain Research* 91: 176–180.

Dittus, W. P. J., and S. M. Ratnayeke. 1989. Individual and social behavioral responses to injury in wild toque macaques (Macaca sinica). *International Journal of Primatology* 10: 215–234.

Fehr, E., and U. Fischbacher. 2003. The nature of human altruism. *Nature* 425: 785–791.

Fouts, R., and T. Mills. 1997. *Next of Kin*. New York: Morrow.

Fraser, O., D. Stahl, and A. Aureli. 2008. Stress reduction through consolation in chimpanzees. *Proceedings of the National Academy of Sciences of the United States of America* 105: 8557–8562.

Gallese, V. 2005. "Being like Me": Self-Other identity, mirror neurons, and empathy." In *Perspectives on Imitation*, edited by S. Hurley and N. Chater, 101–18. Cambridge, MA: MIT Press.

Gallup, G. G. 1983. Toward a comparative psychology of mind. In *Animal Cognition and Behavior*, edited by R. L. Mellgren, 473–510. New York: North-Holland.

Goldman, A. 2006. *Simulating Minds: The Philosophy, Psychology, and Neuroscience of Mindreading*. Oxford: Oxford University Press.

Han, S., Y. Fan, and L. Mao. 2008. Gender difference in empathy for pain: An Electrophysiological Investigation. *Brain Research* 1196: 85–93.

Harbaugh, W. T., U. Mayr, and D. R. Burghart. 2007. Neural responses to taxation and voluntary giving reveal motives for charitable donations. *Science* 326: 1622–1625.

Hare, B., J. Call, and M. Tomasello. 2001. Do chimpanzees know what conspecifics know? *Animal Behaviour* 61: 139–151.

Hirata, S. 2006. Tactical deception and understanding of others in chimpanzees. In *Cognitive Development in Chimpanzees*, edited by T. Matsuzawa, M. Tomanaga, and M. Tanaka, 265–76. Tokyo: Springer Verlag.

Hobson, R. P. 1991. Against the theory of "Theory of Mind." *British Journal of Developmental Psychology* 9: 33–51.

Hoffman, M. L. 1975. Developmental synthesis of affect and cognition and its implications for altruistic motivation. *Developmental Psychology* 11: 607–622.

Hoffman, M. L. 1981. Perspectives on the difference between understanding people and understanding things: The role of affect. In *Social Cognitive Development*, edited by J. H. Flavell and L. Ross, 67–81. Cambridge: Cambridge University Press.

Hoffman, M. L. 1982. Development of prosocial motivation: Empathy and guilt. In *The Development of Prosocial Behavior*, edited by N. Eisenberg, 281–313. New York: Academic Press.

Johnson, D. B. 1992. Altruistic behavior and the development of the self in infants. *Merrill-Palmer Quarterly of Behavior and Development* 28: 379–388.

Kagan, J. 2000. Human morality is distinctive. *Journal of Consciousness Studies* 7: 46–48.

Ladygina-Kohts, N. N. 2001 [1935]). *Infant Chimpanzee and Human Child: A Classic 1935 Comparative Study of Ape Emotions and Intelligence,* edited by FBM de Waal. New York: Oxford University Press.

Lakshminarayanan, V. R., and L. R. Santos. 2008. Capuchin monkeys are sensitive to others' welfare. *Current Biology* 18: 999–1000.

Langford, D. J., S. E. Crager, Z. Shehzad, S. B. Smith, S. G. Sotocinal, J. S. Levenstadt, M. L. Chanda, D. J. Levitin, and J. S. Mogil. 2006. Social modulation of pain as evidence for empathy in mice. *Science* 312: 1967–1970.

Lewis, M. 2002. Empathy requires the development of the self. *Behavioral and Brain Sciences* 25: 42.

Lipps, T. 1903. *Einfühlung, innere Nachahmung und Organempfindung. Archiv für die gesammte Psychologie*, vol. I. Leipzig: Engelman.

MacLean, P. D. 1985. Brain evolution relating to family, play, and the separation call. *Archives of General Psychiatry* 42: 405–17.

Mallavarapu, S., T. S. Stoinski, M. A. Bloomsmith, and T. L. Maple. 2006. Postconflict behavior in captive Western lowland gorillas (Gorilla gorilla gorilla)." *American Journal of Primatology* 68: 789–801.

Masserman, J., M. S. Wechkin, and W. Terris. 1964. Altruistic behavior in rhesus monkeys. *American Journal of Psychiatry* 121: 584–585.

Menzel, E. W. 1974. A group of young chimpanzees in a one-acre field. In *Behavior of Non-human Primates*, vol. 5, edited by A. M. Schrier and F. Stollnitz, 83–153. New York: Academic Press.

Mullins-Nelson, J. L., R. T. Salekin, and A. R. Leistico. 2006. Psychopathy, empathy, and perspective-taking ability in a community sample: implications for the successful psychopathy concept. *International Journal of Forensic Mental Health* 5: 133–149.

Niedenthal, P. M. 2007. Embodying emotion. *Science* 316: 1002–1005.

Palagi, E., T. Paoli, and S. Borgognini Tarli. 2004. Reconciliation and consolation in captive Bonobos (Pan paniscus). *American Journal of Primatology* 62: 15–30.

Paukner, A., S. J. Suomi, E. Visalberghi, and P. F. Ferrari. 2009. Capuchin monkeys display affiliation toward humans who imitate them. *Science* 325: 880–83.

Plomin, R., R. N. Emde, J. M. Braungart, J. Campos, R. Corley, D. W. Fulker, J. Kagan, et al. 1993. Genetic change and continuity from fourteen to twenty months: The MacArthur Longitudinal Twin Study. *Child Development* 64: 1354–1376.

Plotnik, J., F. B. M. de Waal, and D. Reiss. 2006. Self-recognition in an Asian elephant. *Proceedings of the National Academy of Sciences of the United States of America* 103: 17053–17057.

Plutchik, R. 1987. Evolutionary bases of empathy. In *Empathy and Its Development*, edited by N. Eisenberg and J. Strayer, 3–46. Cambridge: Cambridge University Press.

Premack, D., and G. Woodruff. 1978. Does the chimpanzee have a theory of mind? *Behavioral and Brain Sciences* 1: 515–526.

Preston, S. D., and F. B. M. de Waal. 2002. Empathy: Its ultimate and proximate bases. *Behavioral and Brain Sciences* 25: 1–72.

Prinz, W. 1997. Perception and action planning. *European Journal of Cognitive Psychology* 9: 129–154.

Reiss, D., and L. Marino. 2001. Mirror self-recognition in the bottlenose dolphin: A case of cognitive convergence. *Proceedings of the National Academy of Sciences of the United States of America* 98: 5937–5942.

Romero, M. T., M. A. Castellanos, and F. B. M. de Waal. 2010. Consolation as possible expression of sympathetic concern among chimpanzees. *Proceedings of the National Academy of Sciences of the United States of America* 107: 12110–12115.

Schino, G., S. Geminiani, L. Rosati, and F. Aureli. 2004. Behavioral and emotional response of Japanese macaque (Macaca fuscata) mothers after their offspring receive an aggression." *Journal of Comparative Psychology* 118: 340–346.

Shillito, D. J., R. W. Shumaker, G. G. Gallup, and B. B. Beck. 2005. Understanding visual barriers: Evidence for Level 1 perspective taking in an orang-utan, Pongo pygmaeus. *Animal Behaviour* 69: 679–687.

Silk, J. B., S. F. Brosnan, J. Vonk, J. Henrich, D. Povinelli, S. Lambeth, A. Richardson, J. Mascaro, and S. Shapiro. 2005. Chimpanzees are indifferent to the welfare of unrelated group members. *Nature* 437: 1357–1359.

Warneken, F., B. Hare, A. P. Melis, D. Hanus, and M. Tomasello. 2007. Spontaneous altruism by chimpanzees and young children. *PLoS Biology* 5: 1414–1420.

Watts, D. P., F. Colmenares, and K. Arnold. 2000. Redirection, consolation, and male policing: How targets of aggression interact with bystanders. In *Natural Conflict Resolution*, edited by F. Aureli and F. B. M. de Waal, 281–301. Berkeley: University of California Press.

Wellman, H. M., A. T. Phillips, and T. Rodriguez. 2000. Young children's understanding of perception, desire, and emotion. *Child Development* 71: 895–912.

Yerkes, R. M. 1925. *Almost Human*. New York: Century.

Zahavi, D. 2008. Simulation, projection and empathy. *Consciousness and Cognition* 17: 514–522.

Zahn-Waxler, C., B. Hollenbeck, and M. Radke-Yarrow. 1984. The origins of empathy and altruism. In *Advances in Animal Welfare Science*, edited by M. W. Fox and L. D. Mickley, 21–39. Washington, DC: Humane Society of the United States.

Zahn-Waxler, C., and M. Radke-Yarrow. 1990. The origins of empathic concern. *Motivation and Emotion* 14: 107–130.

Zahn-Waxler, C., M. Radke-Yarrow, E. Wagner, and M. Chapman. 1992. Development of concern for others. *Developmental Psychology* 28: 126–136.

IV The Development of Empathy

7 Nature and Forms of Empathy in the First Years of Life

Sharee Light and Carolyn Zahn-Waxler

The feelings which they call tender are difficult to analyze. They seem to be compounded of affection, joy, and especially sympathy.
—Charles Darwin, 1872

We are wired to respond emotionally to the joys and sorrows of others. This capacity is present in the first years of life (Knafo et al. 2008). Deeply rooted instincts for empathy become increasingly refined and regulated as attachment and bonding with the caregiver prepare the child for later empathic connections outside the family setting. Expressions of generalized concern for others likely have roots in the complex interplay and sharing of emotions, as well as in cooperation and turn-taking in social interactions between parent and infant during the first year of life. Socialization plays an important role in how young children respond to the suffering of others (Hastings, Utendale, and Sullivan 2007). Less is known about early biological factors and neural circuitry that support the capacity to care for others. This chapter focuses on these latter processes. It also introduces a broadened conception of affective empathy that includes positively valenced responses (Light, Coan et al. 2009).

Motivational and Cognitive Components of Empathy

Children begin to show prosocial behaviors in the second year of life (Zahn-Waxler et al. 1992). What motivates these behavioral expressions of caring and concern for others? What *impels* individuals to help others, to share their resources, to comfort someone in distress, or to protect and defend someone who may be vulnerable to attack? We assume that empathy is a primary driving force. Different theorists (Eisenberg, Fabes, and Miller 1987; Batson and Shaw 1991; Zahn-Waxler 1991; Decety and Jackson 2004) view empathy as an essential underlying mechanism (also see Knafo et al. 2008). Because it is present so early in life, possibly even in the first year, it is important to consider the biological underpinnings at this time.

Empathy for pain includes both affective and cognitive components (Decety and Jackson 2004; Knafo et al. 2008). The affective aspect reflects a vicarious emotional response to others' distress and a feeling of goodwill toward that person. Cognitive empathy entails an ability to comprehend another's distress and to assume that person's perspective. In young children it appears as hypothesis-testing or inquisitiveness, as the child tries to understand the other's problem. Although cognitive and affective components of empathy are interconnected, they are also separable, suggesting that they have certain unique functions as early as the second and third year of life (Knafo et al. 2008). Even at early ages empathy appears as a disposition, is relatively stable across time and consistent across contexts, and predicts subsequent prosocial behaviors (Knafo et al. 2008; Nichols, Svetlova, and Brownell 2009; Vaish, Carpenter, and Tomasello 2009).

Because empathy, as typically construed, is a response to another's suffering, emotions experienced by the empathizer are negatively toned. If one feels another's sorrow, one also feels sad. If one winces while witnessing another's pain, it becomes part of one's own experience. However, empathic concern captures only one aspect of empathy. We consider other forms of empathy that are more positively toned and hence may have different implications both for the empathizer and the person being empathized with.

The Role of Positive Emotions

Two other forms of empathy exist (Light, Coan, et al. 2009). *Empathic happiness* occurs when one vicariously experiences pleasure and goodwill in response to another's positive emotion. *Empathic cheerfulness* is seen when one exudes positive emotion and goodwill toward someone in distress. This can alleviate that person's distress by reducing negative emotions, possibly shifting their mood by catalyzing a positive emotional state within them.

Collectively, *empathic concern, empathic happiness* and *empathic cheerfulness* are "empathy subtypes" that may play both common and unique roles in children's caring actions. Here we elaborate on their affective and cognitive prerequisites seen in the first year of life. We emphasize the affective side based on our interest in the motivational properties of empathy. Next we speculate about early neural correlates and circuitry. Finally, we examine ways to assess biological underpinnings of empathy in the first years of life and consider future directions for theory and research.

Empathy Subtypes

Empathic Concern

Empathy in humans is thought to emerge later in development than basic emotions such as anger, fear, and joy, which are seen in the first year of life (Zahn-Waxler,

Robinson, and Emde 1992). Like other social emotions (guilt, shame, pride, and jealousy) it involves multiple emotions, or blends of emotions expressed in social contexts. In the case of empathic concern the experience of another's distress (e.g., sadness or pain) also conjures up an other-oriented emotion for the victim (e.g., concern, goodwill, or tenderness). In young children it is seen in facial and vocal (consoling, soothing sounds) expressions of concern for others in distress. Thus the observer's emotion is no longer directly congruent with the victim's emotion and is appropriate to the other's condition (some refer to this as sympathy).

What do we know about the precursors, onset, and expression of empathic concern? Empathic concern is thought by most to blossom from reflexive responses to others' distress. Simner (1971) found that newborn babies aged two to three days old cried more in response to the sound of another newborn crying than to white noise. Later, Dondi, Simion, and Caltran (1999) found that newborns also discriminate between the cries of another newborn and their own previously recorded cry. This underscores the inherent social nature of the cry, its extension beyond the parent-infant relationship, and the possibility that empathic concern emerges in the first year of life. The work by Dondi et al. (1999) also suggests that another's cry evokes not only contagion but also a primitive physiological awareness of the self as separate from others (Decety, personal communication).

Early developmental theory was based on the assumption that empathic concern evolves directly from contagion of distress. As the infant's personal distress diminishes, it transforms into empathic concern; that is, one replaces the other, with the latter actually growing out of the former. Several theorists draw sharp distinctions between personal distress and empathic concern that can lead to distinct behavioral patterns; personal distress invites withdrawal and avoidance whereas empathic concern encourages approach and engagement with the person who suffers. These patterns are also seen in different physiological profiles, where heart rate deceleration is associated with approach and heart rate acceleration is associated with avoidance of others in distress (Eisenberg, Fabes, and Miller 1989; Batson and Shaw 1991; Zahn-Waxler et al. 1995; also see Decety and Lamm 2009 regarding different neural processes for empathic concern and personal distress).

Batson and Shaw (1991) have argued that *personal distress* and *empathic concern* differ in fundamental ways. The former is reflexive or instinctual in nature whereas the latter requires social cognition and motivational forces that allow for the instantiation of purposeful, goal-directed caring actions. Other developmental accounts (Zahn-Waxler 1991) acknowledge that personal distress and empathic concern are different, but they question the utility of an either-or approach that precludes personal distress from motivating caring behaviors. Observations of children in naturalistic situations reveal substantial co-variation or intermingling of personal distress and empathic concern when children respond to someone who is suffering. Especially in the first few years children can cycle rapidly between their own distress and concern for the other. Their personal distress does not necessarily interfere with their ability to behave prosocially.

This is consistent with studies of children that find personal distress or anxiety (indexed by higher heart rate) is positively associated with prosocial behaviors (e.g., Zahn-Waxler et al. 1995). Intensity of personal distress likely determines whether it activates approach or withdrawal. Regulation of emotions is important as well. Children who experience personal distress (as seen in higher heart rate) but who are also able to regulate this emotion (as seen in heart rate deceleration during another's distress) may be optimally poised to intervene on behalf of another (Zahn-Waxler et al. 1995). From a developmental standpoint it is worth noting that observed fearfulness in infancy predicted later prosocial behavior in six-year-olds (Rothbart, Ahadi, and Hershey 1994).

Positive Empathy

Empathic happiness is in play when others' expressions of pleasure and joy elicit parallel responses in those who witness the happiness of others. As with *empathic concern,* there is a presumed mirroring or neural resonance to the other's emotions along with an other-oriented feeling of goodwill. Sallquist et al. (2009) found that empathic happiness was associated with preschool children's greater empathy/sympathy. Empathic happiness may be a trait that reflects early signs of social competence, as some children bring a joyful countenance into a variety of interactions with others. Empathic cheerfulness does not involve a mirroring or neural resonance to the other's emotions, but it does involve the use of a basic positive emotion (e.g., joy or contentment) in combination with a higher-order positive emotion such as goodwill.

What then is the nature of positive empathy? Do the onsets and developmental trajectories differ from those for empathic concern? Although rudimentary building blocks of *empathic concern* are present at birth, we lack comparable knowledge of the precursors of *positive empathy.* The development of positive affect may shed light on the processes of positive empathy.

One way to explore the precursors of positive empathy is to examine the emergence and properties of different types of smiles. Duchenne smiles have historically been thought to indicate genuine joy (Frank, Ekman, and Friesen 1993), although non-Duchenne smiles can also signal enjoyment and affiliative emotion in adults (Niedenthal et al. 2010). Duchenne smiles include the contraction of the orbicularis oculi muscle (which results in the formation of "crow's feet" around the eyes) in addition to contraction of the zygomaticus major muscle (which raises the corners of the mouth). Both types of smiles are seen in infants in the first month of life (Wolff 1987;

Dondi et al. 2007). In a sample of one- to six-month-old infants, Duchenne and non-Duchenne smiles closely followed one another (Messinger, Fogel, and Dickson 1999) suggesting "hedonic similarity": both signal true positive emotion and show similar developmental patterns.

It is important to consider the emergence of these basic smiles because they can be thought of as early physical signs of a developing positive affect system. This system is likely crucial for the development of empathy, as each type of empathy involves the expression of positive emotion (e.g., tenderness, goodwill, etc.). It may be that Duchenne versus non-Duchenne smiles signal different types of positive emotion—joy versus contentment, for example. These different types of positive emotion may relate to different forms of empathy with each having a different neural signature.

We can glean further information about probable precursors of *positive empathy* by looking at the emergence of more complex smiles such as the "social smile" and the "reciprocal smile." The "social smile" emerges in full-term infants between the age of one to two months (Ainsfeld 1982). In institutional settings infants exchanged smiles with infants in nearby cribs at five months of age (Buhler 1930), similar to Bridges's (1933) observations of infants at seven to eight months of age. These social smiles are seen even earlier in reciprocal exchanges between mothers and their infants (Trevarthen and Aitken 2001).

Even though newborns do not show social smiles or laugh (in contrast to their ability to cry and show other forms of distress), soon thereafter they show Duchenne and non-Duchenne smiles; these two types of smiles, as noted, may be markers for joy and contentment, respectively. Thus we are wired to express positive as well as negative emotions from birth onward. Initially they are global affective states of contentment or distress. In newborns, pleasure consists mainly of contentment and calm. Therefore, contentment may be the positive emotion that infants use when they respond in an empathic manner. Other positive emotions come into play over time as the positive affect system develops and differentiates.

Empathic Happiness

Infants can respond to the positive affect of others by showing vicarious happiness. Ten-week-old infants' responses to images of happy, sad, and angry faces made by their mothers elicited distinct matching responses (Haviland and Lelwica 1987), most frequently in response to mothers' expression of joy. By seven months, infants can differentiate levels of happiness (Ludemann and Nelson 1988); that is, they can detect changes in other's positive affect enabling them to respond in an appropriate manner. The extent to which early reflexive mimicry reflects felt emotion is unclear.

Empathic Cheerfulness

The active use of positive emotion to relieve another's distress has roots in infancy too. Infants as young as four months attempt to reengage their mothers using positive affect when the mother makes a still-face display (Cohn, Campbell, and Ross 1991), indicating that they are beginning to discriminate and respond to changes in the affective displays of other people. We do not know, however, whether this reflects an effort to make the mother feel better or to relieve their own distress.

Relationship between Positive Empathy and Empathic Concern

Empathic concern and empathic happiness both involve mirroring the other's emotions. The opposite is true for empathic cheerfulness (which calls for the display of a countervailing emotion). Nevertheless, empathic concern and both forms of positive empathy have one important thing in common. They are all grounded in emotions that appear very early in life. Also, all forms of empathy relate to positive emotion. For example, young children who are friendly, cheerful and enjoy the company of others are also likely to resonate to the pleasure of others. Furthermore, general positive emotion and *empathic happiness* may facilitate both *empathic concern* and *empathic cheerfulness*, which are interrelated in older children (Light, Coan et al. 2009). Sociability (e.g., Volbrecht et al. 2007), dispositional cheerfulness (Robinson, Emde, and Corley 2001), and positive hedonic tone (Robinson, Zahn-Waxler, and Emde 1994) are associated with empathic concern in the first three years of life. In one longitudinal study positive affect observed in four-month-olds predicted empathic concern when children were two years old (Young, Fox, and Zahn-Waxler 1999).

Self-Awareness, Self-Recognition, and Self-Other Discrimination

To be empathic, the child must have a rudimentary awareness that self and other are separate entities. Traditionally this has been studied in terms of self-recognition and self-other differentiation. Certain experimental tasks showed that these qualities emerged around eighteen months of age accompanied by a spurt in prosocial behaviors (Bischof-Kohler 1991; Zahn-Waxler et al. 1992). This in conjunction with Hoffman's theory (Hoffman 1975) led many to believe that true empathy and caring could not be seen prior to eighteen months of age and therefore need not be studied during the first year of life.

Others have been more receptive to the notion that other-directed empathic concern can occur earlier in life, leading them to question whether self-other differentiation is essential (Ungerer et al. 1990). Based on their work with twelve-month-olds Ungerer et al. (1990) concluded that advances in cognitive development during the second year were not *necessary* for achieving an other-oriented response. Recently,

Kartner, Keller, and Chaudhary (2010) found that self-other differentiation was not a universal prerequisite for concerned prosocial behavior in very young children. When children from Western and Eastern cultures were compared, the association was seen only for the Western sample suggesting culture may play a role in our conceptions of self and other. Even within a culture views and measures of self-other differentiation differ. This is why studies have varied in terms of when the differentiation first appears.

There is further evidence for a rudimentary ability for self-other differentiation in the first year of life. For example, the newborn infant already reacts differently to tactile stimulation by the mother as compared with self-stimulation that he/she does not respond to (Rochat 2003; Lagercrantz and Changeux 2009). Furthermore, newborn infants can, as noted earlier, discriminate between their own cry and the cry of another newborn infant (Dondi, Simion, and Caltran 1999). Rochat and Striano (2002) found that four-month-olds smile more and look longer at the mirror image of someone imitating them, compared to looking at a mirror image of themselves, showing that they can discriminate between the specular image of themselves and the specular image of a mimicking other.

Also during the first year of life children exhibit basic *joint attention* and *social referencing* abilities that likely pave the way for affective perspective-taking. Joint attention refers to the ability of two or more people to look at the same object with the shared understanding that this is a mutual process. By three months infants can discriminate between dyadic (face to face) and joint attention (infant-other-object) interactions (Striano and Stahl 2005). This ability likely supports the development of an ability to form mutual ideas about the characteristics of objects and people.

Infants also develop the ability to learn what an object is like by reading the adult's attentional focus when the adult is expressing a positive or negative emotional reaction to it. This process is called *social referencing* (Hornik, Risenhoover, and Gunnar 1987). Interestingly, older infants sometimes try to manipulate other people's emotional responses rather than, as in social referencing, just reading these responses for information about reacted-to objects. This process likely plays an important role in positive empathy, particularly empathic cheerfulness. As young children learn that their affective displays can change the affect of others, they may learn to harness this power in different empathic ways that include comforting others.

Summary

The preceding review provides evidence that a number of different elements of empathy are present in the first year of life. This leads to consideration of what might be the neural underpinnings. MacLean (1985) was one of the first to propose a relevant theory. He viewed empathy as a quality that evolved from parental care for the young whose distress cries elicited responsive care-giving. Empathy was based on

interconnections between the limbic system and the prefrontal cortex, linked origi-
nally to parental concern for the young. Neural connections between brain areas
involving emotion and foresight made the expression of a broader sense of responsibility possible; that is, parental concern for the young generalized to other members
of the species through the higher reaches of the brain. Our ability to share affective
states thus is based on phylogenetically old structures that develop very early in
ontogeny in humans (Singer 2006). MacLean also wrote about the role of positive
emotions and play in the parent-infant relationship, paving the way for consideration
of positive forms of empathy. What is known about relevant neural processes at
this time?

Neural Structures and Circuitry Implicated in Early Empathy

Neural Structures

Bottom-up and top-down processing contribute to our capacity to resonate with
each other emotionally and experience empathy. Bottom-up processes allow for the
rapid processing of an affective signal, such as someone in pain (Decety 2010);
and top-down processes allow for the perceiver's intentions, motivations, and
feelings to be attached to the feeling state initiated by the bottom-up process.
Circuitry sending information from the amygdala and/or hypothalamus to the orbitofrontal prefrontal cortex are thought to form the basis of bottom-up empathic
processes, while activity originating in prefrontal regions is thought to play an important role in top-down empathic processing (Decety 2010). There are four structures
that we propose are involved in the very early development of empathy, and together
they form a largely bottom-up process. However, we argue for the rudimentary presence of a top-down route in infancy in that the medial aspect of the orbitofrontal
prefrontal cortex is not only involved in processing the initial affective signal
generated by the amygdala (i.e., the emotional state of the other) as proposed by
Decety (2010), but it also plays a role in generating an other-oriented feeling of goodwill in the perceiver (a top-down process). The four structures hypothesized to
be involved in early empathy are: the amygdalae, the ventral striatum/nucleus
accumbens, the hypothalamus, and the medial network of the orbitofrontal cortex
(see figure 7.1).

Amygdalae

The amygdalae are located deep within the medial temporal lobes. They help orches-
trate emotional reactions and are part of the limbic system. The role of the amygdala
in negative emotion is well characterized. The sight of a sad or fearful face activates
the amygdala in healthy adults. Therefore, the amygdala likely contributes to our
ability to vicariously experience negative affect when presented with others' negative

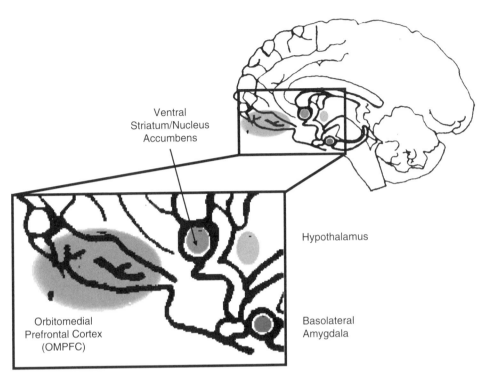

Figure 7.1
Brain structures involved in early empathy.

emotional displays. Recent research indicates that the amygdala also is responsive to positive stimuli. Observing and executing smiles activates the amygdala in adults (Hennenlotter et al. 2005). Thus the amygdala likely plays a role in "reading" happiness from others' faces, contributing to our ability to share positive affect behaviorally (e.g., via smiling).

Ventral Striatum/Nucleus Accumbens

The nucleus accumbens is a collection of neurons within the ventral striatum that play an important role in reward and pleasure. The ventral striatum is important for empathy because there is a rewarding component to empathy. It can feel good to care for others. Also, positive empathy explicitly involves the use and expression of positive affect. Therefore, it is likely that reward centers are activated during certain empathy processes. The role of the smile in the expression of empathy has already been noted; the execution of a smile also activates the ventral striatum (Hennenlotter et al. 2005). Subjective feelings of well-being and goodwill likely correlate with activity in the ventral striatum.

Hypothalamus

Oxytocin, a peptide that is both a hormone and neurotransmitter, has broad influences on social and emotional processing throughout the body and brain. Oxytocin is implicated in social bonding and empathy in adults (e.g., Rodrigues et al. 2009; Tost et al. 2010). It is produced in the supraoptic and paraventricular nuclei of the hypothalamus. There are oxytocin receptors in the nucleus accumbens and orbitomedial prefrontal cortex (PFC). Some oxytocin-producing neurons in the paraventricular nucleus project to other parts of the brain such as the amygdala and orbitomedial PFC. Reduced levels of oxytocin in mice are related to social deficits such as fearlessness and enhanced aggressive behavior (Winslow et al. 2000; Higashida et al. 2010). The effects of oxytocin secretion on the central nervous system may play a prominent role in the early development of empathy, given the importance of social bonding for this process. Oxytocin levels are reduced in children who experience social deprivation and neglect (Wismer Fries et al. 2005). Hurlemann et al. (2010) found that intranasal oxytocin administration acted as an empathogen for emotional empathy but not cognitive empathy in adult men.

The Prefrontal Cortex in the Infant

Because areas of the PFC are some of the last to show neuroanatomical *change* in postnatal life, the region has mostly been related to abilities that emerge at age one or later. The "interactive specialization view" of social brain development, however, predicts earlier activation of the PFC, even if response properties are less well tuned than in adults (Grossmann and Johnson 2007). Therefore, the PFC could play a significant role in empathy development in infancy.

Prefrontal Cortex Development and Structure

Maturation of the PFC occurs in an "inside-out" pattern, beginning with layer V (Fuster 2008). Layer V contains large pyramidal neurons that are the primary excitation units of the mammalian PFC. It is the main source of subcortical efferents (efferent pathways convey neural information away from layer V to other parts of the brain). Thus, layer-V neurons connect the PFC to subcortical structures such as the nucleus accumbens, amygdala, and hypothalamus. Layer III is the origin and termination of profuse corticocortico connections (corticocortico pathways convey neural information *between* prefrontal regions). Activity in this layer is most correlated with developmental changes in cognition. Layer V connections develop faster than corticocortico connections in layer III and thus likely contribute to the earliest manifestations of empathy. Orbital prefrontal areas develop earlier than do lateral prefrontal areas (Fuster 2008). Gray-matter volume reaches adult levels in the orbitofrontal PFC first, followed by the ventrolateral PFC and then the dorsolateral PFC (Giedd et al. 1999).

Because the orbitofrontal PFC is the most developed area in young infants, early empathy likely coincides with activity here.

Medial Network of the Orbitofrontal Cortex

The medial aspect of the orbitofrontal cortex (MOFC) is a prefrontal cortex region in the frontal lobes of the brain. The medial network of the orbitofrontal cortex (versus the lateral network) projects to the ventromedial striatum and nucleus accumbens, likely conveying information about the positive emotional state of the individual. For example, in adults, orbitofrontal prefrontal cortex activity relates to smiling during a comic video, suggesting that this region relates to the conscious experience of positive emotion (Iwase et al. 2002). Furthermore, orbital neurons fire differentially to rewards depending on the individual's relative preference for each reward (Ferry et al. 2000). Last, the MOFC also plays a role in attachment. For example, the sight of one's own smiling baby activates the orbitofrontal prefrontal cortex (Nitschke et al. 2004); and infants showed increased orbitofrontal cortex activity when looking at their smiling mothers (Minagawa-Kawai et al. 2009). Taken together, activity in the medial part of the OFC likely provides the basis for the generation of feelings of goodwill that are associated with both empathic concern and positive empathy in infants. The medial aspect of the orbitofrontal prefrontal cortex is reciprocally linked to the amygdala. This likely enables swift transmission of emotional information taken in by the amygdala to be transformed or elaborated on by activity in the PFC. This processing in the PFC may ultimately lead to the dampening of a negative emotion in the case of empathic concern or the amplification of a positive emotional state in the case of positive empathy—both of which are initiated by amygdala activation.

Neurocircuitry of Early Empathy

We propose three empathy circuits that involve the medial orbitofrontal prefrontal cortex that are active in infancy.

Empathic Concern

The development of empathic concern may rest in connectivity between the medial network of the orbitofrontal prefrontal cortex, amygdala, and hypothalamus. Reflexive cries may be the basic expression of this circuitry. The more advanced overt expression of this circuitry (i.e., as reflexive crying wanes) involves more modulated facial and vocal expressions of worry, sadness, and sympathy that characterize empathy beginning in the second year of life, although possibly earlier (Zahn-Waxler et al. 1992; Vaish et al. 2009). The amygdala has reciprocal connections with the medial and orbital areas of the PFC (Fuster 2008) and also projects to the hypothalamus. The amygdala has oxytocin receptors as does the OFC, so both of these nodes in the circuit can be influenced by the release of oxytocin from the hypothalamus. Because the amygdala is a key structure involved in the frontline generation of negative and positive affect, activity in this region may trigger the activation of the circuit.

In an infant who is prone to experience empathic concern, the negative emotion of another person may trigger the amygdala to initiate those negative emotions that likely accompany empathic concern. A signal may then be sent from the amygdala to the hypothalamus and orbitomedial prefrontal cortex. This signal may prompt the release of oxytocin from the hypothalamus, which could impact receptors in the orbitomedial prefrontal cortex and amygdala. When the signal from the amygdala reaches layer V of the orbitomedial prefrontal cortex, orbitomedial activity may trigger a rudimentary feeling of concern and goodwill that fuses with the amygdala-generated feeling of sadness that already took hold in the infant.

Information about the generation of a feeling of goodwill by orbitomedial prefrontal cortex can be sent back to the amygdala via connections between it and the amygdala. This top-down signal may ultimately prevent the occurrence of personal distress because amygdala activity can be modulated by orbitomedial PFC activity. If the amygdala did not receive this input from the orbitomedial PFC, the infant's response would likely remain negatively toned, reflecting personal distress rather than empathic concern. Oxytocin release may intensify feelings of affiliation, well-being, and social interest that would encourage subsequent caring behaviors via activation of receptors in orbitomedial PFC and amygdala.

Empathic Happiness

The development of empathic happiness may lie in connectivity between the amygdala, medial network of the orbitofrontal prefrontal cortex, hypothalamus, and the nucleus accumbens. The orbitomedial prefrontal cortex projects to the nucleus accumbens via layer V. The amygdala is reciprocally connected to the nucleus accumbens, orbitofrontal PFC, and the hypothalamus. In an infant prone to experience empathic happiness, another's positive emotion may trigger the amygdala to initiate a happy, pleasant feeling. A signal may then be sent from the amygdala to the: (1) nucleus accumbens, (2) hypothalamus, and (3) orbitomedial prefrontal cortex. This could prompt the release of oxytocin from the hypothalamus. Release of oxytocin could impact receptors in the orbitomedial prefrontal cortex and amygdala. When the signal from the amygdala reaches the orbitomedial prefrontal cortex, orbitomedial activity may trigger the formation of a rudimentary feeling of goodwill in addition to the amygdala-generated feeling of happiness already taking hold in the infant. Activation of the nucleus accumbens by the amygdala may prompt the release of opioids and dopamine, which would amplify feelings of joy and goodwill. Additional signals from the orbitomedial prefrontal cortex to the nucleus accumbens may further support the release of these neurotransmitters. Oxytocin release may further generate feelings of affiliation, well-being, and social interest via receptor binding in the orbitomedial PFC and the amygdala.

Empathic Cheerfulness

The biological precursors of empathic cheerfulness likely involve interactions between the medial network of the orbitofrontal prefrontal cortex, amygdala, nucleus accumbens, and hypothalamus. The most rudimentary expression of this circuitry may be reflected in the social smile. The OFC projects to the nucleus accumbens via layer V and has reciprocal connections with the hypothalamus and amygdala (Rempel-Clower and Barbas 1998). This circuitry operates similarly to the circuitry for empathic happiness except that the amygdala initially registers the *distress* of another person, but orbitomedial PFC activity ultimately sends excitatory signals to the nucleus accumbens, which lead to the generation of positive affect and feelings of goodwill (opposed to negative affect) via the release of dopamine and/or opioids by neurons in the nucleus accumbens. Oxytocin receptors in the orbitomedial PFC may be particularly important for empathic cheerfulness because the orbitomedial PFC must override the signal generated by the amygdala in order to produce a positive emotion. Oxytocin release is a likely result of activation of the hypothalamus by the amygdala.

Empathy Neurocircuitry Later in Development

Later, lateral and anterior prefrontal areas may become more important in the empathy process as corticocortico connectivity in layer III develops. For example, the working memory functions of the dorsolateral prefrontal cortex may contribute to developmental changes in cognitive empathy, and this region's connectivity with the ventral striatum may facilitate positive empathy in childhood. In support of this hypothesis Light, Coan, et al. (2009) found that lateral and anterior-most prefrontal cortex activity in children aged six to ten years related to empathic concern and positive empathy. Further evidence comes from a recent fMRI study showing that younger children utilized medial orbitofrontal PFC during another's expression of pain whereas older participants utilized lateral orbitofrontal PFC (Decety and Michalska 2010). These data provide evidence that different prefrontal regions are involved in empathy depending on the developmental stage of the individual being tested.

Conclusions

There is a wealth of knowledge about how the adult human brain processes the social world, including about empathy. However, although several forms of empathy have their roots in infancy, we remain uninformed about relevant neural processes in this early period of social and emotional development. Because fMRI is unlikely to be used with infants, alternative approaches need to be considered. Recent work on the social brain network in infancy—based mainly on electroencephalography (EEG and ERP) methods—has begun to examine biological underpinnings in domains that include face and eye-gaze processing, perception of emotions, perceiving human actions, and joint attention (Grossmann and Johnson 2007). These procedures could be used to study early empathy as well. Although EEG and ERP have relatively poor spatial resolution compared to neuroimaging techniques, they can still provide valuable information. For example, EEG can be used to measure valence/approach motivation of emotion via brain lateralization (Fox and Davidson 1988; Light, Goldsmith, et al. 2009). This might help to distinguish empathic happiness (symmetrical frontal activity) from empathic cheerfulness (left-frontal asymmetry) and empathic concern (rapid switches between right and left frontal asymmetry) (see Light, Coan, et al. 2009).

High density EEG has been used to measure the infant mirror neuron system (Nystrom 2008; also see Lepage and Théret 2007 for a discussion of a mirror neuron system in infancy). One neural index of empathy measured with EEG is mu suppression, an indirect measure of mirror neuron activity, which captures sensory-motor resonance to others' emotions (Yang et al. 2009). Near-infrared spectroscopy measures cerebral hemoglobin oxygenation in response to brain activation and has been used to study infant visual, language, and memory abilities (see Aslin and Mehler 2005). It could potentially be used to study early emotions including empathy.

It may be possible to use urine (Wismer Fries et al. 2005) and saliva (Rodrigues et al. 2009) to assess neurotransmitters and neurohormones (e.g., oxytocin) associated with empathy. In addition to the potential enhancing effects of oxytocin on empathy, hormones such as testosterone can have inhibiting effects. Prenatal testosterone has been linked to lower levels of empathy in preschool boys and girls (Chapman et al. 2006). Other peripheral measures implicated in empathy such as autonomic nervous system activity (e.g., heart rate, vagal tone, heart-rate acceleration and deceleration during an empathy mood induction) could now be done with children in the first years of life because of advances in technology.

Conceptual and methodological advances in assessment of relevant neural activity will make it possible to address more delineated questions about the nature of empathy. Ideally these advances will allow us to come closer to understanding human awareness and the nature of consciousness as manifested in our empathic ties to others. We enter this world equipped to experience a rudimentary sense of ourselves in relation to others as well as to resonate with others' emotions. The first years of life provide an opportunity to learn more about early origins of these processes and their brain-behavior correlates. Infancy is a time period when emotions are expressed openly and candidly before children learn to mask or stifle feelings, especially those that reflect tenderness and vulnerability.

Even if improved methods show more clearly how neural events co-vary with processing of social stimuli early in development, multiple possible interpretations of the data will pose challenges for theory development (Grossmann and Johnson 2007). Problems may be lessened, however, to the extent that (1) well-developed paradigms successfully approximate real-life circumstances for assessing empathy, and (2) reliable and valid behavioral coding systems are used to score young children's emotions and actions. We are beginning to develop better markers of phenotypic expressions of emotions, behaviors, and language related to different empathic processes.

One challenge will be the ability to capture with accuracy through direct observation the many subtle variations in positive and negative emotions expressed when children are exposed to another's distress or pleasure. We have already noted the potential value of coding different types of smiles. In addition it will be important to capture the intensity of positive emotions and blends with negative emotions that are antithetical to empathy. Contemptuous smiles (more often seen in older children) and hearty laughter reflect a form of enjoyment of the other's distress. Taking pleasure from another's plight is a sign of active disregard for the other, sometimes also referred to as *Schadenfreude*. Because positive affect is not typically measured during empathy inductions, there are few coding guidelines except for older children (see Light, Coan, et al. 2009). These systems could be adapted for younger children.

Patterns of neurocircuitry of empathy are typically inferred from highly controlled experiments that use neuroimaging techniques. In the natural environment empathic expressions comingle with other emotions and states of arousal. We have described three types of empathy, two of which occur in the context of another's distress (*empathic concern* and *empathic cheerfulness*). One or the other may predominate or some children may show both, which means that they will rapidly cycle between positive and negative feelings. How are these variations represented in neurocircuitry? What other biological factors (e.g., child temperament) interact with neural processes? To further complicate matters, as children grow older, their potentials for empathy begin to compete with other social emotions, motives, and desires. Interactions with siblings and playmates can evoke empathy, sharing, caring, and cooperation. But they also create occasions for conflict, envy or jealousy, and self-interest. This highlights the need to study empathy in ecologically valid contexts not only in young children but also throughout development.

The neural processes and pathways described in this chapter are speculative. This is the first foray, to our knowledge, into the neurobiology of empathy in infancy. Box 7.1 summarizes the main points of this chapter. It is intended as a starting point for generating testable hypotheses about the underlying origins. Without such research we will continue to have theories of empathy based on older children, adolescents,

Box 7.1
Key Concepts

There are three types of empathy: *empathic concern*, a vicarious emotional response that involves sadness (or other negative affect) and an other-oriented feeling of goodwill or tenderness toward the victim; *empathic cheerfulness*, an emotional response that involves the display of positive affect in response to someone in distress as means to cheer the victim up; and *empathic happiness*, a vicarious emotional response that involves happiness (or a similar positive affect) and an other-oriented feeling of goodwill toward the other person.

All forms of empathy are hypothesized to have an element of positive affect in them. In *empathic concern*, this takes the form of tenderness, whereas in *empathic cheerfulness* and *empathic happiness*, more overt happiness is present.

Early theory and research on empathy held that self-other differentiation, a presumed prerequisite for empathic concern, was not present before eighteen months. More recent work suggests that both of these capacities are present in the first year of life, as well as the relevant affective neurocircuitry to support their expression.

The medial aspect of the orbitofrontal cortex is hypothesized to be a key region involved in all three forms of empathy in infancy and is active in the newborn. It has active connections with relevant subcortical areas (amygdala, hypothalamus, and nucleus accumbens). The circuitry between these brain regions varies across the different subtypes of empathy. The amygdala, hypothalamus, and nucleus accumbens are hypothesized to be important for *empathic happiness* and *empathic cheerfulness* in infancy. The amygdala and hypothalamus are thought to be important to *empathic concern* in infancy.

The *empathic happiness* circuit can be differentiated from the *empathic cheerfulness* circuit in that the amygdala registers a positive emotion in the case of *empathic happiness* but a negative emotion in the case of *empathic cheerfulness*. *Empathic concern* can be differentiated from *empathic cheerfulness* and *empathic happiness* in that the nucleus accumbens is not hypothesized to be involved in *empathic concern*.

and adults for whom empathy is more cognitively layered. Studies that begin with infants allow for a developmental model that can ultimately provide an enriched understanding of empathy that also includes its inception.

The biological processes considered here do not occur in a vacuum. They need to be examined within the social worlds children occupy. The formation of social attachments is a critical component of human relationships. Infants begin to bond with their caregivers from the moment of birth, and social bonds continue to provide regulatory functions throughout life (Wismer Fries et al. 2005). Because children undergo both brain development and accumulate social experience at the same time, it is essential that we study the role of early experience and socialization on the brain systems implicated in empathy and on children with different temperaments

(Robinson, Zahn-Waxler, and Emde 1994). Empathy's social significance is that it motivates caring acts (Zahn-Waxler et al. 1992). Thus, it is important to understand the intricacies of how feelings of concern for the well-being of others become translated into those acts of caring for others that are integral to the maintenance of human social bonds.

According to Darwin (1872), expressions of empathy appear to involve the quality of tenderness. For him, the components of tenderness included affection, joy and sympathy, thus bringing in the importance of positive emotions in all aspects of empathy. Tenderness is a more global construct that is often equated with goodwill, kindness, and goodness, all of which include positive emotions. Future investigations into the nature and neural correlates of different empathy subtypes will necessarily need to involve the study of positive emotions.

Acknowledgments

This work was supported in part by a grant to the second author from the Fetzer Foundation.

References

Ainsfeld, E. 1982. The onset of social smiling in preterm and full-term infants from two ethnic backgrounds. *Infant Behavior and Development* 5: 387–395.

Aslin, R. N., and J. Mehler. 2005. Near-infrared spectroscopy for functional studies of brain activity in human infants: Promises, prospects, and challenges. *Journal of Biomedical Optics* 3: 1–3.

Batson, C. D., and L. L. Shaw. 1991. Evidence for altruism: Toward a pluralism of prosocial motives. *Psychological Inquiry* 2: 107–122.

Bischof-Kohler, D. 1991. The development of empathy in infants. In *Infant Development: Perspectives from German Speaking Countries*, edited by M. E. Lamb and H. Keller, 245–73. Hillsdale, NJ: Lawrence Erlbaum Associates.

Bridges, K. M. 1933. A study of social development in early infancy. *Child Development* 4: 36–49.

Buhler, C. 1930. *The First Year of Life*. New York: John Day.

Chapman, E., S. Baron-Cohen, B. Auyeung, R. Knickmeyer, K. Taylor, and G. Hackett. 2006. "Fetal testosterone and empathy: Evidence from the Empathy Quotient and the "Reading the Mind in the Eyes" Test. *Social Neuroscience* 1 (2): 135–148.

Cohn, J. F., S. B. Campbell, and S. Ross. 1991. Infant response in the still-face paradigm at 6 months predicts avoidant and secure attachment at 12 months. *Development and Psychopathology* 3: 367–376.

Darwin, C. 1872. *The Expression of Emotion in Man and Animals*. London: John Murray.

Decety, J. 2010. The neurodevelopment of empathy in humans. *Developmental Neuroscience* 32: 257–267.

Decety, J., and P. L. Jackson. 2004. The functional architecture of human empathy. *Behavioral and Cognitive Neuroscience Reviews* 3: 406–12.

Decety, J., and C. Lamm. 2009. Empathy versus personal distress: Recent evidence from social neuroscience. In *The Social Neuroscience of Empathy*, edited by J. Decety and W. Ickes, 199–213. Cambridge, MA: MIT Press.

Decety, J., and K. J. Michalska. 2010. Neurodevelopmental changes in the circuits underlying empathy and sympathy from childhood to adulthood. *Developmental Science* 13: 886–899.

Dondi, M., D. Messinger, M. Colle, A. Tabasso, F. Simion, B. Dalla Barba, and A. Fogel. 2007. A new perspective on neonatal smiling: Differences between the judgments of expert coders and naive observers. *Infancy* 12: 235–55.

Dondi, M., F. Simion, and G. Caltran. 1999. Can newborns discriminate between their own cry and the cry of another newborn infant? *Developmental Psychology* 35: 418–426.

Eisenberg, N., R. Fabes, and P. A. Miller. 1987. Relation of sympathy and personal distress to prosocial behavior: A multi-method study. *Journal of Personality* 57: 55–66.

Ferry, A. T., D. Ongur, X. An, and J. L. Price. 2000. Prefrontal cortical projections to the striatum in Macaque monkeys: Evidence for an organization relation to prefrontal networks. *Journal of Comparative Neurology* 425: 447–470.

Fox, N., and R. J. Davidson. 1988. Patterns of brain electrical activity during facial signs of emotion in 10-month-old infants. *Developmental Psychology* 24: 230–236.

Frank, M. G., P. Ekman, and W. V. Friesen. 1993. Behavioral markers and recognizability of the smile of enjoyment. *Journal of Personality and Social Psychology* 64: 83–93.

Fuster, J. M. 2008. *The Prefrontal Cortex*. San Diego, CA: Academic Press.

Giedd, J. N., N. O. Blumenthal, F. X. Jeffries, L. Castellanos, A. Hong, and J. Zijdenbos. 1999. Brain development during childhood and adolescence: A longitudinal MRI study. *Nature Neuroscience* 2: 861–863.

Grossmann, T., and M. H. Johnson. 2007. The development of the social brain in human infancy. *European Journal of Neuroscience* 25: 909–919.

Hastings, P. D., W. T. Utendale, and C. Sullivan. 2007. The socialization of prosocial development. In *Handbook of Socialization: Theory and Research*, edited by J. E. Grusec and P. D. Hastings. New York: Guilford Press.

Haviland, J. M., and M. Lelwica. 1987. The induced affect response: 10-week-old infants' responses to three emotion expressions. *Developmental Psychology* 23: 97–104.

Hennenlotter, A., U. Schroedr, P. Erhard, F. Castrop, B. Haslinger, et al. 2005. A common neural basis for receptive and expressive communication of pleasant facial affect. *NeuroImage* 26: 581–591.

Higashida, H., O. Lopatina, T. Yoshihara, Y. A. Pichugina, A. A. Soumarokov, T. Munesue, Y. Minabe, M. Kikuchi, Y. Ono, N. Korshunova, and A. B. Salmina. 2010. Oxytocin signal and social behaviour: Comparison among adult and infant oxytocin, oxytocin receptor and CD38 gene knockout mice. *Journal of Neuroendocrinology* 22: 373–379.

Hoffman, M. L. 1975. Developmental synthesis of affect and cognition and its interplay for altruistic motivation. *Developmental Psychology* 11: 607–622.

Hornik, R., N. Risenhoover, and M. Gunnar. 1987. The effects of maternal positive, neutral, and negative affective communications on infant responses to new toys. *Child Development* 58: 937–944.

Hurlemann, R., A. Patin, O. A. Onur, M. X. Cohen, T. Baumgartner, S. Metzler, I. Dziobek, J. Gallinat, M. Wagner, W. Maier, and K. M. Kendrick. 2010. Oxytocin enhances amygdala-dependent, socially reinforced learning and emotional empathy in humans. *Journal of Neuroscience* 30: 4999–5007.

Iwase, M., Y. Ouchi, H. Okada, C. Yokoyama, S. Nobezawa, E. Yoshikawa, H. Tsukada, M. Takeda, K. Yamashita, M. Takeda, K. Yamaguti, H. Kuratsune, A. Shimizu, and Y. Watanabe. 2002. Neural substrates of human facial expression of pleasant emotion induced by comic films: A PET study. *NeuroImage* 17: 758–768.

Kartner, J., H. Keller, and N. Chaudhary. 2010. Cognitive and social influences on early prosocial behavior in two sociocultural contexts. *Developmental Psychology* 46: 905–914.

Knafo, A., C. Zahn-Waxler, C. Van Hulle, J. L. Robinson, and S. Rhee. 2008. The developmental origins of a disposition toward empathy: Genetic and environmental contributions. *Emotion (Washington, DC)* 8: 737–752.

Lagercrantz, H., and J. Changeux. 2009. The emergence of human consciousness: From fetal to neonatal life. *Pediatric Research* 65: 255–260.

Lepage, J. F., and H. Théret. 2007. The mirror neuron system: Grasping others' actions from birth? *Developmental Science* 10: 513–523.

Light, S. N., J. A. Coan, C. Zahn-Waxler, C. Frye, H. H. Goldsmith, and R. J. Davidson. 2009. Empathy is associated with dynamic change in prefrontal brain electrical activity during positive emotion in children. *Child Development* 80: 1210–1231.

Light, S. N., H. H. Goldsmith, J. A. Coan, C. Frye, and R. J. Davidson. 2009. Dynamic variation in pleasure in children predicts non-linear change in lateral frontal activity. *Developmental Psychology* 45: 525–533.

Ludemann, P., and C. A. Nelson. 1988. Categorical representation of facial expressions by 7-month-old infants. *Developmental Psychology* 24: 492–501.

MacLean, P. D. 1985. Brain evolution relating to family, play, and the separation call. *Archives of General Psychiatry* 42: 405–417.

Messinger, D. S., A. Fogel, and K. L. Dickson. 1999. What's in a smile? *Developmental Psychology* 35: 701–708.

Minagawa-Kawai, Y., S. Matsuoka, I. Dan, N. Naoi, K. Nakamura, and S. Kojima. 2009. Prefrontal activation associated with social attachment: facial-emotion recognition in mothers and infants. *Cerebral Cortex* 19: 284–292.

Nichols, S. R., M. Svetlova, and C. A. Brownell. 2009. The role of social understanding and empathic disposition in young children's responsiveness to distress in parents and peers. *Cognition, Brain, Behavior* 13: 449–478.

Niedenthal, P. M., M. Mermillod, M. Maringer, and U. Huss. 2010. The simulation of smiles (SMS) model: Embodied simulation and the meaning of facial expression. *Behavioral and Brain Sciences* 33: 417–480.

Nitschke, J. B., E. E. Nelson, B. D. Rusch, A. S. Fox, T. R. Oakes, and R. J. Davidson. 2004. Orbitofrontal cortex tracks positive mood in mothers viewing pictures of their newborn infants. *NeuroImage* 21: 538–592.

Nystrom, P. 2008. The infant mirror neuron system studied with high density EEG. *Social Neuroscience* 3: 334–347.

Rempel-Clower, N. L., and H. Barbas. 1998. Topographic organization of connections between the hypothalamus and prefrontal cortex in the rhesus monkey. *Journal of Comparative Neurology* 398: 393–419.

Robinson, J. L., R. N. Emde, and R. P. Corley. 2001. Dispositional cheerfulness: Early genetic and environmental factors. In *Infancy to Early Childhood: Genetic and Environmental Influences*, edited by R. N. Emde and J. Hewett, 163–177. Oxford: Oxford University Press.

Robinson, J. L., C. Zahn-Waxler, and R. Emde. 1994. Patterns of development in early empathic behavior: Environmental and child constitutional influences. *Social Development* 3: 125–143.

Rochat, P. 2003. Five levels of self-awareness as they unfold early in life. *Consciousness and Cognition* 12: 717–31.

Rochat, P., and T. Striano. 2002. Who's in the mirror? Self-other discrimination in specular images by 4 and 9 month-old infants. *Child Development* 73: 35–46.

Rodrigues, S. M., L. R. Saslow, N. Garcia, O. P. John, and D. Keltner. 2009. Oxytocin receptor genetic variation relates to empathy and stress reactivity in humans. *Proceedings of the National Academy of Sciences of the United States of America* 106: 21437–21441.

Rothbart, M. K., S. A. Ahadi, and K. L. Hershey. 1994. Temperament and social behavior in childhood. *Merrill-Palmer Quarterly* 40: 21–39.

Sallquist, J., N. Eisenberg, T. L. Spinrad, N. D. Eggum, and B. M. Gaertner. 2009. Assessment of preschoolers' positive empathy: Concurrent and longitudinal relations with positive emotion, social competence, and sympathy. *Journal of Positive Psychology* 4: 223–233.

Simner, M. L. 1971. Newborn's response to the cry of another infant. *Developmental Psychology* 5: 136–150.

Singer, T. 2006. The neuronal basis and ontogeny of empathy and mindreading: Review of literature and implications for future research. *Neuroscience and Biobehavioral Reviews* 30: 855–863.

Striano, T., and D. Stahl. 2005. "Sensitivity to triadic attention in early infancy. *Developmental Science* 4: 333–343.

Tost, H., B. Kolachana, S. Hakimi, H. Lemaitre, B. A. Verchinski, V. S. Mattay, D. R. Weinberger, and A. Meyer-Lindenberg. 2010. A common allele in the oxytocin receptor gene (OXTR) impacts prosocial temperament and human hypothalamic-limbic structure and function. *Proceedings of the National Academy of Sciences of the United States of America* 107: 13936–13941.

Trevarthen, C., and K. J. Aitken. 2001. Infant intersubjectivity: Research, theory and clinical implications. *Journal of Clinical Psychology & Psychiatry* 42: 3–48.

Ungerer, J. A., R. Dolby, B. Waters, B. Barnett, N. Kelk, and V. Lewin. 1990. The early development of empathy: Self-regulation and individual differences in the first year. *Motivation and Emotion* 14: 93–106.

Vaish, A., M. Carpenter, and M. Tomasello. 2009. Sympathy through affective perspective taking and its relation to prosocial behavior in toddlers. *Developmental Psychology* 45: 534–543.

Volbrecht, M.M., Lemery-Chalfont, K., Askan, N., Zahn-Waxler, C., and Goldsmith, H.H. 2007. Examining the familial link between positive affect and empathy development in the second year. *Journal of Genetic Psychology* 168 (2): 105–129.

Winslow, J. T., E. F. Hearn, J. Ferguson, L. J. Young, M. M. Matzuk, and T. R. Insel. 2000. Infant vocalization, adult aggression, and fear behavior of an oxytocin null mutant mouse. *Hormones and Behavior* 37: 145–155.

Wismer Fries, A. B., T. E. Ziegler, J. R. Kurian, S. Jacoris, and S. Pollak. 2005. Early experience in humans is associated with changes in neuropeptides critical for regulating social behavior. *Proceedings of the National Academy of Sciences of the United States of America* 102: 17237–17240.

Wolff, P. H. 1987. *The Development of Behavioral States and the Expression of Emotions in Early Infancy: New Proposals for Investigation*. Chicago: University of Chicago Press.

Yang, C., J. Decety, S. Lee, C. Chen, and Y. Cheng. 2009. Gender differences in mu rhythm during empathy for pain: An EEG study. *Brain Research* 1251: 176–184.

Young, S., N. A. Fox, and C. Zahn-Waxler. 1999. The relations between temperament and empathy in 2-year-olds. *Developmental Psychology* 35: 1189–1197.

Zahn-Waxler, C. 1991. The case for empathy: A developmental perspective. *Psychological Inquiry* 2: 155–158.

Zahn-Waxler, C., P. M. Cole, J. D. Welsh, and N. A. Fox. 1995. Physiological correlates of empathy and prosocial behaviors in preschool children with behavior problems. *Development and Psychopathology* 7: 27–48.

Zahn-Waxler, C., M. Radke-Yarrow, E. Wagner, and M. Chapman. 1992. Development of concern for others. *Developmental Psychology* 28: 126–136.

Zahn-Waxler, C., J. L. Robinson, and R. N. Emde. 1992. The development of empathy in twins. *Developmental Psychology* 28: 1038–1047.

8   Social-Cognitive Contributors to Young Children's Empathic and Prosocial Behavior

Amrisha Vaish and Felix Warneken

Humans, even as young children, act prosocially, that is, in ways that benefit other individuals. Quite early in ontogeny, for instance, children help, comfort, and share resources with others (Hay and Cook 2007; Warneken and Tomasello 2009). A question that has occupied psychologists for a long time concerns the mechanisms and motivations underlying such prosocial behavior. Investigating this issue is essential to understanding prosociality: first, people might engage in prosocial behaviors for a number of reasons, including selfish ones—to gain approval, be rewarded, or because acting prosocially relieves the stress induced by witnessing another person's plight. Therefore, despite the commonality among prosocial behaviors to increase another person's welfare broadly construed, we might actually be dealing with quite disparate motivations underlying these behaviors. Second, to understand the development of prosocial behavior in children, it seems critical to understand what psychological mechanisms are required for different prosocial behaviors. In particular, observed developmental trends toward greater prosocial behavior might not be explained by a change in the motivational component of prosocial behavior alone but also by emerging social-cognitive abilities that enable older children to respond in prosocial ways in situations that are still beyond the scope of young children. The question thus arises, what affective, cognitive, and motivational abilities must be in place in order for children to act prosocially?

One mechanism underlying prosocial behavior that has gained a substantial following is empathy (Batson 1991; Hoffman 2000). Empathy and the associated process, sympathy, have been defined in a number of ways (Feshbach 1978; Hoffman 1982; Wispé 1986, 1987; Eisenberg and Strayer 1987; Batson 1998; Preston and de Waal 2002; Decety and Jackson 2006). Here, we will adopt a conceptualization offered by Nancy Eisenberg and colleagues (Eisenberg et al. 1994; Eisenberg, Spinrad, and Sadovsky 2006; see also Hoffman 1982, 2000) in which *empathy* is an affective response that stems from the apprehension or comprehension of another's emotional state and is similar to what the other person is feeling or would be expected to feel. *Sympathy*, on the other hand, is an affective response that stems from the apprehension or comprehension of another's emotional state but is not the same as the other's state, consisting instead of feelings of sorrow or concern for the other (Batson 1987; Eisenberg et al. 1991). Empathy and especially sympathy are thought to lead to prosocial behaviors such as helping and away from antisocial behaviors such as aggression (Hoffman 1982; Eisenberg and Miller 1987; Miller and Eisenberg 1988; Batson et al. 1991; Batson 1998; Hoffman 2000).

The principal approach to investigating the ontogenetic development of this prosocial mechanism has been to assess how infants and young children respond to a victim's observable (visible or audible) emotional cues. In the typical paradigm children are presented with a person (infant, mother, or stranger) displaying pain or distress, and children's empathic, sympathetic, and prosocial responses toward the victim (as evident in their facial, vocal, gestural, or physiological reactions) are assessed. This research suggests that soon after birth infants automatically cry in response to other infants' cries (e.g., Simner 1971; Sagi and Hoffman 1976). This *global empathy* is thought to be a precursor of empathy (Hoffman, 1982, 2000). Around twelve to fourteen months of age, infants show *egocentric empathic distress*, in which they respond to another's distress as if they themselves were in distress because they still lack a clear differentiation between self and other.

True or *veridical empathy* emerges in the second half of the second year, when children more fully differentiate between self and other and thereby understand that others are separate beings (as seen in their ability to recognize themselves in the mirror) (Lewis et al. 1989). With this important cognitive development toddlers realize that others have independent inner states, and now, when they see a person in distress after, say, bumping her knee or after her toy breaks, they show increasing empathic and sympathetic responses to others' visible distress as well as appropriate, other-directed comforting and prosocial behavior (e.g., Zahn-Waxler and Radke-Yarrow 1982; Bischof-Köhler 1991; Zahn-Waxler et al. 1992; Eisenberg and Fabes 1998; see Hoffman 2000 for a detailed account of the developmental stages of empathic responding). Young children's empathy and sympathy have been found to relate positively with their prosocial behavior (Hoffman 1982; Eisenberg and Miller 1987) and negatively with their antisocial and aggressive behavior (Miller and Eisenberg 1988), suggesting that empathic responding does indeed serve as a prosocial motive in early childhood.

Empathic responding to a victim's perceptible emotional cues can be aroused by multiple preverbal and automatic processes including motor mimicry of the victim's emotional cues, emotional contagion, classical conditioning, and direct association of cues from the victim with one's own painful past experience (see Hoffman 2000). These processes are argued to arouse an involuntary affective response and to require only a shallow level of cognitive processing (Hoffman 2000). According to Hoffman these modes are crucial for arousing empathy in early childhood, but they continue to provide an involuntary route to empathy throughout life, especially in face-to-face situations in which the victim's distress is directly perceptible. Indeed, there is ample evidence to suggest that adults do empathize and sympathize with those in distress and that these empathic processes motivate their prosocial behavior (Batson 1981; Batson et al. 1991; Decety and Jackson 2006; Singer and Lamm 2009).

As all of this research shows, it is critical and extremely fruitful to investigate the emergence of children's empathic and prosocial responding toward a victim's emotional cues. Importantly, however, it has also been noted that empathic arousal is an especially important and reliable prosocial motivator because it is *multi*determined (e.g., Hoffman 2000). That is, empathic arousal can result in response to numerous types of distress cues by relying on several different modes of arousal, ranging from basic affective modes to cognitively sophisticated modes. This enables observers to respond empathically to whatever distress cues are available. Certainly, adults display a variety of empathic and prosocial behaviors, ranging from donating money to charities overseas to picking up a dropped object and handing it back to the owner, none of which requires responding to overt emotional cues from the individuals in need. Our aim in this chapter is to present some recent work assessing young children's responses to such "situational cues," which we contrast with the overt emotional cues employed in much of the prior research on empathic and prosocial development. Furthermore, we will suggest that responding to such situational cues calls on relatively sophisticated social-cognitive skills in addition to the affective and social-cognitive processes needed to respond to overt emotional cues.

We focus on two types of situational cues. First, we consider children's empathic and prosocial responses to distressing situations but in the absence of distress signals from the victim. We then present evidence that children in the second year can nevertheless sympathize with the victim and subsequently act prosocially toward her. Next, we consider children's responses to concrete instrumental problems that may not require an apprehension of the other's emotional state but of the other's unfulfilled action-goal. We present evidence that children in the second year of life respond by helping the person fulfill her goal. We also consider the social-cognitive skills required to respond to each type of situational cues.

Distressing Situations in the Absence of Distress Cues

Although most prior work on the development of empathic responding has involved assessing children's responses to overt emotional cues, there are two lines of developmental research relevant to the question of how young children respond in the absence of overt distress signals. However, both lines of research are problematic. The first involves the use of picture and story assessments (Feshbach and Roe 1968;

Eisenberg-Berg and Lennon 1980; Iannotti 1985) in which the child is typically told brief stories while being shown pictures of hypothetical protagonists in emotion-eliciting situations (e.g., a child has lost her dog or a child is at a birthday party) but is given no information about the protagonists' feelings. After each story, the child is asked to indicate verbally or by pointing to pictures of facial expressions how she herself feels. The assumption is that the child has responded empathically if her reported emotion is similar to that of the protagonist. Eisenberg and Miller (1987) argue, however, that among other problems, these assessments create strong demand characteristics and thus tap children's inclination to provide the socially appropriate response rather than their empathic responses (see also Eisenberg and Lennon 1983; Eisenberg, Spinrad, and Sadovsky 2006).

The second relevant line of research has examined children's affective perspective-taking skills. Similar to the picture and story assessments, affective perspective-taking tasks typically involve the child being told stories about a character's situations and then being asked how the character feels. By 2.5 to 3 years of age, children are quite successful at these tasks, suggesting that young children have some understanding of others' affective states (Wellman and Woolley 1990; Dunn and Hughes 1998; Wellman, Phillips, and Rodriguez 2000; Harwood and Farrar 2006). However, these tasks do not test children's sympathy; that is, it remains unclear whether, having comprehended the other's affective state, the child feels concern for the other and would act prosocially toward the other. Finally, a problem common to both lines of research is that the tasks used require relatively sophisticated cognitive abilities (e.g., the ability to understand hypothetical stories) and linguistic skills, which limits the age testable using these tasks.

We thus conducted a study to assess young children's empathic responses (specifically sympathy) toward a victim who shows no overt distress signals (Vaish, Carpenter, and Tomasello 2009). For this purpose we adapted and modified a task developed by Hobson et al. (2009). In our study, eighteen-month-old and two-year-old children first viewed an adult either harming another adult by destroying or taking away her possessions (harm condition) or else doing something similar that did not harm her (neutral condition). Importantly, the "victim" expressed no emotions in either condition, that is, she simply watched the other adult's harmful or harmless actions without displaying any emotional cues. Children viewed four such *sympathy situations*, during which we coded (1) the pattern of children's looks to the victim (e.g., the duration, latency, and number of looks, as well as the number of trials in which children looked to the victim), and (2) the quality of children's looks to the victim (whether each look was a concerned look or not; see Vaish, Carpenter, and Tomasello 2009 for details of the coding scheme).

Following these sympathy situations we assessed children's prosocial behavior toward the victim in a subsequent *prosocial situation*. Recall that empathy and sympathy are thought to give rise to prosocial behavior, and infants' and children's empathic responding toward a victim displaying overt distress has previously been found to correlate with children's prosocial behavior toward the victim. Our reasoning was thus that if children are really sympathizing with a victim even in the absence of any distress cues (i.e., during our sympathy situations), then they should also subsequently show greater prosocial behavior toward the victim. In our prosocial situation all children were given two balloons, and the adult who had played the victim during the sympathy situations was given one balloon. After about a minute of individual play the victim "accidentally" let go of her balloon (which floated to the ceiling) and was then vocally and facially (i.e., overtly) sad. Children's prosocial behavior was coded during the next two minutes (see Vaish, Carpenter, and Tomasello 2009 for details).

The results of this study showed clear differences in children's behavior across the two conditions. With regard to the pattern of looks, children in the harm condition looked to the victim more often, more quickly, and for longer than those in the neutral condition. Moreover, children also showed greater sympathy for the victim in the harm condition than in the neutral condition. Specifically, more children showed concerned looks in the harm than in the neutral condition, and children showed concerned looks in a significantly greater number of the four harm situations than the four neutral situations.

Children's subsequent prosocial behavior toward the victim also differed significantly across conditions: significantly more children acted prosocially toward (i.e., helped, comforted, or shared with) the victim if they had previously observed the victim in the harm rather than in the neutral condition. Furthermore, we found a significant correlation between children's sympathy and their subsequent prosocial behavior.

These findings are noteworthy for at least two reasons. First, they show that even very young children sympathize with victims and act prosocially toward them. This is in line with prior work, which showed that infants empathize and sympathize with those who overtly display distress and that this empathic responding mediates their prosocial behavior (Zahn-Waxler et al. 1992; Eisenberg and Fabes 1998). More importantly, our findings show that by the middle of the second year of life, children can sympathize with a person in a distressing or harmful situation *even if* that person does not display overt distress signals and that this sympathy also mediates children's subsequent prosocial behavior toward the victim.

What mechanisms are needed to respond sympathetically to such situational (rather than overt emotional) cues? Obviously, sympathy in the present study did not result directly from exposure to the victim's emotional cues (e.g., via mechanisms such as mimicking the emotional cues, emotional contagion, etc.), as such cues were not provided. It thus seems likely that sympathy in our study resulted at least partially from more sophisticated social-cognitive processes. One candidate social-cognitive process is affective perspective-taking, that is, drawing inferences about the other's affective state by putting oneself in the other's place and basing one's responses on those inferences (Hoffman 1984; Eisenberg et al. 1991). In the absence of emotional cues one way to make this inference is via simulation, which involves imagining oneself in another's situation (e.g., Harris 1995; Decety and Sommerville 2003). An alternative but related possibility is that the observer can feel her way into the experience of and feel for the other person because she identifies with that person's attitudes (Hobson et al. 2009). In either case one eventually takes the other's perspective and apprehends the other's affective state, which can activate affective responses such as sympathy and can thereby motivate prosocial behavior (Feshbach 1978; Krebs and Russell 1981; Batson, Fultz, and Schoenrade 1987). Plausibly, then, in the present study, children apprehended the victim's state by taking her affective perspective, which motivated their sympathy and prosocial behavior.

Depending on how familiar children were with situations like our sympathy situations, they might additionally have relied on their past experiences to infer the victim's affect. That is, if children had previously directly or vicariously experienced such situations on multiple occasions, perhaps they had formed scripts about people's responses to such situations and, in our study, were partially relying on these scripts to infer the victim's affect. On the other hand, if the situations were novel for children, then children likely engaged in perspective-taking (see Karniol 1982; Eisenberg et al. 1991; Blair 2005). Thus, perhaps some children in the harm condition (those familiar with such situations) relied less on affective perspective-taking and more on scripts than did children who were unfamiliar with such situations. However, even if the situations were to some degree familiar to children, it is highly unlikely that children had ever witnessed precisely the situations that they witnessed in our study (e.g., an adult tearing up another adult's drawing), and so although they might have had some scripts to rely on, they also had to engage in some affective perspective-taking.

In sum, our study demonstrates the flexible nature of empathy-related processes even in young children. As noted earlier, empathic arousal is thought to be a reliable prosocial motivator because it is multidetermined: the many modes of empathic arousal enable observers to respond empathically to whatever distress cues are available (Hoffman 2000). Typically, victims are present and providing clear distress signals; in this case any or several of the arousal mechanisms may be operating, ranging from the most basic and automatic forms of mimicry to the most advanced forms of cognitive reappraisal. However, when a victim is absent or is not providing distress signals for some reason, the cognitively advanced modes of empathic arousal still enable one to empathize, thus adding scope to one's empathic capability (Hoffman 2000). Indeed, adults do empathize and sympathize with victims, both when they have direct access to the victims' distress cues and when they must engage more sophisticated cognitive processes, and these empathic processes do motivate their prosocial behavior (Batson et al. 1981, 1991; Ruby and Decety 2004; Decety and Jackson 2006; Singer and Lamm 2009). Our findings show that this multidetermined nature of empathy-related responses is already functional in early development. This suggests that empathy-related responses are indeed reliable proximate mechanisms underlying prosocial behavior even early in human ontogeny.

Instrumental Helping

Beyond situations in which children respond and intervene to change the emotional states of others, young children also engage in acts of instrumental helping: a person is having trouble achieving a concrete goal (such as reaching for an out-of-reach object or being unable to open a door), and the child helps her achieve it (by moving the object closer or holding the door open for her). These instrumental helping behaviors are interesting motivationally, as they can provide insight into young children's willingness to act on behalf of others, especially in those cases where the child's actions are aimed at assisting with the other's goal attainment rather than a benefit for oneself. These helping behaviors are also interesting cognitively, as they require the social-cognitive ability to represent other people's goals and intentions, rather than apprehending or resonating with the (presumed) emotional states of others. Thus, similar to the experiments on empathy and sympathy described above, instrumental helping critically depends on children's ability to respond to situational cues and not facial expressions alone with the difference that, rather than inferring an emotional state, children have to be able to represent another person's action-goal.

It is a well-established phenomenon that by at least twelve to eighteen months of age children are able to represent other people's actions in terms of their underlying goals. Specifically, young children are able to differentiate between purposeful and accidental actions, highlighted for example in their tendency to imitate those aspects of an action that a person has done on purpose over those aspects the person has done only accidentally (Carpenter, Akhtar and Tomasello 1998). Moreover, they are able to infer what a person was trying but failing to do even without actually witnessing the intended outcome (Meltzoff 1995). Would young children utilize this social-cognitive capacity to read others' goals also to help others with their instrumental problems? A series of recent experiments show that from around fourteen to eighteen months of age, children begin to engage in instrumental helping, and they do so in increasingly sophisticated ways over the second year of life.

In an initial study we tested eighteen-month-old infants in a variety of situations in which an experimenter had trouble achieving his goal and the child had the opportunity to help (Warneken and Tomasello 2006). These situations presented the children with a variety of difficulties in discerning the person's goals. For instance, in one such situation, the person was hanging towels on a line, accidentally dropped a clothespin on the ground, and was unsuccessfully reaching for it. In another situation the person was trying to put a stack of magazines into a cabinet, but he could not open the door because his hands were full, and he bumped into the doors helplessly. Children helped in these situations by performing behaviors such as picking up the dropped object, opening the door, or completing the person's action after the failed attempt of stacking books. Importantly, children did not perform these actions in matched control conditions, in which the same basic situation and objects were presented, but there was no indication from the person that this constituted a problem for him (e.g., he dropped a clothespin on purpose). Therefore, these results indicated that children were able to infer the other person's goal in various contexts and knew how to intervene appropriately to help him achieve that goal. Another experiment showed that even fourteen-month-olds are willing and able to help instrumentally, although almost exclusively in situations in which helping consisted in handing over an out-of-reach object and not in more complex situations involving less salient goals and more complex forms of intervention (Warneken and Tomasello 2007).

The sophistication with which toddlers help instrumentally is also highlighted by the finding that they take into account what another person does or does not know. Specifically, in one helping test (Buttelmann, Carpenter, and Tomasello 2009) a protagonist put a toy into box A, after which the toy was moved to box B while the protagonist was either absent (ignorant condition) or present (knowledge condition). When the protagonist now unsuccessfully tried to open box A, eighteen-month-old children in the ignorant condition did not join him in trying to open box A but instead opened box B in which the toy actually resided, indicating that they inferred that what the protagonist was actually trying to do was to get to the toy. Opening box A would not have helped him. However, children from the knowledge condition were more likely to open box A, presumably reasoning that the protagonist was not trying to get the toy that he knew had been moved to box B, and must thus have a new goal in mind for trying to open box A. This shows that these young children actually help others with their goals (which they infer based on the other's state of knowledge) and do not blindly assist in completing any concrete action that another person (falsely) pursues.

Toddlers not only know when to help and how, but also whom. Specifically, twenty-one-month-old children will selectively help a person who was willing but unable to share a toy with them (because it rolled away) rather than a person who was unwilling to share a toy with them (i.e., she offered but then teasingly withdrew it) in a previous encounter (Dunfield and Kuhlmeier 2010). That is, even though during the previous encounter the results of both individuals' actions were the same (the child did not receive a toy from either of them), they had attended to the "nice" person's intention to give them a toy and the "mean" person's intention to not give them a toy. Therefore, children kept track of how each person had behaved toward them, and altered their own helping behavior accordingly. Moreover, three-year-olds have also been shown to be selective in their helping behavior depending on how two individuals have behaved or intended to behave toward another person (rather than toward the children themselves). In this study (Vaish, Carpenter, and Tomasello 2010) three-year-olds selectively withdrew help from a person who had harmed another person or even intended (but failed) to harm another person. These studies thus demonstrate that young children rely on others' behaviors and intentions when selecting the beneficiaries of their helping acts.

Taken together, these experimental studies show that already early in ontogeny, children display impressive helping behaviors by intervening prosocially in a variety of ways. These findings highlight the sophisticated social-cognitive capacities that young children recruit to adequately represent other people's instrumental problems that go well beyond responding solely to others' overt distress cues.

Conclusions and Implications

Empathic arousal is argued to be one of the most reliable and important motivators of prosocial behavior because it is multidetermined, that is, because it can be reached in response to many different types of cues, via various affective and cognitive routes (Hoffman 2000). Yet until very recently our understanding of the ontogenetic emergence of this motivator was limited to children's empathic and prosocial responses to overt, perceptible emotional cues and thus to only a few and perhaps only the most basic affective mechanisms underlying empathic arousal. In this chapter we aimed to go beyond this focus to present some recent work on young children's responses to situational cues and to explore the social-cognitive skills needed to respond to such cues.

Concerning the development of prosocial behavior, what is clear from the work we have presented is that already young children respond empathically and intervene prosocially toward others based on situational cues. By at least eighteen months of age, toddlers are able to be concerned for a person in a distressing situation but displaying no distress (Vaish, Carpenter, and Tomasello 2009). The social-cognitive skills required in order to respond in these ways include something akin to perspective-taking whereby, because the victim displays no distress, children must take her perspective in order to apprehend how she perceives the situation, which in turn enables them to sympathize with her. They cannot simply catch her emotion via emotional contagion, and they cannot simply identify how she feels by reading her overt emotional cues. Empathic responding in such a situation thus requires different if not greater social-cognitive processing than does empathic responding to overt distress cues.

Starting shortly after their first birthday toddlers begin to engage in instrumental helping (Warneken and Tomasello 2006). Helping in these ways again requires different social-cognitive skills than empathic responding to overt distress cues: it requires appropriately inferring others' goals as well as the empathic or prosocial motivation to assist them in reaching their goals. In fact, already by fourteen months infants help others instrumentally in situations in which the goals are clear and in which intervention is simple, such as giving an object that is out of reach (Warneken and Tomasello 2007). By at least eighteen months of age, they can intervene fairly flexibly in different kinds of situations with more complex actions, such as when someone fails to open a door or uses the wrong means to achieve a goal (Warneken and Tomasello 2006).

Thus, by fourteen to eighteen months of age children display empathic responding to others' overt distress as well as in the absence of such distress but in the presence of other types of cues. Empathy and its related responses can thus motivate prosocial behavior in response to multiple cues, both emotional and situational, and via multiple routes, both affective and cognitive, even in early ontogeny, and are thus reliable prosocial motivators even in early ontogeny (see Hoffman 2000).

These findings demonstrate the impressive flexible nature of empathic responding even in early childhood. Infants seem to come into the world equipped to automatically respond resonantly with others' emotions, as evident in their emotional contagion responses at birth (Simner 1971; Sagi and Hoffman 1976). This way of responding to overt cues continues to function as a bottom-up and an at least partially involuntary route to empathy throughout life (Hoffman 2000; Singer and Lamm 2009). However, with affective and cognitive development and experience, young children become better at apprehending others' inner states from increasingly varied types of cues, regulating their own inner states, keeping others' and their own inner states separate, and even inhibiting empathic and prosocial responding based on what they know about the beneficiary. By adulthood empathic responding has become a highly flexible phenomenon that can be influenced by numerous top-down factors, including contextual (re)appraisal, the interpersonal relationship between empathizer and other, and the perspective adopted during observation of the other (Ruby and Decety 2004; Decety and Jackson 2006; Decety and Lamm 2006; Singer and Lamm 2009).

Furthermore, although we have focused here on the social-cognitive and affective contributors to empathic responding, to gain a fuller understanding it is imperative to also consider the contributions of culture and experience. Indeed, research shows that the developmental context likely plays a critical and fascinating role. Although a comprehensive review of this work is beyond the scope of this chapter, it is worthwhile to consider a few examples to demonstrate the point. One recent study by Kärtner, Keller, and Chaudhary (2010), for instance, showed that although self-other differentiation has been thought for so long to be the critical requirement for true empathic responding (Hoffman 1975) and has been shown to correlate with empathic responding in toddlers (e.g., Bischof-Köhler 1991; Zahn-Waxler et al. 1992), in fact, this correlation only holds for children in cultural contexts in which parents emphasize individuality, autonomy, and self-reliance (in the case of Kärtner, Keller, and Chaudhary 2010, Germany). The correlation did not emerge in India, where parents emphasize social relationships and interpersonal responsiveness (obedience, prosocial behavior) over autonomy. Thus, Kärtner, Keller, and Chaudhary (2010) argue that whereas empathic responding in Germany (and other cultures in which socialization goals concern autonomy) is grounded in perceiving the distinct subjective state that the other is in, in India (and other cultures with relational socialization goals) it has its origins in jointly experiencing the other person's distress. Perceiving the self as distinct from others may thus not be a universal requirement for the emergence of empathic responding.

There is also evidence of cultural and experiential influences on children's prosocial behavior (see Eisenberg 1989, 1992). For instance, a recent study of five-year-olds' spontaneous prosocial behavior revealed that German and Israeli children displayed more prosocial behavior toward a distressed adult as compared to Indonesian and Malaysian children (Trommsdorff, Friedlmeier, and Mayer 2007). The researchers propose that, in cultures that promote face-saving values and respect for hierarchical relations (such as Indonesia and Malaysia), ignoring the mishap of another person (especially an authority figure) can be more valued than attempting to help and thereby risking that the other person lose face. Moreover, there is evidence that toddlers from abusive homes are much less likely to respond empathically or prosocially, and much more likely to respond with anger, fear, or physical attacks, to distressed peers than are toddlers from nonabusive homes (Main and George 1985). Such findings of variation across contexts are provocative because they highlight the ways in which culture and experience fundamentally shape empathic responding, and they demonstrate vividly that empathic responding is not a unitary process but rather is open to a diverse set of influences. More generally, we propose that the relative automaticity of infants' initial affective response is transformed, with development, into a much more complex affective and cognitive response, one that is flexible and open to control, allowing us, in time, to experience forcefully and to respond effectively and in contextually appropriate ways to others' plight without being enslaved to those responses.

Finally, an important implication of the work we have presented is that both affect and cognition are important contributors to empathy-related responding. For instance, children in the Vaish, Carpenter, and Tomasello (2009) study were affectively involved in (and concerned about) a victim's plight; that, after all, was what we measured during the sympathy situations. However, since the victim provided no observable emotional cues, children likely had to rely on social-cognitive processes such as perspective-taking or relevant scripts in order to engage affectively with the victim. Moreover, they would also have needed to rely on the basic cognitive processes required for sympathizing and empathizing, such as self-other differentiation (although see Kärtner, Keller, and Chaudhary 2010). This shows the integral link between affective and cognitive processes in producing empathic responding. Similarly, in Warneken and Tomasello's (2006, 2007) studies on instrumental helping, children had to rely on social-cognitive processes such as inferring unfulfilled goals but also needed a basic empathic or prosocial motivation to help the other fulfill his goals. Indeed, even empathic responding to overt, perceptible distress cues relies on both affective (e.g., catching and experiencing the other's emotion) and cognitive processes (e.g., self-other differentiation in order to keep the other's and one's own emotion separate). Thus, empathic responding in general is a complex, multifaceted process. It is our hope that future work will continue to explore how flexible and sophisticated this mechanism underlying prosocial behavior truly is, especially in early childhood.

References

Batson, C. D. 1987. Prosocial motivation: Is it ever truly altruistic? In *Advances in Experimental Social Psychology*, vol. 20, edited by L. Berkowitz, 65–122. New York: Academic Press.

Batson, C. D. 1991. *The Altruism Question: Toward a Social-Psychological Answer*. Hillsdale, NJ: Lawrence Erlbaum Associates.

Batson, C. D. 1998. Altruism and prosocial behavior. In *The Handbook of Social Psychology*, vol. 2, edited by D. T. Gilbert, S. T. Fiske, and G. Lindzey, 282–316. Boston: McGraw-Hill.

Batson, C. D., J. G. Batson, J. K. Slingsby, K. L. Harrell, H. M. Peekna, and R. M. Todd. 1991. Empathic joy and the empathy-altruism hypothesis. *Journal of Personality and Social Psychology* 61 (3): 413–426.

Batson, C. D., B. D. Duncan, P. Ackerman, T. Buckley, and K. Birch. 1981. Is empathic emotion a source of altruistic motivation? *Journal of Personality and Social Psychology* 40 (2): 290–302.

Batson, C. D., J. Fultz, and P. A. Schoenrade. 1987. Adults' emotional reactions to the distress of others. In *Empathy and Its Development*, edited by N. Eisenberg and J. Strayer, 163–85. Cambridge: Cambridge University Press.

Bischof-Köhler, D. 1991. The development of empathy in infants. In *Infant Development: Perspectives from German Speaking Countries*, edited by M. E. Lamb and H. Keller, 245–73. Hillsdale, NJ: Lawrence Erlbaum Associates.

Blair, R. J. R. 2005. Responding to the emotions of others: Dissociating forms of empathy through the study of typical and psychiatric populations. *Consciousness and Cognition* 14: 698–718.

Buttelmann, D., M. Carpenter, and M. Tomasello. 2009. Eighteen-month-old infants show false belief understanding in an active helping paradigm. *Cognition* 112: 337–342.

Carpenter, M., N. Akhtar, and M. Tomasello. 1998. Fourteen- to 18-month-old infants differentially imitate intentional and accidental actions. *Infant Behavior and Development* 21: 315–330.

Decety, J., and P. L. Jackson. 2006. A social-neuroscience perspective on empathy. *Current Directions in Psychological Science* 15 (2): 54–58.

Decety, J., and C. Lamm. 2006. Human empathy through the lens of social neuroscience. *The Scientific World Journal* 6: 1146–1163.

Decety, J., and J. A. Sommerville. 2003. Shared representations between self and other: A Social Cognitive Neuroscience View. *Trends in Cognitive Sciences* 7: 527–533.

Dunfield, K. A., and V. A. Kuhlmeier. 2010. Intention-mediated selective helping in infancy. *Psychological Science* 21: 523–527.

Dunn, J., and C. Hughes. 1998. Young children's understanding of emotions within close relationships. *Cognition and Emotion* 12: 171–190.

Eisenberg, N. 1989. *The Roots of Prosocial Behavior in Children*. Cambridge: Cambridge University Press.

Eisenberg, N. 1992. *The Caring Child*. Cambridge, MA: Harvard University Press.

Eisenberg, N., and R. A. Fabes. 1998. Prosocial development. In *Handbook of Child Psychology, Vol. 3: Social, Emotional, and Personality Development*, edited by N. Eisenberg, 5th ed., 701–778. New York: John Wiley & Sons.

Eisenberg, N., R. A. Fabes, B. Murphy, M. Karbon, P. Maszk, M. Smith, C. O'Boyle, and K. Suh. 1994. The relations of emotionality and regulation to dispositional and situational empathy-related responding. *Journal of Personality and Social Psychology* 66: 776–797.

Eisenberg, N., and R. Lennon. 1983. Sex differences in empathy and related capacities. *Psychological Bulletin* 94: 100–131.

Eisenberg, N., and P. A. Miller. 1987. The relation of empathy to prosocial and related behaviors. *Psychological Bulletin* 101: 91–119.

Eisenberg, N., C. L. Shea, G. Carlo, and G. P. Knight. 1991. Empathy-related responding and cognition: A "chicken and the egg" dilemma. In *Handbook of Moral Behavior and Development, Vol. 2: Research*, edited by W. Kurtines and J. Gewirtz, 63–88. Hillsdale, NJ: Lawrence Erlbaum Associates.

Eisenberg, N., T. L. Spinrad, and A. Sadovsky. 2006. Empathy-related responding in children. In *Handbook of Moral Development*, edited by M. Killen and J. G. Smetana, 517–49. Mahwah, NJ: Lawrence Erlbaum Associates.

Eisenberg, N., and J. Strayer. 1987. Critical issues in the study of empathy. In *Empathy and Its Development*, edited by N. Eisenberg and J. Strayer, 3–13. Cambridge: Cambridge University Press.

Eisenberg-Berg, N., and R. Lennon. 1980. Altruism and the assessment of empathy in the pre-school years. *Child Development* 51: 552–557.

Feshbach, N. D. 1978. Studies of empathic behavior in children. In *Progress in Experimental Personality Research*, vol. 8, edited by B. A. Maher, 1–47. New York: Academic Press.

Feshbach, N. D., and K. Roe. 1968. Empathy in six- and seven-year-olds. *Child Development* 39: 133–145.

Harris, P. L. 1995. From simulation to folk psychology: The case for development. In *Folk Psychology: The Theory of Mind Debate*, edited by M. Davies and T. Stone, 207–31. Oxford: Blackwell.

Harwood, M. D., and M. J. Farrar. 2006. Conflicting emotions: The connection between Affective Perspective Taking and theory of mind. *British Journal of Developmental Psychology* 24: 401–418.

Hay, D. F., and K. V. Cook. 2007. The transformation of prosocial behavior from infancy to childhood. In *Socioemotional Development in the Toddler Years*, edited by C. A. Brownell and C. B. Kopp, 100–131. New York: Guilford Press.

Hobson, J. A., R. Harris, R. García-Pérez, and P. Hobson. 2009. Anticipatory concern: A study in autism. *Developmental Science* 12 (2): 249–263.

Hoffman, M. L. 1975. Developmental synthesis of affect and cognition and its implications for altruistic motivation. *Developmental Psychology* 11 (5): 607–622.

Hoffman, M. L. 1982. Development of prosocial motivation: Empathy and guilt. In *The Development of Prosocial Behavior*, edited by N. Eisenberg, 281–338. New York: Academic Press.

Hoffman, M. L. 1984. Interaction of affect and cognition in empathy. In *Emotion, Cognition, and Behavior*, edited by C. E. Izard, J. Kagan, and R. B. Zajonc, 103–31. Cambridge: Cambridge University Press.

Hoffman, M. L. 2000. *Empathy and Moral Development: Implications for Caring and Justice*. Cambridge: Cambridge University Press.

Iannotti, R. J. 1985. Naturalistic and structured assessments of prosocial behavior in preschool children: The influence of empathy and perspective taking. *Developmental Psychology* 21 (1): 46–55.

Karniol, R. 1982. Settings, scripts, and self-schemata: A cognitive analysis of the development of prosocial behavior. In *The Development of Prosocial Behavior*, edited by N. Eisenberg, 251–78. New York: Academic Press.

Kärtner, J., H. Keller, and N. Chaudhary. 2010. Cognitive and social influences on early prosocial behavior in two sociocultural contexts. *Developmental Psychology* 46 (4): 905–914.

Krebs, D. L., and C. Russell. 1981. Role-taking and altruism: When you put yourself in the shoes of another, will they take you to their owner's aid? In *Altruism and Helping Behavior*, edited by J. P. Rushton and R. M. Sorrentino, 137–65. Hillsdale, NJ: Lawrence Erlbaum Associates.

Lewis, M., M. W. Sullivan, C. Stanger, and M. Weiss. 1989. Self development and self-conscious emotions. *Child Development* 60 (1): 146–156.

Main, M., and C. George. 1985. Responses of young abused and disadvantaged toddlers to distress in agemates. *Developmental Psychology* 21 (3): 407–412.

Meltzoff, A. N. 1995. Understanding the intentions of others: Re-enactment of intended acts by 18-month-old children. *Developmental Psychology* 31(5): 838–850.

Miller, P. A., and N. Eisenberg. 1988. The relation of empathy to aggressive and externalizing/ antisocial behavior. *Psychological Bulletin* 103: 324–344.

Preston, S. D., and F. B. M. de Waal. 2002. Empathy: Its ultimate and proximate bases. *Behavioral and Brain Sciences* 25: 1–72.

Ruby, P., and J. Decety. 2004. How would you feel versus how do you think she would feel? A neuroimaging study of perspective-taking with social emotions. *Journal of Cognitive Neuroscience* 16: 988–999.

Sagi, A., and M. L. Hoffman. 1976. Empathic distress in newborns. *Developmental Psychology* 12: 175–176.

Simner, M. L. 1971. Newborns' response to the cry of another infant. *Developmental Psychology* 5: 136–150.

Singer, T., and C. Lamm. 2009. The social neuroscience of empathy. *Annals of the New York Academy of Sciences* 1156: 81–96.

Trommsdorff, G., W. Friedlmeier, and B. Mayer. 2007. Sympathy, distress, and prosocial behavior of preschool children in four cultures. *International Journal of Behavioral Development* 31 (3): 284–293.

Vaish, A., M. Carpenter, and M. Tomasello. 2009. Sympathy through affective perspective-taking and its relation to prosocial behavior in toddlers. *Developmental Psychology* 45 (2): 534–543.

Vaish, A., M. Carpenter, and M. Tomasello. 2010. Young children selectively avoid helping people with harmful intentions. *Child Development* 81: 1661–69.

Warneken, F., and M. Tomasello. 2006. Altruistic helping in human infants and young chimpanzees. *Science* 311: 1301–1303.

Warneken, F., and M. Tomasello. 2007. Helping and cooperation at 14 months of age. *Infancy* 11 (3): 271–294.

Warneken, F., and M. Tomasello. 2009. The roots of human altruism. *British Journal of Psychology* 100 (3): 455–471.

Wellman, H. M., A. T. Phillips, and T. Rodriguez. 2000. Young children's understanding of perception, desire, and emotion. *Child Development* 71: 895–912.

Wellman, H. M., and J. D. Woolley. 1990. From simple desires to ordinary beliefs: The early development of everyday psychology. *Cognition* 35: 245–275.

Wispé, L. 1986. The distinction between sympathy and empathy: To call forth a concept, a word is needed. *Journal of Personality and Social Psychology* 50: 314–321.

Wispé, L. 1987. History of the concept of empathy. In *Empathy and Its Development*, edited by N. Eisenberg and J. Strayer, 17–37. New York: Cambridge University Press.

Zahn-Waxler, C., and M. Radke-Yarrow. 1982. The development of altruism: Alternative research strategies. In *The Development of Prosocial Behavior*, edited by N. Eisenberg, 109–37. New York: Academic Press.

Zahn-Waxler, C., M. Radke-Yarrow, E. Wagner, and M. Chapman. 1992. Development of concern for others. *Developmental Psychology* 28: 126–136.

9 Relations of Empathy-Related Responding to Children's and Adolescents' Social Competence

Nancy Eisenberg, Snjezana Huerta, and Alison Edwards

Empathy frequently is viewed as a basic human capacity that contributes to people's abilities to understand and respond to others' emotional states in appropriate ways. Thus, empathy and related vicarious reactions such as sympathy often have been viewed as capacities that foster positive human interactions—such as helping and sharing (e.g., Hoffman 2000; Eisenberg, Fabes, and Spinrad 2006)—and preclude harmful human interactions such as aggression (e.g., Mehrabian and Epstein 1972; Feshbach 1978; Miller and Eisenberg 1988). In addition, some behavioral scientists (e.g., Eisenberg and Miller 1987) have argued that empathy-related reactions provide information that fosters socially competent behavior more generally. In this chapter we examine the evidence for the latter, less frequently examined supposition. First, however, conceptual distinctions in regard to the definition of empathy are discussed, as are reasons for expecting some types of empathy-related reactions to contribute to the development of social competence.

In recent decades empathy has been defined in diverse ways. In developmental and social psychology, definitions of empathy typically include the abilities to understand others' emotions and perspective or situation and, often, to resonate with or experience the other's emotional state. Expanding on the work of Hoffman (2000) and Batson (1991), Eisenberg and colleagues (e.g., Eisenberg et al. 1991; Eisenberg, Fabes, and Spinrad 2006) have defined empathy as an affective response stemming from an understanding or apprehension of another's emotional state or condition that is identical, or very similar, to what the other person is feeling or might be expected to feel given the context. So if, for example, a girl observes a sad boy and consequently recognizes the boy's situation and feels sad herself, she is viewed as experiencing empathy. Thus, we define an emotional response consistent with the other's emotional state or situation as a central component of empathy. Empathy, however, is not mere contagion of affect without understanding the source of the vicariously induced emotion; to experience empathy the individual must realize that the emotion he or she is responding to affectively is another's emotion. Especially for young children, this understanding of another's emotion or state that underlies empathy may be fairly rudimentary and may not involve complex cognitive inferences.

Eisenberg and colleagues (1991) argued that after the first year or so of life, if feelings of empathy are not so weak as to be fleeting, they often elicit other emotional responses including sympathy or personal distress. Sympathy is defined as an affective response that often stems from empathy, but can derive solely (or partly) from perspective-taking or other cognitive processes (e.g., thinking about how it would be to experience a negative event), including the retrieval of relevant information from memory. Sympathy, like empathy, involves an understanding of another's emotion. It also involves an emotional response consisting of sorrow or concern for the distressed or needy other rather than simply feeling the same emotion the other person is experiencing or is expected to experience. Thus, the girl who saw the sad boy might first experience empathic sadness and subsequently feel sympathetic concern for him. This definition of sympathy is similar to Batson's (1991) and Hoffman's (2000) conceptualization of empathy.

In contrast, personal distress—which also is believed to stem from empathy, cognitions regarding another's emotional state or condition, or both—is defined as a self-focused, aversive emotional reaction to the vicarious experiencing of another's emotion (Batson 1991; Eisenberg et al. 1991). For example, if another's sadness or upset makes a viewer uncomfortable or anxious, the viewer is experiencing personal distress. Batson (1991) argued that personal distress is associated with the egoistic motivation to make oneself, not necessarily the other person, feel better—that is, to alleviate one's own aversive affective state. Thus, the social and moral concomitants and consequences of sympathy and personal distress are expected to differ.

Empathy-Related Responding and Social Behavior

Empathy orients an individual to another's emotional state and helps one to better understand that state. Sympathy, however, is likely to provide the affective motivation to improve the condition of the other person. Batson (1991) argued that feelings of sympathy (albeit labeled empathy) provide the motivation that underlies other-oriented helping. There is a considerable body of research, reviewed elsewhere, consistent with the view that the experience of sympathy increases the probability of prosocial behavior (i.e., intentional behavior motivated by the desire to benefit another) in a given context, especially altruism, that is, other-oriented prosocial behavior based on sympathy or moral values (e.g., Batson 1991; Eisenberg et al. 2006). Moreover, individuals who are prone to sympathy are more likely to engage in prosocial behavior than are less sympathetic individuals (e.g., Eisenberg and Miller 1987; Davis 1994; Eisenberg et al. 2006; Eisenberg, Eggum, and Di Giunta 2010).

In addition, people prone to empathy, sympathy, or both appear generally to be somewhat less likely than their less responsive peers to engage in externalizing behaviors such as aggression (Miller and Eisenberg 1988; Zhou et al. 2002; Eisenberg, Eggum, and Di Giunta 2010). It has been suggested that feelings of empathy inhibit aggressive behavior (Mehrabian and Epstein 1972; Feshbach 1978). This body of work has been reviewed elsewhere (e.g., Miller and Eisenberg 1988; Eisenberg, Fabes, and Spinrad 2006; Eisenberg, Eggum, and Di Giunta 2010), and in general there is some support for this argument.

Certainly, engaging in prosocial actions and abstaining from harmful behaviors can be viewed as socially competent behavior, especially if such behavior fosters positive interpersonal relationships. Indeed, prosocial actions tend to be positively associated with individual differences in social competence (see Eisenberg, Fabes, and Spinrad 2006), whereas aggression and externalizing problems often are negatively related with social competence (see Rubin, Bukowksi, and Parker 2006). However, there are a number of other aspects of social competence that pertain to the quality of one's behavior with others (e.g., if it is socially appropriate), one's social status, or the quality and nature of one's relationships with others. Relations of empathy-related responding with these aspects of social competence, as well as the tendency to engage in social behavior, have been examined less frequently and are the foci of this chapter.

Empathy-Related Responding and Social Competence: Conceptual Arguments

It is logical to assume that experiencing others' emotional states generally makes one more sensitive to others' feelings and needs and, hence, increases the probability of engaging in socially appropriate behaviors toward them. However, the distinction between sympathy and personal distress implies that the relation is more nuanced than this simple assumption would imply. Experiences of personal distress due to empathic overarousal are expected to engender avoidance of the empathy-inducing person and engaging in behavior that makes oneself feel better (Batson 1991; Hoffman 2000). Thus, feelings of personal distress, which may stem from empathy, are expected to culminate in self-focused behavior that may be socially insensitive behavior. In contrast, sympathy is expected to foster socially appropriate and socially sensitive behavior and, hence, positive interpersonal relationships due to a focus on the circumstances of the other rather than oneself. Moreover, because people tend to like other people who are socially appropriate and socially sensitive (see Rubin, Bukowski, and Parker 2006), it is reasonable to expect individuals who generally are sympathetic to be fairly well liked by peers.

A conceptual linkage between empathy or sympathy and children's sociability—often viewed as an aspect of social competence in Western cultures—is somewhat less intuitive than for other indices of social competence. An individual could be sociable—a characteristic believed to have a temperamental basis (see Rothbart and Bates

2006)—and not be particularly sensitive to others' emotional states or situations. However, it would seem that people who are sympathetic would generally engage in higher-quality social interactions with others than would less sympathetic people or those prone primarily to personal distress. In turn, these high-quality social interactions would encourage the person to engage in further social interactions and would increase the probability of others seeking social interaction with the individual. Thus, it is possible that sympathetic individuals elicit more positive social encounters and, consequently, engage in, and value, social interactions more than would individuals who are less sympathetic.

Relations of Empathy-Related Responding to Socially Competent Responding

In an early review, Eisenberg and Miller (1987) computed a meta-analysis for ten studies assessing the relation between empathy-related responding (usually empathy and not sympathy) and cooperation, sociability, or socially competent behavior. They found a very modest but significant positive relation. However, the relations of empathy-related responding may vary for different indices of socially competent functioning. In the remainder of this chapter we briefly summarize research findings on the relations of empathy-related responding to various aspects of children's and adolescents' social functioning. Readers interested in such relations in adulthood might consult various reviews (e.g., Davis 1994; Dovidio et al. 2006).

Empathy-Related Responding and Socially Appropriate Behaviors

In general, investigators have found evidence that both empathy and sympathy are positively related to children's socially appropriate behavior, although the association may change with age and vary somewhat with type of empathy-related responding and the measure of the construct. In terms of empathy, for example, in a longitudinal study of children in grades 2 to 5 (Time 1 [T1]), Zhou et al. (2002) found that children's observed (facial) and reported empathy with others' negative emotions/condition at T1 usually was not significantly correlated with their social competence (i.e., socially appropriate behavior and popularity) concurrently or two years later (Time 2 [T2]). However, at T2 children's observed and reported empathy with negative emotions were generally positively related to parents' and teachers' reports of social competence. Children's reports of empathy with others' positive emotions at T1 were not related to teacher-reported social competence concurrently, but they were positively related to teacher- (but not parent-) reported social competence at T2. Moreover, reported empathy with positive emotions at T2 was positively related to teacher- and parent-reported socially appropriate behavior at T2. Observed facial empathy with others' positive emotion at T1 or T2 was not significantly related to parent or teacher reports of socially appropriate behavior. Thus, reported empathy was more consistently related to socially appropriate behavior than was observed empathy, and, in general, relations of empathy with socially appropriate behavior were more evident with age and for empathy with others' negative than positive emotion.

In a separate study using the same sample as Zhou et al. (2002), Liew et al. (2003) examined physiological measures of children's empathy (i.e., heart rate [HR] and skin conductance [SC]) in relation to their socioemotional functioning. Boys' (but not girls') HR during negative empathy-inducing slides was negatively related to a measure of adult-reported maladjustment (i.e., a composite of teacher-reported socially appropriate behavior and popularity [reversed] and mother- and teacher-reported externalizing behavior). HR and SC arousal were positively related to boys' self-regulation. Because the slides were not very evocative and personal distress was not expected, any level of physiological response was considered to reflect empathy. Liew et al. (2003) also found that boys' and girls' HR during positive slides was not related to their positive emotionality, regulation, or maladjustment. For boys, higher SC was negatively related to intense dispositional positive and negative emotionality, but was not related to maladjustment. (In addition, girls' SC responses were positively related to their maladjustment, but this sole finding was likely due to chance.) Thus, especially for boys, physiological responding in reaction to mildly evocative empathy stimuli generally—especially stimuli depicting others' negative emotions—was associated with variables related to social competence.

In a longitudinal study assessing children's positive empathy in relation to their social competence (i.e., a composite of imitation/play and compliance), Sallquist et al. (2009) found that children's mother-reported positive empathy at fifty-four months was positively related to children's social competence as reported by mothers and nonparental caregivers (but not as reported by fathers) concurrently and one year prior (although the correlation for caregivers at the younger age was only nearly significant). Children's observed positive empathy at fifty-four months when the experimenter received a gift was unrelated to adult-reported social competence. These results mirror Zhou et al.'s (2002) results in which the observed measure of positive empathy was not found to be significantly related to social competence.

Sympathy has generally been positively related to indices of children's socially appropriate behavior. For example, in a study of kindergarten to second graders, Eisenberg et al. (1996) found that teacher- and self-reported sympathy were positively related to teachers' reports of concurrent social functioning (a composite of social skills, aggression [reversed], and disruptive behavior [reversed], which they called nonaggressive socially appropriate behavior), teacher-reported social skills two years earlier (although this relation held only for boys), and teacher-reports of prosocial/socially competent behavior (a composite of popularity, social insecurity [reversed], and prosocial behavior). Children's self reports of sympathy were positively related to teacher-reported social skills two years earlier, but only for girls. In addition, children's enactment of socially competent behaviors during a puppet procedure in which children responded to social conflict situations with peers was, in general, positively related to teachers' and children's reports (especially for boys) of the children's sympathy. In a follow-up of this sample four years later, Murphy et al. (1999) found that teachers' (but not parents') reports of children's sympathy generally were positively related to teacher-reported social competence at school (including social skills, popularity, and prosocial rather than aggressive behavior), both concurrently (for both sexes) and two, four, or six years prior for girls. Similarly, when these children were four to six years old, Eisenberg and Fabes (1995) found that concerned facial reactions (i.e., a measure of observed sympathy) in response to an empathy-inducing film were positively related to teachers' reports of social skills and constructive anger reactions.

Similar results have been obtained in other samples. In a sample of Indonesian sixth graders, teacher-reported sympathy and social skills (combined with low problem behavior) were substantially positively related within time; moreover, for boys only, reports of sympathy (by parents or teachers) and social functioning in third grade correlated positively with reports of social functioning or sympathy, respectively, in sixth grade (Eisenberg, Liew, and Pidada 2004). Likewise, Laible and Carlo (2004) found a positive correlation between self-reported sympathy/perspective taking and self-reported social competence in a sample of adolescents. In addition, Björkqvist, Österman, and Kaukiainen (2000) found that self-reported empathy was positively related to adolescents' peaceful conflict resolution.

Empathy, Sympathy, and Children's Peer Relationships

A variety of schemas are available for evaluating and quantifying children's peer relationships and peer group status including, but not limited to, the constructs of social preference, social impact, and friendship (see Ladd 2005). In this section we focus on the relations of empathy and sympathy with a sampling of group-level (i.e., social preference, popularity, and roles in bullying incidents) and dyad-level (i.e., friendship quality and quantity) peer variables. Of note, Benenson, Tricerri, and Hamerman (1999) found that the propensity to engage in these different levels of social organization (i.e., dyads versus groups) was not related to empathy.

Group-level variables are typically based on peer nominations or ratings. Sociometric status (e.g., being rejected or popular) is assessed as a function of nominations or ratings of a student being liked most or liked least. Social impact is operationalized as the sum of positive and negative nominations (i.e., liked most and liked least, respectively), whereas social preference is quantified as the sum of the negative nominations subtracted from the sum of the positive nominations (see Coie, Dodge, and Coppotelli 1982, 1983, for discussion of different sociometric statuses; and Lease, Musgrove, and Axelrod 2002, and Caravita, Di Blasio, and Salmivalli 2009, for the distinction between social status and perceived popularity).

Children's group-level peer relationships may also be examined in light of the roles they assume in bullying incidents. Bullying is a group process that involves bullies, their reinforcers, and their assistants; victims; defenders; and outsiders (i.e., those not involved, a passive bystander; see Salmivalli et al. 1996, for their delineation of participant roles). As a dyadic level variable, friendship typically is operationalized as the quantity or quality of children's affiliative ties with specific peers (Ladd 2005), sometimes only when reciprocated (i.e., when both peers name the other as a friend) and sometimes not.

Social Status and Peer Popularity

Data collected to date suggest that popularity (peer liking) is significantly associated with empathy. Children who are well liked have been found to have higher levels of empathy than those who are rejected by their peers (Deković and Gerris 1994). Moreover, children's sympathy has been positively related to ratings of liking by peers at an earlier age, as well as teachers' ratings of children's popularity with peers (Eisenberg et al. 1996; Murphy et al. 1999). Significant positive relations also have been found for adolescents' ratings of being liked, both for empathy (Lewis and Spilka 1960, although it is unclear if these authors assessed empathy or sympathy) and sympathy (Loban 1953). Studies in which ratings of being liked have been combined with social behavior have produced similar findings; for instance, sympathy was positively associated with positive sociometrics (i.e., being prosocial and being liked) and significantly negatively associated with negative sociometrics (i.e., fighting and being disliked) for ten- to thirteen-year-old Indonesian boys (but not girls) (Eisenberg, Liew, and Pidada 2004).

In contrast, some other investigators have found nonsignificant zero-order correlations between empathy and self- and peer-rated popularity (Coleman and Byrd 2003; Caravita, Di Blasio, and Salmivalli 2009, 2010).[1] The conflicting responses may be partly explained by gender and age. Caravita et al. (2009) and Adams (1983), for instance, found not only a significant correlation between gender and popularity but also different relations of empathy with measures of peer liking for males and females. Additionally, age was negatively associated with empathy in Caravita, Di Blasio, and Salmivalli (2009) and Schonert-Reichl (1993); the former authors also found that different relations held in middle childhood and early adolescence: some positive relations were found in late elementary school, whereas a negative relation was found for adolescent boys' ratings of perceived popularity. Of course, differing measures of peer status may also contribute to contradictory findings.

Friendship

In samples combining males and females, the number of best-friend nominations obtained for adolescents has not been significantly related to sympathy (Gleason, Jensen-Campbell, and Ickes 2009, using reciprocated nominations with an adolescent sample) or empathy (Coleman and Byrd 2003, using self-reported data with twelve- to fourteen-year-olds). Moreover, no significant association was found between empathy and the number of self-reported close friends (i.e., unreciprocated) in partial correlations controlling for age, in either adolescents with behavior problems or those without (Schonert-Reichl 1993). However, when relations were examined separately for males and females, Coleman and Byrd (2003) found a significant positive zero-order correlation between empathy and number of friends for males but a nonsignificant negative correlation for females.

In contrast to the findings for number of friends, sympathy has been positively associated with adolescents' evaluations of friendship quality (Barr and Higgins-D'Alessandro 2007, but only for males; Gleason et al. 2009). This relation has held across differing operationalizations of friendship quality (e.g., evaluations in terms of whether the relationship was positive, respectful, friendly, and helpful [Barr and Higgins-D'Alessandro 2007], or sharing secrets and private thoughts with that person, depending upon them for assistance and support, spending time with them, and having them advocate for the participant [Gleason, Jensen-Campbell, and Ickes 2009]). A substantial relation between empathy and friendship quality was also found by Schonert-Reichl (1993), even when taking into account age and socioeconomic status (SES), but only for adolescents without behavior problems. Moreover, Soenens et al. (2007) found a positive zero-order correlation between adolescents' self-reported sympathy and friendship quality, although this association was not significant when the relation between cognitive perspective taking and friendship quality was taken into account (sympathy and perspective taking were significantly related and apparently accounted for overlapping variance in friendship quality). In addition, security of peer attachment has been positively associated with sympathy (Laible, Carlo, and Raffaelli 2000; Laghi et al. 2009). Taken together, the findings suggest that sympathy generally is related to friendship quality, whereas the relation between empathy or sympathy and number of friends is weak at best. However, findings sometimes have varied depending on the sex or other characteristics (e.g., problem behavior) of the child.

Participant Roles in Bullying Incidents

Although much of the research examining the relations between empathy and participant roles has focused on bullying, only a small sample of this research is described herein. Of more relevance to this review, some investigators have also examined the relations of empathy or sympathy with other participant roles, including defending victims and being a victim. Defending peers from bullying can be considered a measure of social skills and, consequently, is of particular interest in this review. Empathy has been inversely related to being nominated as a bully by peers (Schultze-Krumbholz and Scheithauer 2009),[2] although only for males, but positively associated with defending victims (Caravita, Di Blasio, and Salmivalli 2009, 2010). Sympathy has likewise been negatively associated with being nominated as a bully by peers but positively associated with defending victims (Gini et al. 2007, 2008; see also Laible, Eye, and Carlo 2008, who combined sympathy with shame, guilt, and empathic anger). These significant correlations have also held for self-reported bullying and defending (Correia and Dalbert 2008; Raskauskas et al. 2010) even after controlling for gender (Correia and Dalbert 2008; see also Nickerson, Mele, and Princiotta 2008). Sympathy has also been positively correlated with being an outsider in the bullying situation (Gini et al. 2008; see also Laible, Eye, and Carlo 2008).

There are, however, some inconsistencies across studies. Some data suggest that bullying is not significantly related to lower levels of empathy (Woods et al. 2009; Caravita, Di Blasio, and Salmivalli 2009, 2010). Woods et al. (2007) found that all the bullies in their study reported sympathy for victims in vignettes. Warden and Mackinnon (2003) found that differences in empathy between children who bully and prosocial children were no longer significant when gender was added as a covariate. Woods et al. (2009) also found that, having controlled for gender, the differences in empathy among the participant roles of bully, victim, and uninvolved were not significant. The latter findings suggest that at least some of these inconsistent results may be due to differences in the treatment of gender as a variable.

Interactions with other variables may also play an important role. Caravita, Di Blasio, and Salmivalli (2010), for instance, found a marginally significant interaction between empathy and theory of mind when predicting boys' defending behavior. In follow-up analyses, the relation between theory of mind and boys' defending was not significant for boys low in empathy, whereas this relation was significant for boys with average and high empathy.

Being a victim of bullying can be considered an indicator of low social status, social competence, or both. Some investigators have found that empathy is not significantly related to self-reported victim status or teacher-rated victimization (Correia and Dalbert 2008; Coleman and Byrd 2003). Gleason, Jensen-Campbell, and Ickes (2009) similarly found that sympathy was not related to peer-reported overt or relational victim nominations. There are studies, however, in which significant relations were obtained, although the direction of the relations is not consistent. Raskauskas et al. (2010) found that children who reported being a victim were higher in empathy than their self-reported bully and bully-victim counterparts, although the zero-order correlation between amount of victimization and empathy was virtually zero. Schultze-Krumbholz and Scheithauer (2009), however, found that both cyberbullies and their victims had significantly lower empathy than those not involved in cyberbullying.

A host of variables may account for these conflicting results including gender, age, SES, and methodological differences. For example, Caravita, Di Blasio, and Salmivalli (2010) found a significant positive correlation between empathy and being a peer-nominated victim, although the relation held only for females and not for the sample when sexes were considered together. SES has been associated with sympathy (Malti, Perren, and Buchmann 2010, but it was not related to change in sympathy), albeit sometimes for only one sex (Loban 1953, only for males). However, Caravita, Di Blasio, and Salmivalli (2009) did not find evidence that SES was related to empathy or influenced the relations among the variables in structural equation models.

Data suggesting age is another relevant variable was provided in a longitudinal study conducted by Malti, Perren, and Buchmann (2010), who found that sympathy in kindergarten was neither related to peer victimization in kindergarten nor in the subsequent school year. Sympathy in first grade, however, was significantly negatively related to both peer victimization in first grade and the change in peer victimization from kindergarten to first grade. Moreover, an increase in sympathy between kindergarten and first grade was negatively related to victimization in first grade and was related to a decline in peer victimization from kindergarten to first grade.

Methodological choices, however, may also account for conflicting findings. In addition to the use of different measures of empathy and sympathy, the selection of contrast groups can also influence results. Raskauskas et al. (2010), for example, found that children who reported being uninvolved differed significantly in empathy from those who reported being a bully or reported being both a bully and a victim, but not those who were victims only. They further found that the empathy of bully-victim was more in line with that of bullies than of victims and uninvolved children. A possible explanation for the contrary findings of Schultze-Krumbholz and Scheithauer (2009), then, is the high degree of overlap between bully and victims in their sample.

Sociability and Shyness

Inhibition in the early years has been associated with low levels of empathy and associated prosocial behavior with strangers (Young, Fox, and Zahn-Waxler 1999; Liew et al. 2011). Although shyness and inhibition seem to undermine some types of prosocial behavior involving social contact (see Suda and Fouts 1980; Stanhope, Bell, and Parker-Cohen 1987), children who are shy may not suffer from deficits in empathy or sympathy. Rather, they may be easily overwhelmed by their vicarious emotion or inhibited in enacting helping behavior motivated by their sympathy or empathy. In contrast to research involving strangers, shy children may be sympathetic and helpful toward people they know. Volling (2001) found that preschoolers who were prone to social fear were relatively likely to provide caregiving to a younger sibling during a period in which the sibling was separated from their mother; perhaps they were especially prone to experience their sibling's distress or were not inhibited in interactions with the sibling.

There is relatively little research on the relation between dispositional sociability or shyness and empathy-related responding in childhood and adolescence. Eisenberg, Liew, and Pidada (2004) found that parents' and teachers' reports of Indonesian elementary school children's sympathy tended to be negatively related across time to their reports of the children's shyness, sometimes across reporters (although relations within time were not significant). Consistent with the notion that individuals prone to personal distress are not well regulated, Davis and Franzoi (1991) found that social anxiety was positively related to adolescents' dispositional personal distress but was unrelated to sympathy. In contrast, Carlo, Roesch, and Melby (1998) observed no zero-order correlation between self-reported sympathy and parents' reports of youths' sociability; adolescents' sympathy was predicted by the combination of high paternal support, low adolescent anger, and low adolescent sociability. A similar interaction effect was not obtained for maternal support. It is likely that sociability has at best a weak relation with sympathy, whereas social anxiety and shyness, which may reflect problems with emotion regulation, predict a proneness to empathic overarousal and low sympathy, at least in some social situations.

Conclusions

A review of the relevant literature indicates that individual differences in children's and adolescents' empathy-related responding are related to some aspects of socially competent responding beyond its relations with high prosocial behavior and low levels of aggression and externalizing problems. Children who are high in empathy, sympathy, or both tend to be socially appropriate and well liked by peers; moreover, they tend to have high-quality friendships and to defend peers from bullies. These associations sometimes vary, however, with the sex or age of the child and how empathy-related responding and social competence are assessed. Inconsistent associations were found between empathy-related responding and quantity of friends, children's sociability/shyness, and being victimized. Thus, although the quality of social interactions appears relevant to empathy-related responding, the number of best friends nominations does not.

Because the data are not experimental, it is impossible to assess causal relations. It is possible that sympathy and empathy affect the quality of social interactions and that children with higher-quality social interactions also have more opportunities to develop and experience sympathy and empathy. Moreover, Eisenberg and colleagues (Eisenberg and Fabes 1992; Eisenberg and Morris 2002; Eisenberg, Fabes, and Spinrad 2006) hypothesized that deficits in emotion-related self-regulation can undermine both sympathetic responding and socially competent social behavior, especially for children prone to experience negative emotions. From this perspective, a deficit in regulation also might produce problems in both the capacity to experience sympathy and in the quality of social behavior and relationships. Thus, an association between empathy-related responding and quality of social functioning could be due to multiple mechanisms and processes.

Too little attention has been paid to the role of development in the relation of empathy-related responding to social competence. Some initial evidence suggests that this association might increase with age (Zhou et al. 2002; Malti et al. 2010), which might be expected if the ability to sympathize improves with age (see Hoffman 2000; Eisenberg, Fabes, and Spinrad 2006). Moreover, it is important in future work to examine the ways that gender and SES affect this association. It may be difficult to obtain a highly consistent pattern of results when researchers use measures of empathy-related responding that likely reflect some combination of empathy, sympathy, personal distress, cognitive perspective-taking, and sometimes other skills. A more nuanced conceptualization of both empathy-related responding and social competence is likely to result in more consistent findings in regard to the relation between these two constructs. Finally, examination of the effects of experimental interventions designed to foster empathy or sympathy on various aspects of social competence (or the effects of training social skills on subsequent empathy/sympathy) is needed to test causal relations between the two constructs.

Acknowledgments

Writing of this chapter was supported by grants from the National Institute of Mental Health and the National Institute of Child Health and Development to the first author.

Notes

1. Some of the items on the measure of empathy might also be interpreted as a measure of sympathy; for example, "It makes me sad to see a lonely stranger" does not clearly distinguish between the speaker's feeling sad as a congruent feeling or feeling concern for the state of the other individual. This is the case for the measures of empathy utilized by Adams (1983), Correia and Dalbert (2008), Deković and Gerris (1994), Raskauskas et al. (2010), Schonert-Reichl (1993), Warden and Mackinnon (2003), and Woods et al. (2009). In deference to the authors' use of these measures, we have interpreted them as representing empathy. Many of these measures also include cognitive perspective-taking.

2. Insufficient information is available to assess whether this measure is best construed as empathy or sympathy under our rubric.

References

Adams, G. R. 1983. Social competence during adolescence: Social sensitivity, locus of control, empathy, and peer popularity. *Journal of Youth and Adolescence* 12: 203–211.

Barr, J. J., and A. Higgins-D'Alessandro. 2007. Adolescent empathy and prosocial behavior in the multidimensional context of school culture. *Journal of Genetic Psychology* 168: 231–250.

Batson, C. D. 1991. *The Altruism Question: Toward a Social-Psychological Answer*. Hillsdale, NJ: Lawrence Erlbaum Associates.

Benenson, J. F., M. Tricerri, and S. Hamerman. 1999. Characteristics of children who Interact in groups or in dyads. *Journal of Genetic Psychology* 160: 461–475.

Björkqvist, K., K. Österman, and A. Kaukiainen. 2000. Social Intelligence – Empathy = Aggression? *Aggression and Violent Behavior* 5: 191–200.

Caravita, S. C. S., P. Di Blasio, and C. Salmivalli. 2009. Unique and Interactive Effects of empathy and Social Status on involvement in bullying. *Social Development* 18: 140–163.

Caravita, S. C. S., P. Di Blasio, and C. Salmivalli. 2010. Early adolescents' participation in bullying: Is ToM involved? *Journal of Early Adolescence* 30: 138–170.

Carlo, G., S. C. Roesch, and J. Melby. 1998. The multiplicative relations of parenting and temperament to prosocial and antisocial behaviors in adolescence. *Journal of Early Adolescence* 18: 266–290.

Coie, J. D., K. A. Dodge, and H. Coppotelli. 1982. Dimensions and types of social status: A cross-age perspective. *Developmental Psychology* 18: 557–570.

Coie, J. D., K. A. Dodge, and H. Coppotelli. 1983. Dimensions and types of social status: A cross-age perspective [correction]. *Developmental Psychology* 19: 224.

Coleman, P. K., and C. P. Byrd. 2003. Interpersonal correlates of peer victimization among young adolescents. *Journal of Youth and Adolescence* 32: 301–314.

Correia, I., and C. Dalbert. 2008. School bullying: Belief in a personal just world of bullies, victims, and defenders. *European Psychologist* 13: 248–254.

Davis, M. H. (1994). *Empathy: A Social Psychological Approach*. Madison, WI: Brown & Benchmark.

Davis, M. H., and S. L. Franzoi. 1991. Stability and change in adolescent self-consciousness. *Journal of Research in Personality* 25: 70–87.

Deković, M., and J. R. M. Gerris. 1994. Developmental analysis of social cognitive and behavioral differences between popular and rejected children. *Journal of Applied Developmental Psychology* 15: 367–386.

Dovidio, J. F., J. A. Piliavin, D. A. Schroeder, and L. Penner. 2006. *The Social Psychology of Prosocial Behavior*. Mahwah, NJ: Lawrence Erlbaum Associates.

Eisenberg, N., N. D. Eggum, and L. Di Giunta. 2010. Empathy-related responding: Associations with prosocial behavior, aggression, and intergroup relations. *Social Issues and Policy Review* 4 (1): 143–80.

Eisenberg, N., and R. A. Fabes. 1992. Emotion, regulation, and the development of social competence. In *Emotion and Social Behavior: Vol. 14. Review of Personality and Social Psychology*, edited by M. S. Clark, 119–150. Newbury Park, CA: Sage.

Eisenberg, N., and R. A. Fabes. 1995. The relation of young children's vicarious emotional responding to social competence, regulation, and emotionality. *Cognition and Emotion* 9: 203–228.

Eisenberg, N., R. A. Fabes, B. Murphy, M. Karbon, M. Smith, and P. Maszk. 1996. The relations of children's dispositional empathy-related responding to their emotionality, regulation and social functioning. *Developmental Psychology* 32: 195–209.

Eisenberg, N., R. A. Fabes, and T. L. Spinrad. 2006. Prosocial development. In *Handbook of Child Psychology: Vol. 3. Social, Emotional, and Personality Development*, edited by N. Eisenberg (Vol. Ed.) and W. Damon and R. M. Lerner (Series Eds.), 6th ed, 646–718. New York: Wiley.

Eisenberg, N., J. Liew, and S. U. Pidada. 2004. The longitudinal relations of regulation and emotionality to quality of Indonesian children's socioemotional functioning. *Developmental Psychology* 40: 790–804.

Eisenberg, N., and P. A. Miller. 1987. The relation of empathy to prosocial and related behaviors. *Psychological Bulletin* 101: 91–119.

Eisenberg, N., and A. S. Morris. 2002. Children's emotion-related regulation. In *Advances in Child Development and Behavior*, vol. 30, edited by R. Kail, 190–229. Amsterdam: Academic Press.

Eisenberg, N., C. L. Shea, G. Carlo, and G. Knight. 1991. Empathy-related responding and cognition: A "chicken and the egg" dilemma. In *Handbook of Moral Behavior and Development: Vol. 2. Research*, edited by W. Kurtines and J. Gewirtz, 63–88. Hillsdale, NJ: Lawrence Erlbaum Associates.

Feshbach, N. D. 1978. Studies of empathic behavior in children. In *Progress in Experimental Personality Research*, Vol. 8, edited by B. A. Maher, 1–47. New York: Academic Press.

Gini, G., P. Albiero, B. Benelli, and G. Altoè. 2007. Does empathy predict adolescents' bullying and defending behavior? *Aggressive Behavior* 33: 467–476.

Gini, G., P. Albiero, B. Benelli, and G. Altoè. 2008. Determinants of adolescents' active defending and passive bystanding behavior in bullying. *Journal of Adolescence* 31: 93–105.

Gleason, K. A., L. A. Jensen-Campbell, and W. Ickes. 2009. The role of empathic accuracy in adolescents' peer relations and adjustment. *Personality and Social Psychology Bulletin* 35: 997–1011.

Hoffman, M. L. 2000. *Empathy and Moral Development: Implications for Caring and Justice*. New York: Cambridge University Press.

Ladd, G. W. 2005. *Children's Peer Relations and Social Competence: A Century of Progress*. New Haven: Yale University Press.

Laghi, F., M. D'Alessio, S. Pallini, and R. Baiocco. 2009. Attachment representations and time perspective in adolescence. *Social Indicators Research* 90: 181–194.

Laible, D. J., and G. Carlo. 2004. The differential relations of maternal and paternal support and control to adolescent social competence, self-worth and sympathy. *Journal of Adolescent Research* 19: 759–782.

Laible, D. J., G. Carlo, and M. Raffaelli. 2000. The differential relations of parent and peer attachment to adolescent adjustment. *Journal of Youth and Adolescence* 29: 45–59.

Laible, D., J. Eye, and G. Carlo. 2008. Dimensions of conscience in mid-adolescence: Links with Social behavior, parenting, and temperament. *Journal of Youth and Adolescence* 37: 875–887.

Lease, A. M., K. T. Musgrove, and J. L. Axelrod. 2002. Dimensions of social status in preadolescent peer groups: Likability, perceived popularity, and social dominance. *Social Development* 11: 508–533.

Lewis, M. N., and B. Spilka. 1960. Sociometric choice status, empathy, assimilative and disowning projection. *Psychological Record* 10: 95–100. Retrieved from www.csa.com.

Liew, J., N. Eisenberg, S. H. Losoya, R. A. Fabes, I. K. Guthrie, and B. C. Murphy. 2003. Children's physiological indices of empathy and their socioemotional adjustment: Does caregivers' expressivity matter? *Journal of Family Psychology* 17: 584–597.

Liew, J., N. Eisenberg, T. L. Spinrad, N. D. Eggum, R. Haugen, A. Kupfer, M. R. Reiser, C. L. Smith, K. Lemery-Chalfant, and M. E. Baham. 2011. Physiological regulation and fearfulness as predictors of young children's empathy-related reactions. *Social Development* 20: 111–134.

Loban, W. 1953. A study of social sensitivity (sympathy) among adolescents. *Journal of Educational Psychology* 44: 102–112.

Malti, T., S. Perren, and M. Buchmann. 2010. Children's peer victimization, empathy, and emotional symptoms. *Child Psychiatry and Human Development* 41: 98–113.

Mehrabian, A., and N. A. Epstein. 1972. A measure of emotional empathy. *Journal of Personality* 40: 523–543.

Miller, P., and N. Eisenberg. 1988. The relation of empathy to aggressive and externalizing/antisocial behavior. *Psychological Bulletin* 103: 324–344.

Murphy, B. C., S. A. Shepard, N. Eisenberg, R. A. Fabes, and I. K. Guthrie. 1999. Contemporaneous and longitudinal relations of dispositional sympathy to emotionality, regulation, and social functioning. *Journal of Early Adolescence* 19: 66–97.

Nickerson, A. B., D. Mele, and D. Princiotta. 2008. Attachment and empathy as predictors of roles as defenders or outsiders in bullying interactions. *Journal of School Psychology* 46: 687–703.

Raskauskas, J. L., J. Gregory, S. T. Harvey, F. Rifshana, and I. M. Evans. 2010. Bullying among primary school children in New Zealand: Relationships with prosocial behaviour and classroom climate. *Educational Research* 52: 1–13.

Rothbart, M. K., and J. E. Bates. 2006. Temperament. In *Handbook of Child Psychology: Vol. 3. Social, Emotional, and Personality Development*, edited by N. Eisenberg (Vol. Ed.) and W. Damon and R. M. Lerner (Series Eds.), 6th ed., 99–166. New York: Wiley.

Rubin, K. H., W. M. Bukowksi, and J. G. Parker. 2006. Peer interactions, relationships, and groups. In *Handbook of Child Psychology: Vol. 3. Social, Emotional, and Personality Development*, edited by N. Eisenberg (Vol. Ed.) and W. Damon and R. M. Lerner (Series Eds.), 6th ed., 571–645. New York: Wiley.

Sallquist, J., N. Eisenberg, T. L. Spinrad, N. D. Eggum, and B. M. Gaertner. 2009. Assessment of preschoolers' positive empathy: concurrent and longitudinal relations with positive emotion, social competence, and sympathy. *Journal of Positive Psychology* 4: 223–233.

Salmivalli, C., K. Lagerspetz, K. Björkqvist, and K. Österman. 1996. Bullying as a group process: Participant roles and their relations to social status within the group. *Aggressive Behavior* 22: 1–15.

Schonert-Reichl, K. A. 1993. Empathy and social relationships in adolescents with behavioral disorders. *Behavioral Disorders* 18: 189–204. Retrieved from www.csa.com.

Schultze-Krumbholz, A., and H. Scheithauer. 2009. Social-behavioral correlates of cyberbullying in a German student sample. *Zeitschrift für Psychologie—Journal of Psychology* 217 (4): 224–226.

Soenens, B., B. Duriez, M. Vansteenkiste, and L. Goossens. 2007. The intergenerational transmission of empathy-related responding in adolescence: The role of maternal support. *Personality and Social Psychology Bulletin* 33 (3): 299–311.

Stanhope, L., R. Q. Bell, and N. Y. Parker-Cohen. 1987. Temperament and helping behavior in preschool children. *Developmental Psychology* 23: 347–353.

Suda, W., and G. Fouts. 1980. Effects of peer presence on helping in introverted and extroverted children. *Child Development* 51: 1272–1275.

Volling, B. L. 2001. Early attachment relationships as predictors of preschool children's emotion regulation with a distressed sibling. *Early Education and Development* 12: 185–207.

Warden, D., and S. Mackinnon. 2003. Prosocial children, bullies and victims: An investigation of their sociometric status, empathy and social problem-solving strategies. *British Journal of Developmental Psychology* 21: 367–385.

Woods, S., L. Hall, K. Dautenhahn, and D. Wolke. 2007. Implications of gender differences for the development of animated characters for the study of bullying behavior. *Computers in Human Behavior* 23: 770–786.

Woods, S., D. Wolke, S. Nowicki, and L. Hall. 2009. emotion recognition abilities and empathy of victims of bullying. *Child Abuse & Neglect* 33: 307–311.

Young, S., N. A. Fox, and C. Zahn-Waxler. 1999. The relations between temperament and empathy in 2-year-olds. *Developmental Psychology* 35: 1189–1197.

Zhou, Q., N. Eisenberg, S. H. Losoya, R. A. Fabes, M. Reiser, I. K. Guthrie, B. C. Murphy, A. J. Cumberland, and S. A. Shepard. 2002. The relations of parental warmth and positive expressiveness to children's empathy-related responding and social functioning: A longitudinal study. *Child Development* 73: 893–915.

V The Neuroscience of Empathy and Caring

10 How Children Develop Empathy: The Contribution of Developmental Affective Neuroscience

Jean Decety and Kalina J. Michalska

Empathy, the natural ability to share, understand and respond to the affective states of another in relation to oneself, plays a critical role in social interactions (Batson, 2011). Understanding the feelings of others forms a central core of moral sensitivity. Very young children attempt to alleviate the distress of others and show concern about other individuals being worried well before they are able to articulate their understanding verbally (Dunn 2006; Zahn-Waxler, Radke-Yarrow, Wagner, and Chapman, 1992). Moreover, lack of empathy and concern for the well-being of others is considered a serious risk factor for the development of hostile, aggressive, or even antisocial behavior in children.

Although the study of empathy has a long history in developmental psychology, the past decade has seen an explosion of research on the neurophysiological underpinnings of emotion processing in general and empathy specifically. More recently, however, research has also begun to address the neurodevelopmental changes in the circuits mediating the experience of empathy.

The goals of this chapter are to provide a comprehensive analysis of the neurological mechanisms underlying empathy and concern for others as well as to demonstrate how developmental research and neuroscience can mutually benefit from one another. We begin by briefly discussing the evolutionary roots of empathy that humans share with other mammals. Then, we argue that the construct of empathy needs to be "broken down" into a model that includes bottom-up processing of affective communication and top-down reappraisal processing in which the perceiver's motivations, intentions, and attitudes influence the extent of an empathic experience. We then discuss each of the components (affective sharing, emotion understanding, and self-regulation) separately. Because behavioral responses to signals of distress and pain are crucial to the survival and well-being of offspring, a section is devoted to the neural circuits implicated in the perception of others' pain. We conclude by discussing the relevance of applying a neurodevelopmental approach to translational research about children who exhibit antisocial behavior.

Evolutionary Roots of Empathy and Concern

Empathy is not unique to humans, and many of the physiological mechanisms underlying its expression are shared with other nonhuman primates. In mammals, empathic concern and helping behavior has evolved from a set of mechanisms that promotes parental care of offspring and not just or only from shared experience with or perceived similarity to a person in need (Decety 2011ab). Females must understand the emotions and needs of their offspring and respond appropriately to ensure their survival (Panksepp 1998). This mechanism has been extended beyond the mother-child bond, especially in social animals, where the ability to understand and respond with care to the affective state of another conspecific is crucial for successful navigation in the social arena, and for group survival too. The thalamocingulate division of the forebrain is believed to have evolved in parallel with social behaviors related to the perception of emotional information involved in securing emotional bonding and social interactions (MacLean 1987). Some directed parental behavior is promoted by built-in rewards such as the oxytocin and dopamine release during suckling associated with maternal care (Panksepp 1998). Empathy-based altruism may have similar intrinsically rewarding qualities in that it offers the individual an emotional stake in the recipient's well being, that is, helping the other ameliorates the helper's internal state. In fact the autonomic and endocrine reactions that accompany empathy in humans derive from neural and hormonal systems mainly involving subcortical pathways, well developed in social mammals (Carter, Harris, and Porges 2009), drawing on the evolutionary history of empathic concern. Considerable overlap exists in these phylogenetically conserved neural circuits that support social behavior and physiological homeostasis, two adaptive traits that are equally critical to survival. Once evolved, behavior often assumes motivational autonomy. Its motivation becomes disconnected from its ultimate goals (de Waal 2008). Once the empathic capacity evolved, it could be applied outside the parental-care context. For example, when people send money to distant victims in Haiti or when a gorilla rescues a child, empathy reaches beyond its context of evolutionary origins.

Moreover, empathy should not be seen as an all-or-nothing phenomenon—many forms of empathy exist between the extremes of mere agitation at another's distress and full understanding of another's predicament (de Waal 2008). For instance, there is evidence that chimpanzees act prosocially toward genetically unrelated conspecifics. Research has also indeed shown that both chimpanzees and human infants help altruistically, regardless of any expectation of reward, even when effort is required and when the recipient is an unfamiliar individual, all features previously thought to be unique to humans (Warneken et al. 2007). The evolutionary roots of human altruism go deeper than previously thought.

Humans, however, are unique in the sense that high levels of cognitive abilities subserved by the prefrontal cortex (PFC): executive functions (working memory, inhibitory control), language, and theory of mind are layered on top of phylogenetically older social and emotional capacities. These evolutionary newer aspects of information processing expand the range of behaviors that can be driven by empathy (such as caring for and helping out group members or even individuals from different species, or donating to charity) within cultural environments.

Mapping Empathy onto Neural Circuits

Empathy is not just one thing. Global psychological constructs, however sound, do not always correspond to specific brain mechanisms. The constructs developed by behavioral and social scientists, such as empathy and prosocial behavior, provide a useful means of understanding highly complex activity without a need to specify each individual action by its simplest components and thereby provide a cognitively efficient way of referring to components of complex systems (Decety and Cacioppo 2010). On the other hand there is no one-on-one relation between psychological constructs and brain processes. Given the complexity of what encompasses the construct of empathy, investigation of its neurobiological underpinnings would be worthless without breaking down this construct into component processes. In reality, empathy, like other social cognitive processes, draws on a large array of brain structures and systems that are not limited to the cortex but also include subcortical pathways, the brainstem, the regulation of the autonomic nervous system and hypothalamic-pituitary-adrenal axis (HPA), as well as endocrine systems that regulate bodily states, emotion, and reactivity (Carter, Harris, and Porges 2009). Moreover empathic concern has multiple antecedents within and across levels of organization. A comprehensive neuroscience theory of empathy requires the specification of various causal mechanisms producing some outcome variable (e.g., helping behavior), moderator variables (e.g., implicit attitudes, in group/out group processes) that influence the conditions under which each of these mechanisms operate, and the unique consequences resulting from each of them.

Further, studying subcomponents of more complex psychological constructs like empathy can be particularly useful from a developmental perspective when only some of its components or precursors may be observable. Developmental studies can provide unique opportunities to see how the components of the system interact in ways that are not possible in adults where all the components are fully mature and operational (De Haan and Gunnar 2009).

Based on theory and evidence from cognitive neuroscience and developmental psychology, Decety and collaborators (Decety and Jackson 2004; Decety 2007; Decety and Meyer 2008; Decety 2011) proposed a model of empathy that includes bottom-up processing of affective sharing and top-down processing in which the perceiver's motivation, intentions, and attitudes influence the extent of an empathic experience and the likelihood of prosocial behavior. Under that working model a number of distinct and interacting components contribute to the experience of empathy: (1) affective sharing, a bottom-up process grounded in affective arousal mediated by the brainstem, amygdala and orbitofrontal cortex (OFC) with reciprocal connections to the superior temporal sulcus (STS), which underlie rapid and prioritized processing of emotion signals; (2) understanding the emotions of self and other, which relies on self- and other-awareness, and involves the medial prefrontal cortex (mPFC) and temporoparietal junction (TPJ); and (3) executive functions instantiated in the PFC that operate as a top-down mediator, helping to regulate emotions and yield mental flexibility. Consequently, this model assumes and predicts that dysfunction in either of these components may lead to an alteration in the experience of empathy and may correspond to selective social cognitive disorders depending on which aspect is disrupted (Blair 2005; Decety and Moriguchi 2007). Although we emphasize the role of neurobiology in empathy, we recognize that this does not imply immutability. Empathic dispositions are shaped by complex reciprocal interactions with the social environment over the course of development. It is, therefore, important to keep in mind that both interpersonal as well as contextual factors impact a person's subjective experience of empathy. In addition, it is essential to consider empathy within a developmental framework that recognizes both the changes and the continuities in social understanding from infancy to adulthood.

Affective neuroscience research with children and adult participants indicates that the affective, cognitive, and regulatory aspects of empathy involve interacting, yet partially nonoverlapping neural circuits. Furthermore there is now evidence for age-related changes in these neural circuits, which together with behavioral measurements reflect how brain maturation influences the experience of empathy and concern for others (Decety and Michalska 2010).

The Neurodevelopment of Empathy

It is usually considered that empathy typically emerges as the child comes to a greater awareness of the experience of others, during the second year of life, and arises in the context of a social interaction. Although reflective awareness of one's and other's emotion is a key characteristic of the experience of human empathy, more implicit and intuitive aspects of empathy are available to infants. For the sake of clarity each of the components of empathy (affective arousal, emotion understanding, and emotion regulation) are considered separately from both developmental and neuroscience perspectives. In reality these components are functionally intertwined and interact in complex ways with social contexts.

Affective Arousal

The basis for human interaction and for understanding others is laid down by certain embodied practices that are emotional, sensory-motor, perceptual, and nonconceptual. Prior to the onset of language the primary means by which infants can communicate with others in their environment, including caregivers, is by reading faces and listening to their voices (Leppanen and Nelson 2009). Thus it is important for an infant not only to discriminate familiar from unfamiliar individuals but also to derive information about the individual's feelings and intentions: for example, whether the caregiver is pleased or displeased, afraid or angry (Ludemann and Nelson 1988). Affective arousal can be considered to be the first component of empathy taking place in development. This component refers to the automatic discrimination of a stimulus— or features of a stimulus—as appetitive or aversive, pleasant or unpleasant, threatening or nurturing, which has evolved to differentiate hostile from hospitable stimuli and to organize adaptive responses to these stimuli. Strong bidirectional connections between the amygdala and sensory cortices associated with complex processing of stimuli with emotional significance, as well as connections with the hypothalamus, hippocampus and OFC (Ghashghaei and Barbas 2002) are the fundamental neural underpinnings of affective arousal. The amygdala plays a critical role in extracting the affective significance of sensory stimuli and, with its reciprocal connections with the OFC and STS, mediates the formation of emotional memories (Hoistad and Barbas 2008). Electrophysiological recordings in human patients show that these three regions belong to a temporally linked triangular network implicated in the rapid and prioritized processing of emotion signals, especially when attention is engaged (Krolak-Salmon et al. 2004).

Affective responsiveness is present at an early age, is involuntary, and relies on somato-sensorimotor resonance between other and self (Decety and Meyer 2008). For instance, newborns and infants become vigorously distressed shortly after another infant begins to cry (Martin and Clark 1987; Dondi, Simion, and Caltran 1999). Discrete facial expressions of emotion have been identified in newborns, including joy, interest, disgust, and distress (Izard 1982). These findings suggest that subcomponents of emotional experience and expression are present at birth and support the possibility that these processes are hard-wired in the brain. Very young infants are able to send emotional signals and to receive and detect the emotional signals sent by others. Very early after birth newborns are capable of imitating expressions of fear, sadness, and surprise (Field et al. 1982; Haviland and Lewica 1987), preparing them for future empathic connections through affective interaction with others.

This motor resonance may be partly based on mirror neurons (sensorimotor neurons in the premotor, motor, and parietal cortex that code the goal of actions), which from electroencephalographic (EEG) studies seem to be already functioning in infants as young as six months (Nystrom 2008; but see Cheng, Hung, and Decety, 2011). Whereas the contribution of mirror neurons to emotion perception is not clearly demonstrated (Blair and Fowler 2008; Decety 2010), research using measures of facial electromyography (EMG) demonstrates that viewing facial expressions triggers distinctive patterns of facial muscle activity similar to the observed expression, even in the absence of conscious recognition of the stimulus (Dimberg, Thunberg, and Elmehed 2000). In one such study participants were shown very briefly (56 ms) pictures of happy or angry facial expressions while EMG was recorded from their faces (Sonnby-Borgstrom, Jonsson, and Svensson 2003). Results demonstrated facial mimicry despite the fact that participants were unaware of the stimuli. A study conducted with school-age boys demonstrated that angry and happy facial stimuli spontaneously elicit different EMG response patterns (de Wied et al. 2006). Angry faces evoked a stronger increase in corrugator activity than happy faces, whereas happy faces evoked a stronger increase in zygomaticus activity than angry faces. One study examined the relation between facial mimicry (measured by facial EMG) and self-reported mood on exposure to static facial expressions of anger and happiness in participants who were categorized as either high or low empathizers. Researchers found that the high-empathy participants produced greater facial mimicry than the low-empathy participants (Sonnby-Borgstrom, Jonsson, and Svensson 2003). Another study, however, did not find any relation between emotion recognition performance and participants' tendency to mimic dynamic displays of emotions (Hess and Blairy 2001). Selective facial EMG responses were detected in participants presented with movie clips of morphed (nonnatural) expressions of happy and angry facial expression, but no correlation between the intensity of facial mimicry and dispositional empathy level was observed (Achaibou et al. 2008). This automatic affective resonance between other and self provides the basic mechanism from which intersubjective feelings develop. Infant arousal in response to the affects and emotions signaled by others can serve as an instrument for social learning, reinforcing the significance of the social exchange, which then becomes associated with the infant's own emotional experience.

Together, these findings indicate that, very early on, infants are able to perceive another's affective state. Infant arousal in response to the affects signaled by others can serve as an instrument for social learning, reinforcing the significance of the social exchange, which then becomes associated with the infant's own emotional experience. Consequently, infants come to experience emotions as shared states and learn to differentiate their own states partly by witnessing the resonant responses that they elicit in others (Nielsen 2002). The extent to which this mechanism relies on mirror neurons is, despite the enthusiasm, still a matter of debate (Blair, 2011; Decety, 2010). Emotion contagion may instead engage very evolutionary ancient circuits in the brainstem, basal ganglia, and thalamus (Watt 2007).

Emotion Understanding

It is clear that from very early on in development infants are capable of emotional resonance, which is one important precursor of empathy (Hoffman 2000). Whereas the capacity for two people to emotionally resonate with each other prior to any cognitive understanding provides a basis for developing shared emotional meanings, it is not enough for the development of empathic understanding. Despite shared affect, one individual may have no sense of what the other is crying or laughing about. Resonance does not generate the shared content. Such an understanding requires forming an explicit representation of the feelings of another person as an intentional agent, which necessitates additional computational mechanisms beyond the emotion-sharing level.

Emotion understanding refers to conscious knowledge about emotion processes or beliefs about how emotions work. Such understanding includes the recognition of emotion expression and knowledge of one's own and others' emotions, the detection of cues for others' feelings, as well as ways of intentionally using emotion expression to communicate with others (or vice versa, e.g., hiding emotions). As cognitive development becomes more advanced, young children become increasingly aware of their own and others' emotions. As a result children begin to develop a more complex understanding of the causes and consequences of emotions, how to control emotions, and the nature of emotional experiences. The cognitive components underpinning emotion understanding have a more protracted course of development than the affective component of empathy and are related to processes involved in mentalizing, the ability to explain and predict behavior by attributing mental states such as desires, intentions, beliefs, and emotions to oneself and others (Astington and Hughes 2011), and executive function. This is not to say that emotion understanding and mind reading totally overlap. Interestingly there are individual differences in mind-reading tasks that differ from those of early success on emotion-understanding tasks. Early skills at understanding emotions have been reported to be associated with later peer popularity, sophisticated understandings of feelings, and aspects of moral sensibility. In contrast, early mind-reading skills have been found to be related to a high degree of connected communication with peers, and to frequent role play (Dunn 2000).

A number of studies have shown that the reliable ability to recognize facial expressions across variations in identity or intensity is not present until the age of five to seven months (Haviland and Lewica 1987). Some questions remain as to whether these early reactions represent recognition of emotion in another, or simple mimicry, but by two years of age most children are using emotion labels for facial expressions and are talking about emotion topics (Gross and Ballif 1991). Recent work has documented that even very young children (eighteen to twenty-five months) can sympathize with a victim even in the absence of overt emotion cues (Vaish, Carpenter, and Tomasello

2009) suggesting that some early form of affective perspective-taking that does not rely on emotion contagion or mimicry is present at a young age. Regarding the causes and effects of emotion and the cues used in inferring emotion, developmental research has detailed a progression from situation-bound, behavioral explanations of emotion to broader, more mentalistic understandings (Harris, Olthof, and Meerum-Terwogt 1981). As children develop, their emotional inferences contain a more complex and differentiated use of several types of information, such as relational and contextual factors and the target child's goals or beliefs (Harris 1994). This development appears to be somewhat slower for complex social emotions like pride, shame, or embarrassment. Development of this understanding proceeds from lack of acknowledgment of multiple emotions in younger children to acknowledgment of different variables such as emotion valence and emotion intensity in older children (Carroll and Steward 1984).

The development of empathy is influenced by cognitive development and particularly the increasing ability to differentiate self and other and to adopt another's perspective. This latter aspect of empathy is closely related to processes involved in mentalizing and executive function such as inhibitory control and working memory. There is growing evidence supporting that executive function and mentalizing are fundamentally linked in development and that their relation is stable throughout the lifespan (Carlson, Mandell, and Williams 2004). Several studies have shown that, by around four years of age, children can understand that the emotion a person feels about a given event depends on that person's perception of the event and his or her beliefs and desires about it. For instance, a longitudinal study with children aged forty-seven to sixty months examined developmental changes in understanding false belief, emotion, and mental-state conversation with friends (Hughes and Dunn 1998). The investigators found that individual differences in understanding of both false-belief and emotion were stable over this time period and were significantly related to each other. Understanding that appraisal can modulate a person's emotional experience to a given situation is initially based on a recognition of desires and gradually incorporates inferences about beliefs. At first, two- and three-year-old children understand the role that desires or goals play in determining a person's appraisal and ensuing emotion (Repacholi and Gopnik 1997). By eighteen months infants can not only infer that another person can hold a desire that may be different from their own, but they can also recognize how desires are related to emotions and understand something about the subjectivity of these desires. By four and five years of age this desire-based concept of emotion develops to include beliefs and expectations. Children at this age begin to understand that an emotion is not necessarily triggered by whether or not a desire and an outcome match but rather whether a desire and an *expected* outcome match. Emotion recognition continues to develop into later adolescence (Tonks et al. 2007), and this improves social cognition as well.

Mentalizing is layered on top of affective processes, and its development depends on the forging of connections between brain circuits for domain-general cognition and circuits specialized for aspects of social understanding. Functional neuroimaging studies have identified a circumscribed neural network reliably associated with the understanding of mental states that links the mPFC, posterior STS at the junction of the parietal cortex (TPJ), and temporal poles (e.g., Brunet et al. 2000).

Frontal activation is particularly important for successful mentalizing (Liu et al. 2009). Preschoolers who consistently pass false belief tasks show a distinctly different pattern of event-related potential (ERP) activity in frontal regions compared to preschoolers who consistently fail these same tasks. Prefrontal regions were activated in children aged six to eleven years while they listened to sections of a story describing a character's thoughts compared to sections of the same story that described the physical context (Saxe et al. 2009). Furthermore, change in response selectivity with age was observed in the right TPJ, which was recruited equally for mental and physical facts about people in younger children but only for mental facts in older children. Results from a study with four-year-old children showed that individual differences in EEG alpha activity localized to the dorsal mPFC and the right TPJ were positively associated with children's mentalizing performance, which suggests that the maturation of dorsal mPFC and right TPJ is a critical constituent of preschoolers' explicit mentalizing development (Sabbagh et al. 2009). Support for age-related changes in brain activity associated with meta-cognition is also provided by a functional MRI investigation of mental state understanding in participants whose ages ranged between nine and sixteen years (Moriguchi et al. 2007). Both children and adolescents demonstrated significant activation in the neural circuits associated with mentalizing tasks, including the TPJ, the temporal poles, and mPFC. Furthermore, the authors found a positive correlation between age and the degree of activation in the dorsal part of the mPFC. Direct evidence for the implication of these regions in accurate identification of interpersonal emotional states was recently documented in a study in which adult participants were requested to rate how they believe target persons felt while talking about autobiographical emotional events (Zaki et al. 2009).

In sum, behavioral and neuroscience research indicate that some of the computational processes implicated in emotion understanding partly overlap with those involved in mentalizing and perspective-taking. Neural circuits underlying the relation between mental and emotional state understanding in relation to oneself include the mPFC, vmPFC and right posterior STS/TPJ. In addition these regions continue to undergo maturation until late adolescence and early adulthood.

Emotion Regulation

The regulation of emotion is the ability to respond to the ongoing demands of experience with a range of emotions in a manner that is socially tolerable and sufficiently flexible to permit or delay spontaneous reactions as needed (Fox 1994). Difficulty inhibiting or reducing an emotional response and excessive attention toward negative emotional information may deplete the resources available for other aspects of self-regulation.

Emotion regulation in infants and children is recognized as an interpersonal process. Developmental changes in emotion regulation are demonstrated as the infant progresses from almost total dependence on parental caregivers to more independent self-regulation of emotions. It is important to note that this individualistic view is challenged in that children are progressively exposed to a broader social circle during adolescence and adulthood (Rime 2009).

Early emotion regulation is influenced mainly by innate physiological mechanisms, and around three months of age some voluntary control of arousal is evident. More purposeful control is evident by twelve months when motor skills and communication behaviors develop (Bell and Wolfe 2007). Empathic concern is strongly related to effortful control with children high in effortful control showing greater empathic concern (Rothbart, Ahadi, and Hershey 1994) as indicated by a number of developmental studies that reported that individual differences in the tendency to experience concern versus personal distress vary as a function of dispositional differences in individuals' abilities to regulate their emotions. Well-regulated children who have control over their ability to focus and shift attention have been found to be relatively prone to sympathy regardless of their emotional reactivity. This is because they can modulate their negative vicarious emotion to maintain an optimal level of emotional arousal. In contrast, children who are unable to regulate their emotions, especially if they are by disposition prone to intense negative emotions, are found to be low in dispositional sympathy and prone to personal distress (Eisenberg and Eggum 2009).

Interestingly, the development of emotion regulation is functionally linked to the development of executive functions and meta-cognition. Indeed, improvement in inhibitory control parallels the improvement of meta-cognitive capacities (Zelazo, Craik, and Booth 2004) as well as the maturation of brain regions that underlie working memory and inhibitory control (Tamm, Menon, and Reiss 2002). The regions of the PFC that are most consistently involved in emotion regulation include the ventral and dorsal aspects of the PFC, as well as the dorsal anterior cingulate cortex (dACC) (Ochsner et al. 2002). Importantly, ventromedial areas of the PFC develop relatively early and are especially involved in the control of emotional behaviors, whereas lateral prefrontal cortical regions develop relatively late, and are principally involved in higher executive functions (Philips, Ladouceur, and Drevets 2008). The PFC and its functions follow an extremely protracted developmental course, and age-related changes continue well into adolescence (Casey et al. 2005). Frontal lobe maturation is associated with an increase in children's ability to activate areas involved in emotional control and exercise inhibitory control over their thoughts, attention, and actions. The maturation of the PFC also allows children to use verbalizations to achieve self-regulation of their feelings (Diamond 2002). It is therefore likely that different parts of the brain may be differentially involved in empathy at different ages. For example, Killgore and Yurgelun-Todd (2007) provided evidence that, as a child matures into adolescence, there is a shift in response to emotional events from using more limbic-related anatomic structures, such as the amygdala, to using more frontal-lobe regions to control emotional responses. Thus, not only may there be less neural activity related to the regulation of cognition and emotion in younger individuals, but the neural pattern itself is likely to differ.

Developmental studies suggest that while young children, like adults, recruit cortical mechanisms of emotion regulation, tapped by ERPs associated with effortful control and information processing, they also undergo some important age-related changes (Lewis et al. 2006). In one study with children five to sixteen years of age, two ERP components associated with inhibitory control, the frontal N2 and frontal P3, were recorded before, during, and after a negative emotion induction when engaged in a simple go/no-go procedure in which points for successful performance earned a valued prize. The temporary loss of all points triggered negative emotions, as confirmed by self-report scales. Both the frontal N2 and frontal P3 decreased in amplitude and latency with age consistent with the hypothesis of increasing cortical efficiency. Amplitudes were only greater in the N2 following the emotion induction for adolescents, but they were greater across the age span for the frontal P3. These findings suggest that there are different, but overlapping, profiles of emotion-related control mechanisms. No-go N2 amplitudes were greater than go N2 amplitudes following the emotion induction at all ages, suggesting a consistent effect of negative emotion on mechanisms of response inhibition. No-go P3 amplitudes were greater than go P3 amplitudes, and they decreased with age, whereas go P3 amplitudes remained low. Finally, source modeling indicated a developmental decline in central-posterior midline activity paralleled by increasing activity in the ACC.

Measures of heart rate variability (HRV) and its variations of respiratory sinus arrhythmia and vagal tone have been linked to emotional reactivity and regulation (Bell and Wolfe 2007). Infants with higher HRV are more emotionally expressive and reactive, and this reactivity produces distress and irritability (Calkins and Fox 2002). As regulatory abilities develop, due to executive functions, the reactivity can lead to concentration when interest is paramount or to more expressive reactivity when other situations take precedent. The HPA axis strongly affects how we react to stressors by increasing sympathetic arousal via the release of stress hormones such as cortisol in humans. Interestingly, the effects of the HPA axis are rather slow and tonic, sometimes persisting over extended periods—acting via changes in gene expression both in the body and in the brain. This is in contrast to the second system involved in stress responses, the sympathetic-adrenomedullary system, which triggers fast mobilization of vital resources by the release of adrenaline and noradrenaline (Tarullo and Gunnar 2006).

To sum up, regulating emotions is crucial in maintaining a connection with ongoing perceptual processes, having access to a greater number of adaptive responses, and enhancing flexible and appropriate responses. Emotion regulation develops throughout early childhood and adolescence and parallels the maturation of executive functions. There is evidence indicating that inhibitory processes recruited for emotion regulation involve different cortical-subcortical/limbic circuits, including autonomic reactivity, as children mature.

Neural Response to Perceiving Other People in Distress

Signals of pain play a crucial function in interpersonal communication. Pain evolved as a protective function not only by warning a person suffering that something is awry but also by impelling expressive behaviors that attract the attention of others. Usually, individuals who experience others' distress and feel concern for them are expected to be motivated to help, at least outside competitive situations. Newborns and very young infants experience self-distress in response to others' distress. Then, as toddlers they gradually differentiate their own and other's distress and begin to display comforting and prosocial behaviors (Hoffman 2000). A number of functional MRI studies with both children (Decety, Michalska, and Akitsuki 2008; Decety and Michalska 2010) and adults (Jackson, Meltzoff, and Decety 2005; Lamm, Batson, and Decety 2007; Zaki et al. 2007; Akitsuki and Decety 2009) demonstrated that the same neural circuit involved in the experience of physical pain is also involved in the perception or even the imagination of another individual in pain. This neural network includes the supplementary motor area (SMA), dACC, aMCC, insula, somatosensory cortex, and periaqueductal gray (PAG) which underpins a physiological mechanism that mobilizes the organism to react—with heightened arousal and attention to threatening situations (Decety 2010).

One study examined the neurodevelopmental changes associated with the perception of pain in others in a group of fifty-seven participants ranging from seven to forty years of age while they viewed short video-clips depicting people accidentally harmed or intentionally injured by another (Decety and Michalska 2010). After scanning, participants were asked to evaluate the level of pain in each of the scenarios. Results at the group level, much like previous studies with adults, showed that attending to painful situations caused accidentally was associated with activation of regions of pain matrix, including the aMCC, insula, PAG, and somatosensory cortex. Interestingly, when watching one person intentionally injuring another, regions that are engaged in mental state understanding and affective evaluation (mPFC, TPJ, and OFC) were additionally recruited. A number of significant age-related changes were observed. The younger the participants, the more strongly the amygdala, posterior insula, and SMA were activated when participants watched the painful scenarios. In addition, whereas participants' subjective ratings of the painful situations decreased with age and were significantly correlated with hemodynamic response in the mPFC, increases in pain ratings were correlated with bilateral amygdala activation.

A significant negative correlation between age and degree of activation was found in the posterior insula. In contrast, a positive correlation was found in the anterior portion of the insula. This posterior-to-anterior progression of increasingly complex rerepresentations in the human insula is thought to provide a foundation for the sequential integration of the individual's homeostatic condition with one's sensory environment and motivational condition. Thus:

• The posterior insula receives inputs from the ventromedial nucleus of the thalamus that is highly specialized to convey emotional and homeostatic information such as pain, temperature, hunger, thirst, itch, and cardiorespiratory activity. This region serves as a primary sensory cortex for each of these distinct interoceptive feelings from the body (Craig 2004). The posterior part has been shown to be associated with interoception due to its intimate connections with the amygdala, hypothalamus, ACC, and OFC (Jackson, Rainville, and Decety 2006).

• The anterior insula serves to compute a higher order meta-representation of the primary interoceptive activity, which is related to the feeling of pain and its emotional awareness (Craig 2003).

In line with evidence that cognitive and regulatory mechanisms continue to develop into late adolescence and early adulthood, greater signal change with increasing age was found in the prefrontal regions involved in executive functions, such as dlPFC and inferior frontal gyrus (Swick, Ashley, and Turkem 2008). Overall, this pattern of age-related change in the amygdala, insula, and PFC can be interpreted in terms of the frontalization of inhibitory capacity, hypothesized to provide a greater top-down modulation of activity within more primitive emotion-processing regions (Yurgelun-Todd 2007). Another important age-related change was detected in the vmPFC/OFC: activation in the OFC in response to pain inflicted by another shifted from its medial portion in young participants to the lateral portion in older participants (see figure 10.1).

The medial OFC appears integral in guiding visceral and motor responses, whereas lateral OFC integrates the external sensory features of a stimulus with its impact on the homeostatic state of the body. The pattern of developmental change in the OFC seems to reflect a gradual shift between the monitoring of somatovisceral responses in young children, mediated by the medial aspect of the OFC, and the executive control of emotion processing implemented by its lateral portion, in older participants. These data support the suggestion that the ventromedial PFC contains two

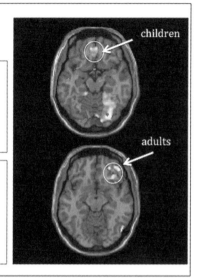

The orbitofrontal cortex

Two interrelated systems, defined on the basis of intrinsic cortico-cortical connections:

- **Medial network** [cortical modulation of visceral function]
  - outputs to visceral control structures in hypothalamus and brainstem
  - interconnected with amygdala, hippocampus and STS
  - involved in mood and emotion behavior

- **Lateral network** [cortical evaluation of affective information]
  - sensory inputs from all sensory modalities, including anterior insula
  - direct projections to sensory cortices, amygdala, ACC
  - involved in affective evaluation, inhibitory control of emotion and reward

Figure 10.1

The orbitofrontal cortex (OFC) and its role in empathy. On the left, a short summary of two interrelated circuits. On the right, the shift in neurohemodynamic activation in the ventromedial prefrontal cortex across age in fifty-seven participants aged from seven to forty years when they are shown video clips depicting another individual being intentionally injured by another. A significant negative correlation ($r = -43$, $p < 0.001$) between age and degree of activation was detected in the medial portion of the OFC (x 10, y 50, z –2), while a significant positive correlation ($r = 0.34$, $p < 0.01$) was found in the lateral portion of the OFC (x 38, y 48, z –8). Note the more diffuse activation of the secondary visual cortex and lingual gyrus in children than in adults, consistent with previous developmental cognitive neuroscience studies that have suggested shifts from diffuse to focal patterns with development. (Adapted from Decety and Michalska 2010.)

feedback-processing systems, consistent with hypotheses derived from anatomical studies (Hurliman, Nagode, and Pardo 2005). One subsystem, situated laterally in the OFC, preferentially processes information from the external environment; the other subsystem, situated medially, preferentially processes interoceptive information such as visceromotor output critical for the analysis of the affective significance of stimuli.

In sum, behavioral evaluations of others in pain combined with measures of brain pattern of brain activation from childhood to adulthood reflect a gradual change from a visceral emotional response critical for the analysis of the affective significance of stimuli to a more evaluative function mediated by different aspects of the vmPFC and its reciprocal connections with the amygdala. Empathic arousal in the young child may be stronger than in adolescents and adults. With age and increased maturation of the PFC and its reciprocal connections with the amygdala, children and adolescents may be better able to internalize moral values and norms by integrating contextual social information, such as in-group versus out-group processes, with motivational and basic emotional states. Thus, individuals become more selective in their responses to others as they age/develop (Warneken and Tomasello 2009).

Empathy Dysfunctions in Children

Lack of empathy is considered a risk factor in a number of developmental disorders, supporting the notion that empathy is a protective factor that, through perspective-taking and empathic concern, decreases the probability of certain types of offending and criminal behavior. A lack of empathy is assumed to have a facilitating influence on offending. Given the complex nature of the empathy construct, the causes and levels of empathy impairments in children and adolescents are likely to vary, and the diagnoses of certain antisocial disorders, such as conduct disorder (CD) and disruptive behavior disorder (DBD), identify individuals with heterogeneous pathologies. Indeed, dysfunctions may occur because of a variety of reasons, such as a lack of emotional responsiveness to distress cues, an insensitivity to punishment and negative feedback, abnormal socioemotional information understanding, or poor emotion regulatory skills. Thus, it is plausible that there are different developmental routes to antisocial disorders, reflecting distinct neurobiological pathways, including functional connectivity and HPA functioning.

It has been postulated that the mechanisms underlying empathy dysfunction in children with DBD children with callous–unemotional traits may be different from those encountered in DBD children without these traits (de Wied, Gispen-de Wied, and van Boxtel 2010). One study that examined dispositional and situational empathy in DBD boys with the use of self-report questionnaires and empathy-inducing vignettes showed impairments in DBD boys' empathic responses to sadness and anger but not to happiness (de Wied, Goudena, and Mathys 2005). Although DBD boys responded less empathically than the normal controls to every sadness vignette, they did not show equally low levels of empathic responses to all vignettes. These findings suggest that DBD boys do not completely lack the capability of feeling empathy with sadness and that situational factors may be involved in DBD boys' reduced responsiveness to other person's sadness.

Another study compared responding to fearful and neutral expressions in DBD children and adolescents with callous unemotional traits (ages ten to seventeen years) relative to comparison children (Marsh et al. 2008). The study employed an implicit emotion-processing task (gender recognition) and found amygdala hyporeactivity to fearful faces in antisocial youth with CD traits compared, not only to typically developing children, but also children with attention-deficit hyperactivity disorder. The study also found reduced functional connectivity between the amygdala and vmPFC in children with DBD relative to comparison children.

In a first attempt to investigate how youth with aggressive CD react to viewing empathy-eliciting situations, Decety et al. (2009) scanned a group of adolescents with aggressive CD and matched controls with no CD symptoms while both groups viewed video-clips depicting other people experiencing pain or not experiencing pain. Furthermore, these situations involved either an individual whose pain was accidentally caused or an individual whose pain was intentionally caused by another person. In both groups the perception of others in pain was associated with activation of the pain matrix, including the ACC, insula, somatosensory cortex, SMA, and PAG. Participants with CD also showed specific amygdala and ventral striatum activation. When watching situations in which pain was intentionally inflicted, control youth exhibited signal increase in the neural networks that process the understanding of social information, including the medial PFC, lateral OFC, and right TPJ. Youth with CD, however, only exhibited activation in the insula and precentral gyrus. Furthermore, connectivity analyses demonstrated that youth with CD exhibited less amygdala/prefrontal coupling when watching pain inflicted by another than did control youth, which is similar to the finding of reduced amygdala/PFC connectivity by Marsh and colleagues (2008). Finally, in youth with CD the extent of amygdala activation to viewing pain in others was significantly correlated in a positive direction to their number of aggressive acts and their ratings of daring and sadism score on the child and adolescent disposition scale (CADS), which quantifies three socioemotional dispositions (i.e., prosociality, daring, and negative emotionality).

The strong and specific activation of the amygdala and ventral striatum in the aggressive youth with CD during the perception of pain in others is an important and intriguing finding. It is possible that this amygdala activation reflects a positive affective response (e.g., "enjoyment" or "excitement"). The finding that CADS ratings of daring items (that reflect enjoyment of novel and risky situations) and sadism items (that reflect enjoyment of hurting others or viewing people or animals being hurt) correlated positively with amygdala response in youth with CD is consistent with this hypothesis. In addition, this interpretation is consistent with the activation of the striatum, which is part of the system implicated in reward and pleasure.

Although these preliminary findings from brain imaging studies are promising in providing possible neurological bases to some of the cognitive and affective differences found across the different developmental pathways to antisocial behaviors, more research is needed. Further research is required in order to better understand the nature of the relations among emotion, cognition, and motivation and to understand how components impact social interaction, taking into account individual differences.

Conclusions

Humans are born with the neural circuitry that implements core affect (that can be described by hedonic valence and arousal) and binds sensory and somatovisceral information to create meaningful representations that can be used to safely navigate the world (Duncan and Barrett 2007). This mechanism is the product of the long evolution of the mammalian brain. Although the intensity of emotional reactions to others' affect may grow at a relatively young age and have a significant biological contribution particularly relying on reciprocal connections between the vmPFC, ACC and amygdala, the ability to understand others' emotional states gradually increases with age. This is crucial for decoding confounded emotions, interpreting situational regulators of affect, and understanding "unexpressed" affect. Part of the developmental process may consist of acquiring more elaborated empathy/concern complex behaviors—more occasions that evoke affect and buffers against such evocation—as well as better distancing, distracting, display, and avoidance patterns (More 1990). With age and increased maturation of the PFC, in conjunction with input from interpersonal experiences that are strongly modulated by various contextual and social factors such as in-group versus out-group processes, children and adolescents become sensitive to social norms regulating prosocial behavior and, accordingly, may become more selective in their responses to others.

We know that brain function and its subsequent influence on behavior processes can be altered by experiences at certain sensitive periods of development that occur across the life course (Cicchetti and Tucker 1994). Therefore, one important future direction in developmental neuroscience is to establish whether there are sensitive periods in the development of the components of empathy, where dysfunctions in developmental processes are most susceptible to impact healthy interpersonal sensitivity, and how this can be restored. For example, there is evidence that normal amygdala functioning is essential during early childhood to develop theory of mind. Lesions of the amygdala have a different impact according to when they occurred. Individuals with early damage to the amygdala are impaired relative to all other groups on more advanced tests of theory of mind reasoning. In contrast, people who acquired damage to the amygdala in adulthood are not impaired in theory of mind reasoning (Shaw et al. 2004). The new finding on the role of the amygdala and reciprocally connected regions of the PFC such as the OFC in empathy suggests a critical role of this circuit in the development of empathy and empathic concern (Decety and Michalska 2010).

The study of the neurocognitive mechanisms underlying empathy from a developmental framework is essential to complement traditional behavioral methods and self-report measures that have been used in empathy research. Developmental affective neuroscience has the potential to provide major breakthroughs in our understanding of the biological underpinning of empathy, social understanding, and social cognition in typically developing children as well as children with sociocognitive disorders.

Acknowledgment

The writing of this chapter was supported by a grant (BCS-0718480) from the National Science Foundation to Jean Decety.

References

Achaibou, A., G. Pourtois, S. Schwartz, and P. Vuilleumier. 2008. Simultaneous recording of EEG and facial muscle reactions during spontaneous emotion mimicry. *Neuropsychologia* 46: 1104–1113.

Akitsuki, Y., and J. Decety. 2009. Social context and perceived agency affects empathy for pain: An event related fMRI investigation. *NeuroImage* 47: 722–734.

Astington, J., and C. Hughes. 2011. Theory of mind: Self-reflection and social understanding. In *Oxford Handbook of Developmental Psychology*, edited by P. D. Zelazo. New York: Oxford University Press.

Batson, C. D. 2011. *Altruism in Humans*. New York: Oxford University Press.

Bell, M. A., and C. D. Wolfe. 2007. The cognitive neuroscience of early socioemotional development. In *Socioemotional Development in Toddler Years*, edited by C. A. Brownell and C. B. Kopp, 345–369. New York: Guilford Press.

Blair, R. J. R. 2005. Responding to the emotions of others: Dissociating forms of empathy through the study of typical and psychiatric populations. *Consciousness and Cognition* 14: 698–718.

Blair, R. J. R. 2011. Should affective arousal be grounded in perception-action coupling? *Emotion Review* 3: 109–110.

Blair, R. J. R., and K. Fowler. 2008. Moral emotions and moral reasoning from the perspective of Affective Cognitive Neuroscience: A selective review. *European Journal of Developmental Science* 2: 303–323.

Brunet, E., Y. Sarfati, M. C. Hardy-Bayle, and J. Decety. 2000. A PET investigation of attribution of intentions to others with a non-verbal task. *NeuroImage* 11: 157–166.

Calkins, S. D., and N. A. Fox. 2002. Self-regulatory processes in early personality development. A multilevel approach to the study of childhood social withdrawal and aggression. *Development and Psychopathology* 14: 477–498.

Carlson, S. M., D. J. Mandell, and L. Williams. 2004. Executive function and theory of mind: Stability and prediction from ages 2 to 3. *Developmental Psychology* 40: 1105–1122.

Carroll, J. J., and M. S. Steward. 1984. The role of cognitive development in children's understandings of their own feelings. *Developmental Psychology* 55: 1486–1492.

Carter, S. S., J. Harris, and S. W. Porges. 2009. Neural and evolutionary perspectives on empathy. In *The Social Neuroscience of Empathy*, edited by J. Decety and W. Ickes, 169–182. Cambridge, MA: MIT Press.

Casey, B. J., N. Tottenham, C. Liston, and S. Durston. 2005. Imaging the developing brain: What have we learned about cognitive development? *Trends in Cognitive Sciences* 9: 104–110.

Cicchetti, D., and D. Tucker. 1994. Development and self-regulatory structures of the mind. *Development and Psychopathology* 6: 533–549.

Cheng, Y., A. Hung, and J. Decety. 2011. Dissociation between affective sharing and emotion understanding in juvenile psychopaths. *Development and Psychopathology*, in press.

Craig, A. D. 2003. Interoception: The sense of the physiological condition of the body. *Current Opinion in Neurobiology* 13: 500–505.

Craig, A. D. 2004. Human feelings: Why are some more aware than others? *Trends in Cognitive Sciences* 8: 239–241.

Decety, J. 2007. A social cognitive neuroscience model of human empathy. In *Social Neuroscience: Integrating Biological and Psychological Explanations of Social Behavior*, edited by E. Harmon-Jones and P. Winkielman, 246–270. New York: Guilford Publications.

Decety, J. 2010. To what extent is the experience of empathy mediated by shared neural circuits? *Emotion Review* 2: 204–207.

Decety, J. 2011a. Dissecting the neural mechanisms mediating empathy. *Emotion Review* 3: 92–108.

Decety, J. 2011b. The neuroevolution of empathy. *Annals of the New York Academy of Sciences*, epub ahead of print.

Decety, J., and J. T. Cacioppo. 2010. Frontiers in human neuroscience: The golden triangle and beyond. *Perspectives on Psychological Science* 5: 767–771.

Decety, J., and P. L. Jackson. 2004. The functional architecture of human empathy. *Behavioral and Cognitive Neuroscience Reviews* 3: 71–100.

Decety, J., and M. Meyer. 2008. From emotion resonance to empathic understanding: A social developmental neuroscience account. *Development and Psychopathology* 20: 1053–1080.

Decety, J., and K. J. Michalska. 2010. Neurodevelopmental changes in the circuits underlying empathy and sympathy from childhood to adulthood. *Developmental Science* 13: 886–899.

Decety, J., K. J. Michalska, and Y. Akitsuki. 2008. Who caused the pain? A functional MRI investigation of empathy and intentionality in children. *Neuropsychologia* 46: 2607–2614.

Decety, J., K. J. Michalska, Y. Akitsuki, and B. Lahey. 2009. Atypical empathic responses in adolescents with aggressive conduct disorder: A functional MRI investigation. *Biological Psychology* 80: 203–211.

Decety, J., and Y. Moriguchi. 2007. The empathic brain and its dysfunction in psychiatric populations: Implications for intervention across different clinical conditions. *BioPsychoSocial Medicine* 1: 22–65.

De Haan, M., and M. R. Gunnar. 2009. The brain in a social environment. Why study development? In *Handbook of Developmental Social Neuroscience*, edited by M. De Haan and M. R. Gunnar, 3–10. New York: Guilford Press.

de Waal, F. B. M. 2008. Putting the altruism back into altruism: The evolution of empathy. *Annual Review of Psychology* 59: 279–300.

de Wied, M., C. Gispen-de Wied, and A. van Boxtel. 2010. Empathy dysfunction in children and adolescents with disruptive behavior disorders. *European Journal of Pharmacology* 626: 97–103.

de Wied, M., P. P. Goudena, and W. Matthys. 2005. Empathy in boys with disruptive behavior disorders. *Journal of Child Psychology and Psychiatry, and Allied Disciplines* 46: 867–880.

de Wied, M., A. van Boxtel, R. Zaalberg, P. P. Goudena, and M. Matthys. 2006. Facial EMG responses to dynamic emotional facial expressions in boys with disruptive behavior disorders. *Journal of Psychiatric Research* 40: 112–121.

Diamond, A. 2002. Normal development of prefrontal cortex from birth to young adulthood: Cognitive functions, anatomy, and biochemistry. In *Principles of Frontal Lobe Function*, edited by D. T. Stuss and R. T. Knight, 446–503. New York: Oxford University Press.

Dimberg, U., M. Thunberg, and K. Elmehed. 2000. Unconscious facial reactions to emotional facial expressions. *Psychological Science* 11: 86–89.

Dondi, M., F. Simion, and G. Caltran. 1999. Can newborns discriminate between their own cry and the cry of another newborn infant? *Developmental Psychology* 35: 418–426.

Duncan, S., and L. F. Barrett. 2007. Affect is a form of cognition: A neurobiological analysis. *Cognition and Emotion* 21: 1184–1211.

Dunn, J. 2000. Mind-reading, emotion understanding, and relationships. *International Journal of Behavioral Development* 24: 142–144.

Dunn, J. 2006. Moral development in early childhood and social interaction in the family. In *Handbook of Moral Development*, edited by M. Killen and J. Smetana, 331–50. Mahwah, NJ: Lawrence Erlbaum Associates.

Eisenberg, N., and N. D. Eggum. 2009. Empathic responding: sympathy and personal distress. In *The Social Neuroscience of Empathy*, edited by J. Decety and W. Ickes, 71–83. Cambridge, MA: MIT Press.

Field, T. M., R. Woodson, R. Greenberg, and D. Cohen. 1982. Discrimination and imitation of facial expression by neonates. *Science* 219: 179–181.

Fox, N. A. 1994. Dynamic cerebral processes underlying emotion regulation. In *The Development of Emotion Regulation: Biological and Behavioral Considerations,* edited by N. A. Fox, 152–166. *Monographs of the Society for Research in Child Development,* 59 (2–3, serial no. 240).

Ghashghaei, H. T., and H. Barbas. 2002. Pathways for emotion: Interactions of prefrontal and anterior temporal pathways in the amygdala of the rhesus monkey. *Neuroscience* 115: 1261–79.

Gross, A. L., and B. Ballif. 1991. Children's understanding of emotion from facial expressions and situations: A review. *Developmental Review* 11: 368–398.

Harris, P. L. 1994. The child's understanding of emotion: Developmental change and the family environment. *Journal of Child Psychology and Psychiatry, and Allied Disciplines* 35: 3–28.

Harris, P. L., T. Olthof, and M. Meerum-Terwogt. 1981. Children's knowledge of emotion. *Journal of Child Psychology and Psychiatry, and Allied Disciplines* 22: 247–261.

Haviland, J. M., and M. Lewica. 1987. The induced affect response: Ten-week old infants' responses to three emotion expressions. *Developmental Psychology* 23: 97–104.

Hess, U., and S. Blairy. 2001. Facial mimicry and emotional contagion to Dynamic Emotional facial expressions and their influence on decoding accuracy. *International Journal of Psychophysiology* 40: 129–141.

Hoffman, M. L. 2000. *Empathy and Moral Development: Implications for Caring and Justice.* Cambridge: Cambridge University Press.

Hoistad, M., and H. Barbas. 2008. Sequence of information processing for emotions through pathways linking temporal and insular cortices with amygdala. *NeuroImage* 40: 1016–1033.

Hughes, C., and J. Dunn. 1998. Understanding mind and emotion: Longitudinal associations with mental state talk between young friends. *Developmental Psychology* 34: 1026–1037.

Hurliman, E., J. C. Nagode, and J. V. Pardo. 2005. "Double dissociation of exteroceptive and interoceptive feedback systems in the orbital and ventromedial prefrontal cortex of humans. *Journal of Neuroscience* 25: 4641–4648.

Izard, C. E. 1982. *Measuring Emotions in Infants and Young Children.* New York: Cambridge University Press.

Jackson, P. L., A. N. Meltzoff, and J. Decety. 2005. How do we perceive the pain of others: A window into the neural processes Involved in empathy. *NeuroImage* 24: 771–779.

Jackson, P. L., P. Rainville, and J. Decety. 2006. To what extent do we share the pain of others? Insight from the neural bases of pain empathy. *Pain* 125: 5–9.

Killgore, W. D. S., and D. A. Yurgelun-Todd. 2007. Unconscious processing of facial affect in children and adolescents. *Social Neuroscience* 2: 28–47.

Krolak-Salmon, P., M. A. Henaff, A. Vighetto, O. Bertrand, and F. Mauguiere. 2004. Early amygdala reaction to fear spreading in occipital, temporal, and frontal cortex: A depth electrode ERP study in human. *Neuron* 42: 665–676.

Lamm, C., C. D. Batson, and J. Decety. 2007. The neural substrate of human empathy: Effects of perspective-taking and cognitive appraisal. *Journal of Cognitive Neuroscience* 19: 42–58.

Leppanen, J. M., and C. A. Nelson. 2009. Tuning the developing brain to social signals of emotions. *Nature Reviews. Neuroscience* 10: 37–47.

Lewis, M. D., C. Lamm, S. J. Segalowitz, J. Stieben, and P. D. Zelazo. 2006. Neurophysiological correlates of emotion regulation in children and adolescents. *Journal of Cognitive Neuroscience* 18: 430–443.

Liu, D., M. Sabbagh, W. Gehring, and H. Wellman. 2009. Neural correlates of children's theory of mind development. *Child Development* 80: 318–326.

Ludemann, P. M., and C. A. Nelson. 1988. Categorical representation of facial expressions by 7-month-old infants. *Developmental Psychology* 24: 492–501.

MacLean, P. 1987. The midline frontal limbic cortex and the evolution of crying and laughter. In *The Frontal Lobes Revisited*, edited by E. Perecman, 121–140. New York: IRBN Press.

Marsh, A. A., E. C. Finger, D. G. V. Mitchell, M. E. Reid, C. Sims, D. S. Kosson, et al. 2008. Reduced amygdala response to fearful expressions in children and adolescents with callous-unemotional traits and disruptive behavior disorders. *American Journal of Psychiatry* 165: 712–720.

Martin, G. B., and R. D. Clark. 1987. Distress crying in neonates: Species and peer specificity. *Developmental Psychology* 18: 3–9.

More, B. S. 1990. The origins and development of empathy. *Motivation and Emotion* 14: 75–79.

Moriguchi, Y., T. Ohnishi, T. Mori, H. Matsuda, and G. Komaki. 2007. Changes of brain activity in the neural substrates for theory of mind in childhood and adolescence. *Psychiatry and Clinical Neurosciences* 61: 355–363.

Nielsen, L. 2002. The simulation of emotion experience: on the emotional foundations of theory of mind. *Phenomenology and the Cognitive Sciences* 1: 255–286.

Nystrom, P. 2008. The infant mirror neuron system studied with high density EEG. *Social Neuroscience* 3: 334–347.

Ochsner, K. N., S. A. Bunge, J. J. Gross, and J. D. E. Gabrieli. 2002. Rethinking feelings: An fMRI study of cognitive regulation of emotion. *Journal of Cognitive Neuroscience* 14: 1215–1229.

Panksepp, J. 1998. *Affective Neuroscience: The Foundations of Human and Animal Emotions*. New York: Oxford University Press.

Philips, M. L., C. D. Ladouceur, and W. C. Drevets. 2008. A neural model of voluntary and automatic emotion regulation: Implications for understanding the pathophysiology and neurodevelopment of bipolar disorder. *Molecular Psychiatry* 13: 833–857.

Repacholi, B. M., and A. Gopnik. 1997. Early reasoning about desires: Evidence from 14- and 18-month olds. *Developmental Psychology* 33: 12–21.

Rime, B. 2009. Emotion elicits the social sharing of emoation: Theory and empirical evidence. *Emotion Review* 1: 60–85.

Rothbart, M. K., S. A. Ahadi, and K. L. Hershey. 1994. Temperament and social behavior in child-hood. *Merrill-Palmer Quarterly* 40: 21–39.

Sabbagh, M. A., L. C. Bowman, L. Evraire, and J. M. B. Ito. 2009. Neurodevelopmental correlates of theory of mind in preschool children. *Child Development* 80: 1147–1162.

Saxe, R. R., S. Whitfield-Gabrieli, J. Scholz, and K. A. Pelphrey. 2009. Brain regions for perceiving and reasoning about other people in school-aged children. *Child Development* 80: 1197–1209.

Shaw, P., E. J. Lawrence, C. Radbourne, J. Bramham, C. E. Polkey, and A. S. David. 2004. The impact of early and late damage to the human amygdala on theory of mind reasoning. *Brain* 127: 1535–1548.

Sonnby-Borgstrom, M., P. Jonsson, and O. Svensson. 2003. Emotional empathy as related to mimicry reactions at different levels of information processing. *Journal of Nonverbal Behavior* 27: 3–23.

Swick, D., V. Ashley, and A. U. Turken. 2008. Left inferior frontal gyrus is critical for response inhibition. *BMC Neuroscience* 9: 102e.

Tamm, L., V. Menon, and A. L. Reiss. 2002. Maturation of brain function associated with response inhibition. *Journal of American Children and Adolescent Psychiatry* 41: 1231–1238.

Tarullo, A. R., and M. R. Gunnar. 2006. Child maltreatment and the developing HPA axis. *Hormones and Behavior* 50: 632–639.

Tonks, J., H. Williams, I. Frampton, P. Yates, and A. Slater. 2007. Assessing emotion recognition in 9- to 15- years olds: Preliminary analysis of abilities in reading emotion from faces, voices and eyes. *Brain Injury : [BI]* 21: 623–629.

Vaish, A., M. Carpenter, and M. Tomasello. 2009. Sympathy through affective perspective-taking, and its relation to prosocial behavior in toddlers. *Developmental Psychology* 45: 534–543.

Warneken, F., B. Hare, A. P. Melis, D. Hanus, and M. Tomasello. 2007. Spontaneous altruism by chimpanzees and young children. *PLoS Biology* 5: e184.

Warneken, F., and M. Tomasello. 2009. The roots of human altruism. *British Journal of Psychology* 100: 455–471.

Watt, D. 2007. Toward a neuroscience of empathy: Integrating affective and cognitive perspectives. *Neuro-psychoanalysis* 9: 119–140.

Yurgelun-Todd, D. 2007. Emotional and cognitive changes during adolescence. *Current Opinion in Neurobiology* 17: 251–257.

Zaki, J., K. N. Ochsner, J. Hanelin, T. D. Wager, and S. C. Mackey. 2007. Different circuits for different pain: Patterns of functional connectivity reveal distinct networks for processing pain in self and others. *Social Neuroscience* 2: 276–291.

Zaki, J., J. Weber, N. Bolger, and K. N. Ochsner. 2009. The neural bases of empathic accuracy. *Proceedings of the National Academy of Sciences of the United States of America* 106: 11382–11387.

Zahn-Waxler, C., M. Radke-Yarrow, E. Wagner, and M. Chapman. 1992. Development of concern for others. *Developmental Psychology* 28: 126–136.

Zelazo, P., F. I. Craik, and L. Booth. 2004. Executive function across the life span. *Acta Psychologica* 115: 167–183.

11 Empathy and Compassion: A Cognitive Neuroscience Perspective

Abigail A. Marsh

A casual viewer might think that the *Star Wars* series focuses more on displays of weaponry than displays of empathy. But aficionados know that the core of the series is a phenomenon called the Force, which is described as binding all living beings together. Barry Benecke II is a *Star Wars* aficionado who exemplifies the Force unusually well. A frequent online contributor to a forum for *Star Wars* collectors, in 2008 Benecke read a post from another young collector named Josh Weisleberg in which he described his rapidly failing kidneys and need for a kidney transplant. Despite having never met Weisleberg, Benecke wrote him back to say he would give him a kidney. Why would the then-forty-five-year-old husband and father volunteer to have one of his internal organs removed and given to a young man he had never met? Benecke had recently lost a number of close friends and family members to cancer and recounted that, "It was because of losing those folks that I was compelled to try to help someone else. The first person who I found that I might be able to help was Josh" (Rosenberg 2010). In other words, Benecke's own distressing experiences influenced his response to another's distress. Although perhaps not *the* Force, an empathic experience like this is clearly a powerful force—one that moved Benecke to risk his own health to save the life of a stranger.

This chapter discusses the neural and psychological forces associated with empathy and the drive to help others in distress. In particular it focuses on recent cognitive neuroscience research that highlights the relation between empathy and the ability to detect and respond to distress in others. Neurocognitive research is discussed that has identified structures involved in empathizing with three distress-related emotions: disgust, pain, and fear. The focus of the chapter then turns to fear, a particularly effective elicitor of concerned or compassionate empathic responses. We conclude by considering how responses to fear cues may be particularly useful in understanding aspects of empathy such as its evolutionary basis and clinical disorders such as psychopathy that are marked by empathy deficits.

The Nature of Empathy

Empathy is a general term for an emotional response to another's emotional state and is sometimes described as "feeling with" another person (Eisenberg and Strayer 1987). Empathic emotional responses include both matching emotional responses—you feel sad, so I feel sad—and compatible responses—you feel pain, so I feel anxiety, or you feel anxiety so I feel compassion (Decety and Meyer 2008; de Waal 2008). Empathy's most basic precursor is the simple ability to detect what another person is feeling (Jackson, Meltzoff, and Decety 2005). Particularly when they are communicated through vivid nonverbal cues like emotional facial expressions or vocalizations, the emotions of others can typically be detected rapidly, perhaps even automatically (Whalen et al. 1998; Öhman 2002; Marsh and Ambady 2007). As such, empathy allows for quick and automatic awareness of others' internal states and may be crucial for regulating social interactions, coordinating behavior, and promoting cooperation among individuals (de Waal 2008).

Neuropsychological evidence indicates that it may be literally true that empathy involves "feeling with" another. A number of theoretical models suggest that when we observe another person's behavior, we make sense of it by activating our own representations of that behavior (Barsalou et al. 2003; Rizzolatti and Craighero 2004; Prinz 2006). This representational mapping appears to occur not only in response to instrumental behaviors such as kicking a ball but in response to emotional behaviors such as facial and body expressions, the observation of which may activate corresponding emotional representations in the observer (Preston and de Waal 2002). For several emotions the brain regions in which this emotional mapping is thought to occur have been identified. Evidence that expressions of disgust, pain, and fear are understood via emotional mapping has been described in detail elsewhere (Adolphs 2002; Goldman and Sripada 2005; Heberlein and Atkinson 2009) and will be summarized here.

Empathy for Disgust, Pain, and Fear

Disgust is an aversive emotional response to distasteful or offensive items (Rozin, Haidt, and McCauley 2000). The neural region most closely associated with the experience of disgust is the insula, a region of cortex underlying the temporal lobes that was identified by Penfield and colleagues. They stimulated the insulae of epileptic patients, who consequently reported experiencing nausea, roiling sensations in their abdomens, or disgusting odors or flavors (Penfield and Faulk 1955). In line with this, weakened experiences of disgust result from damage to the insula, as occurs in neurodegenerative disorders such as Huntington disease (Calder et al. 2000).

If recognizing disgust in others occurs via empathic emotional mapping, common regions should be active both when disgust is experienced and when it is perceived in someone else. This has been confirmed using functional magnetic resonance imaging (fMRI), which shows that regional blood flow to the anterior insula increases when a person experiences, or imagines experiencing, a foul odor or taste (Phillips et al. 1997, 1998). When subjects who experience or imagine tasting something disgusting subsequently witness another person sampling a disgusting fluid and looking disgusted, a striking correspondence in insula activity is observed (Wicker et al. 2003; Jabbi, Bastiaansen, and Keysers 2008). That this emotional mapping is critical to low-level aspects of empathy—like detecting the emotional states of others—is suggested by the fact that insula lesions dampen not only the experience of disgust but the ability to recognize when others are experiencing disgust. Insula lesions cause specific impairments in recognizing disgusted facial expressions (Calder et al. 2000; Adolphs, Tranel, and Damasio 2003; Hennenlotter et al. 2004).

Emotional mapping in the insula together with the anterior cingulate cortex also appears important for empathic experiences of pain. These regions seem primarily involved in the motivational and affective components of painful experiences (Rainville 2002; Jackson, Meltzoff, and Decety 2005). Akin to the case of disgust, both feeling pain and seeing a cue that signals that another person is experiencing pain produce changes in activation in the anterior insula as well as the anterior cingulate cortex (Singer et al. 2004). Work by Decety and colleagues has extended these findings, ascertaining that generating these mental representations of pain allows a person to reconstruct the rich associative network associated with the concept of pain (Jackson, Rainville, and Decety 2006).

That emotional mapping underlies empathy for others' affective experiences remains subject to debate. Discrete regions that subserve empathy for some basic emotions such as sadness and happiness have not been identified. And regions such as the insula are involved in empathic responses to multiple emotional states. This latter concern also applies to empathic fear responses, which appear to rely upon the amygdala. The amygdala is a subcortical structure composed of several nuclei that subserves a wide array of social and emotional functions, not all of which are relevant to fear (LeDoux 2003). However, the amygdala is more active during fear-related events than during other kinds of emotional event (Murphy, Nimmo-Smith, and Lawrence 2003). And accumulating evidence suggests that the amygdala is also important to empathic fear responses.

The amygdala appears to be involved in the generation of fear (Fredrikson and Furmark 2003). Localized damage to the amygdala tends to result in reduced fear responding, as is the case for a patient known as SM. She carries a rare genetic disorder called Urbach-Wiethe that has destroyed her amygdalae bilaterally. Damasio has reported that this individual "Does not experience fear in the same way you or I would in a situation that would normally induce it" (Damasio 1999, 66). Although she is intellectually aware of what fear is and what causes it, her own daily emotional responses are unusually fearless, and she does not exhibit signs of sympathetic arousal during, for example, fear conditioning trials (Bechara et al. 1995). Experimenters working with SM recently attempted to induce fear in her by taking her to a pet store to handle live snakes and to a purportedly haunted house. SM responded to both experiences was intense curiosity and interest, showing no evidence of fear or avoidance in either situation (Feinstein et al. 2011).

If empathic emotional mapping is required to empathize, we would expect amygdala damage to impair the ability to recognize fear in others. Research with SM has found this to be the case. In keeping with the amygdala's many functions, SM shows a variety of impairments related to processing emotion, but her emotion *recognition* impairments are specific to fear (Adolphs et al. 1994). Another amygdala-damaged patient has also been shown to have difficulty recognizing fear conveyed through body postures and sounds as well (Sprengelmeyer et al. 1999). A large study of nine patients with bilateral amygdala damage also found recognition of fearful facial expressions to be significantly impaired (Adolphs et al. 1999). Some of these patients are also impaired in recognizing other emotions. However, with the exception of SM, these other patients sustained extensive damage in regions other than the amygdala, which may be related to their broader emotional deficits. On the opposite end of the spectrum, a large study recently demonstrated that individuals who report experiencing fear most strongly in their own life are best able to identify fearful expressions in others (Buchanan, Bibas, and Adolphs 2010).

Empathy and Simulation

Evidence from neurocognitive studies of disgust, pain, and fear provide the basis for simulation-based explanations of emotion recognition (Goldman and Sripada 2005; Heberlein and Atkinson 2009). Simulation-based models specify that the ability to recognize certain emotions in nonverbal cues such as facial expressions requires observers to be able to simulate the same emotional state in themselves (Heberlein and Atkinson 2009). Simulation theories propose that observers generate emotional attributions by replicating or reproducing in their own mind the same state as an expresser or by attempting to do so (Goldman and Sripada 2005). When circuits that are involved in the experience of comparable emotions are reactivated, this may then allow the observer to retrieve knowledge that links nonverbal cues like facial expressions to the appropriate emotion (Adolphs et al. 2000). Damage to regions like the insula or the amygdala may impair the ability to generate simulated hedonic experiences of, respectively, fear or disgust. Such damage may also thereby impair the ability to recognize these emotions in others' emotional facial expressions

It should be noted that simulation theories have been criticized as insufficiently specific (Zahavi 2008). Zahavi argues that the term "simulation" suggests that the entirety of another's emotional experience is recaptured by the perceiver, which is clearly not the case, as this would lead to simple emotional contagion (e.g., witnessing you disgusted would cause me to actually feel disgusted, rather than simply to recognize your emotional state). Although the recognition of others' emotional expressions is likely associated with activation of some the neural structures involved in emotional experience, emotion recognition probably does not involve the entire network of structures involved in emotional experience (Jabbi, Bastiaansen, and Keysers 2008). Activation in a more limited set of structures is unlikely to capture the entirety of the experience captured by words like "disgust" and "fear," so Zahavi has suggested the term *resonance* to describe the neural-level processes that occur during the perception of others' emotions.

Assuming the basic validity of simulation theories, why does empathy matter? What is the functional significance of being able (or not being able) to create representations of others' emotional states in order to recognize them and respond appropriately? As described above, empathy is thought to be integral to the coordination of various adaptive social behaviors. Empathy also seems essential for moral development (Decety and Meyer 2008). Many have argued that empathy is the primary motivational force behind altruistic behavior (Hoffman 1981; Batson 1990). The form of empathy most conceptually related to altruism and other prosocial behaviors is sympathy, generally considered to be a sorrowful or concerned emotional response to another's distress or need (de Waal 2008). Empirically, do the data suggest that empathic emotional responses are associated with sympathetic concern, moral behavior, and altruism? The answer appears to be yes, but only clearly for one emotion: fear.

Fear Simulation and Compassion

Among the basic emotions, fear is the most vivid communicator of distress. Fear is associated with high arousal and an intensely negative hedonic state. It signifies that harm is impending, unlike sadness, which is generally associated with an unpleasant event that has already happened. It has been suggested that the ability to accurately represent others' distress, particularly fear, is essentially the *only* neurocognitive requirement for generating sympathetic concern (Nichols 2001). Although other empathic abilities, such as cognitive perspective-taking, may be important for devising sophisticated responses to others' distress, perspective-taking abilities and theory of mind do not seem crucial for generating sympathetic concern or compassion. This is suggested by the fact that very young children and autistic children who do not possess sophisticated perspective-taking abilities nevertheless demonstrate basic compassion in response to others' distress (Sigman et al. 1992).

Studies of psychopathy also provide evidence that the ability to generate representations of fear is associated with sympathy. Psychopathy is a disorder characterized by a lack of remorse or compassion, a tendency to use and manipulate other people, and antisocial behaviors (Hare 1991). Psychopaths are also specifically impaired in recognizing fearful facial expressions. A recent meta-analysis concluded that highly antisocial individuals, including psychopaths, are significantly more impaired in recognizing fearful facial expressions than any other expression (Marsh and Blair 2008). This effect is not attributable to the difficulty of recognizing fearful expression and is not associated with gender or age.

Psychopathy also provides evidence that recognizing emotional facial expressions may result from simulation. Psychopathy has long been associated with a fearless temperament (Lykken 1957; Fowles 2000; van Honk and Schutter 2006). Cleckley's original conceptualization of psychopathy suggested that, "Within himself [the psychopath] appears almost as incapable of anxiety as of profound remorse" (Cleckley 1988, 340). Laboratory studies measuring physiological fear responses confirm this. In typical study participants, threats like an impending electrical shock unsurprisingly provoke signs of sympathetic arousal that are associated with fear—sweat on the palms, increased heart rate, increased respiration, and increased blood pressure. Impending threats also exaggerate a person's startle responses. But in similar circumstances psychopaths show reduced sympathetic arousal and reduced startle responses (Levenston et al. 2000). Psychopathic individuals also report attenuated subjective experiences of fear in response to frightening real-life events (Marsh et al. 2010).

Simulation theories predict that someone with diminished experiences of fear and trouble identifying fear in others would exhibit defects in the neural structures that underlie fear responding (Goldman and Sripada 2005). Assuming that the amygdala is integral to fear, this appears to be the case for psychopathy. Functional neuroimaging studies show dysfunction in amygdala activation patterns in psychopathic individuals when they view stimuli that normally elicit fear (Birbaumer et al. 2005; Finger et al. 2008). And anatomical studies have identified structural abnormalities in the amygdalae of psychopaths and in the fibers connecting the amygdala and orbitofrontal cortex (Craig et al. 2009; Yang et al. 2009). This latter finding is interesting in light of the purported role of the orbitofrontal cortex in generating emotional experience (Damasio 2000).

Amygdala dysfunction is also observed in psychopathic subjects when they view fearful facial expressions. Whereas most healthy adults exhibit a greater amygdala response to fearful facial expressions than to any other expression, individuals with psychopathic traits fail to show this response pattern (Marsh et al. 2008; Jones et al. 2009; Dolan and Fullam, 2009). And evidence that psychopaths show reduced electrodermal responses when viewing fearful facial expressions could be interpreted as signifying that psychopaths fail to generate an empathic fear response to others' expressions of fear (Blair et al. 1997). In summary, psychopaths have fearless temperaments, fail to recognize fear in others, and lack sympathy or compassion. A parsimonious explanation for this pattern is that psychopaths do not exhibit the increased amygdala activation and sympathetic nervous system activation in response to fearful expressions that indicate empathic simulation and that would enable emotion recognition.

Empirical evidence also directly links compassionate behavior to the ability to identify fear in others. A recent series of studies assessed the relation between facial expression recognition and altruistic behavior using a classic paradigm developed by Batson and colleagues (Coke, Batson, and McDavis 1978). In this paradigm participants heard a recording featuring an ostensibly real woman named Katie Banks as she described the recent loss of her parents in a car accident and her struggle to raise her young siblings. At the end of the experiment participants were given the option to pledge their time or money anonymously to help Katie if they chose. During the experiment participants also completed a measure of facial expression recognition. The best predictor of participants' pledges of time and money to Katie was their ability to recognize fearful facial expressions. Another experiment in this series found fear recognition to predict prosocial behavior better than gender, mood, responses on a self-reported empathy scale, or the recognition of other emotional facial expressions (Marsh, Kozak, and Ambady 2007). Thus, the evidence is reasonably strong that the ability to detect fear in others is associated with sympathetic concern. People who are particularly good at detecting fear in others seem especially compassionate, and people who are poor at this are more likely to be antisocial, even psychopathic.

Why would empathy for fear in particular be so important for the elicitation of compassionate behavior? In general, accurately perceiving another person to be in distress prompts helping behavior (Clark and Word 1974). And fear expressions are vivid and urgent signifiers of distress, perhaps more so than related expressions like sadness. In addition, perceptual properties of the nonverbal cues associated with fear may be particularly likely to elicit helping behavior. Fearful facial expressions, for example, possess appearance features similar to that of an infantile face, such as high brows, large, round eyes, a flattened brow ridge, and rounded features. Fearful facial expressions and infantile faces also elicit similar attributions, including dependency, warmth, and youth (Marsh, Adams, and Kleck 2005).

In this sense, fearful facial expressions are analogous to distress cues displayed by other social mammals, which often mimic infantile cues (Lorenz 1966). For example, the subordinate wolf in an aggressive encounter will adopt cues that make him appear more puppyish, including folding his ears back, rolling onto his back, whining, and licking the other wolf's jaws. And the high-pitched distress vocalizations that adult humans and other mammals make when distressed appear to be retained from infancy (de Waal 2008). By mimicking the characteristics of an infant, expressions of fear may thereby generate the nonaggressive, protective responses that actual infants usually elicit in adults. The neural correlates of human responses to infants are not yet well understood, but likely they include subcortical structures involved in parental care, such as the periacqueductal gray and the oxytocin-producing hypothalamus (Lonstein and Stern 1997; Numan 2006).

Would the detection of fear in others always lead to a compassionate response? One could generate an alternative scenario under which expressions of fear, because they signal weakness and helplessness, would lead to attack behavior. This may well be the case among species that are not reliant on the formation of strong social bonds for survival. But among social carnivores, adaptive success is associated with adults forming social groups in which the adults mutually care for the young and helpless, resulting in "fitness interdependent" group members (Brown and Brown 2006). In species like these it may be adaptive for adults to have developed a general set of responses to infantile features (Zebrowitz 1997). Simmons (1991) has suggested empathy developed as a mechanism that prompts caregivers to recognize distressed infants' needs, and that this response generalizes to others in need and results in a caregiver's desire to help them as well. That human adults respond to a variety of stimuli that look vaguely infantile is well established (Zebrowitz 1997). If fearful expressions are also infantile in appearance, this may explain why the ability to process these cues is associated with a tendency to provide care and refrain from aggression.

Unanswered Questions

Thus far, the evidence seems reasonably strong that empathy for others' fear is a good predictor of compassionate behavior and that the ability to empathize with others' fear relies on the intact functioning of neural structures involved in generating a fear response, particularly the amygdala. However, many questions remain unanswered.

In particular a complete understanding of the neural mechanisms that underlie empathy and compassion is still lacking. Although amygdala activation may be necessary to generate sympathetic concern, it is certainly not sufficient. Prior research has highlighted the role of other regions involved in recognizing and responding to emotion in others. Right somatosensory-related cortex may play an important role, given that it is involved in the general recognition of emotion (Adolphs et al. 2000) and that activation in this region has been linked to self-reported altruism (Adolphs et al. 2000; Tankersley, Stowe, and Huettel 2007). This region may be important for generating the somatic sensation associated with emotional states; when this ability is impaired, the recognition of emotion in faces is impaired as well (Adolphs et al. 2000). Another critical region may be the inferior frontal operculum, which has also been linked to the simulation of bodily feeling states during social cognition (Jabbi, Bastiaansen, and Keysers 2008). Better understanding of the role of activation in these structures and functional connectivity among them is vital to a complete understanding of empathic responding (Jabbi, Bastiaansen, and Keysers 2008).

The mechanisms underlying empathy for other distress-related emotional states such as pain and sadness also merit further exploration. Identifying conditions that reduce the experience of these emotions may illuminate their role in fostering compassionate social behavior. Rare congenital syndromes exist that result in insensitivity to pain caused by external stimulation. However, data regarding empathy in this population are ambiguous. Adults with this syndrome underestimate others' pain when emotional cues are lacking, but they can accurately recognize painful facial expressions (Danziger, Prkachin, and Willer 2006). They also show normal insula and anterior cingulate cortex activation in response to images of hands and feet being injured but significantly less anterior cingulate cortex activation than controls in response to pained facial expressions (Danziger, Faillenot, and Peyron 2009). However, individuals with congenital pain insensitivity can still experience pain due to internal causes such as spontaneous electrical discharges or migraine headaches (Danziger, Prkachin, and Willer 2006). Additionally, they experience psychological pain, which activates similar neural circuits as physical pain (Eisenberger, Lieberman, and Williams 2003). It is not known whether individuals with congenital pain insensitivity are unusually likely to inflict pain on other people.

It is not clear whether any population exists in which the experience of other distress-related emotions like that of sadness is impaired. Evidence that this is the case in psychopaths is mixed. Finally, it should be noted that the same large study that found an association between fear experience and recognition found no equivalent association for some other emotions, including surprise (Buchanan, Bibas, and Adolphs 2010). This suggests that simulation may be a more important mechanism for the recognition of some emotions than others.

Another question to be addressed is the role of dynamic social behaviors such as eye gaze in responding to fearful facial expressions. The eye region is the region of the face most important to recognizing fear (Adolphs et al. 2005). Convergent evidence suggests that the amygdala is involved in directing gaze toward the eye region of fearful faces. Patient SM's impaired fear recognition improves when she is directed to focus on the eye region of emotional facial expressions (Adolphs et al. 2005). This technique also improves fear recognition in children with psychopathic traits (Dadds et al. 2006). This accords with other evidence that redirecting attention to distress cues may be an effective means of improving social processing in individuals with psychopathic traits (van Baardewijk et al. 2009). Perhaps the amygdala's role in fear recognition includes responding to the presence of certain facial features, such as the eyes, and directing attention to further processing of those features (Heberlein and Atkinson 2009).

Conclusions

Psychologists, philosophers, economists, and biologists have argued for centuries whether humans can be moved to genuinely care for the welfare of family members, friends, or even strangers. Convincingly explaining the behavior of individuals like *Star Wars* aficionado and kidney donor Barry Benecke, who risked his health to help a stranger in a display of seemingly genuine altruism, is difficult enough to make even supernatural forces sound plausible. But recent neurocognitive research has begun to reveal the neural mechanisms that underlie empathy. The systems that generate the experience of emotion appear to respond to equivalent emotions in others, which allows emotion recognition, the most fundamental form of empathy, to occur. When the neural systems responsible for generating one particular emotion—fear—are intact, the empathic response may result in sympathetic concern and, in some cases, altruism. The breakdown of this process is associated with psychopathy. This suggests that the typical person may be equipped to respond empathically to the distress of others. It remains for ongoing research to determine how best to foster and enhance this response.

References

Adolphs, R. 2002. Neural systems for recognizing emotion. *Current Opinion in Neurobiology* 12 (2): 169–177.

Adolphs, R., H. Damasio, D. Tranel, G. Cooper, and A. R. Damasio. 2000. A role for somatosensory cortices in the visual recognition of emotion as revealed by three-dimensional lesion mapping. *Journal of Neuroscience* 20 (7): 2683–2690.

Adolphs, R., F. Gosselin, T. W. Buchanan, D. Tranel, P. Schyns, and A. R. Damasio. 2005. A mechanism for impaired fear recognition after amygdala damage. *Nature* 433 (7021): 68–72.

Adolphs, R., D. Tranel, and A. R. Damasio. 2003. Dissociable neural systems for recognizing emotions. *Brain and Cognition* 52 (1): 61–69.

Adolphs, R., D. Tranel, H. Damasio, and A. Damasio. 1994. Impaired recognition of emotion in facial expressions following bilateral damage to the human amygdala. *Nature* 372 (6507): 669–672.

Adolphs, R., D. Tranel, S. Hamann, A. W. Young, A. J. Calder, E. A. Phelps, et al. 1999. Recognition of facial emotion in nine individuals with bilateral amygdala damage. *Neuropsychologia* 37 (10): 1111–1117.

Barsalou, L. W., P. M. Niedenthal, A. K. Barbey, and J. A. Ruppert. 2003. Social embodiment. *Psychology of Learning and Motivation* 43: 43–92.

Batson, C. D. 1990. How social an animal? The human capacity for caring. *American Psychologist* 45 (3): 336–346.

Bechara, A., D. Tranel, H. Damasio, R. Adolphs, C. Rockland, and A. R. Damasio. 1995. Double dissociation of conditioning and declarative knowledge relative to the amygdala and hippocampus in humans. *Science* 269 (5227): 1115–1118.

Birbaumer, N., R. Veit, M. Lotze, M. Erb, C. Hermann, W. Grodd, et al. 2005. Deficient fear conditioning in psychopathy: A functional magnetic resonance imaging study. *Archives of General Psychiatry* 62 (7): 799–805.

Blair, R. J., L. Jones, F. Clark, and M. Smith. 1997. The psychopathic individual: A lack of responsiveness to distress cues? *Psychophysiology* 34 (2): 192–198.

Brown, R. M., and S. Brown. 2006. Selective investment theory: Recasting the functional significance of close relationships. *Psychological Inquiry* 17 (1): 1–29.

Buchanan, T. W., D. Bibas, and R. Adolphs. 2010. Associations between feeling and judging the emotions of happiness and fear: Findings from a large-scale field experiment. *PLoS ONE* 5 (5): e10640.

Calder, A. J., J. Keane, F. Manes, N. Antoun, and A. W. Young. 2000. Impaired recognition and experience of disgust following brain injury. *Nature Neuroscience* 3 (11): 1077–1078.

Clark, R. D., and L. E. Word. 1974. Where is the apathetic bystander? Situational characteristics of the emergency. *Journal of Personality and Social Psychology* 29: 279–287.

Cleckley, H. 1988. *The Mask of Sanity: An Attempt to Clarify Some Issues about the So-Called Psychopathic Personality*, 5th ed., privately printed.

Coke, J. S., C. D. Batson, and K. McDavis. 1978. Empathic mediation of helping: A two-stage model. *Journal of Personality and Social Psychology* 36: 752–766.

Craig, M. C., Catani, M., Deeley, Q., Latham, R., Daly, E., Kanaan, R., et al. 2009. Altered connections on the road to psychopathy. *Molecular Psychiatry* 14: 946–953.

Dadds, M. R., Y. Perry, D. J. Hawes, S. Merz, A. C. Riddell, D. J. Haines, et al. 2006. Attention to eyes reverses fear recognition deficits in child psychopathy. *British Journal of Psychiatry* 189: 280–281.

Damasio, A. 1999. *The Feeling of What Happens*. New York: Harcourt Brace.

Damasio, A. 2000. A neural basis for sociopathy. *Archives of General Psychiatry* 57: 128–129.

Danziger, N., I. Faillenot, and R. Peyron. 2009. Can we share a pain we never felt? Neural correlates of empathy in patients with congenital insensitivity to pain. *Neuron* 61 (2): 203–212.

Danziger, N., K. M. Prkachin, and J. C. Willer. 2006. Is pain the price of empathy? The perception of others' pain in patients with congenital insensitivity to pain. *Brain* 129 (9): 2494–2507.

Decety, J., and M. Meyer. 2008. From emotion resonance to empathic understanding: A social developmental neuroscience account. *Development and Psychopathology* 20 (4): 1053–1080.

de Waal, F. B. 2008. Putting the altruism back into altruism: the evolution of empathy. *Annual Review of Psychology* 59: 279–300.

Dolan, M. C., and R. S. Fullam. 2009. Psychopathy and functional magnetic resonance imaging blood oxygenation level-dependent responses to emotional faces in violent patients with schizophrenia. *Biological Psychiatry* 66 (6): 570–577.

Eisenberg, N., and J. Strayer. 1987. Critical issues in the study of empathy. In *Empathy and Its Development*, edited by N. Eisenberg and J. Strayer, 3–16. Cambridge: Cambridge University Press.

Eisenberger, N. I., M. D. Lieberman, and K. D. Williams. 2003. Does rejection hurt? An FMRI study of social exclusion. *Science* 302 (5643): 290–292.

Feinstein, J. S., R. Adolphs, A. Damasio, and D. Tranel. 2011. The human amygdala and the induction and experience of fear. *Current Biology* 21 (1): 1–5.

Feldman Barrett, L., E. Bliss-Moreau, S. L. Duncan, S. L. Rauch, and C. I. Wright. 2007. The amygdala and the experience of affect. *Social Cognitive and Affective Neuroscience* 2 (2): 73–83.

Finger, E. C., A. A. Marsh, D. G. Mitchell, M. E. Reid, C. Sims, S. Budhani, et al. 2008. Abnormal ventromedial prefrontal cortex function in children with psychopathic traits during reversal learning. *Archives of General Psychiatry* 65 (5): 586–594.

Fowles, D. C. 2000. Electrodermal hyporeactivity and antisocial behavior: Does anxiety mediate the relationship? *Journal of Affective Disorders* 61 (3): 177–189.

Fredrikson, M., and T. Furmark. 2003. Amygdaloid regional cerebral blood flow and subjective fear during symptom provocation in anxiety disorders. *Annals of the New York Academy of Sciences* 985: 341–347.

Goldman, A. I., and C. S. Sripada. 2005. Simulationist models of face-based emotion recognition. *Cognition* 94 (3): 193–213.

Hare, R. D. 1991. *The Hare Psychopathy Checklist-Revised*. Toronto: Multi-Health Systems.

Heberlein, A. S., and A. P. Atkinson. 2009. Neuroscientific evidence for simulation and shared substrates in emotion recognition. *Emotion Review* 1 (2): 162–177.

Hennenlotter, A., U. Schroeder, P. Erhard, B. Haslinger, R. Stahl, A. Weindl, et al. 2004. Neural correlates associated with impaired disgust processing in pre-symptomatic Huntington's disease. *Brain* 127 (Pt 6): 1446–1453.

Hoffman, M. L. 1981. Is altruism part of human nature? *Journal of Personality and Social Psychology* 40 (1): 121–137.

Jabbi, M., J. Bastiaansen, and C. Keysers. 2008. A common anterior insula representation of disgust observation, experience and imagination shows divergent functional connectivity pathways. *PLoS ONE* 3 (8): e2939.

Jackson, P. L., A. N. Meltzoff, and J. Decety. 2005. How do we perceive the pain of others? A window into the neural processes involved in empathy. *NeuroImage* 24 (3): 771–779.

Jackson, P. L., P. Rainville, and J. Decety. 2006. To what extent do we share the pain of others? Insight from the neural bases of pain empathy. *Pain* 125 (1–2): 5–9.

Jones, A. P., K. R. Laurens, C. M. Herba, G. J. Barker, and E. Viding. 2009. Amygdala hypoactivity to fearful faces in boys with conduct problems and callous-unemotional traits. *American Journal of Psychiatry* 166: 95–102.

LeDoux, J. 2003. The emotional brain, fear, and the amygdala. *Cellular and Molecular Neurobiology* 23 (4–5): 727–738.

Levenston, G. K., C. J. Patrick, M. M. Bradley, and P. J. Lang. 2000. The psychopath as observer: Emotion and attention in picture processing. *Journal of Abnormal Psychology* 109 (3): 373–385.

Lonstein, J. S., and J. M. Stern. 1997. Role of the midbrain periaqueductal gray in maternal nurturance and aggression: c-fos and electrolytic lesion studies in lactating rats. *Journal of Neuroscience* 17 (9): 3364–3378.

Lorenz, K. 1966. *On Aggression*. London: Methuen.

Lykken, D. T. 1957. A study of anxiety in the sociopathic personality. *J Abnorm Psychol* 55 (1): 6–10.

Marsh, A. A., R. B. Adams Jr., and R. E. Kleck. 2005. Why do fear and anger look the way they do? Form and social function in facial expressions. *Personality and Social Psychology Bulletin* 31 (1): 73–86.

Marsh, A. A., and N. Ambady. 2007. The influence of the fear facial expression on prosocial responding. *Cognition and Emotion* 21 (2): 225–247.

Marsh, A. A., and R. J. Blair. 2008. Deficits in facial affect recognition among antisocial populations: A meta-analysis. *Neuroscience and Biobehavioral Reviews* 32: 454–465.

Marsh, A. A., E. C. Finger, D. G. Mitchell, M. E. Reid, C. Sims, D. S. Kosson, K. E. Towbin, D. S. Pine, and R. J. Blair. 2008. Reduced amygdala response to fearful expressions in children and adolescents with callous-unemotional traits and disruptive behavior disorders. *American Journal of Psychiatry* 165 (6): 712–720.

Marsh, A. A., E. C. Finger, J. C. Schechter, I. T. N. Jurkowitz, M. E. Reid, and R. J. R. Blair. 2010. Adolescents with psychopathic traits report reductions in physiological responses to fear. *Journal of Child Psychology and Psychiatry* E-pub ahead of print December 14.

Marsh, A. A., M. N. Kozak, and N. Ambady. 2007. Accurate identification of fear facial expressions predicts prosocial behavior. *Emotion (Washington, D.C.)* 7 (1): 239–251.

Murphy, F. C., I. Nimmo-Smith, and A. D. Lawrence. 2003. Functional neuroanatomy of emotions: A meta-analysis. *Cognitive, Affective & Behavioral Neuroscience* 3 (3): 207–233.

Nichols, S. 2001. Mindreading and the cognitive architecture underlying altruistic motivation. *Mind & Language* 16 (4): 425–455.

Numan, M. 2006. Hypothalamic neural circuits regulating maternal responsiveness toward infants. *Behavioral and Cognitive Neuroscience Reviews* 5 (4): 163–190.

Öhman, A. 2002. Automaticity and the amygdala: Nonconscious responses to emotional faces. *Current Directions in Psychological Science* 11 (2): 62–66.

Penfield, W., and M. E. J. Faulk. 1955. The insula; further observations on its function. *Brain* 78 (4): 445–470.

Phillips, M. L., A. W. Young, S. K. Scott, A. J. Calder, C. Andrew, V. Giampietro, et al. 1998. Neural responses to facial and vocal expressions of fear and disgust. *Proceedings of the Royal Society of London. Series B. Biological Sciences* 265 (1408): 1809–1817.

Phillips, M. L., A. W. Young, C. Senior, M. Brammer, C. Andrew, A. J. Calder, et al. 1997. A specific neural substrate for perceiving facial expressions of disgust. *Nature* 389 (6650): 495–498.

Preston, S. D., and F. B. M. de Waal. 2002. Empathy: Its ultimate and proximate bases. *Behavioral and Brain Sciences* 25: 1–72.

Prinz, W. 2006. What re-enactment earns us. *Cortex* 42 (4): 515–517.

Rainville, P. 2002. Brain mechanisms of pain affect and pain modulation. *Current Opinion in Neurobiology* 12 (2): 195–204.

Rizzolatti, G., and L. Craighero. 2004. The mirror-neuron system. *Annual Review of Neuroscience* 27: 169–192.

Rosenberg, R. S. 2010. The Superheroes: Inside the Mind of Batman and Other Larger-Than-Life Heroes. *Psychology Today Blogs* <http://www.psychologytoday.com/blog/the-superheroes/201006/helping-others-helping-ourselves>.

Rozin, P., J. Haidt, and C. R. McCauley. 2000. Disgust. In *Handbook of Emotions*, 2nd ed., edited by M. Lewis and J. M. Haviland-Jones, 637–653. New York: Guilford Press.

Sigman, M. D., C. Kasari, J. H. Kwon, and N. Yirmiya. 1992. Responses to the negative emotions of others by autistic, mentally retarded, and normal children. *Child Development* 63 (4): 796–807.

Simmons, R. G. 1991. Presidential address on altruism and sociology. *Sociological Quarterly* 32 (1): 1–22.

Singer, T., B. Seymour, J. O'Doherty, H. Kaube, R. J. Dolan, and C. D. Frith. 2004. Empathy for pain involves the affective but not sensory components of pain. *Science* 303 (5661): 1157–1162.

Sprengelmeyer, R., A. W. Young, U. Schroeder, P. G. Grossenbacher, J. Federlein, T. Buttner, et al. 1999. Knowing no fear. *Proceedings of the Royal Society of London. Series B. Biological Sciences* 266 (1437): 2451–2456.

Tankersley, D., C. J. Stowe, and S. A. Huettel. 2007. Altruism is associated with an increased neural response to agency. *Nature Neuroscience* 10 (2): 150–151.

van Baardewijk, Y., H. Stegge, B. J. Bushman, and R. Vermeiren. 2009. Forthcoming. Psychopathic traits, victim distress and aggression in children. *Journal of Child Psychology and Psychiatry, and Allied Disciplines* 50: 718–725.

van Honk, J., and D. J. Schutter. 2006. Unmasking feigned sanity: A neurobiological model of emotion processing in primary psychopathy. *Cognitive Neuropsychiatry* 11 (3): 285–306.

Whalen, P. J., S. L. Rauch, N. L. Etcoff, S. C. McInerney, M. B. Lee, and M. A. Jenike. 1998. Masked presentations of emotional facial expressions modulate amygdala activity without explicit knowledge. *Journal of Neuroscience* 18 (1): 411–418.

Wicker, B., C. Keysers, J. Plailly, J. P. Royet, V. Gallese, and G. Rizzolatti. 2003. Both of us disgusted in my insula: The common neural basis of seeing and feeling disgust. *Neuron* 40 (3): 655–664.

Yang, Y., A. Raine, K. L. Narr, P. Colletti, and A. W. Toga. 2009. Localization of deformations within the amygdala in individuals with psychopathy. *Archives of General Psychiatry* 66 (9): 986–994.

Zahavi, D. 2008. Simulation, projection and empathy. *Consciousness and Cognition* 17: 514–522.

Zebrowitz, L. A. 1997. *Reading Faces: The Window to the Soul?* Boulder, CO: Westview Press.

12   The Cognitive Neuroscience of Sharing and Understanding Others' Emotions

Jamil Zaki and Kevin Ochsner

For the vast majority of human beings, empathy—understanding and responding to others' internal states—is more than an ability. It is a preoccupation. We exert an enormous amount of energy thinking and talking about other people (Dunbar 2004) and spend much of our free time engulfed in the lives of fictional others presented in novels and films (Mar and Oatley 2008). This preoccupation with others is well advised: without a keen grasp of other people's internal states—including their beliefs, intentions, and emotions—we would have difficulty managing cooperative endeavors ranging from group hunting trips to building suspension bridges, and without a tendency to share other peoples' states, we would be disconnected from the vital bonds of social life. These types of interpersonal difficulties plague individuals with illnesses that include deficits in sharing or understanding other people's internal mental states, such as autism spectrum disorders and psychopathy (Blair 2005). The experiences of these disordered populations drive home the point that the social world may provide the most affectively taxing and cognitively challenging experiences we face, and our skills in this domain are honed to a primarily social environment (Humphrey 1976).

Given the importance of empathy, it is unsurprising that a quickly growing number of cognitive neuroscientists have devoted their energy to exploring the neural mechanisms underlying sharing and understanding others' internal states. Perhaps more surprisingly, these studies have, by and large, been conducted in two different ways and published in two different kinds of papers: one focusing on the neural mechanisms involved in vicariously sharing or taking on the states of others (known as *experience sharing*) and the other focusing on the systems involved in cognitively appraising other people's internal states (known as *mental state attribution*).

Experience sharing and mental state attribution are subcomponents of the multifaceted construct that is empathy. As such, we might imagine that they would be intimately linked. And indeed the relationship between these processes and their joint contribution to empathy in complex social situations has been the focus of several emerging theories (Decety and Jackson 2004; Singer 2006; Keysers and Gazzola 2007; Uddin et al. 2007; Zaki and Ochsner 2009). However, whereas empirical energy continues to be focused on the valuable work of characterizing subcomponents or "pieces" of empathy such as experience sharing and mental state attribution, fewer data have been gathered on how those pieces actually come together.

This chapter examines the evolution of cognitive neuroscience research on empathy. Toward this end, the chapter is divided into three parts. First, we briefly chronicle research over the last decade that has characterized the separate neural systems underlying experience sharing and mental state attribution using highly controlled—but also highly simplified and nonnaturalistic—social cues. Second, we describe problems inherent to overemphasizing the separability of these systems based on data designed to functionally isolate them. Third, we describe newer research (largely published in the last four years) demonstrating that these systems are not as isolated as they first appeared, and instead coactivate, interact, and jointly support social cognitive behavior. These data highlight empathy as a multicomponent process, where varying situational constraints and requirements determine which components come into play.

A Tale of Two Systems

Although the term "the social brain" was coined only two decades ago (Brothers 1990), the neuroscience of social cognition has grown quickly into a predominant research topic. This topic has been approached in two ways, each with a distinct line of empirical research and theorizing.

The Shared Representation System

The first line of research deals with the mechanisms through which one person comes to vicariously experience, or share, the internal states of another. Work exploring this question borrows conceptually from many sources, ranging from eighteenth century moral philosophy (Smith 1790/2002) to aesthetic theory (Lipps 1903), to contemporary models of motor cognition (Prinz 1997; Dijksterhuis and Bargh 2001). The common thread uniting various proponents of this approach is the idea that when *perceivers* (individuals focusing on another person's internal state) observe *targets* (individuals who are the focus of perceivers' attention) experiencing an internal state, perceivers engage many of the cognitive and somatic processes they would engage while experiencing those states themselves. This link between perception of others and one's own experience has been supported by demonstrations that perceivers automatically adopt the bodily postures (Chartrand and Bargh 1999), facial expressions (Dimberg, Thunberg, and Elmehed 2000), autonomic arousal (Vaughan and Lanzetta 1980), and self-reported emotional states (Neumann and Strack 2000) of targets. These data led to the supposition that various forms of experience-sharing may be subserved by a "perception-action matching" system in which observed bodily states are automatically mapped onto an observer's own sensory, motor, and affective representations (Preston and de Waal 2002). In many ways this "shared representa-tions" approach borrows from the more general idea of "embodied cognition," which posits that concepts related to physical states (including, presumably, those of other people) are processed through sensory and motor representations (Decety 1996; Kosslyn, Thompson, and Alpert 1997; Niedenthal et al. 2005; Barsalou 2008).

Neuroscience research has identified regions thought to support shared representa-tions that are engaged both when perceivers experience an internal state themselves and when they observe targets experiencing those states, a phenomenon we refer to as *neural resonance*. The localization of neural resonance depends on the type of inter-nal state being shared. For example, when both executing and observing motor acts, perceivers engage the so-called mirror neuron system, encompassing premotor, infe-rior frontal, and inferior parietal cortex (Rizzolatti and Craighero 2004). When expe-riencing and observing nonpainful touch, perceivers engage somatosensory cortex (Keysers et al. 2004; Keysers, Kaas, and Gazzola 2010). When experiencing pain and observing targets in pain, perceivers also engage somatosensory cortex (Avenanti et al. 2005), but they additionally recruit activity in regions related to the interoceptive and affective components of pain, including the anterior insula and anterior cingulate cortex (Morrison et al. 2004; Singer et al. 2004; Jackson, Meltzoff, and Decety 2005; Ochsner et al. 2008). Newer data suggest that even the hippocampus and posterior medial frontal cortex exhibit resonant properties during action imitation (Mukamel et al. 2010). Hereafter, we refer to all brain regions demonstrating this property as the *shared representation system*, or SRS, with the understanding that this is a loose, func-tional definition and not one based on cytoarchitectonic properties or connectivity.

Regardless of the specific states being observed and experienced, the general prop-erty of neural resonance has generated a great deal of excitement for at least two reasons. First, as noted above resonance has been put forward as the likely neural basis of shared representations. Second, resonance often has been nominated as the primary mechanism of empathy, social cognition, and even language (Gallese and Goldman 1998; Gallese, Keysers, and Rizzolatti 2004). The first of these claims is plausible and well supported, but the second is not. Although resonance likely plays a part in social cognition in some situations, it is a much less likely mediator of interpersonal under-standing in other situations. This is because targets' "higher level" intentions and beliefs cannot be translated into motor or somatic states; for example, the identical motor program of pushing someone could be employed for the very different high-level purposes of starting a fight or saving someone from an oncoming bus (Jacob and Jeannerod 2005). Further, there are many instances in which a target's state diverges from that of a perceiver (e.g., when a target falsely believes something that a perceiver does not or is trying to hide or control expression of his or her true beliefs/feelings); in these cases, relying on one's own internal states to understand a target can hinder interpersonal understanding. Indeed, overascription of one's internal states (especially one's own knowledge) to others is a common social cognitive error (Gilovich, Medvec, and Savitsky 2000; Epley et al. 2004), which is especially pronounced in autism spectrum disorders (Baron-Cohen 1994).

The Mental State Attribution System

Errors arising from imputing one's own internal states onto others, in fact, spurred early research in a very different social cognitive tradition: the study of "mentalizing" or "theory of mind." Since Premack and Woodruff's (1978) pioneering work with chimpanzees, the term *theory of mind* has been used to denote the ability of humans (and some other animals) to ascribe unique mental states to others and to utilize those mental state attributions during social interactions (an ability we refer to as *mental state attribution*, or MSA). In various forms MSA has been a major topic of research for decades, with special attention being paid to the developmental trajectory of this ability (Flavell 1999) and to its breakdown in autism spectrum disorders (Baron-Cohen, Leslie, and Frith 1985).

Cognitive neuroscience research on MSA over the last fifteen years has utilized a number of paradigms borrowed from these developmental and clinical traditions, usually asking perceivers to draw inferences about the beliefs, knowledge, intentions, and emotions of others based on written vignettes, pictures, or cartoons. Related work has adapted social psychological paradigms on person perception, for example, asking perceivers to judge the stable traits (as opposed to transient states) of themselves and of targets. Regardless of the type of judgment being made about others or the medium in which target cues are presented, such tasks produce a strikingly consistent pattern of activation in a network that includes medial prefrontal cortex (MPFC), temporo-parietal junction (TPJ), posterior cingulate cortex (PCC), and temporal poles. As with the SRS, we refer to this set of regions as the mental state attribution system, or MSAS, understanding that this categorization is loose and functional (for more descriptions of the MSAS and its functions, see Fletcher et al. 1995; Goel et al. 1995; Baron-Cohen et al. 1999; Castelli et al. 2002; Mitchell, Heatherton, and Macrae 2002; Saxe and Kanwisher 2003; Ochsner et al. 2004; Olsson and Ochsner 2008; Peelen, Atkinson, and Vuilleumier 2010). The specific roles of these cortical regions are, of course, not limited to MSA-related computations. For example, the TPJ is likely related to orienting attention based on exogenous cues (Corbetta, Patel, and Shulman 2008; Mitchell 2008); the PCC's position as a convergence point for both sensory and motor information may support a role in assessing the salience of social stimuli (Vogt, Vogt, and Laureys 2006); and the MPFC may be related to the formation of higher-order or conceptual appraisals of internal states based on input from these other regions, including the more general ability to "project" one's self into a hypothetical scenario and make judgments about currently nonobservable stimuli encompassed by distal scenarios or points of view (including the past, future, and uncertain or counterfactual concepts, as well as targets' nonobservable mental states) (see Buckner, Andrews-Hanna, and Schacter 2008; Mitchell 2009a, 2009b; Spreng, Mar, and Kim 2009). Overall, the MSAS likely instantiates a suite of stimulus-general cognitive processes that need to come together in order for perceivers to form explicit cognitive appraisals of targets' internal states.

Dissociation and Its Discontents

The tale of these two systems—the SRS, involved in sharing others' internal states, and the MSAS, involved in appraising and understanding those states—offers much valuable information about each ability and how it is subserved by the brain. But perhaps the most striking feature of this story is how distant the two systems seem from each other. Indeed, it is a tale of systems divided, not united, and as readers may have noticed, the brain regions making up the SRS and the MSAS are almost completely nonoverlapping. This dissociation holds up under meta-analytic scrutiny: studies engaging one system rarely concurrently engage the other (van Overwalle and Baetens 2009). Further, even within individual studies, these systems can be made to "compete" for control over behavior. For example, perceivers asked to *not* imitate the movements of targets attenuate activity in the mirror neuron system but increase activity in the MPFC and TPJ (Brass, Ruby, and Spengler 2009). In another demonstration of cross-system competition, we asked perceivers to rate target emotion based on the combined presentation of two types of social cues: silent videos of targets talking about emotional events, whose perception is known to engage the SRS, and verbal cues conveying contextual information (sentences ostensibly summarizing the event targets were describing), which are known to engage the MSAS. These cues sometimes presented competing ideas about targets' affect (e.g., a target appeared to be happy based on nonverbal cues, but was ostensibly describing a negative event). As a consequence, perceivers' had to decide how to weigh the importance of these cues, and their subsequent judgments reflected their relative "reliance" on one cue-type or the other. For example, a perceiver who decides that the above-mentioned target is happy based on her positive nonverbal cues and negative contextual cues could be said to have relied predominantly on this nonverbal information. Results indicated that, to the extent that perceivers based their judgments on nonverbal information, they engaged the SRS, including sensorimotor cortex, and showed less activity in the MSAS. However, to the extent that they relied on contextual information, they displayed the opposite pattern (Zaki et al. 2010).

Thus, at first blush, empathy seems to fractionate into two disparate forms of computations—experience sharing and mental state attribution—instantiated in two dissociable neural systems. Yet ostensibly both of these processes and neural systems serve the same ends: understanding and sharing targets' internal states. If this is true, then what specific role does each system play in supporting these outcomes? Extant research can only go so far in answering this question because the studies designed to examine each individual system typically are designed in such a way that there is no need or cause for the other system to come into play. For example, studies designed to examine the SRS typically involve passive perception of dynamic stimuli (e.g., videos of targets displaying real social cues); whereas studies of the MSAS typically require explicit ratings of a target's internal states based on static, verbal, or abstract stimuli.

These differences between tasks suggest that the historical division between studies of the SRS and MSAS is both helpful and unhelpful to understanding empathy. On the one hand, it is useful to the extent that a careful (and preferably within-subjects) approach to exploring the specific tasks and contexts in which each system is engaged can provide a more complete model of the functional architecture of empathy, including when and how each system will be engaged by social information and underlie subsequent social behavior. On the other hand, it is unhelpful insofar as focusing on the SRS or MSAS in isolation leads only to overly constrained, theories of social cognition and empathy that only describe the perception of a small subset of social stimuli.

Critically, the social cues perceivers encounter outside the lab are often substantially different than those employed by the lion's share of extant research. Specifically, "real-world" social information typically contains features that would be likely to engage *both* the MSAS and SRS, including dynamic, multimodal target cues and the need to translate those cues into explicit inferences about internal states (Keysers and Gazzola 2007; Zaki and Ochsner 2009). Theories that emphasize the dissociability of the MSAS and SRS run the risk of either missing or glossing over this complexity, and as a consequence, formulating theories of empathy that rest too heavily on a single process. For example, two competing and well-known theories have claimed that interpersonal cognition can be largely localized to *either* the SRS *or* MSAS (Gallese, Keysers, and Rizzolotti 2004; Saxe 2005). The resulting debate, although provocative, is likely fatuous, because each side bases its argument on evidence derived from studies examining highly simplified "pieces" of social information processing rather than the complex social cues we might see in everyday situations.

Putting the Pieces Together

More recent research has begun to move beyond either/or theories of empathy by examining neural responses to complex social cues and by updating methods and tasks to characterize the role of brain activity in social behavior in a more ecologically valid manner. This work has capitalized on previous characterizations of the SRS and MSAS to study how these systems respond when "pieces" of isolated social information (e.g., dynamic biological movement and linguistic cues about beliefs or emotions) must be put together to form a coherent whole.

This resulting picture differs dramatically from prior depictions of the SRS and MSAS as isolated and dissociable. Instead, an emerging consensus demonstrates that these systems are intimately related in at least three ways: (1) both systems are concurrently engaged by naturalistic, complex social information, although their engagement can be mapped to sometimes dissociable task demands; (2) regions in the MSAS and SRS become functionally connected to regions in the other system when they are responding to complex social cues; and (3) engagement of regions within both of these systems predicts interpersonal outcomes, such as accurate understanding of targets' emotions. We now describe each of these newer findings in turn.

Coactivation

Although early data emphasized separable engagement of the SRS and MSAS, these data were based on perceivers' responses to highly simplified social cues. Outside the lab, social targets more often than not present us with a barrage of multimodal social cues that unfold over time (e.g., a friend looks uncomfortable, then reveals that she has just lost her job, and then leans forward and begins crying). Such cues tap all of our social-perceptive capacities simultaneously and demand that we integrate over many social signs and signals in forming a coherent representation of targets' emotional states.

Consistent with this, several studies that have used multimodal social cues such as videos of social targets, and also required participants to draw inferences about those cues (closely approximating the demands of social interactions), have almost unanimously engaged aspects of both the SRS and MSAS. Two recent illustrative studies (de Lange et al. 2008; Spunt, Satpute, and Lieberman 2010) presented participants with videos of moving targets, and asked perceivers to draw either relatively low- or high-level inferences about targets. For example, while watching a target reading a book, perceivers might have been asked "how" the target accomplished this (e.g., by turning a page) or "why" the target accomplished the task (e.g., to learn more about cognitive neuroscience). In both cases dynamic social cues engaged areas within the SRS (and specifically, regions making up the putative mirror neuron system) regardless of condition. However, drawing high level "why" as opposed to low-level "how" inferences led to additional engagement of regions within the MSAS.

Two other studies have examined perceivers' brain activity while they observe targets in naturalistic social interactions. In one of these experiments (Wolf, Dziobek, and Heekeren 2010) perceivers were instructed to attend either to targets' internal states ("How does Kenneth feel during the following conversation?") or to properties of the physical world ("Was the door open or closed when Tracy arrived?"). The authors found that attending to and judging mental states based on complex, dynamic stimuli engaged regions within both the MSAS and SRS (and again, specifically regions in the mirror neuron system). Another study involving the viewing of complex social interactions (Iacoboni et al. 2004) found similar engagement of areas within both systems even during passive viewing of social stimuli. These data suggest that—in the absence of an explicit nonsocial judgment—perceivers may "default" to drawing inferences about internal states while observing social interactions (Mitchell 2009a, 2009b).

These findings are not shocking by any means: the mirror neuron system and MSAS have been associated, respectively, with observing dynamic target behaviors and drawing explicit inferences about targets for over ten years across scores of studies. It is only sensible that combining stimulus and task characteristics that engage each individual system would lead to engagement of both systems.

Nonetheless, these data make an important point about how theories of empathy and social cognition should discuss prior data. That is, the fact that the SRS and MSAS *can be* dissociated using simplified stimuli and tasks does not necessitate, or even imply, that those systems *are* dissociable in the majority of social contexts. In fact studies employing naturalistic methods suggest that the demands of most social situations would engage these systems—and the processes they underlie—simultaneously. This probability motivates a shift away from an either/or argument about whether the MSAS or SRS is central to empathy, and toward a "when and how" approach to better discriminating the situations likely to engage one or both of these systems.

Interaction

In addition to being concurrently activated during many social tasks, the MSAS and SRS likely interact with each other during many tasks in a feedback loop that informs social information-processing as it unfolds. For example, perceivers who share the sensorimotor states of social targets could use that sharing to inform their inferences about targets. Similarly, some level of inference about targets' situations and their likely responses to those situations is likely necessary to many types of emotion sharing.

Consistent with this idea, a handful of studies has typically found increased functional connectivity between areas in the SRS and MSAS during social cognitive tasks. For example, we (Zaki et al. 2007) examined connectivity during a standard empathy for pain task in which perceivers either experienced pain themselves or observed targets in pain. Consistent with previous studies, both self- and other pain engaged anterior portions of the insula and cingulate (Ochsner et al. 2008). However, each type of pain caused the AI and ACC to exhibit very different patterns of functional connectivity. On the one hand, when perceivers observed targets in pain—but not when they experienced it themselves—the ACC and AI became functionally connected with the MPFC and STS, two regions involved in mental state attribution.

On the other hand, when perceivers experienced pain themselves, the ACC and AI were functionally coupled with midbrain and posterior insula regions involved in somatosensation and low-level nociception. Thus, during empathy for pain (i.e., when observing others in pain), regions involved in shared representations exhibited unique connectivity with those involved in drawing high-level inferences about internal states.

One study has tested the other side of this equation: examining the connectivity of areas in the MSAS during an explicit social inference task. Lombardo et al. (2010) asked perceivers to draw inferences about their own preferences and those of targets. Both of these conditions engaged many regions classically making up the MSAS, including the MPFC, PCC, and TPJ. Interestingly, during both types of inference the MPFC and TPJ were also functionally connected with many regions involved in sharing lower-level physical and affective states with targets, including areas within the mirror neuron system, as well the anterior insula. This is consistent with the idea that, when attempting to understand others, perceivers draw on a system of neural regions involved in such tasks, which in turn likely receive information from areas involved in sharing internal states.

Interactions need not be tested only within individuals. In a recent study Schippers et al. (2010) examined the communication of information from the brain of a target to that of a perceiver. Gesturers manually pantomimed simple actions (in a task approximating a game of charades) while being scanned using fMRI, and perceivers were later scanned while they guessed what gesturers were attempting to communicate. The researchers then examined how gesturers' brain activity at a given time point predicted perceivers' brain activity moments after they had observed gesturers, focusing on the connectivity between participants' mirror neuron systems. In line with their predictions, activity in the gesturer's premotor and inferior parietal cortex predicted subsequent activity in the same regions in observers. However, engagement of these regions in gesturers also predicted perceivers' engagement of the MPFC and PCC, areas typically involved in explicit mental state attribution, suggesting that to make sense of the pantomimed actions perceivers both needed to represent those actions in the SRS and then to draw explicit inferences about them using the MSAS.

Functional connectivity studies provide important insights about the neural mechanisms of human empathy. Although observing targets in pain and drawing inferences about targets' preferences engage dissociable neural systems (the SRS and MSAS, respectively), these regions interact with regions in the other system in both cases. Thus, even seemingly isolated psychological processes (sharing another person's visceral and affective states versus drawing "cold" cognitive inferences about those states) are likely more intimately connected than the first wave of data on the neuroscience of empathy suggested.

Relationship to Outcomes

The engagement of brain regions during social tasks provides a window into the potential cognitive mechanisms involved in such tasks, but it could also represent additional processing extraneous to successfully sharing or understanding targets' internal states.

One way to address this problem is through convergent data from studies of lesion patients that offer a partial—but not complete—remedy. For example, demonstrations that MPFC damage produces difficulty inferring the mental states of targets (e.g., Shamay-Tsoory, Aharon-Peretz, and Perry 2009) provide compelling evidence of the necessary role of this region in at least one empathic sub-process. However, some MPFC lesion patients are still able to understand others' internal states (e.g., Bird et al. 2004). Further, lesions can affect the function of intact brain regions that form a functional circuit with the lesioned area.

Another way to gain additional insights about the functional role of specific brain regions in empathy is to directly examine the relation between activity in these regions and subsequent social outcomes. For example, researchers could examine whether perceivers' engagement of a specific region predicts the amount that they share targets' emotions or understand those emotions. This approach is analogous to the well-known "subsequent memory" paradigm, in which memory researchers used brain activity at encoding to predict accurate retrieval of memoranda (Brewer et al. 1998; Wagner et al. 1998; Paller and Wagner 2002).

Several studies have begun to apply this approach to the study of social cognitive outcomes. Some of the earliest work in this area explored the social-reference effect in memory: the fact that encoding trait adjectives using a social, as opposed to non-social, strategy (e.g., "Does the word 'honest' describe you?" or "Does the word 'honest' describe Barack Obama?" as compared to "How many syllables does the word 'honest' contain?") results in better memory performance at retrieval. Three imaging studies demonstrated that this effect may reflect unique neural correlates of encoding social—as opposed to nonsocial—information. Specifically, successful encoding of social information—unlike nonsocial memory performance—is linked to activity (and intersubject correlation) in many areas within the MSAS, including the MPFC and PCC (Macrae et al. 2004; Mitchell, Macrae, and Banaji 2004; Hasson et al. 2008). This likely reflects the fact that successful social encoding of information requires MSA-like computations about the chronic mental and emotional states of targets.

Another approach to this issue has been to study how neural activity predicts the specific impressions we form about others' traits. In a recent imaging study perceivers were scanned while they viewed pictures of targets and read multiple sentences conveying trait-diagnostic information about those targets (e.g., "He stepped on his partner's feet during the dance"). Importantly, perceivers read both positive and negative sentences and later rated their overall impressions of targets, allowing the experimenters to differentiate between information that perceivers later deemed relevant, as compared to irrelevant, to their subsequent overall judgments. This comparison revealed that PCC activity when perceivers first encountered social cues predicted their later decision that those cues were relevant to overall judgments about perceivers (Schiller et al. 2009).

Thus, ascribing traits to targets—as well as remembering those traits—relies on regions within the MSAS but not the SRS. However, this does not mean that the MSAS alone tracks with subsequent social judgments and behavior. Instead, MSAS involvement here may reflect the largely verbal social cues presented in—and abstracted, general social judgments demanded by—the tasks in these studies. Other social outcomes, especially those related to sharing and judging emotional states, could additionally recruit areas within the SRS. Although there are few data to speak to this issue, a few studies offer provocative evidence that the SRS indeed predicts affect-relevant social outcomes. For example, whereas the relationship between activity in the ACC or AI and self-reported sharing of others' pain and emotion has not been tested, activity in these regions does predict the amount of pain perceivers believe targets to be in (Jackson, Meltzoff, and Decety 2005; Saarela et al. 2007) and how unpleasantly perceivers feel while watching targets in pain (Constantini et al. 2008; Singer et al. 2008).

Our group has taken another approach to measuring brain-behavior relationships in empathy. We have explored brain activity that predicts perceivers' accuracy about targets' emotions over time by adapting an "empathic accuracy" paradigm previously used in behavioral and psychophysiological research (Levenson and Ruef 1992; Ickes 1997; Zaki, Bolger, and Ochsner 2008; Zaki and Ochsner in press). Perceivers watched videos of targets describing emotional autobiographical events, and continuously rate how positive or negative they believed targets felt. Importantly, targets themselves had previously rated their emotions at each moment using the same scale perceivers employed. This allowed us to operationalize accuracy about emotions as the correlation between perceivers' ratings of targets emotions and targets' self-ratings of their emotion and to search for brain activity tracking with perceivers' accuracy on a block-by-block basis. The results of this analysis indicated that accuracy was predicted by activity in regions related to explicit attributions about mental states, including the MPFC and temporal poles, and in regions putatively related to shared sensorimotor states, including premotor and inferior parietal regions (Zaki et al. 2009).

Although studies of brain-behavior relationships in empathy remain rare, their findings are promising. This is primarily because they afford the ability to understand not only the tasks and stimuli that engage neural systems related to social perception but also how this brain activity maps onto the actual goals of social perceivers: demonstrably sharing or understanding targets' emotions in situations approximating the demands of real-world social interaction. Preliminary work taking this approach suggests that accuracy and retention of certain types of social information (especially about traits) are subserved by areas in the MSAS, whereas accuracy and perception of transient emotional states are additionally related to activity in the SRS.

Conclusions and Future Directions

The study of emotion perception, sharing, and understanding is among the fastest growing domains in social cognitive and affective neuroscience. This reflects both the intuitive importance of social perception in our every day lives and the utility of neuroimaging for characterizing the cognitive and neural processes underlying these complex human abilities.

Given the short history of this field of research, the amount of evolution it has gone through is especially impressive. This evolution can be broadly categorized into two "waves" of research. In the first wave researchers characterized two separable neural systems involved in different empathic subprocesses: the SRS, which is involved in sharing targets' sensorimotor and visceral states, and the MSAS, which is engaged when perceivers draw explicit inferences about targets' internal states. This work was foundational because it characterized the neural bases of basic empathic processes with a high degree of consistency. However, it was also limited in its use of highly simplified, nonnaturalistic stimuli and a lack of data connecting brain activity to behavior. These limitations sometimes—though by no means always—led to theories positing that extremely complex phenomena such as empathy are supported by *either* one neural system *or* the other instead of the more likely possibility that these processes tap multiple neural systems simultaneously.

The second wave of research in the neuroscience study of empathy is complementary to the first in that it has capitalized on characterizations of the MSAS and SRS to further demonstrate (1) that these systems are concurrently engaged by "naturalistic," multimodal social cues, (2) that they interact with each other when processing such stimuli, and (3) that their engagement can predict subsequent social-behavioral outcomes such as remembering and understanding targets' internal states. This work provides an integrative view of the brain bases of sharing and understanding others' emotions, seeing theses abilities as flexibly tapping multiple, functionally connected systems of brain regions to translate complex social cues into inferences about others' internal states.

How might we apply insights gained from the second wave of neuroscience research on empathy to future work? The first, most general point is that either/or theories for understanding the cognitive and neural bases of empathy as based on a single process (such as self/other overlap or theory of mind) are outdated, and a more productive approach would be to emphasize subtler questions about when and how each of these systems is involved in processing social information. For example, viewing a target in pain could engage the SRS, MSAS, or both, depending on the structure of the cues presented about that pain (visual or auditory, dynamic, or static), the task involved (simply watching the target vs. drawing an inference about how that target is feeling), or other features of the situation. Related to this, other recent work has examined how SRS and MSAS activity are modulated by contextual factors ranging from the attributions made about targets (Singer et al. 2006; Lamm, Batson, and Decety 2007) to the experiences of perceivers (Cheng et al. 2007) to the differences or similarities between targets and perceivers (Mitchell, Macrae, and Banaji 2006; Mobbs et al. 2009; Xu et al. 2009); interested readers can find reviews of this specific set of studies elsewhere (Hein and Singer 2008; Mitchell 2009a, 2009b).

Another important application of second-wave research on empathy will be to expand and refine the study of deficits in illnesses such as autism spectrum disorders (ASD). ASD is centrally characterized by abnormalities in reciprocal social interaction, which have often been tied to more proximate difficulties in processing and responding to social cues. Social cognitive abnormalities in ASD have been broadly categorized as being of two types: (1) failures to imitate movements, which could represent difficulties in forming shared motor representations (Rogers et al. 2003); and (2) failures to correctly ascribe complex mental states to others (Baron-Cohen 1994). Not surprisingly, early imaging studies of ASD linked each of these deficits to abnormal processing (usually hypofunction) in the SRS and MSAS, respectively (Baron-Cohen et al. 1999; Hadjikhani et al. 2004; Dapretto et al. 2006; Wang 2006). These data have been extremely fruitful in characterizing social cognitive deficits in ASD, but—much like the cognitive neuroscience study of empathy in typically developing populations— studies of neural hypofunction in ASD have typically employed simplified tasks designed to engage each type of neural system in isolation. Importantly, the data reviewed here suggest that ASD could involve additional abnormalities in social information processing that cannot be tapped by studying single neural systems such as the MSAS or SRS in isolation. For example, individuals with ASD may have increased difficulties integrating multiple pieces of social information when faced with complex, multimodal social cues; such a deficit could reflect not only on hypo-function *within* single neural systems, but also on hypo-connectivity *between* these systems. This possibility is supported by more recent data characterizing ASD as involving problems in synaptogenesis during development that lead to abnormal patterns of interregional connectivity later in life (e.g., Courchesne and Pierce 2005). Employing second-wave techniques and paradigms in studying ASD could allow researchers to better understand possible difficulties individuals with this illness may have in integrating social information through concurrent engagement of multiple neural systems.

Conclusions

The study of empathy has produced one of the most exciting subfields in neuroscience research. Programmatic work in this field has allowed empathy to be decomposed into multiple computational "pieces" that rely on separate systems of brain regions to meet separate computational goals. Newer work, however, is also emphasizing the way that these pieces come together to form whole impressions of others' internal states. Future work will help further clarify how disparate types of social cues enable us to share others' emotions, to form insightful, high-level appraisals of what others are experiencing, and to use the abilities in concert.

Acknowledgments

This work was supported by Autism Speaks Grant 4787 (to J.Z.) and NIDA Grant 1R01DA022541–01 (to K.O.).

References

Avenanti, A., D. Bueti, G. Galati, and S. M. Aglioti. 2005. Transcranial Magnetic Stimulation Highlights the sensorimotor side of empathy for pain. *Nature Neuroscience* 8 (7): 955–960.

Baron-Cohen, S. 1994. *Mindblindness*. Cambridge, MA: MIT Press.

Baron-Cohen, S., A. M. Leslie, and U. Frith. 1985. Does the autistic child have a "theory of mind"? *Cognition* 21 (1): 37–46.

Baron-Cohen, S., H. A. Ring, S. Wheelwright, E. T. Bullmore, M. J. Brammer, A. Simmons, et al. 1999. Social intelligence in the normal and Autistic Brain: An fMRI study. *European Journal of Neuroscience* 11 (6): 1891–1898.

Barsalou, L. W. 2008. Grounded cognition. *Annual Review of Psychology* 59: 617–645.

Bird, C. M., F. Castelli, O. Malik, U. Frith, and M. Husain. 2004. The impact of extensive medial frontal lobe damage on "theory of mind" and cognition. *Brain* 127 (Pt 4): 914–928.

Blair, R. J. 2005. Responding to the emotions of others: Dissociating forms of empathy through the study of typical and psychiatric populations. *Consciousness and Cognition* 14 (4): 698–718.

Brass, M., P. Ruby, and S. Spengler. 2009. Inhibition of imitative behaviour and social cognition. *Philosophical Transactions of the Royal Society of London. Series B, Biological Sciences* 364 (1528): 2359–2367.

Brewer, J. B., Z. Zhao, J. E. Desmond, G. H. Glover, and J. D. Gabrieli. 1998. Making memories: Brain Activity that predicts how well visual experience will be remembered. *Science* 281 (5380): 1185–1187.

Brothers, L. (1990). The social brain: A project for integrating primate behavior and neurophysiology in a new domain. *Concepts in Neuroscience* 1: 27–51.

Buckner, R. L., J. R. Andrews-Hanna, and D. L. Schacter. 2008. The brain's default network: Anatomy, function, and relevance to disease. *Annals of the New York Academy of Sciences* 1124: 1–38.

*Castelli, F., C. Frith, F. Happe, and U. Frith. 2002. Autism, Asperger syndrome and brain mechanisms for the attribution of mental states to animated shapes. *Brain* 125 (Pt 8): 1839–1849.

Chartrand, T. L., and J. A. Bargh. 1999. The chameleon effect: The perception-behavior link and social interaction. *Journal of Personality and Social Psychology* 76 (6): 893–910.

Cheng, Y., C. P. Lin, H. L. Liu, Y. Y. Hsu, K. E. Lim, D. Hung, et al. 2007. Expertise modulates the perception of pain in others. *Current Biology* 17 (19): 1708–1713.

Constantini, M., G. Gaspare, G. L. Romani, and S. Aglioti. 2008. Empathic neural reactivity to noxious stimuli delivered to body parts and non-corporeal objects. *European Journal of Neuroscience* 28: 1222–1230.

Corbetta, M., G. Patel, and G. L. Shulman. 2008. The reorienting system of the human brain: From environment to theory of mind. *Neuron* 58 (3): 306–324.

Courchesne, E., and K. Pierce. 2005. Why the frontal cortex in autism might be talking only to itself: Local over-connectivity but long-distance disconnection. *Current Opinion in Neurobiology* 15 (2): 225–230.

Dapretto, M., M. S. Davies, J. H. Pfeifer, A. A. Scott, M. Sigman, S. Y. Bookheimer, et al. 2006. Understanding emotions in others: Mirror neuron dysfunction in children with autism spectrum disorders. *Nature Neuroscience* 9 (1): 28–30.

Decety, J. 1996. Do imagined and executed actions share the same neural substrate? *Brain Research. Cognitive Brain Research* 3 (2): 87–93.

Decety, J., and P. L. Jackson. 2004. The functional architecture of human empathy. *Behavioral and Cognitive Neuroscience Reviews* 3 (2): 71–100.

de Lange, F. P., M. Spronk, R. M. Willems, I. Toni, and H. Bekkering. 2008. Complementary systems for understanding action intentions. *Current Biology* 18 (6): 454–57.

Dijksterhuis, A., and J. Bargh. 2001. the perception-behavior expressway: automatic effects of social perception on social behavior. *Advances in Experimental Social Psychology* 33: 1–40.

Dimberg, U., M. Thunberg, and K. Elmehed. 2000. Unconscious facial reactions to emotional facial expressions. *Psychological Science* 11 (1): 86–89.

Dunbar, R. 2004. Gossip in evolutionary perspective. *Review of General Psychology* 8: 80–100.

Epley, N., B. Keysar, L. Van Boven, and T. Gilovich. 2004. Perspective taking as egocentric anchoring and adjustment. *Journal of Personality and Social Psychology* 87 (3): 327–339.

Flavell, J. 1999. Cognitive development: Children's knowledge about other minds. *Annual Review of Psychology* 50: 21–45.

Fletcher, P. C., F. Happe, U. Frith, S. C. Baker, R. J. Dolan, R. S. Frackowiak, et al. 1995. Other minds in the Brain: A functional imaging study of "theory of mind" in story comprehension. *Cognition* 57 (2): 109–128.

Gallese, V., and A. Goldman. 1998. Mirror neurons and the simulation theory of mind-reading. *Trends in Cognitive Sciences* 2 (12): 493–501.

Gallese, V., C. Keysers, and G. Rizzolatti. 2004. A Unifying View of the basis of social cognition. *Trends in Cognitive Sciences* 8 (9): 396–403.

Gilovich, T., V. H. Medvec, and K. Savitsky. 2000. The spotlight effect in Social Judgment: An egocentric bias in estimates of the salience of one's own actions and appearance. *Journal of Personality and Social Psychology* 78: 211–222.

Goel, V., J. Grafman, N. Sadato, and M. Hallett. 1995. Modeling other minds. *Neuroreport* 6 (13): 1741–1746.

Hadjikhani, N., R. M. Joseph, J. Snyder, C. F. Chabris, J. Clark, S. Steele, et al. 2004. Activation of the fusiform gyrus when individuals with autism spectrum disorder view faces. *NeuroImage* 22 (3): 1141–1150.

Hasson, U., O. Furman, D. Clark, Y. Dudai, and L. Davachi. 2008. Enhanced intersubject correlations during movie viewing correlate with successful episodic encoding. *Neuron* 57 (3): 452–462.

Hein, G., and T. Singer. 2008. I feel how you feel but not always: The empathic brain and its modulation. *Current Opinion in Neurobiology* 18 (2): 153–158.

Humphrey, N. 1976. The social function of intellect. In *Growing Points in Ethology*, edited by P. Bateson and R. Hinde. Cambridge: Cambridge University Press.

Iacoboni, M., M. D. Lieberman, B. J. Knowlton, I. Molnar-Szakacs, M. Moritz, C. J. Throop, et al. 2004. Watching social interactions produces dorsomedial prefrontal and medial parietal bold fMRI signal increases compared to a resting baseline. *NeuroImage* 21 (3): 1167–1173.

Ickes, W. 1997. *Empathic Accuracy*. New York: Guilford Press.

Jackson, P. L., A. N. Meltzoff, and J. Decety. 2005. How do we Perceive the pain of others? A window into the neural processes involved in empathy. *NeuroImage* 24 (3): 771–779.

Jacob, P., and M. Jeannerod. 2005. The motor theory of social cognition: A critique. *Trends in Cognitive Sciences* 9 (1): 21–25.

Keysers, C., and V. Gazzola. 2007. Integrating simulation and theory of mind: From self to social cognition. *Trends in Cognitive Sciences* 11 (5): 194–196.

Keysers, C., J. H. Kaas, and V. Gazzola. 2010. Somatosensation in social perception. *Nature Reviews. Neuroscience* 11 (6): 417–428.

Keysers, C., B. Wicker, V. Gazzola, J. L. Anton, L. Fogassi, and V. Gallese. 2004. A touching sight: SII/PV activation during the observation and experience of touch. *Neuron* 42 (2): 335–346.

Kosslyn, S. M., W. L. Thompson, and N. M. Alpert. 1997. "Neural Systems Shared by Visual Imagery and Visual Perception: A Positron Emission Tomography Study." *NeuroImage* 6 (4): 320–334.

Lamm, C., C. D. Batson, and J. Decety. 2007. "The Neural Substrate of Human Empathy: Effects of Perspective-Taking and Cognitive Appraisal." *Journal of Cognitive Neuroscience* 19 (1): 42–58.

Levenson, R. W., and A. M. Ruef. 1992. "Empathy: A Physiological Substrate." *Journal of Personality and Social Psychology* 63 (2): 234–246.

Lipps, T. 1903. Einfühlung, innere Nachahmung und Organempfindung. *Archiv für die Gesamte Psychologie* 1: 465–519.

Lombardo, M. V., B. Chakrabarti, E. T. Bullmore, S. J. Wheelwright, S. A. Sadek, J. Suckling, MRC AIMS Consortium, and S. Baron-Cohen. 2010. Shared neural circuits for mentalizing about the self and others. *Journal of Cognitive Neuroscience* 22: 1623–1635.

Macrae, C. N., J. M. Moran, T. F. Heatherton, J. F. Banfield, and W. M. Kelley. 2004. Medial prefrontal activity predicts memory for self. *Cerebral Cortex* 14 (6): 647–654.

Mar, R. A., and K. Oatley. 2008. The function of fiction is the abstraction and simulation of social experience. *Perspectives on Psychological Science* 3: 173–192.

Mitchell, J. P. 2008. Activity in right temporo-parietal junction is not selective for theory-of-mind. *Cerebral Cortex* 18 (2): 262–271.

Mitchell, J. P. 2009a. Inferences about mental states. *Philosophical Transactions of the Royal Society of London. Series B, Biological Sciences* 364 (1521): 1309–1316.

Mitchell, J. P. 2009b. Social psychology as a natural kind. *Trends in Cognitive Sciences* 13 (6): 246–251.

Mitchell, J. P., T. F. Heatherton, and C. N. Macrae. 2002. Distinct neural systems subserve person and object knowledge. *Proceedings of the National Academy of Sciences of the United States of America* 99 (23): 15238–15243.

Mitchell, J. P., C. N. Macrae, and M. R. Banaji. 2004. Encoding-specific effects of social cognition on the neural correlates of subsequent memory. *Journal of Neuroscience* 24 (21): 4912–4917.

Mitchell, J. P., C. N. Macrae, and M. R. Banaji. 2006. Dissociable medial prefrontal contributions to judgments of similar and dissimilar others. *Neuron* 50: 1–9.

Mobbs, D., R. Yu, M. Meyer, L. Passamonti, B. Seymour, A. J. Calder, et al. 2009. A key role for similarity in vicarious reward. *Science* 324 (5929): 900.

Morrison, I., D. Lloyd, G. di Pellegrino, and N. Roberts. 2004. Vicarious responses to pain in anterior cingulate cortex: Is empathy a multisensory issue? *Cognitive, Affective & Behavioral Neuroscience* 4 (2): 270–278.

Mukamel, R., A. D. Ekstrom, J. Kaplan, M. Iacoboni, and I. Fried. 2010. Single-neuron responses in humans during execution and observation of actions. *Current Biology* 20 (8): 750–756.

Neumann, R., and F. Strack. 2000. "Mood contagion": The automatic transfer of mood between persons. *Journal of Personality and Social Psychology* 79 (2): 211–223.

Niedenthal, P., L. W. Barsalou, F. Ric, and S. Krauth-Gruber. 2005. Embodiment in the acquisition and use of emotion knowledge. In *Emotion and Consciousness*, edited by L. Feldman Barrett, P. Niedenthal, and P. Winkielman, 186–210. New York: Guilford Press.

Ochsner, K. N., K. Knierim, D. H. Ludlow, J. Hanelin, T. Ramachandran, G. Glover, et al. 2004. Reflecting upon feelings: an fMRI study of neural systems supporting the attribution of emotion to self and other. *Journal of Cognitive Neuroscience* 16 (10): 1746–1772.

Ochsner, K. N., J. Zaki, J. Hanelin, D. H. Ludlow, K. Knierim, T. Ramachandran, et al. 2008. Your pain or mine? Common and distinct neural systems supporting the perception of pain in self and others. *Social Cognitive and Affective Neuroscience* 3 (2): 144–160.

Olsson, A., and K. N. Ochsner. 2008. The role of social cognition in emotion. *Trends in Cognitive Sciences* 12 (2): 65–71.

Paller, K. A., and A. D. Wagner. 2002. Observing the transformation of experience into memory. *Trends in Cognitive Sciences* 6 (2): 93–102.

Peelen, M. V., A. P. Atkinson, and P. Vuilleumier. 2010. Supramodal representations of perceived emotions in the human brain. *Journal of Neuroscience* 30 (30): 10127–10134.

Premack, D., and G. Woodruff. 1978. Does the chimpanzee have a theory of mind? *Behavioral and Brain Sciences* 1: 515–526.

Preston, S. D., and F. B. de Waal. 2002. Empathy: Its ultimate and proximate bases. *Behavioral and Brain Sciences* 25 (1): 1–20, discussion 20–71.

Prinz, W. 1997. Perception and action planning. *European Journal of Cognitive Psychology* 9 (2): 129–154.

Rizzolatti, G., and L. Craighero. 2004. The mirror-neuron system. *Annual Review of Neuroscience* 27: 169–192.

Rogers, S. J., S. L. Hepburn, T. Stackhouse, and E. Wehner. 2003. Imitation performance in toddlers with autism and those with other developmental disorders. *Journal of Child Psychology and Psychiatry, and Allied Disciplines* 44 (5): 763–781.

Saarela, M. V., Y. Hlushchuk, A. C. Williams, M. Schurmann, E. Kalso, and R. Hari. 2007. The compassionate brain: Humans detect intensity of pain from another's face. *Cerebral Cortex* 17: 230–237.

Saxe, R. 2005. Against simulation: The argument from error. *Trends in Cognitive Sciences* 9 (4): 174–179.

Saxe, R., and N. Kanwisher. 2003. People thinking about thinking people: The role of the temporo-parietal junction in "theory of mind." *NeuroImage* 19 (4): 1835–1842.

Schiller, D., J. B. Freeman, J. P. Mitchell, J. S. Uleman, and E. A. Phelps. 2009. A neural mechanism of first impressions. *Nature Neuroscience* 12 (4): 508–514.

Schippers, M. B., A. Roebroeck, R. Renken, L. Nanetti, and C. Keysers. 2010. Mapping the information flow from one brain to another during gestural communication. *Proceedings of the National Academy of Sciences of the United States of America* 107 (20): 9388–9393.

Shamay-Tsoory, S. G., J. Aharon-Peretz, and D. Perry. 2009. Two systems for empathy: A double dissociation between emotional and cognitive empathy in inferior frontal gyrus versus ventromedial prefrontal lesions. *Brain* 132 (Pt 3): 617–627.

Singer, T. 2006. The neuronal basis and ontogeny of empathy and mind reading: Review of literature and implications for future research. *Neuroscience and Biobehavioral Reviews* 30 (6): 855–863.

Singer, T., B. Seymour, J. O'Doherty, H. Kaube, R. J. Dolan, and C. D. Frith. 2004. Empathy for pain involves the affective but not sensory components of pain. *Science* 303 (5661): 1157–1162.

Singer, T., B. Seymour, J. P. O'Doherty, K. E. Stephan, R. J. Dolan, and C. D. Frith. 2006. Empathic neural responses are modulated by the perceived fairness of others. *Nature* 439 (7075): 466–469.

Singer, T., R. Snozzi, G. Bird, P. Petrovic, G. Silani, M. Heinrichs, et al. 2008. Effects of oxytocin and prosocial behavior on brain responses to direct and Vicariously Experienced Pain. *Emotion (Washington, DC)* 8 (6): 781–791.

Smith, A. [1790] 2002. *The Theory of Moral Sentiments*. Cambridge: Cambridge University Press.

Spreng, R. N., R. A. Mar, and A. S. Kim. 2009. The common neural basis of autobiographical memory, prospection, navigation, theory of mind, and the default mode: A quantitative meta-analysis. *Journal of Cognitive Neuroscience* 21 (3): 489–510.

Spunt, R. P., A. B. Satpute, and M. D. Lieberman. 2010. Identifying the what, why, and how of an observed action: An fMRI study of mentalizing and mechanizing during action observation. *Journal of Cognitive Neuroscience* 23: 63–74.

Uddin, L. Q., M. Iacoboni, C. Lange, and J. P. Keenan. 2007. The self and social cognition: The role of cortical midline Structures and mirror neurons. *Trends in Cognitive Sciences* 11 (4): 153–157.

van Overwalle, F., and K. Baetens. 2009. Understanding others' actions and goals by mirror and mentalizing systems: A meta-analysis. *NeuroImage* 48 (3): 564–584.

Vaughan, K. B., and J. T. Lanzetta. 1980. Vicarious instigation and conditioning of facial expressive and autonomic responses to a Model's Expressive Display of pain. *Journal of Personality and Social Psychology* 38 (6): 909–923.

Vogt, B. A., L. Vogt, and S. Laureys. 2006. Cytology and functionally correlated circuits of human posterior cingulate areas. *NeuroImage* 29 (2): 452–466.

Wagner, A. D., D. L. Schacter, M. Rotte, W. Koutstaal, A. Maril, A. M. Dale, et al. 1998. Building memories: Remembering and forgetting of verbal experiences as predicted by brain activity. *Science* 281 (5380): 1188–1191.

Wang, A. T., S. S. Lee, M. Sigman, and M. Dapretto. 2006. Neural basis of irony comprehension in children with Autism: The Role of prosody and context. *Brain* 129 (Pt 4): 932–943.

Wolf, I., I. Dziobek, and H. R. Heekeren. 2010. Neural correlates of social cognition in naturalistic settings: A model-free analysis approach. *NeuroImage* 49 (1): 894–904.

Xu, X., X. Zuo, X. Wang, and S. Han. 2009. Do you feel my pain? Racial group membership modulates empathic neural responses. *Journal of Neuroscience* 29 (26): 8525–8529.

Zaki, J., N. Bolger, and K. Ochsner. 2008. It takes two: The interpersonal nature of empathic accuracy. *Psychological Science* 19 (4): 399–404.

Zaki, J., K. Hennigan, J. Weber, and K. N. Ochsner. 2010. Social cognitive conflict resolution: Contributions of domain-general and domain-specific neural systems. *Journal of Neuroscience* 30 (25): 8481–8488.

Zaki, J., and K. Ochsner. 2009. The need for a cognitive neuroscience of naturalistic social cognition. *Annals of the New York Academy of Sciences* 1167: 16–30.

Zaki, J., and K. N.. Ochsner. In press. Re-integrating the study of accuracy into social cognition research. *Psychological Inquiry*.

Zaki, J., K. N. Ochsner, J. Hanelin, T. Wager, and S. C. Mackey. 2007. Different circuits for different pain: Patterns of functional connectivity reveal distinct networks for processing pain in self and others. *Social Neuroscience* 2 (3–4): 276–291.

Zaki, J., J. Weber, N. Bolger, and K. Ochsner. 2009. The neural bases of empathic accuracy. *Proceedings of the National Academy of Sciences of the United States of America* 106 (27): 11382–11387.

VI Empathy in Clinical Practice

13 Clinical Empathy in Medical Care

Jodi Halpern

Medical practice is a particularly important yet challenging setting for empathy. Empathy is necessary because patients may be reluctant to discuss, or may not be able to identify, their most concerning problems, so that discerning their needs requires excellent listening skills. Empathy is also crucial because the biggest obstacle to effective medical care is patients not adhering to treatment recommendations, and the biggest determinant of adherence is trust in the physician. Empathy plays a crucial role in establishing that trust.

Empathy is challenging, however, because doctors are dealing with the most emotionally distressing of situations—illness, dying, suffering in every form. These situations would normally make an empathic person anxious, perhaps too anxious to be helpful. As Decety and others have shown, when initial empathy is coupled with too much self-related anxiety, a person may in fact employ a variety of psychological processes that interfere with perspective-taking and other aspects of empathy (Jackson, Meltzoff, and Decety 2005; Decety and Ickes 2009).

Empathy is also challenging because physicians are expected to provide equally reliable services to everyone, and yet people ordinarily empathize more with some people than others. Furthermore, doctors are particularly at risk of phases of "compassion fatigue" in which it is hard for them to muster much empathy for anyone at all.

For all these reasons, the question we are asking is a difficult one: What kind of empathy, if any at all, should we expect doctors to provide for their patients?

Clinical Empathy as "Detached Concern"

Until very recently, doctors thought that they had solved this problem. They wanted a version of empathy that they could deploy reliably even in difficult situations such as the following:

Mr. Smith, a fifty-eight-year-old businessman, suddenly paralyzed from the neck down with (potentially reversible) Guillain-Barré syndrome, is refusing necessary care. He will not speak further with the doctors and nurses, saying their care is "useless, a waste." The whole medical team is fed up with him, and his wife is panicked.

Ron, a nineteen-year-old star college athlete is refusing life-saving colon surgery because, he says, he cannot live with a colostomy because it would keep him from "being active." His medical team tries in vain to reassure him that he can play many sports with a colostomy. They feel extremely frustrated, label him "irrational," and call psychiatry.

In these cases physicians' feelings of frustration, helplessness, and anger decreased their clinical effectiveness. Doctors view such cases as professional disasters. Thus, it is perhaps not surprising that physicians have developed their own emotion-free conception of professional empathy—one of detached concern. Note that this conception is quite radical, not like ordinary cognitive empathy or Zen mindfulness. Rather, the ideal of detached concern is that the physician needs to first overcome basic human responses such as fear and disgust in order to cut into human bodies and face death. This utter neutralization of emotion then enables special objective insight into patients' suffering. Thus, the term "detached concern" was coined, denoting a pathway to empathy *through* detachment.

Medical graduations to this day continue to honor Sir William Osler, father of medical residency training, and quote his essay *"Aequanimitas,"* written in 1904, as an inspiration to new physicians. He writes that the doctor should be so emotionally neutral that "his blood vessels don't constrict and his heart rate remains steady when he sees terrible sights." This neutrality in witnessing human suffering gives him a special glimpse into the "inner life" of patients (Osler 1963). Fast-forwarding two generations to 1963, Rene Fox and Howard Lief write their classic essay "Training for Detached Concern." They describe how medical students equate the detachment required to dissect a cadaver to the stance they need to listen empathically without becoming emotionally involved (Fox and Lief 1963). The seeming inconsistency —in which it is detachment from all human emotion that makes one especially skilled at empathy—hints at the unconscious, wishful thinking motivating the ideal of detached concern.

Yet physicians have developed increasingly sophisticated, less problematic versions of detached concern over the past forty years. They rightfully distinguish empathy, which aims for understanding the patient, from sympathy and show how trying to "share" the patient's feelings in sympathy invites errors of projection and overidentification (Aring 1958; Blumgart 1964; Coulehan 1995; Halpern 2001). These concerns have motivated some to define clinical empathy as strictly cognitive empathy. Consider for example, the Society for General Internal Medicine's statement that: "Empathy is the act of correctly acknowledging the emotional state of another *without* experiencing that state oneself" (Markakis et al. 1999).

In sifting through all the justifications for avoiding emotional empathy, three strong, if empirically unvalidated, arguments emerge. The first is that emotions interfere with the cognitive assessment of the patient—that a physician needs a fully objective mindset to obtain a thorough history and make an accurate diagnosis. Second, emotions undermine the ability to provide effective care during difficult circumstances. Third, they increase the risk of burnout (Coulehan 1995; Roter et al. 1997b). In this chapter we challenge each of these claims and argue that a richer clinical empathy, involving emotional and cognitive empathy, makes for more effective medical care.

Finding a New Norm for Clinical Empathy

There has been an upsurge of research on clinical empathy in recent years, but this research has had several problems. First, most of the studies include little or no precise definition of "empathy," and the term seems to be used to describe very different things, ranging from sympathy to self-related concern. Second, the most frequent quantitative method is self-report, which is especially problematic when empathy is not clearly defined. Third, most of the studies involve questionnaires in which the questions are about general tendencies, rather than anchored in concrete circumstances. Fourth, real patients are rarely asked to evaluate physician empathy, although in a few recent studies simulated or standardized patients evaluate physicians. Overall, looking at the 206 studies done over the past ten years, none probe for "concrete details about what the patient or physician understood/misunderstood" (Pedersen 2009).

Simply doing more research without clearly defining and operationalizing empathy is unlikely to be helpful. Rather, to make empirical progress we first need to put forward a clear conception of clinical empathy, which can then be tested and refined empirically. My goal in this chapter is to lay the groundwork for such a conception. To do this, I go to the roots of each of the basic arguments used to rationalize detachment and consider what, if any, kind of empathic stance best meets the goals of medical care.

Let us state that the purpose of clinical empathy is to understand the patient's emotions well enough to help her address her medical problem therapeutically. This is already a complex goal, involving both understanding and addressing the patient's concerns. This dual purpose conception of empathy has been described in other settings as well. As Daniel Batson points out, there are two distinct, if related, tasks of empathy in our personal relationships: understanding how another person is feeling and having an appropriately caring response (Batson 2009). In the case of physicians the second aim is not just to have a caring response but to have a therapeutic response. I say more about this below.

Given this definition, we can break down our inquiry into the conception of clinical empathy into four precise questions we need to address:

1. What (if any) is the cognitive role of empathy in clinical care?
2. What (if any) other ways does empathy contribute to medical care?
3. How can doctors avoid errors of empathy, such as projection and overidentification?
4. How can doctors provide "reliable" empathy? How can they deal with situations that evoke negative emotions? How does empathy relate to burnout?

Note that these questions are not merely descriptive: they are also normative. They ask: what forms of engagement are *good* for medical care? The normative goes beyond describing what *is* to describe how things *might be*. Of course this normative conception needs to be realistic; so empirical findings form the building blocks of this account. However, unlike a simple descriptive project, empirical findings are used here to address questions about the goals that we think empathy *ought* to serve when things are going well.

What (if Any) Is the Cognitive Role of Empathy in Clinical Care?

Many research studies and medical educators presume that the cognitive aim of clinical empathy is to help the physician label the patient's emotion type correctly—recognizing for example, when a patient is angry or worried. However, I would argue that this labeling is only a very beginning step. It is often fairly obvious that a patient is angry or sad, but what needs to be understood is what, in particular, his anger or sadness *is about*.

Emotions are characteristically *about* something in the way that thought is about something. Sometimes an emotion contains a full-fledged belief, and sometimes it involves a less-focused point of view that shapes a person's other beliefs. Thus if I am angry at you, I believe you have wronged me. If I am feeling happy, I may not have one specific belief, but my view of the world as pleasurable and good shapes how I interpret and form many other beliefs (Schwarz 1983).

Importantly, emotional beliefs and views have different properties from detached beliefs. They can arise on less evidence—which makes them crucial shortcuts for sensing danger, and so forth. For example, I may feel suspicious toward someone for reasons that I do not yet recognize, and this could prove to be self-protective. However, the fact that emotional views are less evidence-based can also create problems. It can be difficult to get someone to shift his emotional view by logic alone. For example, if a patient is afraid that he will have a rare complication from an important medical intervention, telling him that his objective risk is quite low, even anchoring this in understandable data (lower than having a car accident on your way to work) might not be helpful enough. Finding out that he is afraid of what happened to his friend, who had a bad outcome from a similar treatment, would be crucial for addressing his concerns.

Further, when doctors themselves are involved in conflicts with patients, as in the difficult situations described at the beginning of this chapter, labeling the patient's emotion is likely to exacerbate the conflict, whereas understanding what in particular the patient is upset about is likely to help (Halpern 2007). For example, in Mr. Smith's case, it was quite obvious that he was feeling terribly depressed about his condition, and his doctors telling him sympathetically that they recognized that he felt hopeless only made things worse.

I was called to take care of him. When I first entered his hospital room I noticed a flicker of interest in his eyes as he saw me. He did try to say something to me but when he tried to speak through his tracheotomy tube, his voice was too feeble to hear. I suddenly felt terribly sorry for this man, and also ashamed at imposing on him, and I spoke very gently to him. Almost immediately, this turned him off; I felt his withdrawal from me. His wife, sitting at the bedside, looked very uncomfortable, and I left his room.

On reflection, awareness of his initial interest and then his withdrawal when I showed sympathy made me realize that feeling sorry for him was the worst thing I could do. Further, I began to wonder why I felt such overwhelming hopelessness about him when he had at least a 50 percent chance of full recovery and another 20 to 30 percent chance of significant recovery, much better odds than most of my ICU patients faced. But his full recovery depended on his participating in physical therapy, which he was rejecting along with all of his other treatment.

This realization led me to reenter his room with a different tone. I asked him directly and assertively what he meant by saying that treatment was "useless, a waste"? My tone was business-like, trying to find his bottom line so that we could negotiate. He immediately responded, looking right into my eyes. He gave a long, angry tirade (whispered but audible) about how disrespected he felt, his body essentially splayed on the bed in front of his wife, his nurses and doctors and therapists entering his room at all hours without permission or notice, and all for what? As I listened, I found myself imagining going from being a virile leader of my family, a titan of industry, to being so helpless that I couldn't even protect my wife. This felt so enraging that I understood his global rejection of all of us and our treatment. Thus began an effective therapeutic alliance.

In Mr. Smith's case, the cognitive challenge was to shift from labeling his emotion from a third-person perspective to imagining how he experienced feelings from an insider perspective. The crucial mental process for shifting in this way was curiosity—wondering about both his responses and my own. Curiosity helped me avoid the error of taking my immediate sympathetic response to him at face value. Rather than seeing him as a man in despair who needed to be treated with kid gloves, I came to see how such treatment actually felt to him. Although the fact that he felt unhappy with his medical care was obvious, what I needed to learn was that he specifically hated the way all of us on his medical team were speaking softly and gently to him. He hated our obvious sympathy; it exacerbated his feelings of shame. We needed to understand this to treat him effectively. This case illustrates how *an important cognitive aim for clinical empathy is to understand what, in particular, a patient is concerned about.*

The cognitive aims of medical care are, of course, much broader than understanding how a patient feels. The overarching cognitive aims include making an accurate diagnosis, and not missing important needs that can be addressed to help the patient. The pathway to meeting these goals is to take a "good" history—a history that tracks important needs and leads to correct diagnosis. It turns out that listening in a non-verbally attuned way, which is another aspect of clinical empathy, plays a crucial role in taking a good history.

Direct observational research shows that patients wait to sense that a physician is nonverbally attuned before they disclose their most concerning symptoms. Careful videotaped studies show that when expert physicians ask all the right questions but lack such attunement, patients refrain from bringing up their anxiety-provoking symptoms. In contrast when doctors ask good questions and their body language and gestures show emotional attunement, patients give fuller histories (Suchman et al. 1997; Finset 2010).

There are even more subtle ways that emotional engagement contributes to understanding a patient's history that have yet to be adequately studied. A patient's specific words and anecdotes trigger images and associations for an empathic listener. For example, Mr. Smith's words that treatment was "useless, a waste" guided me to imagine how he now saw his own body as useless, a waste. And attuning to another's shifts in mood provides a kind of stage lighting for imagining what it is like to be in the patient's world. Attuning to mood works in synergy with the capacity to associate to another's images to help one follow the narrative flow of another person's subjective experiences. A patient of mine was describing her insomnia, which began when she started staying up too late at night. She had recently lost her husband and moved into her daughter's home, sleeping in an attic bedroom. As she told me about her life, I found myself picturing her staying up late, watching television in the living room just to hear voices and avoid the lonely walk up to the attic by herself. This understanding led to an empowering conversation, which resulted in her getting music to listen to upstairs, going to sleep on time, and sleeping well.

Following another's experiences narratively can contribute to making a correct diagnosis, since what is often needed is not just a list of symptoms but a temporal unfolding. Even in taking a simple history of a new patient who says that she feels as though she cannot get out of bed, and who appears sad and demoralized, it would be premature to label her as depressed. What is needed is to imagine how her feelings unfold in real time. Does she first feel hopeless or highly anxious about what the day might bring, or does she first feel weak or as if her limbs are too heavy to move, and then feel discouraged? These distinctions are crucial for distinguishing possible depression from anemia or hypothyroidism or neuromuscular problems.

There are thus multiple empathic processes serving multiple cognitive aims in providing ordinary medical care. These processes include curiosity about what in particular the patient is concerned about and related cognitive empathy; nonverbal attunement, including attuning to mood; and associating to another's associations to imagine the other's experiences. These processes contribute to multiple aspects of healthcare: patients give fuller medical histories to attuned listeners, attunement working in synergy with curiosity and imagination contributes to a narrative understanding of the medical history, and all of these processes together lead to a more individualized understanding of the patient's concerns.

Empathy Improves Therapeutic Effectiveness

Beyond helping with the cognitive aspects of medical care, empathic relating improves therapeutic effectiveness directly. "Evidence supports the physiological benefits of empathic relationships, including better immune function, shorter post-surgery hospital stays, fewer asthma attacks, stronger placebo response, and shorter duration of colds" (Reiss 2010). Perhaps the most well-understood pathway through which empathy improves health outcomes is the relation between patient perception of physician concern and trust.

In a large meta-analysis of all the factors that predict treatment adherence, the dominant factor was trust in the physician. And the largest predictor of trust was whether the patient felt that the physician seemed genuinely worried about the patient when discussing serious matters (Roter et al. 1997a). Note that in the same meta-analysis, friendliness was not a predictor of trust. Given that the largest single factor in treatment failure is nonadherence to treatment (approximately 50 percent of prescribed medications are not taken as prescribed), empathic concern is very important for effective medical care (Sabate 2003).

Additionally, research in oncology shows that physicians' emotional engagement reduces patients' anxiety when receiving cancer diagnoses and even influences whether the patient is able to take early steps to get into treatment. Physicians delivering bad news in an emotionally detached fashion impacts both the patient's self-reports of feeling confused and overwhelmed afterward and the patient's readiness to seek treatment options, attend support groups, and otherwise becomes agential regarding his or her cancer (Ptacek and Ptacek 2001).

Note that empathic concern is quite distinct from the other two empathic processes already mentioned—engaged listening seeking to understand what in particular is troubling the patient and nonverbal attunement. We might ask skeptically why patients actually need their physicians to feel emotional concern for them. Why is it not enough for their doctors to be committed to helping them but not be emotionally invested? Daniel Batson emphasizes a central role for protective feelings of concern in empathy (Batson et al. 2007). And there are obvious reasons for valuing such concern as the basis for empathy in intimate relationships—such concern is crucial for survival of the young, and may help cement commitment between spouses over time. Patient-provider interactions, though, are rarely long-lasting enough to require such a foundation. My hypothesis (which needs testing) is that patients understand this and care less about having their doctors feel deep personal affection for them and more about receiving attentive care. That is, my guess is that patients want their doctors to show actual concern because this shows them that their doctor has an emotional reason to believe that their suffering is real and therefore take their needs to be important. Outside of medicine, we do know that people recovering from psychological trauma during war and other catastrophes describe how an emotionally neutral listener makes them feel insignificant, even unreal (Halpern 2001).

In any case, emotions contribute to clinical empathy in a variety of ways. Both curiosity and nonverbal attunement serve cognitive aims, and feelings of concern influence patient trust. Thus clinical empathy is not one simple psychological process, but a complicated one, which may involve different types of emotional engagement to meet different clinical needs.

Seeking Empathic Accuracy

How can doctors become more accurate in their understanding of patients and, in particular, avoid errors of projection and over-identification? Importantly, although affective attunement and associating to another's associations are, in my view, important contributors to empathic understanding, these mental processes may not be sufficiently focused, nor are they self-correcting enough to lead to an accurate understanding of a patient. Rather, what is also needed is to be genuinely curious to learn more about what the patient is experiencing. Curiosity is a crucial metacognitive organizing theme for clinical empathy (Halpern 2001).

Curiosity is, in my view, crucial for increasing empathic accuracy. At the very least clinicians need to be on the lookout for instances in which we *think* we already understand what a patient is upset about when we do not yet grasp the patient's concerns . . . Consider the case of Ron, the college athlete who was not reassured by his doctors telling him that he could still be physically active. One clinician finally listened more carefully to him—and empathically recognized that what Ron was most concerned about was *sexual* activity (Ron felt too embarrassed to raise this concern directly). This realization quickly led to a referral to a nurse who had herself adjusted well to living with a colostomy. After she and Ron had a private conversation about his sexual future, he accepted the surgery.

We need to be equally cautious about situations in which we experience emotional empathy for a patient going through a similar medical problem or personal loss to something that we ourselves have experienced. In such situations it can be tempting for the doctor to imagine *herself* in a patient's shoes and think that she knows how the patient feels because of how *she* (the doctor) would feel. Given that each person has a different personal history and personality and is likely to be affected by similar medical diseases in very different emotional ways, this is usually a clinical mistake. Curiosity about how another person with an entirely distinct life is experiencing his or her illness is a crucial corrective to over-identification. I always recommend that physicians avoid saying to patients "I know how you feel," and rather that they learn to say "tell me what I'm missing" (Coulehan and Williams 2003).

Curiosity also protects us from being naively sympathetic and taking our initial resonance at face value or from projecting our concerns onto patients. The team treating Mr. Smith felt so helpless witnessing his predicament that we saw his situation as overwhelming and lost sight of his very realistic chance of significant recovery. We might instead have been curious about how his sense of the future was collapsed at the present moment and helped him become aware that this was the case (Halpern 2010).

Finally, patients seem to appreciate their physician's curiosity even when the physician is having a hard time fully understanding the patient. My psychotherapy patients have referred to instances in which I misunderstood them, but stayed interested as they corrected and guided me, as especially therapeutic. Despite older authoritarian norms of the omniscient physician, or perhaps because patients now find it hard to trust this stance, inviting the patient to let you know what you are missing or getting wrong is a very important way to build trust and a therapeutic alliance (Halpern 2007).

At this point let me summarize and suggest that we conceptualize clinical empathy as, first and foremost, *engaged curiosity*. This involves a real interest in going beyond surface emotions and easy sympathetic identifications—seeking to invite and understand a patient's whole range of emotions.

"Reliable" Empathizing and Emotional Engagement

How can doctors empathize "reliably" even when they face conflicts with patients? How does emotional engagement affect burnout and compassion fatigue?

These issues are perhaps the most clinically daunting. After all, our emotions are not under our direct control. For a variety of sociological reasons ranging from too much time pressure to the complexity of treatment options, doctors are increasingly facing conflicts with patients, often leading to frustration and anger on both sides (Halpern 2007). I have just suggested that a new concept for clinical empathy ought to involve genuine concern for the patient. However, basic psychology research suggests that, when we feel concern for another, it can be especially difficult to empathize during a conflict (Steins 2000). Especially relevant here is Decety's recent work suggesting that unreflective emotional resonance with another's pain can lead to self-related anxiety (Jackson, Meltzoff, and Decety 2005; Decety and Ickes 2009; Watson and Greenberg 2009). When a physician feels responsible for a patient who is refusing care, she may feel self-related anxiety, guilt, shame, and so forth. These feelings can decrease the physician's ability to see the patient's perspective.

However long-standing it has been, the medical culture of doctors avoiding their own negative emotions may not be as hard to change as some think. Doctors are people. Basic psychology research suggests that negative emotions (besides rage) tend to make people *more* inquisitive about the basis for their own emotional views (Schwarz 1983, 2000). Although physicians are socialized against self-reflection, early research suggests that they can learn to be mindful of their own negative feelings and, in so doing, improve their clinical care and professional satisfaction (Novack et al. 1997; Shapiro, Schwartz, and Bonner 1998; Epstein 1999; Meier, Back, and Morrison 2001; Gockel 2010).

Still, self-reflection does not automatically lead to curiosity about another's views, especially when that person causes distress. Psychotherapists bridge the two by becoming curious about what clues their own uncomfortable feelings provide about patients' feelings. Psychiatry educators teach residents specific ways to think about their own "negative countertransference" (anxiety or other difficult feelings in response to a patient). Practicing psychiatrists easily recognize subtle negative feelings and use them as important clues to how a patient might affect other important people in the patient's life (Rossberg et al. 2010). By becoming genuinely curious about what their own painful feelings might be showing them about a patient, expert psychiatrists learn to decenter from self-related anxiety to focus on their patient's feelings. This is perhaps why therapists with highly skilled empathy can work in trauma centers and other highly noxious settings and show low rates of burnout (Harrison and Westwood 2009).

Consider the role of curiosity in the following situation: Sam, a nineteen-year-old is blocking the door to his dying mother's room and threatening to shoot the oncology nurses if they give his mother sedating pain medication. The entire team is terrified of him and call psychiatry to admit him involuntarily for "dangerousness to others." How was the situation resolved? First, we asked hospital security to ascertain that Sam had no gun, no way to obtain one at present, and no history of violence (all confirmed). Once the team was reassured that he was not a physical threat, they shifted to recognizing how sad his situation was. He could not face permanently losing contact with his mother. We met as a team, and each member spoke about what this situation evoked in him or her regarding losing loved ones. Immediately after this reflection, everything changed. No one was angry at the young man anymore; most felt sad for him, and a few began to wonder why his response was so severe, thus developing genuine clinical curiosity coupled with their concern. In this frame of mind, a representative team member met with the young man, showing genuine concern about his grief, and listening to him in an attuned way. Sam responded by trusting her for the first time and telling her that he felt terrible for going away across the country for college the year before, when his mother had already been diagnosed with breast cancer. This confession enabled him to recognize how anxious he was, and he stopped making threats. He then phoned his father, who, despite his grief, was staying home because he could not deal with his son. When the mother died (comfortably medicated), the father held his son in his arms, and they grieved together.

Notably, this was a receptive team of caregivers ready to discuss their own emotions. In many subcultures in medicine it would take much more time to establish this sort of self-awareness. For example, I was asked by a Medical Intensive Care Unit (MICU) team to help them with the following problem: transplant surgeons were selectively ignoring those of their patients who had poor medical outcomes and wound up in the MICU. These were patients whom the surgeons had met with daily during their pre- and posttransplant hospital stay but who now were severely ill and dying because their organs had been rejected. The patients or their families noticed the neglect and were very upset about it. It took several months of ongoing weekly shared rounds with both the medical teams before the transplant team's culture began to shift. As they came to trust the other medical team members, they began to express, often through humor, their feelings that they had "killed" their patients. Gradually they became less avoidant of their dying patients in the MICU.

This experience speaks not only to the importance of self-awareness for clinical empathy but also to the question of how to prevent burnout. We might hypothesize that holding such painful feelings and never expressing them might contribute to burnout. What we do know is that physicians whose long-standing styles emphasize receptivity to psychological needs tend to burn out less and enjoy their jobs more. Over the past thirty years a field of research on patient-physician communication has developed, yielding empirical evidence that, indeed, doctors miss important information and are less effective when they are emotionally detached. Further, there are suggestions that emotional engagement makes medical practice more fulfilling for doctors themselves and actually protects against burnout (Jackson et al. 2008; Morse, Mitcham, and van Der Steen 1998; Shanafelt et al. 2005). Those with especially skilled empathy show less burnout (Kearny et al. 2009; Maguire and Pitceathly 2003; Wear and Bickel 2000). This observation begs the question of whether those with skilled empathy might have less self-related anxiety. We do have findings that those with less self-related anxiety are better at perspective-taking/cognitive empathy (Morse, Mitcham, and van Der Steen 1998; Shanafelt et al. 2005; Jackson et al. 2008). Thus, a virtuous cycle could be supported through the integration of skillful empathy in medical practice.

Recently, a new term has emerged—"compassion fatigue"—that may shed important light on barriers to sustaining clinical empathy. Whereas burnout refers to a more global loss of interest in doing one's job, "compassion fatigue" is specifically a lack of empathy when one would expect to feel it. We need research on what specifically causes compassion fatigue. Notably, we see a surprising lack of compassion fatigue in some settings in which we might expect it—hospice physicians, pain-management teams (Kearny et al. 2009). In these settings physicians are immersed in a culture that, unlike the usual medical culture, emphasizes that caregiving requires self-care and conscious attention to grieving and supporting each other. This suggests a positive role for self-care and a culture of connectedness and support in preventing compassion fatigue (Coster and Schwebel 1997; Salston and Figley 2003; Perry 2008; Harrison and Westwood 2009).

A New Model of Clinical Empathy

In conclusion, although empirical research on empathy in medical settings is still at an early stage, we can propose a coherent model for clinical empathy in terms of four basic mutually sustaining aims:

• The first goal is for physicians to *cultivate genuine curiosity* about the complexity of human emotional lives, avoiding too simplistic a view. This curiosity will foster attentive listening and help physicians invite patients to share more complicated feelings.

• The second goal is *nonverbal attentiveness* with the aim of nonverbal attunement. The path to this goal is through practices that instill self-awareness and mindfulness so that physicians can be calm enough to attune to their patients. This attentiveness will support history-taking for accurate and full diagnoses and could improve patient adherence to treatment leading to better clinical outcomes. It can also play a crucial role in giving a patient a sense that she is accompanied when having to face painful issues (Halpern 2001).

• The third goal is maintaining *genuine, proportional concern for one's patients*, so that when something serious is occurring one can convey genuine worry without becoming overly anxious. This skill will promote trust and therapeutic effectiveness, helping patients regain a sense that they truly matter in an often dehumanizing medical system.

• The fourth goal, essential for meeting the third, is instilling a *culture of social support and self-care in clinicians*. Providing support can help doctors and nurses empathize with patients while continuing to enjoy their profession over time.

My hope is that others will take these goals, all of which can be operationalized, and study them empirically. Several important issues need to be examined. These include (1) the pathways through which these processes improve history-taking, diagnosis, and the establishment of effective therapeutic alliances; (2) how feasible it is to engage in such processes in various settings and situations; (3) how patient-physician dyads and group dynamics contribute to the occurrence of empathy; and (4) how any or all of these processes affect health outcomes.

From my own experience the first question that will be asked is not any mentioned above but whether empathic listening takes too much time? Given that empathy improves trust and treatment adherence and helps prevent ruptures in treatment, patient transfers, lawsuits, and burnout, it likely improves the ultimate efficiency as well as the effectiveness of medical care. I have suggested to medical students that, rather than compartmentalizing empathy into an additional task, they think of empathy as an adverb describing *how* they take a history, perform a physical exam, discuss treatment options, resolve conflicts, and so forth. They can listen with curiosity, touch the patient with sensitivity and attunement, and discuss treatment options with respect and concern.

Learning these skills will take time in the physician's education, but does using these skills add time to patient interviews? The only way to answer this question will be through empirical research. Notably, physicians have long assumed that letting patients talk without interruption at the beginning of an office visit would take significantly more time. When this hypothesis was finally tested, it turned out that the median length of time patients spoke for was a mere ninety seconds (Langewitz et al. 2002). Yet this open-ended listening has many benefits. Patients reveal clinically important information and are much more comfortable with their doctor, both of which are likely to make treatment more effective.

In closing, I have laid out a proposal for a *normative* model for clinical empathy that involves engaged curiosity, nonverbal attentiveness, genuine proportional concern for the patient, and self-awareness. By no means should this full or aspirational conception of clinical empathy be used to devalue the variety of empathies that actually occur in clinical practice. It is likely that even the best doctors cannot do all of this well, all of the time. Utilizing some of these skills even in the absence of others—employing cognitive empathy, or attuning nonverbally or feeling appropriate concern—may still be helpful (Larson and Yao, 2005). On the other hand these skills can also work in synergy—often curiosity about another's perspective invites her to tell one details about her life that naturally move one to resonate nonverbally, which leads one to feeling appropriate concern. When physicians become skillful at empathy they find these processes not only mutually sustaining but centering and meaningful (Halpern 2001; Kearny et al. 2009). A final challenge requiring empirical research is how we can educate more physicians to gain the skill to engage in full clinical empathy, thus enhancing both the effectiveness of their care for patients and their own career fulfillment.

References

Aring, C. D. 1958. Sympathy and empathy. *Journal of the American Medical Association* 167:448–452.

Batson, D. 2009. These things called empathy: Eight related but distinct phenomena. In *The Social Neuroscience of Empathy*, ed. J. Decety and W. Ickes, 3–5. Cambridge, MA: Massachusetts Institute of Technology.

Batson, C. D., J. H. Eklund, V. L. Chermok, J. L. Hoyt, and B. G. Ortiz. 2007. An additional antecedent of empathic concern: Valuing the welfare of the person in need. *Journal of Personality and Social Psychology* 93 (1):65–74.

Blumgart, H. L. 1964. Caring for the patient. *New England Journal of Medicine* 270:449–456.

Coster, J. S., and M. Schwebel. 1997. Well-functioning in professional psychologists. *Professional Psychology, Research and Practice* 28 (1):5–13.

Coulehan, J. L. 1995. Tenderness and steadiness: Emotions in medical practice. *Literature and Medicine* 14 (2):222–236.

Coulehan, J., and P. C. Williams. 2003. Conflicting professional values in medical education. *Cambridge Quarterly of Healthcare Ethics* 12:7–20.

Decety, J., and W. Ickes. 2009. *The Social Neuroscience of Empathy*. Cambridge, MA: MIT Press.

Epstein, R. 1999. Mindful practice. *Journal of the American Medical Association* 282 (9):833–839.

Finset, A. 2010. Emotions, narratives and empathy in clinical communication. *International Journal of Integrated Care*. 10 (Suppl. e020).

Fox, R., and H. Lief. 1963. Training for "detached concern.". In *The Psychological Basis of Medical Practice*, ed. H. Lief, 12–35. New York: Harper & Row.

Gockel, A. 2010. The promise of mindfulness for clinical practice education. *Smith College Studies in Social Work* 80 (2):248–268.

Halpern, J. 2001. *From Detached Concern to Empathy: Humanizing Medical Practice*. New York: Oxford University Press.

Halpern, J. 2007. Empathy and patient–physician conflicts. *Journal of General Internal Medicine* 22 (5):696–700.

Halpern J. 2010. When concretized emotion-belief complexes derail decision-making capacity. *Bioethics* E-pub ahead of print.

Harrison, R. L., and M. J. Westwood. 2009. Preventing vicarious traumatization of mental health therapists: Identifying protective practices. *Psychotherapy, Theory, Research. Training (New York, N.Y.)* 46 (2):203–219.

Jackson, P. L., A. N. Meltzoff, and J. Decety. 2005. How do we perceive the pain of others? A window into the neural processes involved in empathy. *NeuroImage* 24 (3):771–779.

Jackson, V. A., J. Mack, R. Matsuyama, M. D. Lakoma, A. M. Sullivan, R. M. Arnold, J. C. Weeks, and S. D. Block. 2008. A qualitative study of oncologists' approaches to end-of-life care. *Journal of Palliative Medicine* 11 (6):893–906.

Kearny, M. K., M. L. S. Vachon, R. L. Harrison, and B. M. Mount. 2009. Self-care of physicians caring for patients at the end of life. *Journal of the American Medical Association* 301 (11):1155–1164.R. B. Weininger

Langewitz, W., M. Denz, A. Keller, A. Kiss, S. Rüttimann, and B. Wössmer. 2002. Spontaneous talking time at start of consultation in outpatient clinic: Cohort study. [Clinical Research Edition] *BMJ (Clinical Research Ed.)* 325:682–683.

Larson, E. B., and X. Yao. 2005. Clinical empathy as emotional labor in the patient-physician relationship. *Journal of the American Medical Association* 293:1100–1106.

Maguire, P., and C. Pitceathly. 2003. Managing the difficult consultation. *Clinical Medicine (London)* 3 (6):532–537.

Markakis, K., R. Frankel, H. Beckman, and A. Suchman. 1999. Teaching Empathy: It Can Be Done. Working paper presented at the Annual Meeting of the Society of General Internal Medicine, San Francisco, CA, April 29–May 1, 1999.

Meier, D. E., A. L. Back, and R. S. Morrison. 2001. The inner life of physicians and care of the seriously ill. *Journal of the American Medical Association* 286:3007–3014.

Morse, J. M., C. Mitcham, and W. J. van Der Steen. 1998. Compathy or physical empathy: Implications for the caregiver relationship. *Journal of Medical Humanities* 19 (1):51–65.

Novack, D. H., A. L. Suchman, W. Clark, R. M. Epstein, E. Najberg, and C. Kaplan. 1997. Calibrating the physician: Personal awareness and effective patient care. *Journal of the American Medical Association* 278:502–509.

Osler, W. 1963. *Aequanimitas*. New York: Norton.

Pedersen, R. 2009. Empirical research on empathy in medicine—A critical review. *Patient Education and Counseling* 76 (3):307–322.

Perry, B. 2008. Why exemplary oncology nurses seem to avoid compassion fatigue. *Canadian Oncology Nursing Journal* 18 (2):87–99.

Ptacek, J. T., and J. J. Ptacek. 2001. Patients' perceptions of receiving bad news about cancer. *Journal of Clinical Oncology* 19:4160–4164.

Reiss, H. 2010. Empathy in medicine—A neurobiological perspective. *Journal of the American Medical Association* 304 (14):1604–1605.

Rossberg, J. I., S. Karterud, G. Pedersen, and S. Friis. 2010. Psychiatric symptoms and counter-transference feelings: An empirical investigation. *Psychiatry Research* 178 (1):191–195.

Roter, D., J. A. Hall, R. Merisca, B. Nordstrom, D. Cretin, and B. Svarstad. 1997a. Effectiveness of interventions to improve patient compliance: A meta-analysis. *Medical Care* 36 (8):1131–1161.

Roter, D., S. Stewart, N. Putnam, and M. Lipkin. 1997b. Communication patterns of primary care physicians. *Journal of the American Medical Association* 277:350–356.

Sabate, E. 2003. *Adherence to Longterm Therapies—Evidence for Action.* Geneva: WHO.

Salston, M., and C. R. Figley. 2003. Secondary traumatic stress effects of working with survivors of criminal victimization. *Journal of Traumatic Stress* 16 (2):167–174.

Schwarz, N. 1983. Mood, misattribution, and judgments of well-being: Informative and directive functions of affective States. *Journal of Personality and Social Psychology* 45 (3):513–523.

Schwarz, N. 2000. Emotion, cognition and decision-making. *Cognition and Emotion* 14 (4):433–440.

Shanafelt, T. D., C. West, X. Zhao, P. Novotny, J. Kolars, T. Habermann, and J. Sloan. 2005. Relationship between increased personal well-being and enhanced empathy among internal medicine residents. *Journal of General Internal Medicine* 20 (7):559–564.

Shapiro, S., G. Schwartz, and G. Bonner. 1998. Effects of mindfulness-based stress reduction on medical and premedical students. *Journal of Behavioral Medicine* 21 (6):581–599.

Steins, G. 2000. Motivation in person perception: The role of the other's perspective. *Journal of Social Psychology* 140 (6):692–709.

Suchman, A. L., K. Markakis, H. B. Beckman, and R. Frankel. 1997. A model of empathic communication in the medical interview. *Journal of the American Medical Association* 277:678–682.

Watson, J. C., and L. S. Greenberg. 2009. Empathic resonance: A neuroscience perspective. In *The Social Neuroscience of Empathy,* ed. J. Decety and W. Ickes, 125–137. Cambridge, MA: MIT Press.

Wear, D., and J. Bickel, eds. 2000. *Educating for Professionalism: Creating a Culture of Humanism in Medical Education.* Iowa City, IA: University of Iowa Press.

14   The Costs of Empathy among Health Professionals

Ezequiel Gleichgerrcht and Jean Decety

When perceiving another person experiencing pain or distress, the scope of the observer's reaction, depending on various interpersonal (e.g., mood, goals, and dispositions) and situational factors, can range from concern for personal safety, including feelings of alarm, fear and avoidance, to concern for the other person, including compassion, sympathy, or even to absolute indifference (Goubert, Craig, and Buysse 2009; Decety 2011a). In the context of care-giving environments, medical practitioners such as physicians, nurses, emergency workers, and therapists have no choice but to interact with people suffering or traumatized as part of their everyday activities. For these practitioners, providing care and helping others is the fundamental aspect of their duties. This painful reality may take its toll on these people and can lead to compassion fatigue, burnout, professional distress and can result in a low sense of accomplishment and severe emotional exhaustion. A better understanding of the neurocognitive mechanisms that underlie interpersonal sensitivity can contribute to preventing such serious health hazards and risks. It also may shed light on the medical profession's longstanding struggle to achieve an appropriate balance between empathy and clinical distance. Such a detachment is often seen as necessary for doctors not only to avoid burning out or fear of losing control but, more importantly, to provide objective medical care. However, as argued by Halpern (2001), physicians' own emotions may help them attune to and empathically understand patients' emotional states and have therapeutic impact. There is growing evidence from psychoneuroimmunology suggesting that care givers who assist in the healing process by truly paying heed to their patients and respecting their integrity enhance rather than hamper their technical skill (Milligan and More 1994).

Central to health care and the patient-physician relationship is the complex construct of *empathy*, which is usually defined as the capacity to understand or appreciate how someone else feels. Unfortunately, this term is applied to various phenomena that cover a broad spectrum, ranging from feelings of concern for other people that create the motivation to help them, to experiencing emotions that match another individual's emotions, knowing what the other is thinking or feeling, to blurring the line between self and other (Batson 2009). This conceptual diversity explains the difficulties in measuring empathy. In fact none of the attempts to quantify it with self-reports, peer ratings, or patient ratings has been able to capture the entire range of affective, cognitive, and behavioral components of empathy. Given the complexity of this construct, and the fact that there is no one-to-one relationship between psychological constructs and brain processes, it should come as no surprise that empathy is implemented by a network of distributed, often recursively connected interacting neural regions and systems (Decety 2011a, 2011b). Converging evidence from animal behavior, functional imaging studies in normal individuals, and lesion studies in neurological patients shows that empathy draws on a wide array of brain structures and systems that are not limited to the cortex, but also extend to, the subcortical nuclei, autonomic nervous system, hypothalamic-pituitary-adrenal (HPA) axis, and endocrine systems that regulate bodily states, emotion, and reactivity (Carter, Harris, and Porges 2009).

In this chapter we begin by setting empathy in the context of medicine and clinical practice by briefly dissecting this complex construct into some of its underlying components as they relate to clinical practice. We then explore the ways in which excessive levels of empathic arousal and poor emotion regulation can lead to professional distress and compassion fatigue, and we present several ways to regulate empathy to avoid such negative and devastating consequences. We conclude by highlighting the importance of balanced levels of empathic responses in health professionals for successful interactions with patients.

The Components of Empathy

In attempting to understand the role of empathy in medical practice, it is crucial first to identify what empathy is about and how it operates in the clinical practice. In doing so, it is useful to distinguish between the affective arousal (also called empathic arousal) elicited by the perception of others' suffering or in distress that helps physicians attune to patients' emotions and the more complex cognitive forms of empathy associated with perspective-taking, mental state understanding, and self-regulation that enable the ability to take the subjective view point of the other while one maintains a sufficient sense of self to permit cognitive structuring of that experience (Decety 2011b). Research in affective neuroscience indicates that affective arousal is a bottom-up process in which the amygdala, hypothalamus, and orbitofrontal cortex (OFC) underlie rapid and prioritized processing of emotion signal; whereas perspective-taking involves the medial prefrontal cortex (mPFC), ventromedial prefrontal cortex (vmPFC), and posterior superior temporal sulcus. Emotion regulation depends on executive functions instantiated in the intrinsic cortico-cortical connections of the OFC, mPFC, and dlPFC as well as connections with subcortical limbic structures such as the amygdala and hypothalamus implicated in processing affective information (Decety and

Jackson 2004; Decety and Meyer 2008; Decety 2010a, 2010b). These networks operate as top-down mediators, crucial in regulating emotions and thereby enhancing flexible and appropriate responses. Finally, empathic concern involves a set of other-oriented emotions felt for someone in need that can produce a motivation to help. Caring for others draws on general mammalian neural systems of social attachment and reward (Watt 2000; Moll et al. 2007), and has its underpinnings in subcortical neural systems similar to those known to regulate parental behavior in other nonhuman mammals including circuits in the brain stem, midbrain connected with the hypothalamus, and ventral tegmental area dopamine systems (Panksepp 1998). Importantly and contrary to what is often thought, empathic concern is not necessarily a product of perceived similarity of the other to the self nor is it elicited by affective sharing or arousal (Batson 2011). We can feel empathic concern for a wide range of others in need, even dissimilar others, as long as we value their welfare. Thus, sharing the affective states of others, understanding their emotional and mental conditions, and caring for them are partly distinct processes, underpinned by interacting, yet specific, neural systems.

Empathy in Medicine

Empathy in medicine has been described in a variety of ways, such as a tool, a skill, a kind of communication, a listening stance, a type of introspection, a capacity, a disposition, an activity, or a feeling (Basch 1983). Most people, especially patients and clients, agree that *being empathic* is a valuable trait in their physician. A growing body of research shows that emotional communication in the patient-physician relationship positively influences healing (Halpern 2001). Thus, empathy has to be conceived as a major *skill* for care providers. But too much sensitivity, may be detrimental to the patient-physician relationship, as well as for the physician's well-being if some aspects of empathy are not well regulated. For example, the emotional intensity of negative arousal that comes from seeing someone with an open fracture may contribute to motivating a physician in aiding the wounded irrespective of his or her own feelings of discomfort or aversion toward a mutilated limb. In accordance for empathic arousal to translate into empathic concern and intervention, care providers must be able to regulate the potential personal distress caused by the situation. Empathic overarousal may promote personal distress to prevail (Eisenberg and Fabes 1992; Eisenberg and Eggum 2009), and thus, the practitioner may tend unconsciously to withdraw him- or herself from the patient in an egoistic motivation to reduce feelings of distress caused by it, therefore decreasing the likelihood of prosocial behavior (Decety and Lamm 2009). Fear of loosing control, of the depleting effects of unguarded openness to one's patients, is a persistent theme in the literature on empathy (Milligan and More 1994).

Empathy is also to be considered an important *cognitive tool* for practitioners them-selves, as they can rely on emotion, reasoning, and understanding in their interactions with their patients. This creates opportunities for knowledge, influencing medical judgment, and therefore contributing to fulfillment of their professional responsibili-ties. It can, naturally, also lead to feelings of comfort, self-appreciation, and reward, which in turn provide further motivation to help others. As we argue later in this chapter, the ability to regulate emotions is crucial for empathy to ultimately have a favorable outcome for both the patient and the care provider.

Empathic concern can further foster a more fruitful *communication process* because patients may be more open to sharing their personal history, symptoms, and suffering with practitioners who they feel are more bound to understanding their subjectivity. This is only possible if the health professional perceives the patient's situation, acknowledges his or her distress, and expresses understanding. Listening while being emotionally engaged not only improves the quality of the patient-physician encounter but also improves the quality of the diagnosis. Clearly, empathy also plays a pivotal role in the consolidation of the patient-doctor relationship. For instance, patients who perceive their doctors as caring are more likely to develop stronger bonds with and have more confidence in them. For a doctor to have his or her patients' *trust* can lead, among other factors, to increased adherence to treatment and increased patient satis-faction (Duberstein et al. 2007; Epstein et al. 2007), thereby contributing to positive patient outcome (see for example, Bennett 2010; Hillen, de Haes, and Smets 2010; Saunders et al. 2010).

Costs to Being Too Empathetic

Although there are many good reasons to be an empathetic physician, there can be too much of a good thing, and there do appear to be costs to being too empathetic.

The ability to adaptively cope with distressing life experiences, and negative emo-tions, is a key self-regulatory challenge. Failing to meet this challenge can be costly, as intrusive and emotionally charged thoughts about these experiences contribute to a variety of clinical disorders. For many health professionals and care providers, the reality of everyday clinical duties—especially the high volume of patients in very reduced timeframes—means continuous exposure to patients in pain or distress. Emo-tional states can transiently enhance or impair high-level cognition. Particularly, the processing of negative emotion is resource competing. A number of studies using experimentally induced approaches and emotional states of withdrawal have demon-strated selective effects on cognitive control (e.g., Gray 2001). Negative emotions may increase the information-processing load and drain attentional resources that otherwise might be devoted to task performance (Ellis and Ashbrook 1988). For instance, after negative emotion induction (exposure to unpleasant pictures from the

International Affective Picture System, such as mutilations), participants made more errors on a task that requires inhibitory control (Sommer et al. 2008). Additionally, negative emotions induced less activation in regions involved in inhibitory control, including the right inferior frontal gyrus, superior frontal gyrus, and anterior cingulate cortex.

Acute sensitivity to the suffering of patients can go beyond occasional feelings of discomfort, anxiety or avoidance, as the constant strain on care providers can lead to the development of compassion fatigue (Figley 2002; Joinson 1992). Health professionals suffering from compassion fatigue exhibit emotional exhaustion, detachment, and a low sense of accomplishment (Maslach, Jackson, and Leiter 1996), which can interfere with their capacity of being of assistance to others (Decety and Lamm 2009). Recently, research devoted to compassion fatigue has demonstrated that it is a complex construct in and of itself and that each symptom may manifest to varying degrees in different individuals (Dyrbye, West, and Shanafelt 2008). Indeed, compassion fatigue constitutes the end result of unregulated affective and empathic responses. Such responses are manifested physiologically by heightened bodily responses that accompany stressful emotions because negative arousal consumes physiological resources at rates greater than baseline (HPA axis, increased sympathetic and cardiovascular responding) (Ehlert and Straub 1998).

Because of the emotional empathetic nature of the work, health professionals working in particular fields are more prone to developing compassion fatigue, including caregivers dealing with patients with chronic conditions, extreme pain, disaster (e.g., terrorist attack) or trauma (e.g., car crash) victims (Palm, Polusny, and Follette 2004). For instance, psychotherapists treating patients who suffered from severe traumatic experiences (e.g., war, sexual abuse) may develop compassion fatigue if they are unable to regulate their capacity to empathize with their patients. Some would argue that compassion fatigue in therapists may result from countertransference—an emotional reaction to the patient—but the latter is a lot more associated with the therapist's personal background than with empathic attachment (Figley 2002; Pearlman and Saakvitne 1995). Nurses working with patients suffering from life-threatening (e.g., cancer) and/or chronic conditions (e.g., AIDS) are also at risk for manifesting compassion fatigue symptoms, especially given the high demands involved in caring for these patients (Omdahl and O'Donnell 1999; Sabo 2006). Physicians working among other fields in emergency units, trauma services, pain clinics, and oncology wards who fail to suppress excessive emotional empathic feeling can develop burnout and/or compassion fatigue. These two concepts have some shared characteristics, but contrary to compassion fatigue, simple burnout is the physical, emotional, and mental exhaustion that comes from long-term exposure to emotionally demanding settings that does not necessarily involve the excessive empathic response to patients in pain or distress (Pines and Aronson 1988). As expected, however, burnout can contribute to the onset of compassion fatigue, which tends to emerge more acutely—especially when it results from an over-sensitive experience with a particular patient or group of patients—and is more strongly associated with feelings of helplessness and trends to professional/social isolation (Figley 2002).

Regulating Empathy

We have argued that there is a cost associated with excessive empathic responses or sensitivity to negative emotion to patients in pain and distress, which can eventually manifest as compassion fatigue and therefore affect the well-being of health practitioners. This, in turn, will most likely interfere with the efficacy of the medical service health professionals are expected to provide. For this reason it is fundamental that caregivers regulate empathy in an attempt to avoid the deleterious effects of excessive caring. In doing so it also is important that an optimal balance be reached between regulation of empathy and caring so that the provider does not suffer from the effects of undershooting empathy toward his or her patients. Excessive regulation has been shown to lead to personal distress and increased anxiety with both physiological and sociopsychological consequences that included increased blood pressure, disrupted communication, and reduced rapport (Butler et al. 2003). In addition, a complete detachment rather than some form of emotional engagement with patients is often believed to protect from burnout, but in fact understanding and influencing patients' emotions positively both influence healing (Halpern 2001).

When healthy individuals are exposed to videos of people expressing pain (facial expressions) or body parts in pain, a neural response is detected in the neural network that processes nociceptive information. This network includes the anterior cingulate cortex, the supplementary motor area (SMA), the anterior insula, the thalamus, the somatosensory cortex, and the periaqueductal gray (PAG) (Jackson, Rainville, and Decety 2006; Lamm, Decety, and Singer 2011). Several dispositional and situational factors have been shown to modulate the perception of pain in others, ranging from cognitive processing and perspective-taking (Jackson et al. 2006; Lamm, Batson, and Decety 2007), and attentional demands (Fan and Han 2008; Gu and Han 2007), to sociopsychological traits, including a priori attitudes toward others (Decety, Echols, and Correll 2010), as well as perceived fairness and social relationship between individuals (Singer et al. 2006). In addition, some evidence exists as to a possible neurobiological predisposition to empathy and stress reactivity. For example, a particular polymorphism of the oxytocin receptor has been linked to decreased "empathy" (more specifically, affective theory of mind) and higher physiological (heart rate) and dispositional (affective reactivity scale) stress (Rodrigues et al. 2009). Similarly, varying levels of alexithymia (deficits in identifying and describing feelings and distinguishing feelings from the bodily sensations of emotional arousal) have been associated with the intensity with which the anterior insula activated in response to the pain of others (Bird et al. 2010).

Among health professionals, however, additional regulation mechanisms may play a central role in modulating empathic response. Two studies have directly investigated how physicians react to the perception of others' pain. One functional MRI study compared the neurohemodynamic response in a group of physicians and a group of matched control participants while they viewed short video clips depicting hands and feet being pricked by a needle (painful situations) or being touched by a Q-tip (nonpainful situations) (Cheng et al. 2007). The results demonstrated that when controls attended to the painful situations relative to the nonpainful ones, a network that overlapped with the so-called pain matrix was activated, which included the anterior insula, anterior cingulate cortex, SMA, somatosensory cortex, and the PAG. This brain network is typically activated when one experiences pain firsthand and might be associated with general survival mechanisms such as aversion and withdrawal when one is exposed to danger and threat (Yamada and Decety 2009; Decety 2010b). Remarkably, a different pattern of signal increase was detected in the physicians when they watched painful procedures. Connectivity analyses showed that cortical regions underpinning executive functions and self-regulation (dorsolateral and medial prefrontal cortex) and executive attention (precentral, superior parietal, and temporoparietal junction) were found to be activated, and unlike in the control group, no signal increase was detected in the pain matrix.

The second study (Decety, Yang, and Cheng 2010) recorded event-related potentials (ERP) from physicians and matched controls as they were presented with the same visual stimuli (needle vs. Q-tip). The results showed early N110 differentiation between pain and no pain, reflecting negative arousal, over the frontal cortex as well as late P3 over the centroparietal regions observed in the control participants. In contrast, no such early ERP response was detected in the physicians, which indicates that affect regulation has very early effects, inhibiting the bottom-up processing of negative arousal arising from the perception of painful stimuli. Taken together, these findings in physicians stress the importance of expertise in modulating the perception of pain in others and their central role in down-regulating the empathic response to pain. Do the results from these studies indicate that physicians have less empathy because they do not activate the pain matrix in response to the perception of others' pain? Probably not. What this research seems to suggest instead is that physicians' down-regulation of the pain response dampens their negative arousal in response to the pain of others, and thus it may have beneficial consequences in freeing up cognitive resources necessary for being of assistance and expressing empathic concern. It is possible that medical practitioners who are most vulnerable to professional distress, which may lead to emotional exhaustion, detachment, and a low sense of accomplishment, are those who have difficulties regulating their negative arousal. It is important to note, however, that a modicum of negative arousal is necessary to help physicians attune to and empathically understand the patient's emotions (Halpern 2001).

The question then remains: Can empathy be regulated, and to what extent does it indeed need to be regulated for the sake of both patients and doctors in medical settings? If we consider that the costs of emotional empathy among health professionals are related to high levels of emotional arousal when one perceives the pain or distress of others, regulation of empathic concern must be achieved by reducing that concern. Several strategies may be used to regulate emotional empathy that vary in the degree of personal effort they demand (Benbassat and Baumal 2004; Hodges and Biswas-Diener 2007) and, more importantly, may carry severe consequences of their own. Perhaps the least effortful mechanism is simply *exposure control*: if we do not expose ourselves to the target of empathy (e.g., a patient in extreme pain), we will automatically reduce emotional empathy just because we are controlling the stimuli inducing the emotional response. In medicine, however, exposure control means being unable to provide medical care, thereby interfering with the responsibilities expected from a professional in the field. This simple mechanism, nonetheless, may prompt for the development and design of clinical shifts that allow for a more balanced exposure. For example, a resident in surgical oncology may be granted two hours of out-patient care for every four hours spent on the surgical floor interacting with the more extreme cases.

Another strategy aimed at regulating emotional empathy is *emotion suppression*, which simply implies not thinking about the empathy-inducing stimuli (e.g., "This patient is suffering no pain whatsoever"). One can imagine, however, that in the context of high affective arousal (e.g., treating an acute trauma patient), emotional suppression may be especially effortful from a cognitive perspective and may actually interfere with one's ability to provide care. Perhaps a less extremist approach is *framing*, which may be achieved in several ways. For instance, one may attempt to reinterpret the entire situation (e.g., "I understand this patient is in extreme pain, but I also believe his reaction may be exacerbated by the psychological trauma and that the pain is not as severe. I am also aware that my intervention is needed to make the patient feel better"). Another approach may be to increase the distinction between the self and the patient in pain or distress, for example, by objectifying the patient. By perceiving the empathy-inducing agent as inhuman, the self versus other distinction increases followed by a decrease in the empathic response. Evidently, these reframing strategies imply high levels of cognitive demand, but over time, they may become easier and more automatic (Hodges and Biswas-Diener 2007).

Whether any, some, or all of these regulatory strategies play a role in the down-regulation of empathic responses observed in physicians is yet to be determined. Some research studies have attempted to determine the way empathy evolves throughout medical training. In a group of internal medicine residents empathy levels were recorded using the Interpersonal Reactivity Inventory (IRI) (Davis 1983) at the beginning and toward the end of their internship year. Relative to the start of the year, significantly lower levels of empathic concern and significantly higher levels of personal distress were observed on internship completion (Bellini, Baime, and Shea 2002). These changes were not without a cost to the residents: they also showed increased depression, anger, and fatigue. It is possible, though, that down-regulation of empathy does not necessarily occur once students have graduated and entered into the real clinical professional world. In academic programs that include exposure to patients during medical school, empathy decreases may be observed during graduate academic training. For instance, in a sample of medical students, empathy was measured using the Jefferson Scale of Physician Empathy (JSPE) (Hojat 2007) throughout the four years of medical school (Hojat et al. 2009). A significant decrease in empathy levels was found during the third year which continued on to the fourth year. Remarkably, the phenomenon remained when distinguishing between genders and across specialties. Not surprisingly, the third year, at least in the United States as well as in other countries, is when students start engaging in patient-care activities. Whether the decrease in empathic response at this stage is an anticipatory regulatory mechanism in face of increased exposure, a premature consequence of early interactions with patients, or both, is worthy of further research. Another intriguing issue is whether decreased empathy in medical students is related with depression induced by the high demands of medical school or with burnout–compassion-fatigue symptoms such as depersonalization. In a large cohort of medical students (Thomas et al. 2007), the latter seemed to be more strongly associated with the decrease of empathy than the former. However, dissociating depression from depersonalization using self-administered questionnaires can limit their potential utility in measuring such complex constructs, so further evidence is needed to determine what factors contribute to empathy decreases throughout academic medical training.

Training for Empathy in Medicine

We have so far acknowledged that there is a down-regulation of empathy that comes with expertise in medical settings. What empirical research seems to suggest is that caregivers' down-regulation of the emotional response dampens their negative arousal in response to the pain or distress of others and may thus have beneficial consequences in freeing up cognitive resources necessary for being of assistance and expressing empathic concern. But again, a complete emotional detachment is detrimental to the patient-physician relationship. It has been argued that detachment does not make medicine more rational; rather, it forces irrationality underground, where it poses as certainty of the future and other irrational assumptions (Halpern 2001, 29). We have also identified possible regulatory mechanisms that will decrease emotional empathy, although they too may be costly if done excessively or too intensively. In general, however, little training is given to care providers in everyday clinical settings to learn how to regulate empathy. For example, in analyzing audiorecorded transcribed consultations between patients with lung cancer and their thoracic surgeons or oncologists, only 10 percent of the empathic opportunities (e.g., patients asking about symptoms, morbidity, or about treatment options) were responded to empathically (Morse, Edwardsen, and Gordon 2008). In training for empathy the main objective should be to achieve the optimal balance between being empathic without suffering from the costs that come from overstimulating negative emotional arousal. We want our health professionals to be able to respond empathically to patients in pain or distress because, as argued above, it will generate the motivation to help these patients, who will most likely show increased adherence to treatment and patient satisfaction. In fact, both higher efficacy of treatment provided and increased professional satisfaction have been recognized in physicians who engage in empathic responses more frequently (Larson and Yao 2005).

Because caring for others is the core element of empathy, identifying the patient's needs and concerns is a fundamental step when one is engaging in an empathic response. Several strategies have been proposed to *train* caregivers for this purpose by focusing on the features of the empathic process that can actually be controlled (Benbassat and Baumal 2004), which include but are not limited to: ensuring as much privacy for the patient as possible when conducting the interview; listening carefully to the patient's story, making eye contact, and avoiding interruptions for at least a couple of minutes; delaying writing up on patient's charts for as long as possible; enquiring further into the patient's concerns; and leaving written accounts of these concerns on the patient's charts. The emotional response to a patient in distress inevitably involves autonomic aspects over which we have no full control (Campbell-Yeo, Latimer, and Johnston 2008). In this sense another key feature of empathy training may involve learning to identify the autonomic changes that come from emotional arousal (e.g., increased heart rate) and ways in which regulatory mechanisms as the ones discussed before can be implemented to dampen high-intensity responses.

The development of empathy-training programs based on empirical evidence is essential, as it may be fairly easy to rely on popular folk wisdom about what helps patients feel more at ease with their caregiver. For instance, there is a common belief that doctors who spontaneously share information about their own physical or mental health or comment on their own beliefs or previous experiences—but not in response to the patient's concern—will have a better rapport with patients. So much so, that in primary care alone, about 30 percent of physicians are talking about themselves during consultation (Beach, Roter, Larson, et al. 2004; Beach, Roter, Rubin, et al. 2004; McDaniel et al. 2007), and yet, these disclosures have not been shown effective in increasing the conveying of understanding, helping patients to engage in improved self-care, or in increasing patient-physician rapport (Morse et al. 2008). On the contrary, incorporating the biopsychological approaches based on empirical studies that we outlined above to patient-care practices has been demonstrated to have multiple positive consequences in patient treatment, including the prescription of fewer medications, ordering fewer laboratory examinations, and it eventually led to higher scores of patient satisfaction (Margalit et al. 2004).

Conclusion

Empathy in medicine, the capacity to take in and appreciate the affective life of another person while maintaining a sufficient sense of self to permit cognitive structuring of that experience, involves sharing and appreciating the emotional and affective states of patients. It plays a central role in the patient-practitioner interaction, as it may foster better communication and lead to increased rapport (see Halpern this volume). These, in turn, may result in stronger adherence to treatment, improved patient satisfaction, and more tailored clinical interventions (Margalit et al. 2004; Epstein et al. 2007). Being too empathic, however, can be costly. When exposed to high levels of negative emotional arousal, health professionals can develop compassion fatigue (Hodges and Biswas-Diener 2007; Decety, Yang, and Cheng 2010), exhibiting depersonalization, a low sense of accomplishment, and fundamentally, severe emotional exhaustion (Maslach, Jackson, and Leiter 1996; Figley 2002). A dramatic illustration was recently provided by a study reporting high prevalence of distress and less altruistic attitudes among medical students (Dyrbye et al. 2010). Importantly, students who suffered from personal distress were more susceptible to engage in dishonest clinical behaviors.

Interacting and providing efficient care for patients can be extremely difficult. In this sense, the empathic response to patients in distress leads almost to a paradoxical scenario: caring is important to be motivated to help others, but caring may also lead to high levels of personal distress that can interfere with one's ability to help others. On the other end, *not* caring can also be costly and manifest through physical and psychological signs that interfere with delivery of treatment (Butler et al. 2003). For these reasons, it is crucial that health professionals develop regulatory mechanisms to dampen the emotional response to suffering patients just enough to avoid the collateral damage that comes from caring excessively (i.e., compassion fatigue), yet not to the extent that they become blunted or insensitive to the affective signal expressed by patients.

Empirical evidence demonstrates that physicians are able to down-regulate their empathic response to pain to a great extent (Cheng et al. 2007; Decety, Yang, and Cheng 2010). Said empathic regulation seems to be associated with activation of brain areas typically related to cognitive control and executive attention, as well as attenuated early and late ERP responses to pain. Whether these mechanisms are the result of conscious or unconscious cognitive control is yet to be elucidated. Noticeably, empathy seems to also suffer erosion during medical school (Thomas et al. 2007; Hojat et al. 2009) and internship-residency (Bellini, Baime, and Shea 2002), as medical students and professionals are increasingly exposed to patients. It is likely that the decrease in empathic responses results, among other factors, from the hectic reality of clinics, overly demanding patients, patients who show little appreciation, issues of malpractice, restrictive decision-making in compliance with hospital guidelines, and increased personal distress (Thomas et al. 2007; Hojat et al. 2009).

As mentioned above, neither of the extreme levels of empathy (i.e., too little or too much) is beneficial for caregivers and, consequently, for patients. For this reason it is fundamental that training programs be designed to *train* empathy based on empirical evidence. There are several regulatory strategies that can be implemented in everyday practice that require training before they can become useful in everyday medical settings. These strategies include patient-oriented approaches, such as the patient-centered interview carefully attending to his or her concerns, and caregiver-oriented approaches, which include empathy-regulation strategies such as exposure control, emotion suppression, reframing, and cognitive control over autonomic responses.

Overall, the medical arena faces the fundamental challenges of designing and tailoring training and clinical programs aimed at providing caregivers with the tools necessary to reach the optimal balance between caring for their patients and regulating the emotional responses to their pain and distress. Not only will this have a direct impact on health professionals' physical and psychological health, but it will also affect the quality and efficacy of treatment, and ultimately, the patient's outcome.

References

Basch, M. 1983. Empathic understanding: A review of the concept and some theoretical considerations. *Journal of the American Psychoanalytic Association* 31: 101–125.

Batson, C. D. 2009. These things called empathy: Eight related but distinct phenomena. In *The Social Neuroscience of Empathy*, edited by J. Decety and W. J. Ickes, 3–15. Cambridge, MA: MIT Press.

Batson, C. D. 2011. *Altruism in Humans*. New York: Oxford University Press.

Beach, M. C., D. Roter, S. Larson, W. Levinson, D. E. Ford, and R. Frankel. 2004. What do physicians tell patients about themselves? A qualitative analysis of physician self-disclosure. *Journal of General Internal Medicine* 19 (9): 911–916.

Beach, M. C., D. Roter, H. Rubin, R. Frankel, W. Levinson, and D. E. Ford. 2004. Is physician self-disclosure related to patient evaluation of office visits? *Journal of General Internal Medicine* 19 (9): 905–910.

Bellini, L. M., M. Baime, and J. A. Shea. 2002. Variation of mood and empathy during internship. *Journal of the American Medical Association* 287 (23): 3143–3146.

Benbassat, J., and R. Baumal. 2004. What is empathy, and how can it be promoted during clinical clerkships? *Academic Medicine* 79 (9): 832–839.

Bennett, J. K., J. N. Fuertes, M. Keitel, and R. Phillips. 2010. The role of patient attachment and working alliance on patient adherence, satisfaction, and Health-Related Quality of life in lupus treatment. *Patient Education and Counseling* E-pub ahead of print.

Bird, G., G. Silani, R. Brindley, S. White, U. Frith, and T. Singer. 2010. Empathic brain responses in insula are modulated by levels of alexithymia but not autism. *Brain* 133: 1515–1525.

Butler, E. A., B. Egloff, F. H. Wilhelm, N. C. Smith, E. A. Erickson, and J. J. Gross. 2003. The social consequences of expressive suppression. *Emotion (Washington, DC)* 3 (1): 48–617.

Campbell-Yeo, M., M. Latimer, and C. Johnston. 2008. The empathetic response in nurses who treat pain: concept analysis. *Journal of Advanced Nursing* 61 (6): 711–719.

Carter, S. S., J. Harris, and S. W. Porges. 2009. Neural and evolutionary perspectives on empathy. In *The Social Neuroscience of Empathy*, edited by J. Decety and W. J. Ickes, 169–182. Cambridge, MA: MIT Press.

Cheng, Y., C. P. Lin, H. L. Liu, Y. Y. Hsu, K. E. Lim, D. Hung, et al. 2007. Expertise modulates the perception of pain in others. *Current Biology* 17 (19): 1708–1713.

Davis, M. H. 1983. Measuring individual differences in empathy: Evidence for a multidimensional approach. *Journal of Personality and Social Psychology* 44 (1): 113–126.

Decety, J. 2010a. The neurodevelopment of empathy in humans. *Developmental Neuroscience* 32 (4): 257–267.

Decety, J. 2010b. To What extent is the experience of empathy mediated by shared neural circuits? *Emotion Review* 2: 204–207.

Decety, J. 2011a. Dissecting the neural mechanisms mediating empathy. *Emotion Review* 3: 92–108.

Decety, J. 2011b. The neuroevolution of empathy. *Annals of the New York Academy of Sciences*. Epub ahead of print

Decety, J., S. Echols, and J. Correll. 2010. The blame game: The effect of responsibility and social stigma on empathy for pain. *Journal of Cognitive Neuroscience* 22 (5): 985–997.

Decety, J., and P. L. Jackson. 2004. The functional architecture of human empathy. *Behavioral and Cognitive Neuroscience Reviews* 3: 71–100.

Decety, J., and C. Lamm. 2009. Empathy versus personal distress—Recent evidence from social neuroscience. In *The Social Neuroscience of Empathy*, edited by J. Decety and W. J. Ickes, 199–213. Cambridge, MA: MIT Press.

Decety, J., and M. Meyer. 2008. From emotion resonance to empathic understanding: A social developmental neuroscience account. *Development and Psychopathology* 20 (4): 1053–1080.

Decety, J., C. Y. Yang, and Y. Cheng. 2010. Physicians down-regulate their pain empathy response: An event-related brain potential study. *NeuroImage* 50 (4): 1676–1682.

Duberstein, P., S. Meldrum, K. Fiscella, C. G. Shields, and R. M. Epstein. 2007. Influences on patients' ratings of physicians: Physicians demographics and personality. *Patient Education and Counseling* 65 (2): 270–274.

Dyrbye, L. N., F. S. Massie, A. Eacker, W. Harper, D. Power, S. J. Durning, M. R. Thomas, C. Moutier, D. Satele, J. Sloan, T. D. Shanafelt. 2010. Relationship between burnout and professional conduct and attitudes among US medical students. *Journal of the American Medical Association* 304: 1173–80.

Dyrbye, L. N., C. P. West, and T. D. Shanafelt. 2008. Defining burnout as a dichotomous variable. *Journal of General Internal Medicine* 24 (3): 440.

Dyrbye, L. N., F. S. Massie, A. Eacker, W. Harper, D. Power, S. J. Durning, M. R. Thomas, et al. 2010. Relationship between burnout and professional conduct and attitudes among US medical students. *Journal of the American Medical Association* 304: 1173–1180.

Ehlert, U., and R. Straub. 1998. Physiological and emotional response to psychological stressors in psychiatric and psychosomatic disorders. *Annals of the New York Academy of Sciences* 851: 477–486.

Eisenberg, N., and N. D. Eggum. 2009. Empathic responding: sympathy and personal distress. In *The Social Neuroscience of Empathy*, edited by J. Decety and W. J. Ickes, 71–83. Cambridge, MA: MIT Press.

Eisenberg, N., and R. A. Fabes. 1992. Emotion regulation and the development of social competence. In *Review of Personality and Social Psychology: Vol. 14. Emotion and Social Behavior*, edited by M. S. Clark, 119–50. Newbury Park, CA: Sage.

Ellis, H. C., and P. W. Ashbrook. 1988. Resource allocation model of the effects of depresses mood states on memory. In *Affect, Cognitive and Social Behavior*, edited by K. Fiedler and J. Forgas, 25–43. Toronto: Hogrefe.

Epstein, R. M., T. Hadee, J. Carroll, S. C. Meldrum, J. Lardner, and C. G. Shields. 2007. "Could this be something serious?" Reassurance, uncertainty, and empathy in response to patients' expressions of worry. *Journal of General Internal Medicine* 22 (12): 1731–1739.

Fan, Y., and S. Han. 2008. Temporal dynamic of neural mechanisms involved in empathy for pain: An event-related brain potential study. *Neuropsychologia* 46 (1): 160–173.

Figley, C. R. 2002. Compassion fatigue: Psychotherapists' chronic lack of self care. *Journal of Clinical Psychology* 58 (11): 1433–1441.

Goubert, L., K. D. Craig, and A. Buysse. 2009. Perceiving others in pain: experimental and Clinical Evidence on the role of empathy. In *The Social Neuroscience of Empathy*, edited by J. Decety and W. Ickes, 153–65. Cambridge, MA: MIT Press.

Gray, J. R. 2001. Emotional modulation of cognitive control: Approach-withdrawal states double-dissociate spatial from verbal two-back task performance. *Journal of Experimental Psychology. General* 130: 436–452.

Gu, X., and S. Han. 2007. Attention and reality constraints on the neural processes of empathy for pain. *NeuroImage* 36 (1): 256–267.

Halpern, J. 2001. *From Detached Concern to Empathy*. New York: Oxford University Press.

Hillen, M. A., de Haes, H. C., and Smets, E. M. 2010. Cancer patients trust in their physician: A review. *Psychooncology* 20: 227–241.

Hodges, S. D., and R. Biswas-Diener. 2007. Balancing the empathy expense account: Strategies for regulating empathic response. In *Empathy in Mental Illness*, edited by T. F. D. Farrow and P. W. R. Woodruff, 389–405. Cambridge: Cambridge University Press.

Hojat, M. 2007. *Empathy in Patient Care: Antecedents, Development, Measurement, and Outcomes*. New York: Springer.

Hojat, M., M. J. Vergare, K. Maxwell, G. Brainard, S. K. Herrine, G. A. Isenberg, et al. 2009. The devil is in the third year: A longitudinal study of erosion of empathy in medical school. *Academic Medicine* 84 (9): 1182–1191.

Jackson, P. L., E. Brunet, A. N. Meltzoff, and J. Decety. 2006. Empathy examined through the neural mechanisms involved in imagining how i feel versus how you feel pain: An event-related fMRI study. *Neuropsychologia* 44: 752–761.

Jackson, P. L., P. Rainville, and J. Decety. 2006. To what extent do we Share the pain of others? Insight from the neural bases of pain empathy. *Pain* 125: 5–9.

Joinson, C. 1992. Coping with compassion fatigue. *Nursing* 22 (4): 116, 118–119, 120.

Lamm, C., C. D. Batson, and J. Decety. 2007. The neural substrate of Human Empathy: Effects of perspective-taking and cognitive appraisal. *Journal of Cognitive Neuroscience* 19 (1): 42–58.

Lamm, C., J. Decety, and T. Singer. 2011. Meta-analytic evidence for common and distinct neural networks associated with directly experienced pain and empathy for pain. *NeuroImage* 54(3): 2492–2502.

Larson, E. B., and X. Yao. 2005. Clinical empathy as emotional labor in the patient-physician relationship. *Journal of the American Medical Association* 293 (9): 1100–1106.

Margalit, A. P., S. M. Glick, J. Benbassat, and A. Cohen. 2004. Effect of a biopsychosocial approach on patient satisfaction and patterns of care. *Journal of General Internal Medicine* 19 (5 Pt 2): 485–491.

Maslach, C., S. E. Jackson, and M. P. Leiter. 1996. *Maslach Burnout Inventory Manual*, 3rd ed. Palo Alto, CA: Consulting Psychologists Press.

McDaniel, S. H., H. B. Beckman, D. S. Morse, J. Silberman, D. B. Seaburn, and R. M. Epstein. 2007. Physician self-disclosure in primary care visits: Enough about you, what about me? *Archives of Internal Medicine* 167 (12): 1321–1326.

Milligan, M. A., and E. S. More. 1994. Introduction. In *The Empathic Practitioner*, edited by E. S. Moore and M. A. Milligan, 1–15. New Brunswick, NJ: Rutgers University Press.

Moll, J., R. de Oliveira-Souza, G. J. Garrido, I. E. Bramati, E. M. Caparelli-Daquer, M. L. Paiva, et al. 2007. The self as a moral agent: Linking the neural bases of social agency and moral sensitivity. *Social Neuroscience* 2 (3–4): 336–352.

Morse, D. S., E. A. Edwardsen, and H. S. Gordon. 2008. Missed opportunities for interval empathy in lung cancer communication. *Archives of Internal Medicine* 168 (17): 1853–1858.

Morse, D. S., S. H. McDaniel, L. M. Candib, and M. C. Beach. 2008. "Enough about me, let's get back to you": Physician self-disclosure during primary care encounters. *Annals of Internal Medicine* 149 (11): 835–837.

Omdahl, B. L., and C. O'Donnell. 1999. Emotional contagion, empathic concern and communicative responsiveness as variables affecting nurses' stress and occupational commitment. *Journal of Advanced Nursing* 29 (6): 1351–1359.

Palm, K. M., M. A. Polusny, and V. M. Follette. 2004. Vicarious traumatization: Potential hazards and interventions for disaster and Trauma Workers. *Prehospital and Disaster Medicine* 19 (1): 73–78.

Panksepp, J. 1998. *Affective Neuroscience*. New York: Oxford University Press.

Pearlman, L. A., and K. W. Saakvitne. 1995. *Trauma and the Therapist: Countertransference and Vicarious Traumatization in Psychotherapy with Incest Survivors*. New York: Norton.

Pines, A., and E. Aronson. 1988. *Career Burnout: Causes and Cures*. New York: Free Press.

Rodrigues, S. M., L. R. Saslow, N. Garcia, O. P. John, and D. Keltner. 2009. Oxytocin receptor genetic variation relates to empathy and stress reactivity in humans. *Proceedings of the National Academy of Sciences of the United States of America* 106 (50): 21437–21441.

Sabo, B. M. 2006. Compassion fatigue and Nursing Work: Can we accurately capture the consequences of caring work? *International Journal of Nursing Practice* 12 (3): 136–142.

Saunders, C., C. Caon, J. Smrtka, and J. Shoemaker. 2010. Factors that influence adherence and strategies to maintain adherence to injected therapies for patients with multiple sclerosis. *Journal of Neuroscience Nursing* 42 (5 Suppl): S10–S18.

Singer, T., B. Seymour, J. P. O'Doherty, K. E. Stephan, R. J. Dolan, and C. D. Frith. 2006. Empathic neural responses are modulated by the perceived fairness of others. *Nature* 439 (7075): 466–469.

Sommer, M., G. Hajak, K. Dohnel, J. Meihardt, and J. L. Muller. 2008. Emotion-dependent modulation of interference processes: An fMRI study. *Acta Neurobiologiae Experimentalis* 68: 193–203.

Thomas, M. R., L. N. Dyrbye, J. L. Huntington, K. L. Lawson, P. J. Novotny, J. A. Sloan, T. D. Shanafelt. 2007. How do distress and well-being relate to medical student empathy? A multicenter study. *Journal of General Internal Medicine* 22 (2): 177–183.

Watt, D. F. 2000. The centrencephalon and thalamocortical integration: Neglected contributions of periaqueductal gray. *Emotion and Consciousness* 1: 93–116.

Yamada, M., and J. Decety. 2009. Unconscious affective processing and empathy: An investigation of subliminal priming on the detection of painful facial expressions. *Pain* 143: 71–75.

15   The Empathic Response in Clinical Practice: Antecedents and Consequences

Charles R. Figley

You've gotta have heart
All you really need is heart. . .
—From the musical *Damn Yankees*

Practitioners without the empathic response fail to promote healing. It is a fact demonstrated time and again by psychologists, physicians, nurses, the clergy, and other "arrow removers."[1]

At my former university I directed the PhD Program in Marriage and the Family and directed the Friday Trauma Clinic. The students who performed very well in the classroom tended to do the same in the clinic. The exceptions were instructive, however. Those top students who underperformed in the clinic were those unable to empathize and unable to take the position of clients, who never would experience vicarious trauma because it requires empathy (Figley 1995).

Purpose

I wrote this chapter with students in mind who may be interested in the psychoneuroimmunology of emotions, a key element of the science of emotion. But I also wanted to write a chapter for my colleagues in other fields under the broad umbrella of this extraordinary book. My purpose, then, is to share my views about the extraordinary importance of emotions and especially the empathic response in clinical practice.

I have four goals, and they largely organize this chapter. First, I define and discuss the importance of the empathic response for mental health professionals and link this with other healers. Second, I discuss vicarious trauma (cause) and compassion fatigue (consequence) as "healer's burdens." Any practitioner working with the traumatized or any other emotionally injured patients will recognize the signs and symptoms.

In the next section I discuss empathy and resilience as a goal to prepare healers for clinical practice and, in turn, to help patients appreciate the importance of sustainable resilience and helping others—other healers and even patients—develop tools for healer or practitioner resilience. The final section discusses some tools for developing and sustaining healer empathic responses and ways of monitoring the success of such responses.

Why the Empathic Response Matters

Empathic response is the opposite of a defensive or reactive response. To give an example, if on seeing the outstretched arm (of a person or of a statue) we feel in the muscles of our own arm the tensions associated with being outstretched, then the response is empathic. If, on the other hand, we react to the outstretched arm by blocking it, our response could be called defensive or reactive.

Empathy, as broadly defined in the social and health sciences, appears to be an important element in the interpersonal repertoire of the human service providers such as social worker child protection workers (Forrester et al. 2007), social workers (Figley, 1993). psychologists (Rogers 1961), rehabilitation professionals (Stebnicki 2000), nurses (White 1997), family therapists (Figley and Nelson 1989), animal care workers (Figley and Roop, 2006) and other human service professions. We define empathy, consistent with Decety and Lamm (2006) as the ability to experience and understand what others feel without confusion between oneself and others. We define empathy as a noun that represents the intellectual identification with or vicarious experiencing of the feelings, thoughts, or attitudes of another.

Some (Langfield 1953) date the origin of the concept of empathy to Lepps who, in 1887, described *Einfrehlung* as the experience of losing one's self-awareness and fusing with an object intellectually and emotionally. Less than thirty years later, Tichener (1924) and then Allport (1937) and others have suggested the critically important role of empathy (and related processes) as an indicator of humanity as well as important markers for understanding and helping others. Rogers (1980, 146) noted that ". . . the ideal therapist is, first of all, empathic." Rogers's model of empathy (1961) led to a program research for measuring empathy and its impact on those seeking counseling. Truax and Carkhuff (1967) designed the first empathy scale, the Truax Accurate Empathy Scale, later revised by Carkhuff (1969).

Tallman and Bohart's (1999) review of the practice literature notes that patients are clearly the most important factor in predicting outcome in psychotherapy practice. These patient factors include faith, optimism, and social resources. Of special interest is the interface between the patient's emotional characteristics and those of the practitioner.

In their chapter on the empirical case for the common factors in therapy, Asay and Lambert (1999) indicated that a correlation exists as high as $r = 0.82$ between empathy and therapeutic outcome and that it is a largely about the therapeutic alliance, the sense of comfort and fit experienced by both the practitioner and the patient. They suggested that there are four major factors that, collectively, account for success as a practitioner of mental health services: client factors, therapeutic alliance factors, psychological expectancy factors, and treatment approach factors.

Each of these factors can play a role in the therapeutic alliance that must develop between patient and practitioner.

Client Factors Asay and Lambert (1999) suggest that, as others (e.g., Bergin and Garfield 1994; Duncan, Miller, and Sparks 2004) noted earlier, client factors are the most important in accounting for successful treatment, ascribing 40 percent of the variance.

Therapeutic Alliance These are the relationship-mediated variables found across treatment approaches that note the importance of team work in reaching client goals; a partnership (Bordin, 1979; Orlinsky, Grawe, and Parks 1994). Asay and Lambert (1999) suggest that these factors account for 30 percent of the variance in clinical outcome.

Psychological Expectancy This is a class of factors associated with the patient's assessment of the credibility of the practitioner's efforts and includes such things as placebo effects and a sense of hope and confidence in the process. Asay and Lambert (1999) suggest that these factors account for 15 percent of the variance in clinical outcome.

Treatment Approach Ironically, the push for evidence-based practice among treatment approaches turns out to be one of the least important in terms of the actual impact of the approaches. Asay and Lambert (1999) suggest that these factors account for 15 percent of the variance in clinical outcome. This is consistent with some earlier theorists who suggested that any treatment approach could be considered simply as a "healing ritual" not unlike Native American rituals following battle or a death (Frank 1973; Rosenzweig 1936). Miller et al. (1995) noted that ". . . 30 years of research evidence . . . makes it clear that the similarities rather than the differences between models" account for most of the change that client outcome. He urged practitioners to be more open minded about change in their patients.

Thus, the key factor or active ingredient in effective helping is imparting the empathic response required to effectively deliver human services. But what about the cost of caring; the downside for practitioners who "fuse with" their patients' experiences and suffering?

The Impact of the Empathic Response on the Practitioner

As a practitioner, the down side of imparting regular and high-quality empathic responses to patients, day after day, can and often does lead to a special kind of strain or stress reaction associated with empathy. This is the cost of caring: the caring continues to occupy the mind of the practitioner and can lead eventually to depression, despair, and hopelessness that can be characterized as *compassion fatigue* (Figley 1995).

Being aware of our emotions and how they affect our actions is a key component to a successful personal relationship such as the one between patient and service provider. Practitioners began to admit the negative, traumatic experiences, and consequences of their work through personal reflection such as those of William James and the origins of modern psychology (Richardson 2006).

The American Psychiatric Association's diagnostic disorders manual DSM IV (American Psychiatric Association 1994) notes that posttraumatic stress disorder (PTSD) is possible only when one is traumatized either directly (in harm's way) or indirectly. Both victims may experience trauma, through different social pathways. The latter pathway is called *compassion fatigue* or secondary traumatic stress reactions. There are few reports of the incidence and prevalence of this type of stress reaction. However, based on secondary data and theory analysis, burnout, countertransference, worker dissatisfaction, and other related concepts may have masked this common problem (Figley 1995). Vicarious traumatization, for example, refers to a transformation in the therapist's (or other trauma worker's) "inner experience resulting from empathic engagement with clients' trauma material. . .[and] vulnerable to the emotional and spiritual effects of vicarious traumatization. . ." (Pearlman and Saakvitne 1995, 151). Alternatively, vicarious trauma can be viewed as secondary traumatic stressors first identified in one person and then in another with whom she or he identifies in an effort to understand and help (Figley 2002).

With the publication of *Compassion Fatigue* (Figley 1995) and the subsequent book (Figley 2002) focusing on the assessment and treatment of compassion fatigue, practitioners began to recognize the impact of this work on themselves and their morale.

The concept of compassion fatigue has been around only since 1992 when Joinson used the term in a nursing magazine. It fit the description of nurses who were worn down by the daily hospital emergencies they faced. That same year Kottler (1992) in his book *Compassionate Therapy* emphasized the importance of compassion in dealing with extremely difficult and resistant patients.

The dictionary meaning of compassion is a "feeling of deep sympathy and sorrow for another who is stricken by suffering or misfortune, accompanied by a strong desire to alleviate the pain or remove its cause" (*Webster's* 1989, 229). Some would argue that it is wrong for a practitioner to have deep feelings of sympathy and sorrow for her or his client's suffering. And certainly practitioners must understand their limitations in helping to alleviate the pain suffered by their clients.

Yet, most systematic studies of the effectiveness of therapy point to the therapeutic alliance between client and clinician, the ability to empathize to understand and help clients (Figley and Nelson 1989). If it is not present, it is highly unlikely that therapeutic change will take place. The most important ingredients in building a therapeutic alliance include the client liking and trusting her or his therapist. And these feelings are directly related to the degree to which the therapist utilizes and expresses empathy and compassion.

Contrasts between Compassion Fatigue and Related Concepts

Compassion fatigue is the latest in an evolving concept that is known in the field as secondary traumatic stress. Most often this phenomenon is associated with the "cost of caring" (Figley 1982) for others in emotional pain. There are a number of terms that describe this phenomenon. It has been described as secondary victimization (Figley 1982), secondary traumatic stress (Figley 1982, 1985, 1989; Stamm 1996, 1997), vicarious traumatization (McCann and Pearlman 1989; Pearlman and Saakvitne 1995), and secondary survivor (Remer and Elliott 1988, 1988b). A similar concept, *emotional contagion*, is defined as an affective process in which "an individual observing another person experiences emotional responses parallel to that person's actual or anticipated emotions" (Miller, Stiff, and Ellis 1988, 254). Also rape-related family crisis (Erickson, 1989) and *proximity effects* on female partners of war veterans (Verbosky and Ryan 1988) are related concepts. The generational effects of trauma (McCubbin et al. 1977; Danieli 1985) and the need for family "detoxification" from war-related traumatic stress (Rosenheck and Thomson 1986) have been noted.

Finally, some view difficulties with client problems as a matter of simple counter-transference, and this has been discussed within the context of PTSD treatment (Danieli 1988; Maroda 1991; Herman 1992; Wilson and Lindy 1994). However, the concept is encased in an elaborate theoretical context that is difficult to measure, and traumatic issues from all others in the client-therapist transactions.

Confronting Healer Burdens

Since vicarious trauma leads to compassion fatigue, the latter is considered the "healer's burdens." Any practitioner working with the traumatized or any other emotionally injured patients will recognize the signs and symptoms.

Figure 15.1 describes the process by which practitioners, drawing on their own levels of empathic ability and interest in helping the patient, can lead to an appropriate empathic response. Such a response draws on all their skills and is discussed in the next section. In the process of position-taking the practitioner becomes more vulnerable to negative consequences represented by *residual compassion stress*.

This is the processing of the demand to be empathic and compassionate during the session. Such stressors are associated with thoughts and feelings by the practitioner about how he or she performed and the identification with the patient and the patient's situation. Such thoughts and feelings are frequently helpful during a session but are the source of considerable consternation for some practitioners—especially

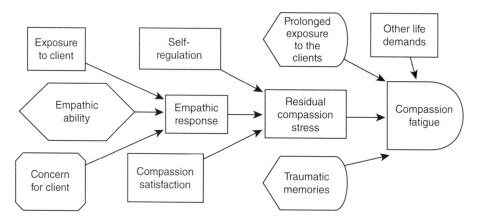

Figure 15.1
The compassion stress/fatigue model.

those who are new to the profession or who are working with an especially provocative patient.

The antecedents of the critically important empathic response include not only the practitioner's empathic ability but also the direct exposure to the suffering and a sufficient level of concern.

Residual compassion stress, in addition to the contribution of empathic response effects, figure 15.1 suggests that two other factors are important but serve as buffers to offset or even prevent such stress: *compassion satisfaction* and *self-regulation*. *Compassion satisfaction* is the enjoyment, fulfillment, or sense of pride as practitioner generally and especially in specific and challenging cases. Like life and work satisfaction, the practitioner is rewarded for her or his empathic response with the satisfaction of knowing the patient is being helped.

Self-regulation, consistent with self-regulation theory (Bandura 1986), is the ability to develop and maintain full control over one's behavior, thoughts, and emotions to enable the practitioner to feel safe and calm in order to effectively perform his or her job as effectively as possible. The power of self-regulation has been demonstrated in hospital settings with patients receiving radiation therapy (Johnson et al. 1997). The nursing research team in this study found that patients who received the self-regulation theory-based nursing interventions experienced less disruption in their usual life activities during and following radiation therapy. Even among those patients who tended to be pessimistic, those who received the self-regulation theory-based interventions had a more positive mood than those who did not receive the interventions.

Self-regulation theory applied to empathy, and especially the avoidance of compassion stress and fatigue, postulates that a practitioner who has high residual compassion stress from clients who touch him emotionally benefits most from self-regulation behaviors. This is because of the increased demand to managing the emotional impact of the experience of practicing efforts to provide relief to the patient.

As noted in Figure 15.1 compassion fatigue is more likely if there is a buildup of residual compassion stress, despite compassion satisfaction and self-regulation, if two factors are present: prolonged exposure to the suffering due to lack of sufficient time and opportunity to relax and process the experiences of the day and active traumatic memories that can be reawakened when one is working with certain patients or the conditions are right to trigger those memories. Finally, various other life demands may promote the development of compassion fatigue when the other causal factors are present.

Developing Practitioner Resilience

With the awareness of the process by which practitioners become distressed from working with suffering patients, what can be done to protect them from such emotionally challenging work? The Internet and libraries are filled with resources to understand and help practitioners' (Figley 2002) overwhelmed by their work. Collectively these strategies of work-related coping can be divided into two main themes or sets of coping.

First is the effort to limit exposure to vicarious trauma through distractions, changes in the work environment, and skills for limiting the encoding of distressing information. Among the skills are being assertive to supervisors and colleagues about the challenges of working with suffering patients. A second set of coping skills is associated with self-regulation. This includes effectively managing the compassion stress emerging from the empathic responses to the suffering through various in vivo strategies that include distraction, talking with colleagues, regular supervision and coaching, socializing, and the use of effective self-soothing and stress-management methods. Another important category of coping and promoting resilience is the developing of a more robust personal life that competes with thoughts of work.

Clearly, the demands and consequences of being compassionate and empathic response resonate with clinicians and therapists who work with suffering patients and apply effective empathic responses frequently. Practitioners drawn to the helping professions are vulnerable to the cost of caring and need to be prepared to be resilient.

Note

1. The origin of healer is Greek for "the remover of arrows."

References

Allport, G. W. 1937. *Personality: A Psychological Interpretation*. New York: Holt.

American Psychiatric Association. 1994. *Diagnostic and Statistical Manual of Mental Disorders*, 4th ed. Washington, DC: American Psychiatric Association.

[REMOVED IF= FIELD]Asay, T. P., and M. J. Lambert. 1999. The empirical case for the common factors in therapy: Quantitative findings. In *The Heart and Soul of Change: What Works in Therapy*, edited by M. A. Hubble, B. L. Duncan, and S. D. Miller, 23–55. Washington, DC: American Psychological Association.

Bandura, A. 1986. *Social Foundations of Thought and Action: A Social Cognitive Theory*. Englewood Cliffs, NJ: Prentice-Hall.

Bergin, A. E., and S. L. Garfield, eds. 1994. *Handbook of Psychotherapy and Behavior Change*, 4th ed. New York: Wiley.

Bordin, E. S. 1979. The generalizability of the psychoanalytic concept of the working alliance. *Psychotherapy: Theory, Research & Practice* 16 (3): 252–260.

Carkhuff, R. R. 1969. *Practice and Research*, Vol. II. *Helping and Human Relations*. New York: Holt, Rinehart & Winston.

Danieli, Y. 1985. The treatment ad prevention of long-term effects and intergenerational transmission of victimization: A lesson from Holocaust survivors and their children. In *Trauma and its Wake*, edited by C. R. Figley, 295–313. New York: Brunner/Mazel.

Danieli, Y. 1988. Treating survivor and children of survivors of the Nazi Holocaust. In *Post-traumatic Therapy and Victims of Violence*, edited by F. Ochberg, 278–294. New York: Brunner/Mazel.

Decety, J., and C. Lamm. 2006. Human empathy through the lens of social neuroscience. *TheScientificWorldJournal* 6: 1146–1163.

Duncan, B. L., S. D. Miller, and J. A. Sparks, eds. 2004. *The Heroic Client: A Revolutionary Way to Improve Effectiveness through Client-Directed, Outcome-Informed Therapy*. San Francisco, CA: Jossey-Bass.

Erickson, C. A. 1989. Rape and the family. In *Treating Stress in Families*, edited by C. R. Figley, 257–290. New York: Brunner/Mazel.

Figley, C. R. 1982. Traumatization and Comfort: Close Relationships May Be Hazardous to Your Health. Keynote Presentation, Families and Close Relationships: Individuals in Social Interaction. Conference held at the Texas Tech University, Lubbock, March.

Figley, C. R., ed. 1985. *Trauma and its Wake: The Study and Treatment of Post-Traumatic Stress Disorders*. In the Psychosocial Stress Book Series. New York: Brunner/Mazel.

Figley, C. R. 1989. *Helping Traumatized Families*. San Francisco: Jossey-Bass.

Figley, C., ed. 1995. *Compassion Fatigue: Coping with Secondary Traumatic Stress Disorder in Those Who Treat the Traumatized*. New York: Brunner/Mazel.

Figley, C. R., ed. 2002. *Treating Compassion Fatigue*. New York: Brunner-Routledge.

Figley, C. R., and T. Nelson. 1989. Basic family therapy skills, I: Conceptualization and initial findings. *Journal of Marriage and Family Therapy* 15 (4): 349–365.

Figley, C. R., and R. Roop. 2006. *Compassion Fatigue in the Animal Care Community*. Washington, DC: The Humane Society Press.

Forrester, D., S. Kershaw, H. Moss, and L. Hughes. 2007. Communication skills in child protection: How do social workers talk to parents? *Child and Family Social Work* 13: 41–51.

Frank, J. D. 1973. *Persuasion and Healing*. Baltimore, MD: Johns Hopkins University Press.

Gerdes, K. E., and E. A. Segal. 2009. A social work model of empathy. *Administration in Social Work* 10 (2): 114–127.

Herman, J. L. 1992. *Trauma and Recovery*. New York: Basic Books.

Hojat, M., J. S. Gonnella, T. J. Nasca, S. Mangione, M. Vergare, and M. Magee. 2002. Physician empathy: Definition, components, measurement, and relationship to gender and specialty. *American Journal of Psychiatry* 159 (9): 1563–1569.

Johnson, J. E., V. K. Fieler, G. S. Wlasowicz, M. L. Mitchell, and L. S. Jones. 1997. The effects of nursing care guided by self-regulation theory on coping with radiation therapy. *Oncology Nursing Forum* 24 (6): 1041–1050.

Joinson, C. 1992. Coping with compassion fatigue. *Nursing* 22 (4): 116–122.

Juslin P. N., and J. Sloboda. 2010. *Handbook of Music and Emotion*. New York: Oxford University Press.

Kottler, J. A. 1992. *Compassionate Therapy: Working with Difficult Clients*. San Francisco: Jossey-Bass.

Langfield, H. S. 1953. Empathy. In *The Problems of Aesthetics*, edited by E. Vivas and M. Krieger. New York, Toronto: Rinehart and Company.

Maroda, K. 1991. Saint or sadist: Who is the self-righteous patient? *The Psychotherapy Patient* 7: 125–135.

McCann, L., and L. Pearlman. 1989. Vicarious traumatization: A framework for understanding the psychological effects of working with victims. *Journal of Traumatic Stress* 3 (1): 131–149.

McCubbin, H. I., B. B. Dahl, G. Lester, and B. Ross. 1977. The returned prisoner of war and his children: Evidence for the origin of second generational effects of captivity. *International Journal of Sociology of the Family* 7: 25–36.

Miller, K. I., J. B. Stiff, and B. H. Ellis. 1988. Communication and empathy as precursors to burnout among human service workers. *Communication Monographs* 55: 250–265.

Miller, S., M. Hubble, and B. Duncan. 1995. No more bells and whistles. *The Family Networker* 19 (2): 53–63.

Myers, S. 2000. Empathic listening: Reports on the experience of being heard. *Journal of Humanistic Psychology* 40: 148–173.

Orlinsky, D. E., K. Grawe, and B. K. Parks. 1994. Process and outcome in psychotherapy. In *Handbook of Psychotherapy and Behavior Change*, 4th ed., edited by S. L. Garfield and A. E. Bergin, 270–376. New York: John Wiley & Sons.

Pearlman, L. A., and K. W. Saakvitne. 1995. Treating therapists with vicarious traumatization and secondary traumatic stress disorder. In *Compassion Fatigue: Coping with Secondary Traumatic Stress Disorder in Those Who Treat the Traumatized*, edited by C. R. Figley. New York: Brunner/Mazel.

Radey, M., and C. R. Figley. 2007. Social psychology of compassion. *Clinical Social Work Journal* 35: 207–214.

Remer, R. and J. E. Elliot. 1988a. Characteristics of secondary victims of sexual assault. *International Journal of Family Psychiatry* 9 (4): 373–387.

Remer, R. and J. E. Elliot. 1988b. Management of secondary victims of sexual assault. *International Journal of Family Psychiatry* 9 (4): 389–401.

Richardson, R. D. 2006. *William James: In the Maelstrom of American Modernism*. New York: Houghton Mifflin Harcourt.

Rogers, C. R. 1957. The necessary and sufficient conditions of therapeutic personality change. *Journal of Counseling Psychology* 21: 95–103.

Rogers, C. R. 1961. *On Becoming a Person*. Boston, MA: Houghton Mifflin.

Rogers, C. R. 1980. *A Way of Being*. Boston, MA: Houghton Mifflin.

Rosenheck, R., and J. Thomson. 1986. "Detoxification" of Vietnam war trauma: A combined family-individual approach. *Family Process* 25 (4): 559–570.

Rosenzweig, S. 1936. some implicit common factors in diverse methods of psychotherapy. *American Journal of Orthopsychiatry* 6: 412–415.

Salston, M., and C. R. Figley. 2003. Secondary traumatic stress effects of working with survivors of criminal victimization. *Journal of Traumatic Stress* 16: 167–174.

Shulman, C. 2001. *The Complete Book of Figure Skating*. Champaign, IL: Human Kinetics.

Stamm, B. H. 1996. Contextualizing death and trauma: A preliminary endeavor. In *Death and Trauma*, edited by C. R. Figley, 3–21. New York: Brunner/Mazel.

Stamm, B. H. 1997. Work-related Secondary Traumatic Stress. PTSD Research Quarterly, (8) 2, Spring. Available on-line http://www.dartmouth.edu/dms/ptsd/RQ_Spring_1997.html.

Stamm, B. H. 2002. Measuring compassion satisfaction as well as fatigue: Developmental history of the Compassion Satisfaction and Fatigue Test. In *Treating Compassion Fatigue*, edited by C. R. Figley, 107–119. New York: Brunner-Routledge.

Stebnicki, M. A. 2000. Stress and grief reactions among rehabilitation professionals: Dealing effectively with empathy fatigue. *Journal of Rehabilitation* 6: 23–29.

Tallman, K., and A. C. Bohart. 1999. The client as a common factor: Clients as self- healers. In *The Heart and Soul of Change: What Works in Therapy*, edited by M. A. Hubble, B. L. Duncan, and S. D. Miller, 91–132. Washington, DC: American Psychological Association.

Tichener, E. 1924 *A Textbook of Psychology*. New York: Macmillan.

Truax, C. 1961. *A Scale for Management of Accurate Empathy*. Discussion Paper 20, Wisconsin Psychiatric Institute, Madison.

Truax, C. B., and R. R. Carkhuff. 1967. *Toward Effective Counseling and Psychotherapy: Training and Practice*. Chicago: Aldine.

Verbosky, S., and D. Ryan. 1988. Female partners of Vietnam veterans: Stress by proximity. *Issues in Mental Health Nursing* 9: 95–104.

Webster's Encyclopedic Unabridged Dictionary of the English Language. New York: Gramercy Books.

White, S. J. 1997. Empathy: A literature review and concept analysis. *Journal of Clinical Nursing* 6 (4): 253–257.

Wilson, J. P. and J. D. Lindy. 1994. *Countertransference in the Treatment of PTSD*. New York: Guilford.

16 The Paradox of Teaching Empathy in Medical Education

Johanna Shapiro

The emotional burden of avoiding the patient may be much harder on the physician than he [*sic*] imagines . . . a doctor's job would be so much more interesting and satisfying if he simply let himself plunge into the patient, if he could lose his fear of falling.
—Anatole Broyard, *Intoxicated by My Illness,* 1992

The Paradox of Empathy in Medical Education

In the domain of medical education, empathy is touted as among the essential attitudes and skills of professionalism. Various educational and professional bodies in medicine, such as the Accreditation Council for Graduate Medical Education (Joyce 2006) and the Association of American Medical Colleges (Anderson et al. 1998) have identified empathy as a key component of professionalism and specify that medical education must include curriculum whose goal is the development of empathy in learners (Larson and Yao 2005). The empathy-altruism hypothesis (Batson et al. 1991) argues that empathic concern is a requisite of altruistic action, another fundamental anchor of a profession that mandates placing the patient's interests above those of self.

Empathy is deemed especially important in medicine because of the crucial role of the physician in creating *representations* of the patient's story through the medical chart (Hyden 2008). At least to some extent, and especially when the patient's voice becomes weak or nonexistent, the patient ends up on the periphery of the medical action, and the vicarious voice of the physician becomes the authoritative depiction of the patient. Under these circumstances the capacity to accurately and honestly resonate to the patient's perspective becomes essential. Further, empathy has been implicated in patient adherence to medical regimens (Kim, Kaplowitz, and Johnston 2004), with research documenting a direct relationship between patient-perceived physician empathy and increased satisfaction and compliance. Other research identifies a strong relationship between empathy and establishing the working alliance necessary to an effective patient-doctor relationship (Fuertes, Boylan, and Fontanella 2009).

Awareness of such connections has led to medical schools across the country providing required courses in communication skills that routinely include the teaching of empathy. Yet research shows that despite recognition of the importance of empathy in a medical student's education, and despite efforts to develop empathic communication through curricular instruction, student empathy actually *declines* significantly during the third year of medical school and continues low throughout the fourth year of training (Newton et al. 2008; Hojat et al. 2009). How is this possible? In a seminal article on medical education, the problem is stated as follows: "North American medical education favors an explicit commitment to traditional values of empathy, compassion, and altruism—and a tacit commitment to an ethic of detachment, self-interest and objectivity" (Coulehan and Williams, 2001). This educational deficiency is not necessarily self-correcting. Rita Charon, professor of internal medicine at Columbia College of Physicians and Surgeons, has written that even experienced "physicians sometimes lack the capacities to recognize the plights of their patients, to extend empathy toward those who suffer, and to join honestly and courageously with patients in their illness" (Charon 2001, 1897). Thus, although there are a plethora of words expended in support of empathy in clinical training and practice, it has not successfully translated into sustainable and effective attitudes and actions. This article analyzes this paradox, identifies possible reasons for its existence, and suggests potential pedagogical alternatives.

What Is Clinical Empathy?

Definitional Complexity

Perhaps surprisingly, given its pervasive appearance in the medical education literature, there is considerable disagreement about the definition of empathy. Traditional definitions used in medical education include emotive, moral, cognitive, and behavioral dimensions (Stepien and Baernstein 2006). A leading medical ethicist, Jodi Halpern, in her book *From Detached Concern to Clinical Empathy* and other writings (Halpern 2001, 2003), emphasized that empathy must involve emotional resonance not simply cognitive comprehension. Other scholars have described empathy as a complex process that starts with gaining insight into the patient's concerns, feelings, and distress; engaging emotionally with the patient's perspective; feeling compassion at the distress of the patient; and finally, taking action motivated by a desire to remove or alleviate the causes of that distress (Benbassat and Baumal 2004). It is apparent that, utilizing these complex, multifaceted definitions, true empathy is difficult to achieve because it may entail the physician being pulled across a boundary she did not want to cross and entering a zone where life is profoundly insecure (Frank 2008).

Why Medicine Has Trouble Successfully Incorporating the Construct of Empathy

Physicians belong to a profession that has increasingly placed itself squarely within the logicoscientific tradition. Medicine's positivist worldview, which prioritizes technological progress, hierarchy, certainty, and efficiency, encourages conceptualizing patients as objects and can lead to the doctor feeling alienated from, rather than empathic toward, the patient (Davis-Floyd and St. John, 1998). Researchers have shown that patients are often referred to in derogatory ways by physician role models, conceptualized as tasks to finish or as objects from which to extract learning (Dyrbye, Thomas, and Shanafelt 2005). The most widely accepted view of medical professionalism is that its practitioners should respond to the suffering of patients with objectivity and detachment (Coulehan 2009a,b). It has also been observed that physicians "place themselves out of their patients' lives" by identifying themselves with heroic invincibility and their patients with illness, suffering, and misfortune (Irvine 2009). In general, medical culture does not acknowledge the physician's need to experience and process personal feelings (Jennings 2009).

The cultural norms of medical education likewise expect that aspiring doctors should not show emotion, especially emotion that helps connect the student-physician to the patient. Like clinical practice itself the medical education process promotes emotional detachment, affective distance, and clinical neutrality (Evans, Stanley, and Burrows 1993; Hojat 2009). Medical pedagogy encourages "detached concern which devalues subjectivity, emotion, relationships, and solidarity" (Coulehan 2005). Medical students are particularly vulnerable to emotional detachment because they are still learning how to modulate their own emotional states in the often stressful and emotionally demanding environment of clinical medicine (Jennings 2009). Since students don't know how to cope with the often intense feelings they experience on a daily basis, they end up denying or ignoring them.

Suppression of the strong emotions that arise in the face of death, disability, medical error, and one's own mortality is exhausting and can lead to burnout and compassion fatigue. In a dysfunctional cycle, this emotional exhaustion prompts further efforts to cope by promoting distancing oneself emotionally from patients (Kearney et al. 2009). In one recent study only 19 percent of a randomized sample of learner-reflective clinical stories included any emotional content whatsoever. The authors concluded that the hidden curriculum (Hafferty and Franks 1994) continues to socialize students to quell their emotions and to reinforce norms against displaying or even feeling/acknowledging emotion (Karnieli-Miller et al. 2010). Because they are unfamiliar with and afraid of their own emotional landscape, medical students are also often embarrassed and uncomfortable when confronted with patient emotion (which triggers emotions in themselves) (Benbassat and Baumal 2001). Students who are not able to examine and come to terms with their own psychological lives find it difficult to connect empathically with others (Medved and Brockmeier 2008).

The Pseudosolution: Taming an Unruly Construct

Understanding this background makes it easier to see that definitions of empathy that include the emotions seem unpredictable and uncontrollable to medical educators. Since there is general consensus that physicians "need" empathy, the pedagogical result is often based on ways of "taming" empathy so that it conforms to reassuringly normative assumptions and practices already extant in medicine. This has meant by and large separating empathy from the unruliness and unpredictability of emotion. Cognitions, having to do with thought processes and critical inquiry, are more comfortable and familiar to academics of all stripes[1], and especially to physicians. Therefore an understanding of empathy that relies solely on cognitive processes seems more controllable, more manageable, more teachable, and more measurable in terms of outcomes. The result has been to promote as empathy a kind of cognitive listening to and apprehension of the patient's concerns while avoiding the perceived "risks" of emotional involvement with the patient.

Cognitive-Behavioral Empathy

In medical education research empathy is defined more and more as a purely cognitive exercise. This is particularly significant because, while precision and meaning restriction are key elements of the scientific method, research also bestows a mantle of "truth" on the constructs it studies and therefore exerts a profound influence on what is taught clinically and how. Definitions such as the one formulated by Hojat (2009) and Hojat et al. (2009) identify empathy as an objective, rational, accurate, intellectual process that is "always" good for both patient and practitioner, at the expense of sympathy, which is vilified as an emotional, self-indulgent, co-dependent, even histrionic practice that will lead to burnout and compassion fatigue. These and similar efforts to separate out the active elements of empathy (Crandall and Marion 2009) have the effect of making the construct easier to recognize and identify—but not necessarily of making it more "empathic" in its clinical manifestations. Nevertheless, empathy is now typically taught as a set of cognitive and behavioral skills (Winefield and Chur-Hansen 2000). This cognitive emphasis translates into cognitive-behavioral approaches in which specific verbal and nonverbal phrases or gestures become stand-ins for empathy: "I understand your concern"; "Your language is expressing sadness"; "I grasp that you don't want to die." Similarly, touching a shoulder or knee also reductively become synonymous with empathy.

Positive Physician Role Models to Teach Empathy

In contemporary medical education, the teaching of empathy is formally incorporated into the curriculum primarily in the preclinical years, usually in the form of a lecture and/or role-playing exercises. When empathy is considered as part of students' learning experience during the clinical years, it is almost entirely addressed through the process of role modeling. This idea assumes a two-step process: First, physicians "model" empathic attitudes on the wards and in clinics. Then, attentive students observe these empathic demonstrations and assimilate them. Although it is true that role modeling has a highly significant influence on students' own empathy (Winseman et al. 2009), there are problems with this approach. Unfortunately, we have learned that physician role modeling can be negative as well as positive. Research on the hidden curriculum (Hafferty 1988) reveals that students frequently encounter physician role models who embody problematic qualities such a rudeness, dismissiveness, and lack of empathy. Further, even positive role models do not always know how to teach what they do (Shapiro 2002), resulting in the "wow" effect: students are suitably impressed by outstanding role models, but they are unable to identify exactly what it is that these role models are doing that they could emulate or incorporate. Thus, we cannot simply rely on the existence of positive role models to convey attitudes, values, and skills of empathy to medical students.

Problematic Unintended Consequences

Fake Empathy

The cognitive-behavioral methods of teaching empathy so widespread in the preclinical years run the risk of becoming mere intellectual exercises for medical students. Exclusively technique-based modes can mean that empathy increasingly is understood by medical students as a means to other, more valuable ends, rather than a morally valuable end in itself. In this construction empathy may sometimes become a means to ends benefiting students (positive evaluation of performance) and sometimes as promoting positive patient outcomes (increased compliance, increased continuity). Of course these are not undesirable ends. However, they remain squarely situated in the ethical position of "getting" and "acquiring." In such formulations empathy becomes a tool to obtain an objective (albeit an appropriate one) rather than a quality that one human being owes another (Levinas 2005). As Pence wrote in his seminal work on compassion (Pence 1983), merely imitating compassionate behavior is not compassion. Much the same could be said for empathy.

In particular, the standardized patient (SP) encounters that form the center of the Objective Structured Clinical Examination (OSCE) increasingly used to evaluate empathy and other "communication skills" among students and residents can encourage learners to merely acquire mimetic displays of empathy, superficial language and gestures that earn them success in an examination context but are detached from underlying emotional connection. Because of the evaluative link, students may infer that there are narrowly correct ways of interacting with patients, which in turn can lead to formulaic, impersonal interactions and, ironically, to an appearance of *lack* of empathy (Case and Brauner 2010). Such artificial assessment situations encourage the appearance of relationship between student and SP while they fail to establish authentic connection (Hanna and Fins 2006). Literary scholars have noted that conventional language is sometimes too familiar, quotidian, and well known to adequately understand the uniqueness of suffering (Brockmeier 2008), suggesting that it is only by *breaking out of* routinized ways of talking and thinking that empathy can be communicated to another. Yet the standardized format of an OSCE works directly counter to such spontaneity and originality in language. Further, scholars have also expressed concern as to whether the behaviors performed in SP interactions actually transfer to practice with actual patients or are sustained over time in the absence of further evaluation, raising the specter of a rigorous, but meaningless, evaluation method (Meitar, Karnieli-Miller, and Eidelman 2009).

Empathic Failures toward Stigmatized Others

A purely cognitive empathy risks lack of emotional engagement and meaningful understanding of the other. Pence pointed out that true compassion must be rooted in deeper internal attitudes and behaviors and must recognize that the suffering of the other *really matters,* and this insight is true for empathy as well. When empathy is viewed more as a performance than as a deeply held commitment to a way of being in the world, it can easily result in "selective" empathy, that is, performance that is generated in response to certain evaluative situations, or something that naturally arises toward certain "likeable" patients or patients similar to the student, *not* as something that needs to be cultivated toward all patients, especially stigmatized, marginalized, or otherwise unappealing patient populations. Cognitive-behavioral empathy leads to rejection of stories that do not look or sound like what the student expects, stories that strike the student as unfamiliar, broken, disjointed, lacking coherence, in short, the kinds of stories that patients who appear as "other" to medical students tend to tell (Bulow 2008). In the absence of core ethical values that trigger pursuit of empathic responses regardless of situational cues, students will likely not feel it necessary to empathize with such stories. In fact, neuroscience research has demonstrated that perceived stigma has a significant effect on expressed empathy for patients (Decety, Echols, and Correll 2009). In clinically based research there is evidence that patients who make physicians emotionally uncomfortable, such as dying patients, tend not to elicit empathy in their physicians. For example, one study of medical encounters between oncologists and patients with advanced disease found that physician responses to empathetic opportunities offered by the patients were infrequent (Pollack et al. 2007). In another study on breaking bad news, students who were distanced/detached or defensive/avoidant in relation to their patients avoided acknowledging patient emotions or expressing empathy for their plight (Meitar, Karnieli-Miller, and Eidelman 2009). Students with little awareness of their own and the patient's emotions set rigid boundaries to try to control the interaction and tended to avoid the expression of empathy.

Devaluing of Empathy

Under these conditions empathy, at best, is something that learners (and practicing physicians) may sometimes undertake but rarely publicly acknowledge or advocate for (Mattingly 2008). Because the culture of medicine does not consistently authorize, support, or approve the attitudes and practices of empathy, the needs to identify and express empathy toward patients tend not to acquire official status in the clinical environment. Since the expression of empathy is not a billable procedure, and since learners rarely see even positive role models reflecting on how to experience and convey empathy, it is easy for students to see empathy as a "nice" but nonessential aspect of practice. Even when they do emerge, empathic responses are potentially fragile and fleeting. They are often viewed by the students who express them as tangential or irrelevant to "real" medicine, a way of engaging with the patient that should be distrusted, discounted, and devalued as often as they are esteemed.

Demoralizing Outcomes of Empathy Training

Not infrequently, medical students are resentful of efforts to teach empathy didactically (Henry-Tillman et al. 2002; Shapiro et al. 2009). Sometimes they express feelings of being patronized by a curriculum that tries to "teach" empathy and related attitudes and draw the conclusion that they are being told that they are not good people. In one study students reported that personal factors (parents, life experience, faith) had already molded their capacity for empathy and compassion at least as much if not more than formalized instruction or role modeling in medical school (Wear and Zarconi 2007). The implication was that these did not need any help in learning how to be empathic, thank you very much. Students in this same study further noted that sometimes their teachers seemed more interested in the appearance of altruism rather than in the actual feeling. Thus, at least to some degree, the performative emphasis on empathy training has backfired, with students resisting what they perceive to be efforts to remold existing values they already consider to be perfectly sound.

A Modest Proposal for Encouraging Empathy in Medical Learners

The Necessity for Culture Change

Ultimately, the overall context of medical practice is more important for teaching empathy than the efforts of any one role-model individual, admirable as such efforts may be. This means, that to effectively communicate the importance of empathy to medical learners, we must do no less than change the culture of medicine (Pence 1983; Coulehan 2005). This is of course a large order; and change can usefully occur on multiple levels, such as economic, political, philosophical, and sociological. In the context of cultivating empathy perhaps the most important change needed is an attitudinal one appreciating the importance of skillfully recognizing and dealing with emotions in the doctor-patient relationship. It is only in this way that the multidimensional complexity of the construct of empathy can be comfortably absorbed into medical education.

Learning to Identify and Work Skillfully with Emotions

Over a decade ago, leading physician scholars recognized that physician emotions and emotional hot buttons, expectations, beliefs, attitudes, assumptions, and needs have an important, but often unacknowledged, impact on how they interact with patients (Suchman et al. 1997), including how they express or avoid empathy. Yet this important insight did not translate into pervasive curricular changes because it could not be supported by the existing cultural norms of medicine. In a more recent study of breaking bad news, researchers found that students who were "involved" and emotionally connected with the patient were able to avoid algorithmic, rote forms of interacting. They were not afraid of the patient's emotional reactions, seemed "well-prepared to harness their emotions in the service of the patient" (Meitar, Karnieli-Miller, and Eidelman 2009, 1589), and were much more likely to express empathy toward the patient than other students in the exercise.

Medical educators often make the assumption that it is easier to work with cognitions than to change emotions (Hojat 2009). However, there are many intriguing curricular initiatives whose goal is to help students become familiar with emotions, both their own and those of their patients. Training in mindfulness (Krasner et al. 2009), narrative medicine (Charon 2006), medical humanities (Shapiro et al. 2006; Foster and Freeman 2008), and reflective writing (Reis et al. 2010) have all shown theoretical and empirical promise as ways of helping students to become more aware of and learn to interrogate critically the role of emotions in clinical practice and, as a result, to express multidimensional empathy.

Emotional Regulation

In this regard the concept of emotional regulation is relevant. When empathic over-arousal occurs in response to another's emotional state or condition, it results in an aversive, self-focused emotional reaction. Individuals who can regulate their emotional state are better able to avoid being overwhelmed by their own emotions and therefore can focus on the needs of the other (Eisenberg et al. 1994; Decety and Meyer 2008). Research in the neurosciences has established that empathy consists of three components: emotion sharing, perspective-taking (taking the point of view of another), and emotion regulation (Decety and Lamm 2006). This means that empathy involves both the capacity to emotionally respond to the suffering of another as well as the capacity to regulate and modulate this experience. This formulation suggests that what is needed is not the ignoring or suppressing of emotion, but its regulation, so that it is present, but modulated.

Putting Empathy Back into the Patient-Doctor Equation

We should not accept that the emotional component of empathy is dangerous and should be exiled from the doctor-patient encounter. On the contrary, purely "cognitive" empathy without the "proper dose" (Balint 2000) of emotion runs the risk of being excessively operationalized, codified, and measured in ways that will become pointless and meaningless. From a pedagogical perspective incorporating empathy into the curriculum may be more of a "restoration project" than one of inculcation (Spiro 1992). In other words we should build on students' existing empathic strengths, their natural human impulses toward identifying with others, impulses that currently are all too often stifled and repressed in the existing medical culture.

Curricular approaches to teaching empathy should aspire to what bioethicist Jodi Halpern almost a decade ago called "clinical empathy" (Halpern 2001). Clinical empathy derives from a detailed experiential as well as cognitive understanding of what the patient is feeling. It is neither detachment nor immersion but, rather, an ongoing double movement of emotional resonance and compassionate curiosity about the meaning of the clinical situation to the patient (Shapiro 2007). This form of empathy involves the capacity to participate deeply in the patient's experience while not losing sight of the fact that this imaginative projection is not, in fact, one's own experience but that of another. In a similar formulation the clinician must possess the negative capability not to be emotionally overwhelmed by the patient's plight while simultaneously being moved by his/her suffering (Coulehan 1995). Neuroscience research confirms that awareness of a distinction between the experiences of self and others constitutes a crucial aspect of empathy. For empathy to be effective individuals must be able to separate their own feelings from the feelings shared with others, so must have self-awareness as well as other-awareness (Decety and Lamm 2006). Without self-awareness physicians lose perspective, and they experience empathy as a liability. Self-aware physicians, on the other hand, experience empathy as a mutually healing connection with patients (Kearney et al. 2009).

A Culture of Empathy

By making room for emotions and a practice of empathy that honors its emotion-based dimension, we might change other aspects of the culture of medicine as well. For example, instead of the emotional detachment routinely encouraged in clinical interactions, we might see physicians and students alike being willing to develop "compassionate solidarity" with the patient's suffering (Coulehan 2009a,), an attitude which Coulehan describes as one comprised of presence, listening, affirmation, and witnessing. Rather than defending against their patients' distress, from a position of empathy physicians could learn to recognize their own vulnerability to suffering and therefore be willing to connect with others, including most radically their patients.

Doctors and patients share in common uncertainty, suffering, sickness, and death (Fantus 2008). Yet Charon has observed that although patients and doctors both suffer, their suffering seems parallel and disconnected (Charon 2006). Rather than pull away from the suffering of their patients, in a futile attempt to emotionally protect and insulate themselves, doctors who adopted an attitude of empathy could acknowledge their similarities with their patients because they could see themselves in their patients' suffering. Instead of distance and objectivity, such physicians could embrace attitudes of affiliation and alliance with patients (Charon 2008). They would be ready, indeed eager and unafraid, to share some small portion of the burdens under which their patients labor, and they would be able to hear their patients' laments without flinching (Bub 2004).

In this empathic medical culture physicians would value and cultivate self-awareness of their own thoughts and feelings, countertransference, and emotional labor (Larson and Yao 2005). They would be interested in developing "insight into how one's life experiences and emotional makeup affect one's interactions with others" and would be able to engage in personal calibration of their own emotional responses to patients (Novack et al. 1997). Such a culture would promote role modeling in physicians that was both self-aware and reflexive—outstanding physicians would bring awareness and critical examination to their own behavior and would be able, for example, to reflect on and illuminate for students how empathy was being created and expressed in any given clinical encounter (Kenny, Mann, and MacLeod 2003). From these role models students would learn that their impulses to connect with their patients are valid and appropriate, rather than foolishly naive (Reisman 2006).

Conclusion

Medicine has tried to have it both ways as far as empathy is concerned. It has acknowledged empathy as an essential cornerstone of the patient-doctor relationship, but it has tried to cleanse empathy of its emotional underpinnings and define it as a purely cognitive-behavioral skill. This is because the emotions of patients and their own emotions seem confusing, overwhelming, unpredictable, and therefore difficult to manage to practitioners schooled in the reductive positivism of the sciences. As a result medical culture has, perhaps unwittingly, promoted attitudes of detachment and distance rather than empathy in both practitioners and learners. Alternatively, medical culture and medical education might consider acknowledging that emotional reactions are an integral—and indeed, potentially valuable—part of clinical practice. Their patients' emotions and their own in large part define how the meanings and implications of biophysical disease are processed and decided on, how treatment decisions are made, and how adherence plays out in daily life. By paying attention to emotions, how to identify them and how to make determinations about what emotional responses are most beneficial to the patient, students and clinicians alike will be able to become familiar and comfortable with the expression of empathy. In fact their willingness to feel and convey empathy may even have the effect of shifting the culture of medicine toward one anchored in attitudes of compassionate solidarity, affiliation, and alliance toward patients.

Note

1. Even medical humanities scholars are likely to describe empathetic imagination as a purely "cognitive skill that helps one to imagine the experiences and responses of another" (Case and Brauner 2010, although these authors also caution against "surface acting" or performance in executing empathic skills).

References

Anderson, M. B., J. J. Cohen, J. E. Hallock, D. G. Kassebaum, J. Turnbull, and M. E. Whitcomb. 1998. The Medical Student Objectives Project. Washington, D.C.: Association of American Medical Colleges.

Balint, M. 2000 [1957]. *The Doctor, His Patient and the Illness*, 2nd ed. London: Churchill Livingstone.

Batson, C. D., J. G. Batson, J. K. Singlsby, K. L. Harrell, H. M. Peekna, and R. M. Todd. 1991. Empathic joy and the empathy-altruism hypothesis. *Journal of Personality and Social Psychology* 61: 413–426.

Benbassat, J., and R. Baumal. 2001. Teaching doctor patient interviewing skills using an integrated learner and teacher-centered approach. *American Journal of the Medical Sciences* 322: 349–357.

Benbassat, J., and R. Baumal. 2004. What is empathy, and how can it be promoted during clinical clerkships? *Academic Medicine* 79: 832–839.

Brockmeier, J. 2008. Language, experience, and the "traumatic gap": how to talk about 9/11. In *Health, Illness, Culture: Broken Narratives*, edited by L.-C. Hyden and J. Brockmeier, 16–35. New York: Routledge.

Bub, B. 2004. the patient's lament: Hidden key to effective communication: How to recognize and transform. *Journal of Medical Ethics* 30: 63–69.

Bulow, P. 2008. "You have to ask a little": troublesome storytelling about contested illness. In *Health, Illness, Culture: Broken Narratives*, edited by L.-C. Hyden and J. Brockmeier, 131–153. New York: Routledge.

Case, G. A., and D. J. Brauner. 2010. The doctor as performer: a proposal for change based on a performance studies paradigm. *Academic Medicine* 85: 159–163.

Charon, R. 2001. Narrative medicine: a model for empathy, reflection, profession, and trust. *JAMA* 286: 1897–1902.

Charon, R. 2006. *Narrative Medicine: Honoring the Stories of Illness*. New York: Oxford University Press.

Charon, R. 2008. What to do with stories. In *Appendix: A Journal of the Medical Humanities. The Medical School for International Health* 2: 42–49.

Coulehan, J. 1995. Tenderness and steadiness: emotions in medical practice. *Literature and Medicine* 14: 222–236.

Coulehan, J. 2005. Viewpoint: Today's professionalism: Engaging the mind but not the heart. *Academic Medicine* 80: 892–898.

Coulehan, J. 2009a. Compassionate solidarity: Suffering, poetry, and medicine. *Perspectives in Biology and Medicine* 52: 585–603.

Coulehan, J. 2009b. Rescuing empathy. *Literature, Arts, and Medicine Blog*, Nov. 30. <http: // medhum.med.nyu.edu/blog>.

Coulehan, J. and P. C. Williams. 2001. Vanquishing virtue: The impact of medical education. *Academic Medicine* 76: 598–605.

Crandall, S. J., and G. S. Marion. 2009. Commentary: Identifying attitudes towards empathy: An essential feature of professionalism. *Academic Medicine* 84: 1174–1176.

Davis-Floyd, R., and G. St. John. 1998. *From Doctor to Healer: The Transformative Journey*. Piscataway, NJ: Rutgers University Press.

Decety, J., S. Echols, and J. Correll. 2009. The blame game: The effect of responsibility and social stigma on empathy for pain. *Journal of Cognitive Neuroscience* 22: 985–97.

Decety, J., and C. Lamm. 2006. Human empathy through the lens of social neuroscience. *TheScientificWorldJournal* 6: 1146–1163.

Decety, J., and M. Meyer. 2008. From emotion resonance to Empathic Understanding: A Social Developmental Neuroscience Account. *Development and Psychopathology* 20: 1053–1080.

Dyrbye, L. N., M. R. Thomas, and T. D. Shanafelt. 2005. Medical student distress: Causes, consequences and proposed solutions. *Mayo Clinic Proceedings* 80: 1613–1622.

Eisenberg, N., R. A. Fabes, B. Murphy, M. Karbon, P. Maszk, M. Smith, C. O'Boyle, and K. Suh. 1994. The relations of emotionality and regulation to dispositional and situational Empathy-Related Responding. *Journal of Personality and Social Psychology* 66: 776–797.

Evans, B. J., R. O. Stanley, and G. D. Burrows. 1993. Measuring medical students' empathy skills. *British Journal of Medical Psychology* 66: 121–133.

Fantus, C. 2008. Looking into the eyes of others: Towards a poiesis of narrative medicine. *Appendix: A Journal of the Medical Humanities. The Medical School for International Health* 2: 35–41.

Foster, W., and E. Freeman. 2008. Poetry in general practice education: Perceptions of learners. *Family Practice* 25: 294–303.

Frank, A. W. 2008. Caring for the dead: Broken narratives of internment. In *Health, Illness, Culture: Broken Narratives*, edited by L.-C. Hyden and J. Brockmeier, 122–130. New York: Routledge.

Fuertes, J. N., L. S. Boylan, and J. A. Fontanella. 2009. Behavioral indices in medical care outcome: The working alliance, adherence and related factors. *Journal of General Internal Medicine* 24: 80–85.

Hafferty, F. W. 1988. Cadaver stories and the emotional socialization of medical students. *Journal of Health and Social Behavior* 29: 344–356.

Hafferty, F. W., and R. Franks. 1994. The hidden curriculum, ethics teaching, and the structure of medical education. *Academic Medicine* 69: 861–871.

Halpern, J. 2001. *From Detached Concern to Clinical Empathy: Humanizing Medical Practice*. New York: Oxford University Press.

Halpern, J. 2003. What is clinical empathy? *Journal of General Internal Medicine* 18: 670–674.

Hanna, M., and J. J. Fins. 2005. Power and Communication: Why simulation training ought to be complemented by experiential and humanist learning. *Academic Medicine* 81: 265–270.

Henry-Tillman, R., L. A. Deloney, M. Savidge, C. J. Graham, and V. S. Klimberg. 2002. The medical student as patient navigator as an approach to teaching empathy. *American Journal of Surgery* 183: 659–662.

Hojat, M. 2009. Ten approaches for enhancing empathy in health and human services cultures. *Journal of Health and Human Services Administration* 31: 412–450.

Hojat, M., M. J. Vergare, K. Maxwell, G. Brainard, S. K. Herrine, G. A. Isenberg, J. Veloski, and J. S. Gonnella. 2009. The devil is in the third year: A longitudinal study of erosion of empathy in medical school. *Academic Medicine* 84: 1182–1191.

Hyden, L.-C. 2008. Broken and vicarious voices in narratives. In *Health, Illness, Culture: Broken Narratives*, edited by L.-C. Hyden and J. Brockmeier, 36–53. New York: Routledge.

Irvine, C. 2009. The ethics of self-care. In *Faculty Health and Academic Medicine: Physicians, Scientists, and the Pressure of Success*, edited by T. Cole, T. Goodrich, and T. Gritz, 127–146. New York: Humana.

Jennings, M. L. 2009. Medical student burnout: Interdisciplinary exploration and analysis. *Journal of Medical Humanities* 30: 253–269.

Joyce, B. Introduction to Competency-Based Residency Education. ACGME Outcome Project: Educating Physicians for the 21st Century, 2006. Available at http://www.acgme.org/outcome/e-learn/Physician_21M1.ppt (accessed March 27, 2011).

Karnieli-Miller, O., R. Vu, M. C. Holtman, S. G. Clyman, and T. S. Inui. 2010. Medical students' professionalism narratives: A window on the informal and hidden curriculum. *Academic Medicine* 85: 124–133.

Kearney, M. K., R. B. Weininger, M. L. Vachon, R. L. Harrison, and B. M. Mount. 2009. Self-care of physicians caring for patients at the end of life: "Being connected... a key to my survival." *Journal of the American Medical Association* 301: 1155–1164, E1.

Kenny, N. P., K. V. Mann, and H. MacLeod. 2003. Role modeling in physicians' professional formation: reconsidering an essential but untapped educational strategy. *Academic Medicine* 78: 1203–1210.

Kim, S. S., S. Kaplowitz, and M. V. Johnston. 2004. The effects of physician empathy on patient satisfaction and compliance. *Evaluation & the Health Professions* 27: 237–251.

Krasner, M. S., R. M. Epstein, H. Beckman, A. L. Suchman, B. Chapman, C. J. Mooney, and T. E. Quill. 2009. Association of an educational program in mindful communication with burnout, empathy, and attitudes among Primary Care Physicians. *Journal of the American Medical Association* 302 (12): 1284–1293.

Larson, E. B., and X. Yao. 2005. Clinical empathy as emotional labor in the patient-physician relationship." *Journal of the American Medical Association* 293 (9): 1100–1106.

Levinas, E. 2005. *Humanism of the Other.* translated by N. Poller. Champaign: University of Illinois Press.

Mattingly, C. 2008. Stories that are ready to break. In *Health, Illness, Culture: Broken Narratives*, edited by L.-C. Hyden and J. Brockmeier, 73–98. New York: Routledge.

Medved, M. I., and J. Brockmeier. 2008. Talking about the unthinkable: neurotrauma and the "catastrophe reaction." In *Health, Illness, Culture: Broken Narratives*, edited by L.-C. Hyden and J. Brockmeier, 54-72. New York: Routledge.

Meitar, D., O. Karnieli-Miller, and S. Eidelman. 2009. The impact of senior medical students' personal difficulties on their communication patterns in breaking bad news. *Academic Medicine* 84: 1582–1594.

Newton, B. W., L. Barber, J. Clardy, E. Cleveland, and P. O'Sullivan. 2008. Is There Hardening of the heart during medical school? *Academic Medicine* 83: 244–249.

Novack, D. H., A. L. Suchman, W. Clark, R. M. Epstein, E. Najberg, and C. Kaplan. 1997. Calibrating the physician: Personal awareness and effective patient care. Working Group on Promoting Physician Personal Awareness, American Academy on Physician and Patient. *Journal of the American Medical Association* 278: 502–509.

Pence, G. E. 1983. Can compassion be taught? *Journal of Medical Ethics* 9: 189–191.

Pollack, K. I., R. M. Arnold, A. S. Jeffreys, S. C. Alexander, M. K. Olsen, A. P. Abernethy, C. Sugg Skinner, K. L. Rodriguez, and J. A. Tulsky. 2007. Oncologist communication about emotion during visits with patients with advanced cancer. *Journal of Clinical Oncology* 25: 5748–5752.

Reis, S. P., H. S. Wald, A. D. Monroe, and J. M. Borkan. 2010. Begin the BEGAN (The Brown Educational Guide to the Analysis of Narrative) - A framework for enhancing educational impact of faculty feedback to students' reflective writing. *Patient Education and Counseling* 80: 253–259.

Reisman, A. B. 2006. Outing the hidden curriculum. Hastings Center Report. 36: 9.

Shapiro, J. 2002. How do physicians teach empathy in the primary care setting? *Academic Medicine* 77: 323–328.

Shapiro, J. 2007. Using literature and the arts to develop empathy in medical students. In *Empathy in Mental Illness*, edited by T. F. D. Farrow and P. W. R. Woodruff, 473–94. Cambridge: Cambridge University Press.

Shapiro, J., J. Coulehan, D. Wear, and M. Montello. 2009. Medical humanities and their discontents: Definitions, critiques, and implications. *Academic Medicine* 84: 192–198.

Shapiro, J., L. Rucker, J. Boker, and D. Lie. 2006. Point-of-view writing: A method for increasing medical students' empathy, identification and expression of emotion, and insight. *Educ Health (Abingdon)* 19: 96–105.

Spiro, H. 1992. What is empathy and can it be taught? In *Empathy and the Practice of Medicine: Beyond Pills and the Scalpel*, edited by H. Spiro, E. Peschel, M. G. McCrea Curnen, and D. St. James, 7–14. New Haven, CT: Yale University Press.

Stepien, K. A., and A. Baernstein. 2006. Education for empathy: A review. *Journal of General Internal Medicine* 21: 524–530.

Suchman, A. L., K. Markakis, H. B. Beckman, and R. M. Frankel. 1997. A model of empathic communication in the medical interview. *Journal of the American Medical Association* 277: 678–682.

Wear, D., and J. Zarconi. 2007. Can compassion be taught? Let's ask our students. *Journal of General Internal Medicine* 23: 946–953.

Winefield, H. R., and A. Chur-Hansen. 2000. Evaluating the outcome of communication skill teaching for entry-level medical students: Does knowledge of empathy increase? *Medical Education* 34: 90–94.

Winseman, J., A. Malik, J. Morison, and V. Balkoski. 2009. Students' views on factors affecting empathy in medical education. *Academic Psychiatry* 33: 484–491.

17   Empathy and Neuroscience: A Psychoanalytic Perspective

David M. Terman

Empathy has become the subject of great interest and investigation to neuroscientists in the last decade. Many investigators have made important discoveries about the nature of a process that, as we have come to learn, is a crucial component of human relationships and even human existence. In this context it is important for neuroscience and all branches of human psychology to be aware of the extensive work on empathy that has been an important part of psychoanalytic theory and practice over the past fifty years.

Freud (1920) had noted in a footnote that empathy or *einfuhlung* "is the mechanism by means of which we are enabled to take up any attitude at all towards another mental life"; he did not elaborate on this idea extensively. Part of the absence of its further elaboration in the English translation of his work is the function of the dislike of the term by James Strachey, the translator of Freud's oeuvre into English. American analysts were more concerned with the elaboration of mechanisms of defense and the psychology of the ego. They focused their attention on the manifestation of defense as "resistance" in the therapeutic situation. Then, Heinz Kohut's 1959 seminal paper, "Introspection, Empathy and Psychoanalysis," brought empathy to the center of psychoanalytic attention. Since then, there has been an outpouring of articles and papers in the psychoanalytic literature[1] that have taken up the questions of empathy's definition, its scientific status, its nature, and its effect on technique and others.

What had Kohut written that inspired such interest and attention? Kohut defined the essential process and essence of empathy as vicarious introspection. To arrive at an accurate understanding of the inner experience of another, one had to refer to some aspect of one's own inner experience. This definition and description stress the similarity of the inner subjective, psychological experience of the two parties. In taking this position Kohut was further emphasizing the importance of the "subjective" in understanding psychological life, and he was extending Freud's reclamation of the subjective for scientific scrutiny. Further, Kohut maintained that what one could observe with empathy defined the extent and limit of psychoanalysis. Hence, Kohut was emphasizing the importance of inner experience of the observer in making sense of the observed. He was emphasizing the centrality of subjective resonance in making sense even of the more "objective" data of free associations and dreams.

Basch (1983) clarified the process further. Adding the more precise findings of affect theory, he stated that one component of the empathic process was the apprehension of the other's affect state by virtue of the fact that one's own affective state duplicates that of the other. But although empathy contains this important feature for Basch, he added that it involves "complex cognitive processes by which we form certain hypotheses about another person's inner experience, hypotheses that are then open to further study so that the judgments can be confirmed or proven false." Basch further cautioned that empathic perception is never a matter of somehow getting a direct look at what goes on inside another mind; rather it is considered judgment that there is a correspondence between what we are feeling and what, in the case of the analytic situation, the analysand is experiencing, consciously or unconsciously. In other words it involves complex cognitive tasks and often prolonged dialogue to establish the correct apprehension of the inner experience of the other—what we call prolonged empathic immersion. Goldberg (2010) has recently elaborated on the nature of prolonged empathic immersion which he sees as unique to the psychoanalytic situation. He contrasts the data and experience of prolonged immersion with the momentary apprehension of another's inner state. The former consists of many aspects of the total personality and so includes those elements that may be sequestered, layered in defense, contradictory feelings and attitudes, and, most importantly, the history of such elements.

Kohut's placement of empathy as the defining phenomenon of the psychoanalytic process was followed by the development of a set of ideas to understand both development and treatment. These came to be known as self-psychology, and he initially believed that they would simply fill out an area that had been neglected in psychoanalytic theory up to that point. However, as the theories evolved they began to offer an additional paradigm for understanding both development and psychoanalytic treatment.[2] One of the central ideas of self-psychology is the *selfobject*. The selfobject refers to the phenomenon of one person serving as a *function* in the psychological organization of another. In the experience of the person for whom the function is being performed, the person doing the job is felt as being a part of the self, hence the term "selfobject." For example, the child who is soothed by the parent may experience the calming effect as something that is part of his/her own psychological function. More profoundly, Kohut held that the functions of approving response and the appearance of strength and effectiveness that become the child's own are central experiences that enable the child to form a cohesive self. The responses are an integral part of the child's experience of him-/herself and they are essential in the creation and development of that self. He labeled these sets of responses as *mirroring* and *idealizing* respectively. These developmental experiences were then reproduced in the analytic situation as mirroring and idealizing transferences.

These theories may seem rather arcane and obscure to the reader who is not familiar with psychoanalytic theory, but I bring them to your attention because these phenomena are very deeply entwined with the phenomenon and understanding of empathy. The selfobject functions and experiences that have played such a central role in both development and therapy are dependent in part or in entirety on empathy. The caretaker's capacity to respond in the ways the child requires depends on the caretaker's understanding of the child's inner state. And the child's experience of response and connection is crucial for his or her growth.

Some analysts have disputed the nature of empathy, and some have been critical of placing it as the defining center of analytic work. Several have concentrated on its origins in early mother-child interactions in which there is an experience of merger (Buie 1981).[3] Hence empathy was seen as based on illusions. Shapiro (1981) thought that empathy was a "new organ" but was not scientific. Empathy was also seen to be instantaneous. Goldberg (1983) had countered with the argument that empathy, which relies on introspection, is no less scientific than data derived from extraception (defined as direct, public observation). The data of introspection are, indeed, subject to error, as are the data of extraception. Both require theories to make sense of the data gathered, and both use inference.

Kohut (1959) wavered in his position about the nature of empathy in respect to its observational or therapeutic functions. At first he was at pains to maintain that empathy is a method of observation only and could be used for good or ill depending on the motivations of the empathizer. He used the example of the terror that Nazis inflicted on the population that he maintained was effective because they had understanding—empathy—for those they were terrorizing. They knew what would make them terrified and helpless. Basch quite emphatically pointed out that the capacity to accurately assess the inner experience of another may be used for neutral or quite nefarious purposes. The con man, for example, may add to his capacity to deceive his victim by knowing that the person who has been understood may feel better for the experience, and he may use that to his or her own advantage. For Basch (1983) empathy was an observational tool only. Kohut (1984), on the other hand, reluctantly acknowledged in his later work that empathy, per se, had a therapeutic effect. Most other self-psychologists have taken the position that empathy is both the essential method of understanding and an important aspect of the therapeutic process. Howard Bacal (1985), Morton and Estelle Shane (1996), Tolpin (2002), and Terman (1988) among many others have all written about the importance of the empathic bond, per se, in fostering the repair and growth of the self. Developmentally, the experience of being empathically understood is an essential requirement for the development of the self. The accurate perception of intention, affect and need, after all, constitutes the positive experience of mirroring. And that essential element of self-construction and self-cohesion becomes enacted and alive in the therapeutic process in the experience of empathy.

When one considers the therapeutic effect of empathy, one then is looking at the object, if you will, of the empathic understanding. We then are in the realm of the experience of being understood. As I have just noted, self-psychology has elaborated its centrality in development and therapy, for this is an important means to establish the experience of the selfobject. Appropriate responsiveness to selfobject needs is often made possible by an empathic grasp of those needs. The experience of being understood occurs after the communication of the empathizer's understanding. And, as Basch had pointed out, the process of more accurate understanding depends, in part, on a dialogue between the empathizer and the empathizee. The positive effects of being understood also occur in many daily situations and are an important component of the bonds between people. It evokes feelings of alikeness, similarity which has a positive effect on the cohesion and the value of the self. The positive effect of understanding in the clinical situation is even greater, for there the focus of the understanding is to both foster a positive bond and to foster the growth and well-being of the patient.

It is interesting to dissect the elements of the phenomenon of empathy into its various components, yet we must beware that there are both gains and losses in such an approach. Like putting experience into linear causal chains or teaching an autistic person to recognize affect, the fragmentation of the experience or the concept loses an essential part of its character. It is important, too, to remember that the discovery, if you will, of the importance and centrality of empathy was done in a clinical setting. And that is not an accident. The apprehension of psychological phenomena by complex cognitive beings has several advantages. One of them is surely that the forest can be distinguished from the trees. The wholes can be seen, and the additional emergent properties of the wholes grasped by the cognitive being that is similarly equipped— that operates and integrates these emergent wholes. So one might say that it was only possible for empathy to have been "discovered" by those who deal with such wholes, that is, by clinicians, and that its existence and importance could not have been identified or understood with neuroscience alone.

That stated, we now have some very interesting findings from the side of the neuroscientists, and it behooves all of us to communicate with each other and learn from one another so that we do not remain in ignorance and each of us benefit from the understandings of the other. We need not live in parallel universes. There has been an outpouring of research on the neural circuits that are activated in the respective parties and on the times and ways inner neural networks are activated. There seems to be a clear correspondence between neuronal events and the varieties of psychological processes we have called empathy. There is a convergence between many neuroscientists' definition of empathy and our own. Notably Decety (Decety and Jackson 2004; Decety 2007; Decety and Meyer 2008; Decety 2011) has proposed three major functional components that dynamically interact to produce the experience of empathy in humans:

1. Affective sharing between the self and the other; based on perception-action coupling that lead to shared representations;
2. Self-other awareness. Even when there is some temporary identification, there is no confusion between self and other;
3. Mental flexibility to adopt the subjective perspective of the other and also regulatory processes.

In other words, for Decety empathy is not simply the sharing or similarity of affect or any other state; it must have the components of awareness of the difference between self and other and the complex cognitive operations that involve the capacity to take the perspective of another.

Looking at the first part of Decety's description of empathy, one starts with the work on mirror neurons that has greatly excited some of our self-psychologists and the psychoanalytic community in general (see Wolf et al. 2000; Gallese 2006). First observed in monkey brains and then widely documented in humans, the mirror neuron system has the property of replicating the activation of the areas of the brain in the observer that correspond to the inner events in the brains of the person whose behaviors are observed. Observer and observed share excitations of congruent areas of the brain. And although these correspondences were first noted in relation to motor acts, they have been subsequently and extensively observed in response to emotions and pain. One of the interesting findings of neuroscience is that perception is a means to action, and action is a means to perception, and apparently this built-in human capacity is present at birth. That is, the observation of action activates the inner experience of action and may lead to action. More important, there is a link of inner experiences from the most rudimentary beginnings of psychological life—or observable neurological activity.

There is a great deal of neurophysiological evidence for affect sharing. The areas of the brain that are congruently activated in the one in pain and the one observing are analogously present in the observing and experiencing of a number of emotions: happiness, sadness, anger, disgust, and surprise among them. In addition to the developmental studies that show that infants can perceive affects of their caretakers, there is evidence from the study of lesions that perception of emotion activates the neural mechanisms that are responsible for the generation of emotions (Decety and Jackson 2004; Decety and Meyer 2008). For example, while watching someone smile the observer activates the same facial muscles involved in producing a smile at a subthreshold level, and this would create the corresponding feeling of happiness in the observer. In his review of studies on empathy Decety summarizes the findings by stating that shared representations between self and other at the cortical level have been found for action understanding, pain processing, and emotion recognition. This mechanism provides the neurophysiological basis for the operation of social cognition by means of the automatic activation of motor representations or emotions. There is no specific cortical site for shared representation; their neural underpinnings are widely distributed, and the pattern of activation varies according to the processing domain, the particular emotion, and the stored information. This finding helps the psychoanalytic theoretician to validate the contention that an element of empathy is, indeed, the congruent experience of affect, and it weighs against those who have dismissed shared affect states as either unreal or illusory.

Turning to Decety's second functional component of empathy, one finds that there is neurological evidence that indicates that certain areas of the brain are necessary for the attribution of intention to others and to develop a "theory of mind"—that is, the capacity to attribute qualities of mind to others. The region concerned is around the paracingulate sulcus in the medial prefrontal cortex in conjunction with the posterior temporal sulcus (Decety 2010). It is activated experimentally in several situations: when people are asked to judge emotion in someone's gaze, attributing intention to cartoon characters, detecting social transgression, and appreciating humor. All of these capacities derive from some kind of awareness of the mind of another. There are also several neural pathways that are shown to be active in differentiating perceptions of affect of others from self, and these differentiations depend, in part, on the inhibition of one's own affect. This is mediated by the right frontopolar cortex (Ruby and Decety 2004). If there were no such inhibition, there would only be affect contagion. Hence, differentiation between self and other partly depends on *self*-regulation.

There has been considerable interest in the development of capacity to control affect among psychologists. For instance, Eisenberg, Valiente, and Champion (2004) did a series of studies of children and adults that measured affective self-regulation and social functioning and levels of empathy and found positive correlations between higher levels of control and empathic capacity. I find that an interesting fact, for although we, as clinicians, assume from our clinical experience that self-regulation is generally part of a developmental process that leads to a capacity to empathize, we do not single out self-regulation as a crucial component of that capacity. This finding of neuroscience and experimental psychology suggests that we look more closely at this issue clinically.

Decety summarizes these sets of findings—and many others that I have not eluci-dated as follows:

Empathy . . . is an intentional capacity. In many cases, the outcome of the simulation mechanism is not empathic feeling. In addition, without self-awareness and emotion regulation processing, there is no true empathy. Indeed, the activation of shared representations would lead to anxiety or discomfort. . . . Forming an explicit representation of another person's feeling as an intentional agent therefore necessitates additional computational mechanisms beyond the shared representation level . . . empathy is not a simple resonance of affect between the self and other. It involves an explicit representation of the subjectivity of the other.

Further, to emphasize the complexity of empathy in its neurological form, Decety declares ". . .we do not assume that there is a unitary empathy system (or module) in the brain. Rather, we consider multiple dissociable systems to be involved in the experience of empathy." Here, too, there is a convergence between clinical observation and theory and neuroscience. Empathic understanding can only occur if one is clear that it is concerning another subjectivity. Vicarious introspection is in service of the apprehension of the other. On the neurophysiological level, this is a system—or systems—that involves much more than mirror neurons.

So far all the studies I have cited have dealt with the empathizer. What about the empathizee? In an interesting study and taking its cue from the neuroscience finding of automatic imitation as a component of empathy, van Baaren et al. constructed a number of ingenious experiments in which they studied the effect of imitation on subsequent social interactions (van Baaren et al. 2009). The subject—called the participant—had his/her behavior imitated by the experimenter—called the confederate—while doing some task. The imitation took place following a several-second delay and consisted of typical involuntary movements like face rubbing, touching one's hair or moving one's limbs. Several groups were examined. One set of participants had been imitated, one had not, and one had contrary movements. The sequelae were interesting. Imitated subjects felt better about their confederates than nonimitated subjects. Another set of experiments found that the imitated subjects thought their imitators shared more of their views about subjects in general than nonimitated people. They felt, in other words, that they were more alike.

In another experiment van Baaren and his group (2009) instructed waitresses in the Netherlands to imitate patrons (or not). The imitators got 50 percent more tips. In yet another situation the experimenter dropped pens after a fictitious task. Those subjects who had been imitated were much more likely to help the experimenter. All of this led the investigators to say that they showed the increased positive feeling for others after they had felt mirrored, established the likeness of. To further test whether such positive fellow feeling went beyond the experimenter, the group members devised several further variations of opportunities to help others, and they found significant differences in the group that had been imitated: they were more helpful. Finally, a preliminary area of research using functional magnetic resonance imaging (fMRI) and fantasy and the projection of congruent or incongruent faces showed that the incongruent faces produced excitation in the areas of the brain that related to "expectancy violation or conflict and self-other distinction." Van Baaren and colleagues (2009) cautiously speculated that the experience of being imitated is the default expectation of human interaction. It is the *absence* of imitation that is *unexpected* and perceived as negative! As Kohut (1959) said, empathy is like the oxygen we need—in development and in the therapeutic process—and when we turn psychologically blue, we have been deprived of something essential that, indeed, causes conflict and rage.

The last set of experiments I cite involve what is labeled as "empathic accuracy." Ickes (2009) has devised ways of measuring the accuracy of the perceptions of the affects of others in various filmed interactions. At selected points in numerous interactions participants are asked what they are feeling. The viewers are not privy to that information, so their speculations about the nature of the inner, affective experience of the subjects could be checked and their accuracy rated. In some confirmation of the importance of dialogue in grasping the inner world of another, the study shows that raters' accuracies increased if they were given feedback about what the subjects said about their own feelings. That is, their accuracy increased in subsequent judgments. Now that is a revelation that may strike a clinician as truly banal. But another—perhaps more interesting—finding arose when the experimenters subtracted various elements from the videotapes and observed its effect on empathic accuracy. The loss of verbal information—the words, themselves, dramatically impaired empathic accuracy. The loss of paralinguistic cues had a more moderate effect; and the loss of visual information had a surprisingly negligible effect. These data suggest that using the couch or having skype analyses may indeed permit analysts to gather the data that are most relevant to the analytic process.

Using this method to measure empathic accuracy, several investigators found some other interesting and suggestive findings. Pairs of mothers and children aged nine to eleven were filmed in conversations about a variety of practical decisions such as planning a trip or making a purchase. Children were then asked about their actual feelings in the situation, and then each mother was asked to infer her child's thoughts. Not surprisingly the children of the mothers who were more accurate about their inferences about the child's feelings had the most positive self-concepts. In another study abusive husbands were found to have had very low empathic accuracy about their wives and saw various women in videotapes as critical and rejecting significantly more than the critical or rejecting instances had occurred. This finding is interesting to me in connection with the work I have done on the nature of what I have called the *paranoid gestalt*. The origin of it lies in the experience of perceived narcissistic injury for either the individual or the group, and one important outcome is the demonization of the evil other with whom there can be no empathy. I have called that attitude a kind of *neg-empathy* (Terman, 2010).

The amount of work on empathy is quite considerable, and I have selected a small portion of it. So what can the analyst add to the question of the value of such an approach in relation to his or her clinical work? First of all I think it is both interesting and promising that there are so many convergences of our disciplines. What we have observed clinically has been borne out in the data that have come from both neurophysiology and experimental psychology. Jean Decety's definition of the elements of empathy quite precisely parallel our own: affective resonance, the distinction between self and other, and a complex cognitive process in which one both differentiates oneself and puts oneself in the place of another (Decety 2010). Finding different areas of the brain that serve discrete aspects of this process underlines the elements that we have delineated. There is emphatic support for importance of alikeness in human psychology. It was Kohut's contention that this basic experience of alikeness was what was central in understanding another. The experience of alikeness seems to also foster feelings of well-being and good feeling for one's fellow humans. It seems that the experience of being understood—or at least being alike—leads to a better attitude toward others. And mothers who are more empathic with their children seem to have children who feel better about themselves.

So our central notions about the nature and effect of empathy seem to be confirmed, or rather, they are quite consistent with that data that is emerging from these other approaches. Have analysts learned anything new? The possible importance of motor acts in both being empathic and being understood is an area that we might investigate. Does this add weight to the clinical observations that some patients really need to see us and that we are depriving them of something essential if we think that they should use the couch? Might we learn more if we paid more conscious attention to both their and our movements? On the other hand, the data of the accuracy study seem to indicate that the verbal communications rather than visual cues, for example, are most important for the therapist's understanding; however, would the *patient* feel more understood if he or she could be aware of our spontaneous and unconscious physical resonance? With respect to empathic capacity, we noted that self-regulation of affect seems to be a crucial factor in the development of empathy. We have to both resonate with another's affect and also to *inhibit* our own affects. And the capacity to do that is an independent developmental phenomenon. There is some work on this aspect of functioning in recent studies of the so-called borderline patient.

It appears that breaking the psychological wholes into neurological or experimental psychological parts both confirms our ideas—at this point—and possibly points to aspects of our experience that we have not yet been aware. And I think this adds to our understanding of empathy. However, I think we should also be aware that we saw the importance and centrality of this phenomenon first. As I noted at the outset I think it would have been impossible for our researchers to have known of the existence of such an entity without the work of clinicians. And that is not because analysts are cleverer but because the nature of the phenomenon in question is at another level of system organization. And it is not phenomenology versus causality. Rather it is causality in an emergent system.

For all we learn from these other approaches, we are still ahead. For these other disciplines are—for the most part—looking at the elements of the isolated mind. Neuroscientists have elucidated a great deal about the empathizer in isolation, but they do not yet know as much about the experience of the empathizee, nor about the system that encompasses both—what self psychological analysts call the self—which encompasses the selfobject. Our understanding of the importance of this system of self-selfobject may help our colleagues in neurology and experimental psychology to fashion studies that look at these systems using their tools. It will be interesting to learn what they will discover with simultaneous and reciprocal fMRI, for example. But whatever we learn we will have to incorporate into our wholistic understandings that include the most subtle and sophisticated ways of apprehending another human and participating in a therapeutic relationship with him or her.

Arnold Goldberg (1983) contends that the phenomenon of prolonged empathic immersion in the psyche of another human—the experience of a psychoanalytic encounter—becomes yet another level of psychological organization and generates a field of data that is of a different order. Perhaps the systems that neuroscience and experimental psychology are delineating are the basic building blocks in a repetitive process that generates emergent structures that have additional properties that are captured in psychoanalytic or clinical psychological language and theory. The analogy may be to the relation between the findings of inorganic chemistry and physiology— the properties of complex molecules and tissues. One cannot understand complex physiological systems with the tools and concepts of inorganic chemistry; one must know about the properties of membranes and enzymes, for example. However, there can be no physiology that is not consistent with the fact that the basic elements of the enzymes and membranes are atoms.

Were analysts to reduce their understandings to some variety of disconnected waving of hands or simplistic, mechanical imitations rather than the complex understandings of prolonged empathic immersion and the layered relatedness of selfobject experience, both approaches would lose. But if we retain our mutual respect and integrity, we can learn from and inform each other.

Notes

1. PEP Web lists 162 articles, chapters and books that contain "empathy" in their titles. All but nine have been published since Kohut wrote his seminal article.

2. Kohut's ideas can be found in the three books he wrote: *The Analysis of the Self* (New York: International Universities Press, 1971); *The Restoration of the Self* (New York: International Universities Press, 1977); and *How Does Analysis Cure* (Chicago: University of Chicago Press, 1984).

3. Daniel Buie, in "Empathy: Its Nature and Limitations," *Journal of the American Psychoanalytic Association,* 29 (1981): 281–307, argues that empathy grows out of a "merger" between the child

and parent and that such mergers are illusions. Hence the data from empathy could not be considered scientific. Steven Levy, "Empathy and Psychoanalytic Technique," *Journal of the American Psychoanalytic Association*, 33 (1985): 353–78, although seeing empathy as important— "the analyst's awareness of and responses to the patient's inner state"—sees Kohut's definition as equal to the early mother-child interactions.

References

Bacal, H. 1985. Optimal responsiveness in the therapeutic process. *Progress in Self Psychology* 1: 202–227.

Basch, M. F. 1983. Empathic understanding: A review of the concept and some theoretical considerations. *Journal of the American Psychoanalytic Association* 31: 101–126.

Buie, D. 1981. Empathy: Its nature and limitations. *Journal of the American Psychoanalytic Association* 29: 281–307.

Decety, J. 2007. A social cognitive neuroscience model of human empathy. In *Social Neuroscience: Integrating Biological and Psychological Explanations of Social Behavior*, edited by E. Harmon-Jones and P. Winkielman, 246–70. New York: Guilford Press.

Decety, J. 2010. The neurodevelopment of empathy in humans. *Developmental Neuroscience* 32: 257–267.

Decety, J. 2011. The neuroevolution of empathy. *Annals of the New York Academy of Sciences*. Epub ahead of print

Decety, J., and P. L. Jackson. 2004. The functional architecture of human empathy. *Behavioral and Cognitive Neuroscience Reviews* 3: 71–100.

Decety, J., and M. Meyer. 2008. From emotion resonance to empathic understanding: A social developmental neuroscience account. *Development and Psychopathology* 20: 1053–1080.

Eisenberg, N., C. Valiente, and C. Champion. 2004. Empathy-related responding: moral, social, and socialization correlates. In *The Social Psychology of Good and Evil: Understanding Our Capacity for Kindness and Cruelty*, edited by A. G. Miller, 386–415. New York: Guilford Press.

Freud, S. 1920 [1955]. *Group Psychology and Analysis of the Ego, XVII,* 2nd ed. New York: Hogarth Press.

Gallese, V. 2006. Mirror neurons and intentional attunement. *Journal of the American Psychoanalytic Association* 54: 47–57.

Goldberg, A. 1983. On the scientific status of empathy. *Annual of Psychoanalysis* 11: 155–69.

Goldberg, A. 2010. A Note on Sustained Empathy. Paper given at a meeting of the Self Psychology Study Group, Chicago, July 2010.

Ickes, W. 2009. Empathic accuracy. In *The Social Neuroscience of Empathy*, edited by J. Decety and W. Ickes, 57–70. Cambridge, MA: MIT Press.

Kohut, H. 1959. Introspection, empathy, and psychoanalysis—An examination of the relationship of the mode of observation and theory. *Journal of the American Psychoanalytic Association* 7: 459–483.

Kohut, H. 1971. *The Analysis of the Self.* New York: International Universities Press.

Kohut, H. 1977. *The Restoration of the Self.* New York: International Universities Press.

Kohut, H. 1984. *How Does Analysis Cure?* Chicago: University of Chicago Press.

Levy, S. 1985. Empathy and psychoanalytic technique. *Journal of the American Psychoanalytic Association* 33: 353–78.

Ruby, P., and J. Decety. 2004. How would you feel versus how do you think she would feel? A neuroimaging study of perspective taking with social emotions. *Journal of Cognitive Neuroscience* 16:988–999.

Shane, M., and E. Shane. 1996. Self psychology in search of the optimal: A consideration of optimal responsiveness, optimal provision, optimal gratification, and optimal restraint in the clinical situation. In *Progress in Self Psychology*, vol. 12, edited by A. Goldberg, 37–54. Hillsdale, NJ: The Analytic Press.

Shapiro, T. 1981. Empathy: A critical reevaluation. *Psychoanalytic Inquiry* 1:423–448.

Terman, D. M. 1988. Optimal frustration: Structuralization and the therapeutic process. *Progress in Self Psychology* 4:113–125.

Terman, D. M. 2010. Fundamentalism and the paranoid Gestalt. In *The Fundamentalist Mindset*, edited by C. B. Strozier, D. M. Terman, and. W. Jones, 47–61. New York: Oxford University Press.

Tolpin, M. 2002. The role of empathy and interpretation in the therapeutic process. *Progress in Self Psychology* 18:113–125.

van Baaren, R. B., J. Decety, A. Dijksterhuis, A. van der Leij, and M. L. van Leeuwen. 2009. Being imitated: Consequences of nonconsciously showing empathy. In *The Social Neuroscience of Empathy*, edited by J. Decety and W. Ickes, 31–42. Cambridge, MA: MIT Press.

Wolf, N. S., M. Gales, E. Shane, and M. Shane. 2000. Mirror neurons, procedural learning, and the positive new experience: a developmental systems self psychology approach. *Journal of the American Academy of Psychoanalysis* 28(3): 409–430.

Contributors

C. Daniel Batson   University of Kansas

Joshua Correll   University of Chicago

Jean Decety   University of Chicago

Frans B. M. de Waal   Emory University

Stephanie Echols   University of Chicago

Alison Edwards   Arizona State University

Nancy Eisenberg   Arizona State University

Charles R. Figley   Tulane University

Ezequiel Gleichgerrcht   Favaloro University, Buenos Aires

Jodi Halpern   University of California, Berkeley

Sara D. Hodges   University of Oregon, Eugene

Snjezana Huerta   Arizona State University

Karyn L. Lewis   University of Oregon, Eugene

Sharee Light   University of Wisconsin, Madison

Abigail A. Marsh   Georgetown University

Kalina J. Michalska   University of Chicago

Kevin Ochsner   Columbia University

Søren Overgaard   University of Copenhagen

Johanna Shapiro   University of California, Irvine

David M. Terman   The Chicago Institute for Psychoanalysis

Amrisha Vaish   Max Planck Institute for Evolutionary Anthropology, Leipzig

Felix Warneken   Harvard University

Allan Young   McGill University

Dan Zahavi   University of Copenhagen

Carolyn Zahn-Waxler   University of Wisconsin, Madison

Jamil Zaki   Columbia University

Author Index

Subject Index